HOW TO WEATHER TOGETHER

Environmental Cultures Series

Series Editors:

Greg Garrard, University of British Columbia, Canada
Richard Kerridge, Bath Spa University, UK

Editorial Board:

Frances Bellarsi, Université Libre de Bruxelles, Belgium
Mandy Bloomfield, Plymouth University, UK
Lily Chen, Shanghai Normal University, China
Christa Grewe-Volpp, University of Mannheim, Germany
Stephanie LeMenager, University of Oregon, USA
Timothy Morton, Rice University, USA
Pablo Mukherjee, University of Warwick, UK

Bloomsbury's *Environmental Cultures* series makes available to students and scholars at all levels the latest cutting-edge research on the diverse ways in which culture has responded to the age of environmental crisis. Publishing ambitious and innovative literary ecocriticism that crosses disciplines, national boundaries, and media, books in the series explore and test the challenges of ecocriticism to conventional forms of cultural study.

Titles Available:

ANTHROPOCENE REALISM
John Thieme

BODIES OF WATER
Astrida Neimanis

CITIES AND WETLANDS
Rod Giblett

CIVIL RIGHTS AND THE ENVIRONMENT IN AFRICAN-AMERICAN LITERATURE, 1895–1941
John Claborn

CLIMATE CHANGE SCEPTICISM
Greg Garrard, George Handley, Axel Goodbody, Stephanie Posthumus

CLIMATE CRISIS AND THE 21ST-CENTURY BRITISH NOVEL
Astrid Bracke

COGNITIVE ECOPOETICS
Sharon Lattig

COLONIALISM, CULTURE, WHALES
Graham Huggan

CONTEMPORARY FICTION AND CLIMATE UNCERTAINTY
Marco Caracciolo

DIGITAL VISION AND ECOLOGICAL AESTHETIC
Lisa FitzGerald

ECOCOLLAPSE FICTION AND CULTURES OF HUMAN EXTINCTION
Sarah E. McFarland

ECOCRITICISM AND ITALY
Serenella Iovino

ECOCRITICISM AND TURKEY
Meliz Ergin

ECOSPECTRALITY
Laura A. White

ENVIRONMENTAL CULTURES IN SOVIET EAST EUROPE
Anna Barcz

FUEL
Heidi C. M. Scott

IMAGINING THE PLAINS OF LATIN AMERICA
Axel Pérez Trujillo Diniz

LITERATURE AS CULTURAL ECOLOGY
Hubert Zapf

READING UNDERWATER WRECKAGE
Killian Quigley

THE LIVING WORLD
Samantha Walton

NERD ECOLOGY
Anthony Lioi

THE NEW NATURE WRITING
Jos Smith

THE NEW POETICS OF CLIMATE CHANGE
Matthew Griffiths

RADICAL ANIMISM
Jemma Deer

RECLAIMING ROMANTICISM
Kate Rigby

TEACHING ENVIRONMENTAL WRITING
Isabel Galleymore

THIS CONTENTIOUS STORM
Jennifer Mae Hamilton

THE TREE CLIMBING CURE
Andy Brown

WEATHERING SHAKESPEARE
Evelyn O'Malley

Forthcoming Titles:

AN ECOPOETICS OF AGENCY
Sarah Bouttier

ANGLOPHONE LITERATURE AND THE FIGHT AGAINST CLIMATE CHANGE
Matthias Stephan

CLIMATE FICTION AND DISCURSIVE AGENCY IN A TIME OF CLIMATE CHANGE
Heidi Toivonen

IMAGES OF THE PLANT HUMANITIES
Danielle Sands and Daniel Whistler

NARRATING NUCLEAR DISASTER
Hannah Klaubert

POLLUTION THEORY
Emily McAvan

SENSORY ECOLOGIES IN CONTEMPORARY LITERATURE
Mirja Lobnik

HOW TO WEATHER TOGETHER

FEMINIST PRACTICE FOR CLIMATE CHANGE

Astrida Neimanis and Jennifer Mae Hamilton
with illustrations by Tessa Zettel

BLOOMSBURY ACADEMIC
LONDON • NEW YORK • OXFORD • NEW DELHI • SYDNEY

BLOOMSBURY ACADEMIC

Bloomsbury Publishing Plc, 50 Bedford Square, London, WC1B 3DP, UK
Bloomsbury Publishing Inc, 1359 Broadway, New York, NY 10018, USA
Bloomsbury Publishing Ireland, 29 Earlsfort Terrace, Dublin 2, D02 AY28, Ireland

BLOOMSBURY, BLOOMSBURY ACADEMIC and the Diana logo are trademarks of Bloomsbury Publishing Plc

First published in Great Britain 2026

Copyright © Astrida Neimanis and Jennifer Mae Hamilton, 2026

Astrida Neimanis and Jennifer Mae Hamilton have asserted their right under the Copyright, Designs and Patents Act, 1988, to be identified as Authors of this work.

For legal purposes the Acknowledgements on pp. 265–269 constitute an extension of this copyright page.

Cover design: Rebecca Heselton
Cover image © Tessa Zettel

All rights reserved. No part of this publication may be: i) reproduced or transmitted in any form, electronic or mechanical, including photocopying, recording or by means of any information storage or retrieval system without prior permission in writing from the publishers; or ii) used or reproduced in any way for the training, development or operation of artificial intelligence (AI) technologies, including generative AI technologies. The rights holders expressly reserve this publication from the text and data mining exception as per Article 4(3) of the Digital Single Market Directive (EU) 2019/790.

Bloomsbury Publishing Plc does not have any control over, or responsibility for, any third-party websites referred to or in this book. All internet addresses given in this book were correct at the time of going to press. The author and publisher regret any inconvenience caused if addresses have changed or sites have ceased to exist, but can accept no responsibility for any such changes.

A catalogue record for this book is available from the British Library.

A catalog record for this book is available from the Library of Congress.

ISBN: HB: 978-1-3504-6750-7
PB: 978-1-3504-6749-1
ePDF: 978-1-3504-6751-4
eBook: 978-1-3504-6752-1

Series: Environmental Cultures

Typeset by RefineCatch Ltd, Bungay, Suffolk
Printed and bound in India

For product safety related questions, contact productsafety@bloomsbury.com.

To find out more about our authors and books, visit www.bloomsbury.com and sign up for our newsletters.

Contents

List of illustrations	xi
Prologue: We are weather, too	1
INSET A: Lucky dip	17
1 Feminist theory for climate change	21
INSET B: Close meteorology	45
2 Weather	49
INSET C: Weathering with and without	73
3 Weathering	77
INSET D: #Haircutsforplanetarysurvival	95
4 Infrastructure (A bridge between theory and practice)	99
INSET E: Reading and listening groups	121
5 Field report: Weathering the university	125
INSET F: Speed-zining	147
6 Field report: Feeling research (Astrida)	151
The FEELed lab	151
INSET G: Market stall	147
7 Field report: Finding community (Jennifer)	151
The community weather station (CoWS)	151
INSET H: Community housework	189
8 Field report: Downscaling planetary health (Jennifer)	193
Armidale climate & health project (ACHP)	193

Contents

INSET I: Walkshops	209
9 Field report: Walking in the fringes (Astrida)	**213**
INSET J: Cosmic weathering	229
Epilogue: Cosmic weathering	**233**
Bibliography	245
Acknowledgements	265
Index	271

Illustrations

Figures

0.1 Tessa Zettel at Water Lesson Nine: The Weathering Collective, 23rd Biennale of Sydney *rīvus*, 2022. Photograph: Maria Louise Boyadgis. Courtesy Biennale of Sydney 11
1.1 "Lucky Dip," or, Mapping the weather (Somatechnics Conference in Byron Bay, 2016). Photograph: Astrida Neimanis 36
2.1 *When we image the earth, we imagine another*, 2022. Illustration by Golrokh Nafisi in collaboration with open-weather for *Ecoes #3*, a publication by Sonic Acts 62
3.1 Stones in the river at the FEELed Lab on unceded syilx territory. Photograph: Astrida Neimanis 81
4.1 On the Princes Highway bridge over Goolay'yari. *The River Ends as the Ocean: Walk the tide out*. Aunty Rhonda Dixon-Grovenor, Clare Britton and Astrida Neimanis. Shanghai Biennale *Bodies of Water*. Sydney, 2021. Photograph: Lucy Parakhina 105
5.1 Lake Madgwick and the Community Weathering Station Stall and Breakfast for the 'Weathering Everything' Symposium University of New England campus, Anaiwan Country, Armidale, February 4, 2020. Photograph: Astrida Neimanis 127
5.2 Jen's Community Weathering Station 'Drought-Friendly Hairstyles' zine makes an appearance at the People's University for Gaza on UBCO campus. Photograph: Astrida Neimanis 141
6.1 Caolan Leander reads from his draft manuscript *Bad Weather* at the FEELed Lab's Welcome the Dark gathering, on unceded syilx territory, December 2022. Photograph: Astrida Neimanis 156
7.1 Community Weathering Station Breakfast Stall at the Compassions, 'A Timely Feeling' Conference at UNE October 26, 2019. The picture includes Jen's partner (Craig) and son (Stan) who were helping out that morning. Photograph: Jennifer Hamilton 174

Illustrations

8.1 The Armidale Climate and Health Project Open Day at the Aboriginal Cultural Centre and Keeping Place, Anaiwan Country, May 15, 2021. The Creek Walk was led by Uncle Steve Widders. Photograph: Stephen Tafra   201
9.1 *Care for the Stranded: A Shoreline Walkshop*, 2022. Photograph: Jonathan Vanderweit, courtesy of the Henry Art Gallery   223
10.1 Jen and Astrida leading the first Cosmic Weathering activity at the Common Worlds Weathering Early Childhood Education Workshop on Rindö, Sweden, 2017. Photograph: Affrica Taylor   238

Plates

Plate 1 Earthenware bowl from *The River Ends as the Ocean: Walk the tide out*. Aunty Rhonda Dixon-Grovenor, Clare Britton and Astrida Neimanis. Shanghai Biennale *Bodies of Water*. Sydney, 2021. Photograph: Victoria Hunt
Plate 2 Bridge over Goolay'yari. Photograph: Astrida Neimanis
Plate 3 Reflected clouds in Goolay'yari. Photograph: Astrida Neimanis
Plate 4 Protest sign at the People's University for Gaza UBCO student encampment. Photograph: Astrida Neimanis
Plate 5 "Sometimes hot" knees at a retreat of the Weathering Collective, 2016. Photograph: Astrida Neimanis

Insets

All Insets in this book have been created, and permissions granted, by Tessa Zettel.

Prologue:
We are weather, too

The day isn't overly hot for a Sydney summer – still under 30°C – but the walk to Goolay'yari feels heavy and humid. The kids passing on their bikes have a thick film of sweat mixed with suncream below the helmet line, and the slightly sour smell of damp bodies and brackish water hangs in the air around us. Goolay'yari's colonial name is Cooks River, after the Captain. The 'river' is now a polluted tidal estuary and a complex place for exploring how human–weather relations have changed here and elsewhere since colonial disruption. It is also a place where we can remake them.

As uninvited guests walking through Wangal, Gadigal and Bidjigal Country that day, we had already learned that this body of water once thrived as a food bowl, sustaining small communities along its banks, before becoming a site for heavy industry.[1] It is now unsafe to eat from or swim in, but some folks still cast a line or hop in a kayak, sharing space with the mangroves that edge the tributaries and pelicans hanging out under the Illawarra Road bridge. The river's Indigenous name translates as *pelican*; apparently 'because he left his footprint there when he crossed the river and the little island there used to be in the shape of the pelican's footprint'.[2] The presence of the birds by the riverside that day evidence the weight of this history and justify calls for the name to be changed back. Goolay'yari – the tidal estuary we call a river – is enigmatic; it motivates historians,[3] ethnographers[4] and artists[5] to spend time with it. It motivated us, too.

We spot a small and sheltered picnic table off the path. Single-file, we veer down a narrow, unsealed track between two lomandra bushes. Here, we find ourselves tucked under the casuarinas. A hand reaches for a near-empty water bottle. Someone fans themself with a piece of paper. Sunglasses fog near the bridge of a nose. We're all wearing hats. We are no longer among footpath traffic, nor are we in the playground on the other side of the small tidal inlet. We're on our own picnic table-sized peninsula.

This was the first 'official' meeting of the Weathering Collective. We – a ragbag group of feminist artists and scholars – wanted to think about the weather.[6] In 2016, 'talking about the weather' contained a bit of climate doom, but it still felt mostly like small-talk filler.[7] Climate change was something bigger. There was a lot of work to do joining the dots between the apocalyptic crisis and mundane experience, especially for people like us, still relatively sheltered from this accelerating upheaval. Official definitions encouraged us to hold the terms 'weather' and 'climate change' apart, but we wanted to pull them together. Our hunch: that approaching the first (weather) with deeper curiosity and rigour could teach us something new about how we experience, and will increasingly come to experience, the second (climate change) individually and together.

So we wondered: What is weather? Where is it? Is it held only in the archived numbers that record temperature and humidity? While useful, maybe these numbers are part of a bigger story that still needs to be written. Maybe weather also shows itself in the feelings it arouses (like the annoyance of wearing sandals in the rain, or the fear of standing under a loose-limbed tree in a windstorm, as we discussed while sitting under that gazebo). Or maybe we find it indexed by the ways that we manage it (umbrellas, parkas, air conditioners). Is weather objective, or always relative in ways that allow us to call a day 'hot' or 'humid' (in comparison to what?)? Or is it most obviously in our embodied experience, revealed by the damp spot nestled in the curve of someone's spine that day as we sat by the river? Does our understanding of weather change depending on the weathers we grew up with?

Sulphur-crested cockatoos squawked as they vaulted overhead. In a few hours, when the daylight would fade, the flying foxes would begin their evening flyover from Wolli Creek to the south, across the dusky skies. Our curiosity swelled. How do non-humans interact with weather, and what could their knowledges teach us? Considering the Western mindset that has long understood 'nature' as something other than or separate to humans, how did this affect our understanding of weather, particularly given hard evidence of anthropogenic climate change?[8] In the worldviews of people who had lived in this place since time immemorial, neither the flying foxes nor the rising breeze coming down the river were fundamentally separate from each other or us. What could we learn by listening better and responding carefully to Country or Land-based knowledges of weather? We had noted with some interest that the word 'weather' does not even appear in early glossaries attached to IPCC (Intergovernmental Panel on Climate Change) reports, whose objectives include providing 'neutral, policy-relevant' and 'comprehensive and balanced' information that guaranteed 'objectivity and transparency'.[9] But surely the cockatoos and the sweat on our brows – not to mention knowledges as old as this river – were part of this story?

Prologue: We Are Weather, Too

Like weather forecasts, climate change predictions are made with a combination of instrumental measurements, observations and analysis of accumulative data sets. Sciences aren't diametrically opposed to arts and humanities; climate science, like feminist theory, is an attempt to describe something about the world and is always a work in progress. But as Blanche Verlie has noted, scientists are most often framed as having expert climate change knowledge, while the rest of us simply consume this expertise.[10] We trust the expert assessment that anthropogenic climate change is real, and we value this science immensely. But as feminist theorists and practitioners, we also have climate expertise that looks to the expression of feelings, the movement of bodies and the meaning of experiences. This expertise is devalued in a world that valorizes so-called rational detachment and observation. So what if we started taking measurements, devising methods for observation and building data sets using our own bodies as our most basic research tools, as a way to understand bodies, weather and climate change together? What does weather smell like? What is its tone, or rhythm or hue? Can my tongue be a rain gauge, or my skin a thermometer? We wondered whether poetry could be a barometer, or whether feeling could be a weathervane. These were the first iterations of the practices you will find in this book.

But researching the weather is a slow pursuit because each experience of weather is both complete in itself and partial in the context of the system we call climate. A hot and humid summer day is a complete example of that particular combination of elements, but what about the ice and snow elsewhere? What about the cold front that will blow in later, changing the whole situation in ways we cannot control? The system is dynamic. We wanted our practice to offer an understanding of climate change that didn't just reinscribe binary and hierarchical ways of knowing, and that could grapple with the imprecise and shifting ways that particulars are part of the system. To know it well, we needed to take time. We needed to keep practising. Intentional practice was our way of joining the dots between everyday life and a big abstract system that was framed as beyond the capacity of everyday folks to feel, sense, know and change.

Was weather maybe also this feeling of community and curiosity? There was no rain in the forecast that January day on the banks of Goolay'yari, but we were all precipitating a little bit from the inside. Weather was not just around us. We were weather, too. We wanted to make these words – weather and climate change – strange to ourselves, so that we could experience them differently. *Might a new understanding of weather eventually change the weather?*

How to Weather Together

Why and how we wrote this book

We did not gather near Goolay'yari that day planning these curiosities as a book. In the years since, our work developed via conventional academic methods of reading, reflecting, writing, surveying and interviewing, as well as more practice-based ones such as group hikes, camp-outs, events, lectures, workshops, walkshops, exhibitions, videos, tutorials and games with a broad range of participants (teachers, artists, community members, students, general publics) in diverse locations around the world. This book responds to the many participants who have asked us where they can read more, or learn more, about our practices. While intended to serve as an archive of our work, we also frame this book as a 'how to' guide. But it is not a conventional step-by-step manual that is replicable 1:1. Instead, we hope that something in the ideas and practices we outline might resonate with you: if *we* did things in a certain way under certain circumstances, how might *you* do related or complementary things? The chapters detail the enabling contexts as well as barriers that determined the particular shape of our experiments. We figure the differences and/or similarities between our experiences and yours might also help you better position your own thinking and practice in relation to the ideas of the book.

In this section we outline the book's objectives, and paint a bit of a picture of how we arrived at our collaboration. The Weathering Collective has shapeshifted over the years, but its academic iterations have been pushed forward primarily by the two of us, together and apart.

As feminist scholars, the main aim of this book is to offer a robust framework that can help us understand climate change from a feminist perspective. The feminism of the book is specific, as we describe in Chapter 1 ('Feminist Theory for Climate Change'). This feminism emerges from decades of work as scholars, engaging with a broad range of feminist debates, as well as our lives lived as feminists. This feminism is both critical (descriptive of what the world is) and prefigurative (taking a stand for some worlds and not others). Our feminist starting point enables our departure from a standard understanding of weather in environmental scholarship. It allows us to see that the atmospheres that texture our daily lives are also historical, cultural and social. We are affected by these weathers, but we are also weathermakers, who also have the capacity to change the climate. As feminist humanists who pay attention to language as world-building, we know this isn't 'just' wordplay or mere metaphor. (We say more about this in Chapter 2, 'Weather.')

Second, this book outlines a feminist environmental humanities methodology for designing and building climate change mitigation and adaptation infrastructures. Here, we make a case for community-engaged practices modelled on our own experiences doing this work. We argue that these practices must be grounded in feminist ethics, as a way to rehearse and seed *the redistribution of shelter and vulnerability*.

This phrase is the refrain for our work and is the goal of our project. You will come across it in many places and in various forms throughout these chapters. We use it to highlight the way different people and communities experience climate change differently. It recognizes there is no one-size-fits-all top-down response to climate change. Our practice has taught us that climate change is about too much shelter for some (e.g. with gas-guzzling vehicles, permanent climate control and literal escape hatches to Mars), but nowhere near enough for others. These differences are colonial, gendered, raced, classed and geographically specific. We develop this proposition iteratively through these chapters: we need to ensure more shelter (which comes in all kinds of forms) for those bearing the brunt of the weather, while challenging misguided dreams of invulnerability and escape.

Finally, this book offers practical guidance on how a weathering methodology can be implemented for communities inside and outside of the university. We present these as 'reports from the field', with examples ranging from community market stalls, to creekside walks to the halls of the university itself. A series of practical 'how-to' guides illustrated by our longtime Weathering Collective collaborator Tessa Zettel are offered as adaptable tools for researching and addressing climate change-related issues within various communities.

The book is also written from a very specific place by two people with particular backgrounds and inheritances. We think sharing how our individual preoccupations came together helps explain this project's investment in the relationship between words and worlds. Conceptually, this work was seeded with a paper Astrida co-authored with Rachel Loewen Walker in 2014 called 'Weathering: Climate Change and the Thick Time of Transcorporeality'.[11] (We revisit the ideas from this essay in Chapter 3.) With the goal of defining the 'weathering' concept for feminist environmental theory, this article emerged from Astrida's PhD training in (primarily Western) feminist theory and philosophy. Among other revelations, this training also reaffirmed for Astrida the usefulness of twentieth-century French phenomenologist Maurice Merleau-Ponty's understanding of language.[12] Merleau-Ponty suggests that mundane words we use every day can radically transform how we experience our world, if we find a way to do new things with those words. Paradoxically, this requires reconnecting words to worldly phenomena in honest and surprising ways. *We find a way to hear the words – and experience the world – anew.* This is the power of poetry, but also of concepts, such as weathering.

Astrida met Jen on a beach writing retreat in early 2015 just after moving to Australia from Canada to take a new job. Jen had finished a PhD on weather in literary studies a couple of years before, and liked interpreting the many different uses of the words we mundanely throw around, specifically weather-words. Jennifer's PhD project and first book, *This Contentious Storm*,[13] reassessed the weather's role in *King Lear*, a story about power and mortality. Jen was also a gender studies student and was specifically interested in how speech act theory and theories of gender performativity might shape emerging debates about the environment: the question of how words iteratively make weather-worlds was key for her.[14] So, when we met we found we were already thinking about weather in strikingly complementary ways, even though we came from different disciplines (and different climates). The 'weathering' concept organically formed the basis of the collaboration that developed gradually following that meeting.

In addition to giving you a sense of our training as researchers, we offer this background to emphasize that this book was birthed by a mutual commitment to wordplay. We were brought together by a word – 'weathering' – or a gerund, to be precise. Gerunds bring together verbs and nouns. The bridging work of gerunds also supports the logic of this book, which connects the beingness of a noun (for example, 'theory') and the activeness of a verb (for example, 'practising'). Weathering as gerund also bridges different fields, subjects and objects. For instance, we use weathering in engineering to talk about the qualities of different materials; in geology, weathering is akin to erosion; in soil science, it is the fallout of geological processes that help create soil. But in social work and public health, weathering helps us talk about hardship. Weathering gathers up duration, materiality, emotion, psychology, bodies, communities and more.[15] This is the power of this word in particular!

We anchor this project in language (words and concepts, but also poetics, interpretation and theory, as you will see) because these have been the tools of *our* trade. We were students of the late twentieth-century 'linguistic turn' in feminist literary and cultural studies, which took seriously the way words act in the world, and their capacity to change how we live in it.

Prologue: We Are Weather, Too

So, the objective of the book's first half is to illuminate for our readers the development and deepening of ideas that occurred through our collaboration. Each of the first four chapters introduces an overarching concept, and works through how that idea has been generative to our work in the Weathering Collective. We take a concept and dig around in it: where did it come from? How is it usually understood (or misunderstood)? How are we hacking or refining the concept to make it do interesting things in the service of creating more equitable and joyful climate futures? We want to demonstrate how concepts and theories, arising within academic spaces, can show up elsewhere in the world to help us make sense of it. Especially as all of our key concepts appear in various academic disciplines and operate in all kinds of situations, we want to show how this plasticity is what allows words to be so potentially powerful. The idea here is that new theories, or new takes on existing concepts, can open to new possibilities for living.

Another objective of this book is to bridge theories of weathering to practices of weathering. Given that the practices we describe in the second half of the book have been the engine of our work, we want to share these with other theorists (most likely academics) who might incorporate versions of these practices in their own research and teaching. We also want to share these with the practitioners who sometimes attend our workshops or read our papers (nurses, architects, community workers, dreamers, mental health workers, doulas, urban planners, parents and so on), and who want some guidance on integrating weathering as a feminist proposition for climate justice in their practices. We purposely touch on situations and examples that will demonstrate the relevance of weathering across many disciplines and professions. We spend a lot of time explaining concepts for people who aren't necessarily steeped in a critical theory or literary studies context. In doing so, we think carefully with the language we are using and hacking. We want to show how this kind of reading/writing/thinking work can translate into different ways to weather the world, for us all.

Among these many possible readers, we also have kept two particular readers in mind as we wrote this book: one who wants to learn how to better address climate change in a very direct sense using creative and community-engaged feminist methods; the other who sees how this climate change stuff is actually about the hard work of building and repairing relationships. This refers to relationships between ourselves and the land (which includes sky, rain, air pressure, and other weathery things), but also among individual humans and our different communities. This latter point is delicate. Communities are more and more isolated, more polarized, and more intransigent in this polarization, all the time. Within this, as environmental scholars interested in global climate change, we must approach our work with a holistic vision for trying to bring folks along with us. We have to be open to conversing with the climate change denying guy. But as feminists, we are committed also to antifascism, anticolonialism and ethical encounters with difference. For those reading this to repair and build relations, we offer strategies for doing so, but we do not champion unconditional love.

These two readers could line up with two different feelings or scenarios that the word weathering invokes: the first is an awareness of meteorological weather, climate change and the specific work that needs to be done to address climate crisis as rising temperatures, wildfires, drought, storms, and more. The second, though, is the more generalized feeling of getting by, making it through, and feeling the marks of the world on our skin. Put otherwise, it is about the broader need for antipolarization work to help us connect with each other across difference.[16] Making more durable and flexible connective tissues better equips us to do specific climate change work, and helps that work actually find purchase. Our friend Laura McLauchlan calls this 'learning and practising relational traction'.[17] So we want this book to be for readers interested in finding and making shelter in both of these ways. *We are always weathering.*

Overview of the book's chapters

We know that the specific connection between climate change and feminism is sometimes murky, so Chapter 1, 'Feminist theory for climate change', explains why climate change is a feminist issue. Here, we argue that any climate response that does not include feminism would simply uphold many miseries of the present. We also get specific about the kind of feminism that our weathering practice requires. This feminism needs to be both antipolarizing and antifascist, and must work through the historically fraught relationship between feminism and 'nature'. This feminism is anchored in an embodied politics of solidarity, but also has clear boundaries. We finish this chapter by insisting on the inextricability of feminist theory and feminist practice.

In Chapter 2, we turn to weather. Weather is most regularly defined as non-human phenomena: hot, cold, wet, dry, thunder, lightning, wind, rain – or, the meteors understood via the methods of meteorology. But this definition does not capture all weathers. To get to a more expansive understanding, we begin by acknowledging the need to unlearn colonial weather. We consider theories of language and metaphor as a way to think critically about the changing meaning of words, and trace the history of how weather came to lose its cultural content within our own colonial contexts. We arrive at a broader understanding of weather as more-than-meteorological – where the word becomes a way of bringing together the domains of environmental climate change on the one hand, and social and cultural forces on the other. The chapter closes with a return to practice, drawing on the work of artists and practitioners that have helped us reimagine what weather is and can be.

Chapter 3 offers a very closely related concept: weathering. The expansive understanding of weather offered in Chapter 2 prepares us to discuss our profound and long-term entanglement with weather as weathering, and how this connects to the uneven distribution of shelter and vulnerability in a time of climate change. Taking the example of stones weathered by water as a guiding example, it tells the story of how 'weathering' as a feminist concept for climate change emerged. Weathering as a durational accumulation of weather in and as bodies is the starting point, but this understanding is supplemented with examples that show how structural disadvantage is also a kind of weather that accumulates. Politically speaking, weathering is also a process of solidarity and resistance.

We end the 'theory' section of the book with a chapter on infrastructure. We begin by discussing how infrastructure creates social worlds and shows up within climate change discourse, mostly in terms of building more 'climate-resilient' mega-projects that attempt to control the weather and preserve the status quo. Here, resilience is mostly used to shore up the status quo of the privileged. We therefore propose feminist infrastructure as an alternative climate change mitigation and adaptation strategy that can help us practice the redistribution of shelter and vulnerability. To help make this point, we talk a lot about bridges – both as a typical kind of infrastructure, but also as connectors of other kinds. Bridges bring together different interests, contexts, or ways of being in the world. Chapter 4 is also a bridge to the chapters on practice.

The second part of the book comprises our 'reports from the field', where we show how the ideas of our work are applied in different contexts. Chapter 5 sets this up by contextualizing weathering within the conditions of our work: namely, the university. This chapter links our weathering practices to the colonial and capitalist weather of the neoliberal university, that shows up in more or less violent ways for those who seek shelter (education, employment, community) there. We use the example of the *Composting Feminisms* reading group as one practice or tactic for weathering the university. The chapter's conclusion reflects on protest on university campuses as another kind of weather front.

The next four reports take up the work that Jennifer has undertaken primarily in Armidale, Australia (Chapter 7, 'Finding community'; Chapter 8, 'Downscaling' planetary health), and that Astrida began in Sydney and then reseeded when she moved to Kelowna, Canada (Chapter 6, 'Feeling research' and Chapter 9, 'Walking in the fringes'). Each of these chapters describes how these experiments came about and illuminates the relationships that we had to build and maintain in order to do this work.

Ten insets with illustrations and instructions

'And what is the use of a book,' thought Alice, 'without pictures?'[18] For Lewis Carroll's *Alice in Wonderland*, the implied answer to this question is 'not much'. In crafting this book, we arrived at a similar answer: the use-value of the book will be improved with visual instructions for how to engage in the practices. To this end, each chapter is accompanied by an inset illustrating a specific practice. These illustrations are the work of artist Tessa Zettel, a longtime part of The Weathering Collective, whose creative practice is an important inspiration for our weathering work and this book.[19] These insets provide pragmatic guidance for building intellectual, artistic and activist community in response to the book's primary question of 'how to weather together?' We also hope these insets will deepen the feeling we want this book to generate – of taking time, working together and finding pleasure and world-changing possibility in small moments.

Some of these insets, like 'Lucky Dip' and 'Weathering with and without', are group-setting games designed to open up the definitions of weather and weathering. Others – 'Market stall', 'Reading groups', 'Walkshops' and 'Community housework' – are pragmatic examples of how to build small-scale social infrastructures for weathering climate change otherwise. Still others, like 'Close meteorology', #haircutsforplanetarysurvival and 'Speed zining'[20] provide examples of collective creative methods that help us pay attention to difference and vulnerability; here, we link them specifically to weather and weathering, but the model can be useful in other contexts. The final inset is called 'Cosmic weathering': a practice inspired by phenomenology, meditation and pleasure activism. It's about grounding in the body to find a safe way of becoming accountable to what's changed, and doing the work required to be a small and significant part of remaking the world.

Prologue: We Are Weather, Too

Figure 0.1 Tessa Zettel at Water Lesson Nine: The Weathering Collective, 23rd Biennale of Sydney *rīvus*, 2022. Photograph: Maria Louise Boyadgis. Courtesy Biennale of Sydney.

All of the insets consider how weathering practices and feminist infrastructures allow us to experiment with being a bit out of our comfort zone. They provide examples of how to practise a 'low-stakes vulnerability', which is a step along the way of considering the redistribution of vulnerability and shelter in a supported and safe environment. Each inset is accompanied by basic instructions and some explanatory notes – specific enough to help you do it; loose enough to let you bring your own thing to the game. We suggest reading the chapters as a complement to these activities because they offer deeper descriptions of where and how we've used them. The chapters will also help attune you to questions that these activities might surface. But you can also use them on their own. The activities can be led in classes, workshops, camps, workplaces and even at home or as part of a personal practice.

Moving back and forth between practice and theory

With four theory chapters preceding five practical case studies, the overarching structure of the book might imply that theory comes before practice, but these interspersed practice-led insets demonstrate one additional aim of this book: namely, to thoroughly wreck the theory–practice distinction and hierarchy. Practice is sometimes the presumed 'opposite' of theory; practice is something that you do versus something that you think, or something done by your body versus something in your brain, which also makes this a very gendered and colonial distinction. Our own text-heavy academic disciplines seem to uphold this hierarchy. But even as scholars in text-centric disciplines, we have always been pretty 'practice-y'. In addition to a background in theatre and performance art, Jennifer's literary studies training focused on theories of performativity (the idea of words *doing* things!),[21] while Astrida's training in body hermeneutics (a kind of phenomenology[22]) was all about field work, and testing philosophical concepts in the world. We have both been doing theory and practice all along.

So while we initially imagined that this book would illustrate the movement from theory to practice, writing it has reminded us of our constant movement between both. It has also made us think more about the idea of practice. Practice could simply mean action, or doing. It could just be a synonym for 'case study' or 'example'– like when weathering wafts from the pages of our journal articles to take a more enlivened physical form in the world. But practice has other meanings too, that we hope inflect what we are trying to say here. Meditation proliferationalist Jeff Warren's working definition of practice is 'any activity or way of being that we engage in regularly and deliberately'. Warren notes that this includes both the disciplined kind of skilling-up (like doing yoga or practising the piano) and the idiosyncratic things we do for comfort and pleasure (like 'pretending to be a tree, hiding tiny skull beads in public, or darning moth holes while listening to Amy Winehouse'). He concludes: 'Practices are the habits we choose. The more we repeat them, the less we seem to choose them. Eventually, our practices choose us. Throughout this process, they have much to teach us about ourselves and the world.'[23]

Maybe this is what we mean by practice.[24] Maybe doing theory in the way we demonstrate here is also a kind of practice. Practice changes theory, and theory changes practice. Both are needed, together, in a climate-changing world.

Notes

1. When Clare Britton and Astrida undertook the 'The River Ends as the Ocean' project with Gadigal, Bidjigal and Yuin Elder Aunty Rhonda Dixon, they

referred to the river as moving through Wangal, Gadigal and Bidjigal Country. Geographical features like waterways are often the borders between different communities. We were on the south-eastern banks of the river that day – near the junction with Wolli Creek and almost directly south of Gumbramorra Swamp. So it is most likely we were on Bidjigal Country, as Gadigal is north-east and Wangal is north-west. But sticking with this hybrid naming also highlights waterways as important meeting points.

2. Margaret Somerville and Frances Bodkin, 'Featherlines: Becoming Human Differently with Earth Others', in *Becoming Earth: A Post Human Turn in Educational Discourse Collapsing Nature/Culture Divides*, ed. Anne B. Reinertsen (Rotterdam: Sense, 2016), 65.

3. Ian Tyrrell, *River Dreams: The People and Landscape of the Cooks River* (Sydney: NewSouth, 2018).

4. Kate Judith, 'The Other Alongside: Suburban Mangroves and the Postcolonial Swampy Gothic', *Gothic in the Oceanic South* (London: Routledge, 2023).

5. Clare Britton, A Week on the River (Sydney, 2021); Rhonda Dixon-Grovenor, *Aunty Rhonda's Walk* (Sydney, 2021). And our own performance art walks: Jennifer Hamilton, 'Walking in the Rain' (2011), and Astrida Neimanis, Aunty Rhonda Dixon-Grovenor and Clare Britton, 'The River Ends as the Ocean: walk the tide out' (2021).

6. That iteration of the Collective included Tessa Zettel, Rebecca Giggs, Kate Wright, Sarah Truman, Stephanie Springgay and ourselves.

7. Astrida Neimanis and Jennifer Hamilton, 'The Weather Is Now Political', *The Conversation*, 21 May 2017, https://theconversation.com/the-weather-is-now-political-77791.

8. The objective of this book is neither to rehearse nor convince the reader of this data, but in case there is any doubt, we refer to the 2023 Report from the Intergovernmental Panel on Climate Change (a body that does not undertake research, but synthesizes research conducted worldwide) that states: 'Human activities, principally through emissions of greenhouse gases, have unequivocally caused global warming, with global surface temperature reaching 1.1°C above 1850–1900 in 2011–2020.' 'Climate Change 2023: Synthesis Report. Contribution of Working Groups I, II and III to the Sixth Assessment Report of the Intergovernmental Panel on Climate Change' (Geneva, Switzerland: IPCC, 2023), https://www.ipcc.ch/report/ar6/syr/downloads/report/IPCC_AR6_SYR_SPM.pdf, 4.

9. Groupe d'experts intergouvernemental sur l'évolution du climat, ed., *Climate Change 2014: Mitigation of Climate Change Working Group III Contribution to the Fifth Assessment Report of the Intergovernmental Panel on Climate Change* (New York, NY: Cambridge University Press, 2014).

10. Blanche Verlie, *Learning to Live with Climate Change: From Anxiety to Transformation* (New York, NY: Routledge, 2022), 92–3.

11. Astrida Neimanis and Rachel Loewen Walker, 'Weathering: Climate Change and the "Thick Time" of Transcorporeality', *Hypatia* 29, no. 3 (2014): 558–75.
12. Maurice Merleau-Ponty, *Phenomenology of Perception*, trans. Colin Smith, reprint edn (London and New York, NY: Routledge and Kegan Paul, 1981), 207.
13. Jennifer Mae Hamilton, *This Contentious Storm: An Ecocritical and Performance History of King Lear* (Bloomsbury Publishing, 2017).
14. The genealogy stems specifically from J.L. Austin's *How to Do Things with Words*, which was picked up in gender and sexuality studies during the 1980s/90s by Judith Butler and Eve Sedgwick and proliferated by the many folks working with their ideas. J.L. Austin, How to do Things with Words. (Cambridge, MA: Harvard University Press, 1975).
15. We have been excited by the many different ways our weathering work has been taken up: for example, in early childhood education (Tonya Rooney and Mindy Blaise, *Rethinking Environmental Education in a Climate Change Era: Weather Learning in Early Childhood* (London: Routledge, 2022)); in thinking about prison abolition and climate change (Stella Maynard, 'Weaponised Weathers: Heat, Don Dale, and "Everything-Ist" Prison Abolition', *Right Now*, 13 August 2019, https://rightnow.org.au/opinion/weaponised-weathers-heat-don-dale-everything-ist-prison-abolition/.); and in climate change psychology (Susan Kassouf, 'Thinking Catastrophic Thoughts: A Traumatized Sensibility on a Hotter Planet', *The American Journal of Psychoanalysis* 82, no. 1 (2022): 60–79, https://doi.org/10.1057/s11231-022-09340-3.).
16. We draw our use of the term 'antipolarization' from new work by Laura McLauchlan, 'Hedgehogs, Conservation and Attachment to other Animals: Embodied Approaches to Anti-Polarisation for Our Shared Worlds' (2024). Here, we also suggest Naomi Klein, *Doppelganger: A Trip into the Mirror World*, 1st edn (New York, NY: Farrar, Straus and Giroux, 2023), and Arlie Russell Hochschild, *Strangers in Their Own Land: Anger and Mourning on the American Right*, paperback edition (New York and London: The New Press, 2018).
17. This is the phrase Laura used when commenting on a first draft of some of these chapters. We really like this wording.
18. Lewis Carroll, *Alice's Adventures in Wonderland and Through The Looking Glass* (New York, NY: Simon and Schuster, 2010), 7.
19. Tessa Zettel's body of work is archived at OuMoPo. We were specifically influenced by 'Making Time', a travelling preservation, recipe exchange and book-making project (2012–14), https://oumopo.com.
20. Pronounced 'zeen-ing', from the word 'zine', in turn derived from the word 'magazine'.
21. As Judith Butler says 'within speech act theory, a performative is that discursive practice that enacts or produces that which it names' (*Bodies That Matter: On the Discursive Limits of 'Sex'* (New York, NY: Routledge, 1993), 13.
22. Samuel B. Mallin, *Art Line Thought* (Dordrecht: Kluwer, 1996).

23. Jeff Warren, 'Practices Are the Habits We Choose', Home Base with Jeff Warren, 26 May 2024, https://www.homebasewithjeff.com/p/practices-are-the-habits-we-choose .

24. The uncritical deployment of the language of meditation and secular Buddhism in the prologue might be jarring to some readers. We find Warren's plain language and non-judgemental understanding of 'habit' incredibly useful. But there is a meaningful connection between secular Buddhist practices of repetition and the body of critical theory this book draws on, especially in Chapter 1 and the Epilogue, in relation to unlearning binary thinking. This connection between critical theory and Buddhist practice is encapsulated in a maxim by founding figure of queer theory, Eve Sedgwick: 'Deconstruction is the theory, buddhism is the practice.' 'Making things, practicing emptiness' in Eve Kosofsky Sedgwick, *The Weather in Proust*, ed. Jonathan Goldberg (Durham, NC: Duke University Press, 2011), 75. More recently – and closer to home – there is a growing number of artist/poet/scholars engaging in meditation and mindfulness methods either as an aspect of creative practice or career change or a bit of both. Pia van Gelder's work 'Relaxation Circuit', *Westspace* 2015, explored energetics and electrical currents by placing people in a circuit together connected by wires; Ju Bavyka's 'Rest your identity' (various sites, 2023–ongoing) is a performative facilitation that uses meditation practices to explore aspects of our identity that become overworked in everyday life; and Kynan Tan was a musician, artist and academic who changed careers to become a community teacher of meditation; see https://kynanmeditation.net/.

Lucky Dip

INSET A

"LUCKY DIP" IS A FEMINIST PRACTICE FOR REIMAGINING THE WEATHER THROUGH THE BODY. PARTICIPANTS EXPLORE WEATHER AS A CULTURAL, TEMPORAL, SPATIAL, COLLECTIVE AND SENSORY PHENOMENON. THROUGH THIS PRACTICE, WE SHIFT, LOOSEN AND EXPAND OUR UNDERSTANDINGS OF WEATHER: WHAT IT IS AND WHAT COULD IT BE?

What You Need

- 20-30 SQUARES OF PAPER + SMALL ENVELOPES
- 2 BOWLS OR VESSELS TO HOLD THE ENVELOPES
- PAPER/JOURNAL + WRITING IMPLEMENT × EACH PARTICIPANT

How To Play

1. WRITE INSTRUCTIONS LIKE THOSE ON THE NEXT PAGES ONTO YOUR SQUARES OF PAPER, AND PLACE EACH IN AN ENVELOPE LABELLED EITHER "A" (PROMPTS THAT ENGAGE CONTEMPLATION, CONVERSATION AND SPECULATION) OR "B" (PROMPTS THAT INVITE EMBODIED EXPERIMENTS).

tip: JUST PHOTOCOPY OUR EXAMPLES AND CUT THEM OUT! FEEL FREE TO ADD YOUR OWN...

2. PUT ALL THE "A" ENVELOPES IN ONE BOWL AND THE "B" ENVELOPES IN THE OTHER. WORKING ALONE OR IN PAIRS, INVITE PARTICIPANTS TO:
- TAKE AN ENVELOPE FROM THE LUCKY DIP
- FOLLOW THE INSTRUCTION
- JOURNAL ABOUT THE EXPERIENCE

REPEAT AS MANY TIMES AS YOU WISH, CHOOSING FROM BOTH "A" AND "B". SOME PROMPTS WILL BE DONE IN A FEW MINUTES, SOME INVITE LONGER OR DEEPER ENGAGEMENT — IT'S UP TO YOU!

3. AFTER A WHILE, HAVE A GENERAL DEBRIEF: HOW DID YOU RESPOND TO THE PROMPTS? WERE SOME EASIER, MORE DIFFICULT, INTERESTING, OR TROUBLING? WHAT DID YOU LEARN ABOUT WEATHER, BODIES, TIME, SPACE, IMAGINATION, MEMORY, MATERIALITY — AND THEIR MANY RELATIONS?

CHAPTER 1
Feminist theory for climate change

Introduction: Feminism for weathering together

Weathering together emerged from our research and our lives as feminists. Feminism's insights and tools have pushed us both to think more closely about environment generally and climate change specifically. Our weathering practice asks us to grapple with questions of bodies, justice, solidarity and difference – feminist mainstays that confirm for us that weathering together is a feminist practice. This practice has reinforced our conviction that climate change is a feminist issue, too.

But the connections between feminism and climate change (and by extension, weathering) are not straightforward. This is partly because feminism's meaning is contested. While feminism is a gender-aware theory and practice of justice, not everyone agrees on (or is even aware of) the fine print. This chapter, as the first of four chapters that lay out the conceptual foundations of the book, therefore has two aims. The first is to offer a more nuanced argument about the connections between weathering, climate change, and feminism. At a general level, this chapter shows that any climate actions without feminism would simply uphold many miseries of the present. More specifically it offers feminist tools and tactics for a robust, joyful and just climate change response.

The chapter's second aim looks more closely at feminism's fine print. Weathering, as we unfurl in the chapters to come, is attention and action towards redistributing shelter and vulnerability in a climate changing world. While we understand weathering as a feminist practice, we need a feminism fit-for-purpose. So what specific kind of feminism does weathering require? We have organized the chapter according to four related responses to this question. The first section of the chapter outlines why weathering's feminism needs to be both antipolarizing and antifascist: this feminism takes a stand for some worlds and not others,[1] even if we can't decide in advance who's with us or against us; our feminism can't be an exclusive identity-based club. The second section argues that we need a feminism that isn't afraid of nature.

Western academic feminism has inherited (and sometimes perpetuated) a fraught relationship to nature, especially when gender inequality has long been seen as a 'natural' product of women's 'naturally' different bodies, capacities and roles. Ecofeminism has often served as the fall guy for this anxiety, but as we discuss, rejecting a relationship to nature won't serve us in a climate-changing world. Third, weathering needs a feminism that is grounded in an embodied politics of solidarity. This links to our commitment to antipolarization, and calls for a feminism that must also be anticolonial, antiracist, queer, gender expansive and multibeing.[2] This feminism also acknowledges how power, desire, joy and contradiction are part of figuring out how to do embodied solidarity well. Part three of this chapter presents these commitments in the form of a listicle: necessarily partial and incomplete, and awaiting your additions and amendments.

Finally, weathering's feminism understands that feminist theory is feminist practice. One of the challenges in writing this chapter has been accounting for all of the *yeses, buts* and *on the other hands* that thwart our attempt to be precise about the feminism we are describing. This futility underscores why we have also needed practice all along. Practice shows us where the theory is too blunt, or too blurry. Practice offers new insights or angles that are seeds from which revised theories grow. The concluding section of the chapter therefore describes the first illustrated Inset in this book (Lucky dip) to show how bringing together embodiment and imagination are at the heart of weathering's feminist practice.

An antipolarizing and antifascist feminism for climate change

This book opens with a straightforward claim: climate change is a feminist issue. Clear evidence shows that environmental harms impact women in specific and often more severe ways than men (the research is mostly framed in binary-gender terms). More women than men die in climate disasters, such as hurricanes. This was well documented in 2005 with Hurricane Katrina,[3] but was also the case both before[4] and since.[5] Domestic violence rates rise amid natural disasters,[6] and sites of massive planetary damage (like man-camps at extraction sites) are also sites of heightened sexual violence.[7] Even though climate change will affect us all, its drivers and impacts do not affect us all the same. We need feminism to help us explain and mitigate these disparities.

Feminist Theory for Climate Change

We also see a connection between climate change and feminism in how both call attention to the commodification and destruction of our bodies and the planet. Powerful men who are pussy-grabbers are often the same powerful men who are land-grabbers, where a sense of entitlement to women's bodies and the earth's resources go hand in hand. Opposition to reproductive justice and sexual rights aligns with support for Big Fossil Fuel. Both tend to align with antifeminist, authoritarian versions of masculinity, perhaps epitomized by the pro-extraction promise to 'Drill, baby, drill!'[8] Feminist concerns and climate concerns seem to simply line up.

Links between mastery over nature and heteropatriarchy are not new. Colonial land-theft has long been enacted through violent repression of Indigenous sexual, gender and kinship systems.[9] Today, increasingly polarized cultural spaces of 'woke' and 'anti-woke' politics mean that anti-environmentalism is often tethered to antifeminism in ways that seem both baffling and intractable. But, as Elizabeth Kolbert writes, 'as a problem, climate change is as bipartisan as it gets'.[10] Climate change denial won't protect you from climate change's devastating effects, but neither will feminist politics in the abstract. So while climate change action needs feminism, it needs a kind of feminism that can chip away at the entrenchment of positions. Instead of reinforcing polarization, it requires a feminism that is expansive and inclusive. Climate change affects everybody, but luckily, to quote bell hooks, 'feminism is for everybody'.[11] Simple.

But the connection between feminism and climate change is also complex because not all feminisms are the same. Indeed, as decolonial feminist Françoise Vergès has noted, 'the term "feminism" is not always easy to claim'.[12] While internal critiques of (academic) feminism's whiteness and class privilege are many decades old, a more recent consolidation of trans-exclusionary radical feminists (TERFs) and other kinds of fascist[13] 'feminisms' into what Sophie Lewis has named 'enemy feminisms'[14] makes it difficult to call oneself a feminist without qualification. In the context of colonial genocide, imperialists calling themselves feminists (sometimes also draped in a pride flag, whereby sexually liberated white feminists will claim to free brown bodies from sexual repression, even if it means bombing them) further frack the foundation of any residual notion of the global 'sisterhood'.[15] 'Why call yourself "feminist," why defend feminism', asks Vergès, 'when these terms are so corrupted that even the far right can appropriate them?'[16]

In specifically environmental terms, we also note that white feminism – or what Vergès calls 'civilizational feminism',[17] that is at equal turns individualist (capitalist, neoliberal) and saviourist (racist, classist) – does not meaningfully redistribute power, or shelter, or vulnerability. Liberal feminists mobilize relative privilege to find political power inside patriarchal and colonial institutions that approve new coal mines and expand existing ones. Relatedly, renewable energy wind farms on stolen Indigenous lands beg the question of which women financially benefit from 'a greener future'. These supposed feminisms are interested neither in difference nor weathering better, *together*. They are more congruent with econationalism and ecofascism than feminism. Here, any simple alliance between climate justice and feminism falters.

If we flip that alliance around, we also see that climate change activism and environmentalism are not always 'feminist-forward' in an inclusive and transformative sense. Consider this thought experiment: what is the point of making homes fully sustainable (say, with solar-passive, zero-waste renewable energy, with composting, with public and active transport commuter options), if there is no accompanying concern for systemic misogyny, private property regimes on stolen Indigenous lands, the gendered division of labour, deeply problematic policing and carceral systems, or the privatization of care? These homes might be green-star rated, and even (someday) more or less affordable, but they will still shelter a domestic violence crisis, exacerbate colonial dispossession[18] and prop up the harms of consumer capitalism. Climate change and related environmentalisms without a commitment to inclusive feminisms will just make the miseries of the present more sustainable.

So weathering together needs feminism, and climate change is a feminist issue. But while the need for feminism in a climate-changing world is real and urgent (simple), all feminisms and environmentalisms do not automatically support a more inclusive and just future (complex). For us, any approach to climate change (research, teaching, art, activism, adaptation, policy and so on) that does not include a transformative, inclusive, justice-oriented, queer, anti-racist and decolonial feminist framework is destined to replicate the problems of the present. bell hooks also tells us that the practice of visionary feminism (even if it is potentially 'for everyone') has to become both 'clearer and more complex'[19] in response to a changing world. Becoming clearer requires making choices, and appraising and reappraising feminist tools as they emerge. 'There are times when we have to stand for justice', hooks writes, 'and in standing for justice, there are times when we have to turn away.'[20] For us this means turning away from things like trans-exclusionary feminisms which use ideas of nature to license hate, or 'green' techno-fixes that use the guise of sustainability to further capitalist expansion and colonial dispossession. As we have argued elsewhere, sometimes you need to break a relation in order to make a relation.[21]

Like Vergès, though, we are still committed to feminism. We need it! Specifically, our weathering project needs a feminism that can build a commons (antipolarizing) *and* navigate dangerous off-ramps into exclusionary and regressive feminisms and environmentalisms (antifascist). We need a feminism that holds both the simple and the complex.

Who's afraid of nature? Ecofeminism and feminist environmental humanities

Feminism is a theory and practice of justice. Although it may begin with sex and gender, it can't end there. Françoise Vergès comments that feminism radicalizes struggles around gendered bodies and rights because feminism's task is 'taking into account the challenges faced by a humanity threatened with extinction'.[22] She does not delve deeply into the connections between climate crisis and feminism, but we read her words as an invitation to this: if ever there were a challenge that threatened humanity with extinction, this is it. But to take Vergès's claim seriously, we also need a feminism that is not afraid of nature. This is not as simple as it sounds, on account of feminism's longstanding fraught relationship to nature. In this section, we trace one path of this relationship. We begin with ecofeminism, then consider poststructuralist challenges to ecofeminism's purported essentialism. We follow this by offering our own response to feminism's 'nature problem' – what we call feminist environmental humanities.

The term 'ecofeminism' was coined by Françoise d'Eaubonne in her 1974 book *Feminism or Death: How the Women's Movement Can Save the Planet*.[23] In its simplest definition, ecofeminism is 'a socio-political theory and movement which associates ecological (esp. environmental) concerns with feminist ones'.[24] Over the last decades, however, ecofeminism has often been reduced to a stereotype associated with essentialism – a claim that women are naturally more in tune with nature, naturally its protectors, and that this naturalness inheres in the (natural, essential) biological substance of women's bodies.[25] We will get to the errors of many of these assumptions shortly, but for now it is important to note that as a result, ecofeminism has sat awkwardly in relation to other academic feminisms that took hold in the 1980s and 90s, specifically those described as 'antiessentialist' or 'poststructuralist'. In the words of Charis Thompson and Sherilyn McGregor, 'cosmopolitan academics distanced themselves from the 'touchy-feely', religious, and reproductive-celebratory strands [of ecofeminism] (jokes about placenta-eating covens of ex-hippies became common)'.[26] Popularized by Judith Butler and their theory of gender performativity,[27] poststructuralist feminisms insist that bodies and nature cannot exist outside of how humans construct them through language. These antiessentialist feminisms also question any 'natural' connection between sex and gender, and the 'essential' dominance of heterosexuality. From this perspective, (the stereotype of) ecofeminism was seen as too simple in how it understood nature. These poststructuralist criticisms and suspicions make a lot of sense in a context where women's 'natural' biology was also the anchor for their 'naturally' inferior social and legal status.

But a rejection of ecofeminism also meant that some poststructuralist feminisms veered too far away from a necessary and nuanced engagement with nature as the material reality of the body. In the words of Stacy Alaimo: 'How could feminisms approach nature without solidifying or cementing gender dichotomies?'[28] Alaimo's work and other antiessentialist feminisms sought ways of navigating these tensions. For example, feminist new materialism, feminist posthumanities, and feminist science and technology studies (STS), among other feminist projects, all grapple with the tricky relationship between gender, nature and culture (and more) in important ways.[29] Many of these feminisms were in turn scrutinized: for being too binary; for being too anthropocentric; for being inattentive to race and colonialism; for being too theoretical, or not theoretical enough; or for not being 'new' at all.[30] In some cases, critiques underlined the tensions between environmental concerns and feminist commitments in these projects.[31] Our point is not to rehash or even adjudicate these criticisms. It is simply that holding nature and feminism together is very difficult.

Yet, when so much of our current crises implicate nature, we *need* a feminism that is not afraid of nature, and is actually deeply invested in it. We need to keep contending with this tension between feminism and environment, even if we never quite get it perfect. It is not surprising, then, to note an ecofeminist resurgence as part of widespread climate justice activism – a broad, coalitional movement led by women in the Global South.[32] Some academic feminists have turned (back) to the term ecofeminism without too many anxieties about its history,[33] and continue to defend its longstanding importance and its continued 'promise.'[34] As Thompson, McGregor and others rightly argue, ecofeminism has always been more than its reductive stereotype, and academic criticism was often 'overdetermined.'[35]

Ecofeminism's dismissers did not pay enough heed of the content of ecofeminist analysis whose analyses provide valuable foundations for contemporary climate justice struggles. One example is the labour- and justice-oriented anticolonial ecofeminism promoted by activist and scientist Vandana Shiva and Marxist feminist Maria Mies, where global ecofeminist solidarity against colonial capitalist extraction shows up in women's leadership of ecological movements (against atomic energy, logging, food pollution and for biodiversity and clean water).[36] Or, from a different angle, Val Plumwood's philosophical ecofeminism gives us key concepts for challenging dominant frames of Western thought – like the binary oppositions of female/male and nature/culture – that help us better understand the logic of domination that links gender oppression and environmental harm.[37]

As these academic feminist disagreements about ecofeminism emerged and solidified, we were both students, researching environmental issues and the materiality of bodies and 'nature.' But although we studied in different places at different times, we were also both academically reared on the liberatory potential of poststructuralist feminism in text-centric disciplines of philosophy and literary studies. Poststructuralism, like ecofeminism, has been criticized, and also caricatured. Some claim it is unhelpfully relativist ('poststructuralists say anything can be true!') and divorced from 'reality' ('poststructuralists say everything is constructed and nothing is real!'). We (along with many others) disagree. Again, we won't rehearse these decades of debates here, but our point is that a fit-for-purpose feminist theory for climate change, as well as being unafraid of nature, also has to be unafraid of culture. This means being prepared to genuinely deal with the way culture imprints on the actual stuff of the world.

We are among those feminists who are turning (back) to ecofeminism after dismissing it too easily in the past, but we also want to hold onto our poststructuralist feminist origins as vital for our weathering project. We believe that poststructuralism can still support a version of social construction (i.e. that worlds are shaped by ideas and language) while maintaining a nuanced view of nature and the material world.[38] (Here, we have learned alongside and as part of many of the antiessentialist feminisms we note above – new materialism, posthuman feminisms, feminist STS, and more.) We also hold onto poststructuralism because it provides a clear line to the antipolarizing and antifascist feminism we stand for. In *Who's Afraid of Gender?*, Judith Butler points out that a fear of gender is actually a fear that words that once felt stable but have now become unmoored.[39] In this way, gender – seen by some as 'code for a political agenda'[40] – becomes the touchstone for increased polarization. Butler is writing this now with some urgency because of the rise of fearful and fascist feminist projects (such as trans-exclusionary reactionary feminism). We think it is important to notice how the fear of gender described by Butler is also related to a fear that nature is no longer 'natural' in the ways some people believed. A fear of bodily diversity is a fear that gender is neither binary nor anchored in nature, and this fear represents nostalgia for a time where the meaning of both gender and nature seemed fixed and controllable. In other words, Butler's adamance that we continue to examine what we mean by gender must be accompanied by an ongoing examination of what we mean by nature.[41] Poststructuralist feminisms give us the tools to open up both of these concepts beyond the narrow ways their meanings have culturally sedimented.

We need a feminism that understands that language can work in two ways: it can oppress and limit what bodies and their worlds can do or be (hence the 'gender policing' we hear about so often), but language can also celebrate and even proliferate difference. A new (or newly configured) language can serve the proliferation of messy, joyful, many gendered, queer, trans, crip and anti-essentialist human and non-human bodies. A new (or newly configured) language can serve the proliferation of a nature that is neither pristine nor wild (as colonial views hold), but deeply cultural, also messy, and always in us and of us, too. (It is worth noting that while our focus here is on language and culture, in many ways this proliferation also aligns with scientifically and empirically grounded understandings of the material properties of both 'gender' and 'nature'.)[42] To come full circle: there is nothing 'essentialist' (static, passive, locked-down-with-no-possibility-of-change) about gender or nature, as both words and material realities.

We maintain that we need the promise of *both* ecofeminism and poststructuralist feminism to land here. As mentioned above, we have started to call our version of this theory *feminist environmental humanities*.[43] For our purposes in this book, feminist environmental humanities let us consider 'climate change' using both ecofeminism's steady commitment to thinking through our relationship with nature, and poststructuralist feminism's interest in language, not for its own sake, but for the way it can refuse fascist positions while remaining open to more inclusive and expansive futures. Feminist environmental humanities lets us approach climate change in non-obvious and non-linear ways, reading for difference, justice, and marginalization, but also coalition, repair, desire and joy.

Frankly, we don't think 'feminist environmental humanities' is the most accurate term for what we do and it certainly isn't a very catchy one (but neither is 'neo-poststructuralist neo-ecofeminism'!). Our term is awkward and sometimes funny, because in doing this work we make a point of questioning and upending what we think 'the environment' is (as it turns out: everything); what we think we mean by 'feminist' (see this chapter!); and what we think 'humanities' are (we liberally work with and as scientists, artists, poets, ethnographers, community workers, and more). At the same time, this framework provides a useful anchor: we are feminists, we are concerned with environments, and we are, fundamentally, humanities scholars. This is why we centre questions of meaning, metaphor, concepts, stories and creativity in this book.

In offering 'feminist environmental humanities' as a feminist framework for our weathering work, nor are we proposing something discrete. Feminist environmental humanities learn from and sit alongside differently named academic and activist feminisms, sometimes doing similar things: Black feminisms, Indigenous feminisms, feminist science and technology studies, queer, trans and crip ecologies, and more. Our feminism is deliberately promiscuous, because there are always new connections to be made in this complex world we inhabit. But it also practises safe promiscuity. Solidarity cannot be easily assumed. We don't want to extract knowledge carelessly from other struggles, so we build relationships slowly.[44]

Our overarching proposal in this book is this: weathering together requires us to be expansive in our feminism in order to build social infrastructure for practising a redistribution of shelter and vulnerability. To do this, we need practices and tools, including theories, concepts and frameworks, that are useful for the task. So we are not claiming that 'feminist environmental humanities' gets the relation between gender and nature 'right', for once and for all; more modestly, we claim that these three words importantly focus our attention. We think our feminist environmental humanities is both provisional and useful (as all good theories should be), and gives us a decent resting place for doing the work we need to do, now.

Feminism as an embodied politics of solidarity: A listicle for weathering together

As an antipolarizing methodology, weathering together requires an embodied politics of solidarity. This means that although our feminism begins in gender, it must also be anticolonial and antiracist, queered and cripped, and multibeing. An embodied politics of solidarity means valuing difference as we live it in and as bodies, and seeking out tactics (which can also be concepts) for connecting across differences that others exploit to divide us. In these ways, the meaning of 'embodied politics of solidarity' as a phrase is very clear to us. At the same time, it has many facets and follows many possibilities, not all of them realized yet by us. That's why we've chosen to describe this dimension of the feminism we need as a listicle.

The listicle – an ostensibly low-brow genre found in magazines and online – presents information in the form of an annotated list. Some people think it is bad journalism, but we like the genre for a few reasons. First, a listicle is non-hierarchical: you can start reading at the middle, or the bottom. Second, a listicle is incomplete and partial, but not entirely arbitrary. This one arises from our combined years researching and teaching at the intersection of feminism and environment in fields that include gender studies, literary studies, cultural studies and environmental studies. Third, a listicle boils things down to key points, but since it is provisional, it provokes lateral thinking. Finally, listicles can create surprise communities. Poet Eileen Myles suggests that listicles are of the time *after* mass culture, where social media's proliferation of styles and trends leads us to 'sort of suspect that nobody has the same list as us'.[45] But what if your listicle is the same as or similar to ours? Or what if you can offer some useful additions or amendments? What communities can we build together?

1. **Feminism as an embodied politics of solidarity starts with bodies**. Many different versions of feminism have argued that all theory – no matter how seemingly abstracted – begins in our bodies, and affects bodies in close and distanced ways. Any suggestion that theory is disembodied is another God Trick![46] Weathering as a feminist practice brings climate change to the scale of the body because that is how we live it, and that is how we, as different bodies, live it differently. As lesbian feminist Adrienne Rich encouraged us, 'Start with the geography closest in – the body'.[47] Feminist tools such as Rich's politics of location allow us to account for our differences as anchors for practising an embodied politics of solidarity. Feminism also understands what's at stake when bodies are deemed insignificant by a false masculinist hierarchy of rational minds over sensing bodies.

2. **Feminism as an embodied politics of solidarity supports Indigenous sovereignty and anticolonial futures.** Acknowledging our own politics of location relates to what Max Liboiron calls 'specificities and obligations'.[48] This means not only listing our

identity markers, but understanding our inheritances as specific obligations and commitments. As a material practice happening in real places, our weathering methodology has a specific commitment to Indigenous sovereignty. We are in a process of reckoning with what it means to be doing this work on stolen Indigenous land. We must work to undo colonialism in large and small ways, where both the feminist and the queer is intentionally oriented towards 'undoing of the indoctrination' of colonialism, as Anaiwan scholar and artist Gabi Briggs puts it.[49] We unpack this more in Chapter 2, 'Weather', but flag it here as a non-negotiable part of an embodied politics of solidarity. There can be no climate solidarity without a commitment to Indigenous sovereignty.

3. **Feminism as an embodied politics of solidarity is about power,** with a specific, but hardly exclusive, interest in cisheteropatriarchal power. It can examine how human systems of power are drivers of climate change. Power, though, has two meanings: it refers to power structures like patriarchy and colonial capitalism, but also to material power like fossil-fuelled energy systems. Feminism offers analyses that bring these kinds of power together – for example, exploring how extraction of resources like coal and oil connects to ideas of 'powerful' masculinity.[50] Feminism can also meaningfully consider the power of non-human agents – say, a hurricane, or a parasite – that scramble existing power orders. These insights are important checks against a Western masculinist hubris that presumes a 'mastery of nature'.[51] But power can also be a ground for solidarity, as it imagines alternatives to omnicidal forms of power, and locates power in persistence,[52] survival,[53] anger,[54] erotics[55] and more. Feminism offers our weathering work different ways to think about and enact power for building new and different worlds as we dismantle some current ones.

4. **Feminism as an embodied politics of solidarity cares about your feelings**. A Western (masculinist) separation of rational minds from feeling bodies privileges detached scientific objectivity as a way of dealing with crises. Still, even with access to lots of rational climate science, climate change is escalating (Kari Norgaard calls this the 'myth of information deficit').[56] This shows why we cannot address the climate crisis just by stating facts and figures. Emotional orientation and how we feel about things matters in terms of changing minds and behaviours (and thus *changing climates*).

Feminist research on affects and emotions gives us tools for examining why differences in feelings must be part of climate responses. For example, how people feel about their own gender identity helps explain why men recycle less (not rational!);[57] how we feel about gender stereotypes more generally helps explain why hurricanes given 'female names' are (sometimes catastrophically) perceived as less dangerous than those with 'male names' (also not rational!).[58] Feminists know feelings are political (where bad feeling is not an individualistic pathology[59]), and relational. We say more about this in Chapter 6 in relation to our weathering practices.

5. **Feminism as an embodied politics of solidarity notices and values difference.** Different bodies (neurodiverse or neurotypical, childbearing or child-free, Black or white, sixteen or sixty-five . . .) experience climate change's effects in different ways. Feminism notices how climate change exacerbates these differences. It is interested in how the unequal distribution of shelter and vulnerability shows up in insecure housing, harsher temperatures or lack of potable water. (We say lots more about this in the following chapters.) Feminism as an embodied politics of solidarity offers nuanced analyses of where differences come from: are they materially given, socially constructed, or (most often) both? We need to account for bodies as made up of both matter (skin, blood, carbon, water) and meaning (how they are shaped by cultural frameworks). Both influence how we will weather climate change. We analyse this at length in Chapter 3.

6. **Feminism as an embodied politics of solidarity *desires*.** Feminism understands the ecological crisis as 'a problem of desire',[60] where many kinds of environmentalism want to manage and curb our material desires. But queer feminists remind us that desire can also be a desire for abundant and flourishing non-human worlds.[61] Moreover, in a context where climate change (plus cis-heteropatriarchy, colonialism and capitalism) is overwhelming and depressing,[62] feminism maintains that desire can be a form of resistance and power, especially when your pleasure has been denied and unvalued by the structures that fuel climate colonialism.[63] Sex positivity, careful consent and intimacies beyond heteronormativity can encourage environmental attachments rooted in desire and accountability. This kind of desire can lead to more ecological and

less destructive relations.⁶⁴ Moreover queerness, as poet Eileen Myles suggests, can be 'a research tool' for thinking more creatively about environments and climates. (Myles cheekily notes: 'If you're all buttoned up about sexuality, can you really think about climate?')⁶⁵

7. **Feminism as an embodied politics of solidarity is no stranger to contradiction and incommensurability.** Desire can also be contradictory. Some desires *do* exacerbate climate change and uphold colonialism, while others are liberatory. Feminist praxis works to constrain some longings in hopes of a 'climate-improved' future, but holds on to joy along the way. A feminism fit-for-purpose for weathering together thus claims we need to both stoke and curb our desires. Two things can be true at once. We are fans of the conjunctive 'both/and'. We appreciate ellipses that indicate there is always more to add . . . We don't not like a double negative. This is also why we can say, despite problems with dominant science, that we are grateful for climate scientists who are sounding the alarm. This is why we can say that human rights, and now the rights of 'nature', despite some troubling Western liberal origin stories, are something we can't not want.⁶⁶ We need lots of levers, especially as most are imperfect or inadequate on their own.

8. **Feminism as an embodied politics of solidarity understands the complexity of 'we'.** Our feminist embodied politics asks how *we* can find solidarity because of, not in spite of, our differences. This is no easy feat in the shadow of the Western liberal universal subject and all of its violences. On the one hand, we earthly beings really are all in this together! But as Max Liboiron points out, 'arguments that "we" are destroying the planet or "we" must all band together as One' fail to describe how climate crisis burdens some groups of people disproportionately.⁶⁷ While it is good to acknowledge the collective nature of the issue, Robyn Wiegman notes that the use of 'we' can also be 'a masterstroke of white-woman speech' that flattens other differences (especially race and class) in service of a liberal feminist agenda.⁶⁸ With all these pitfalls, what's a feminist to do? Wiegman, like other feminists, suggests we need to 'inhabit the error' and find ways of sticking with this false-but-necessary category. Such 'inhabitation' demands accountability. It requires what poet Alexis Pauline Gumbs has called a kind of 'echolocation' whereby all of us (not only whales and bats or other echolocating animals) have to

send out signals across all kinds of bodies and species, and pay attention to what comes back – 'humbly listening and learning to take responsibility for [our] frequencies'.[69] In other words, our 'we' is not a free pass to a make-believe universalism. Solidarity is not easy. We cannot respond well to climate change without committing to the complexity of the 'we' who are in 'this' together.

9. **Feminism as an embodied politics of solidarity is also about gender.** As we've noted above, climate change has gendered effects; climate change evokes gendered responses. But feminism also provides the opportunity to make this 'simple' point complex. Queer and trans feminist theories remind us that gender is not a matter of a simple binary: scientifically speaking, an organism can have thousands of possible genders, depending on how you understand that word.[70] Mutability and proliferation of gender is also connected to climate change and environmental degradation (e.g. rising water temperatures and chemical inflows). Feminism can help us understand these changes not as pathologies to be eradicated, but as creative tactics for climate change mitigation and adaptation.[71]

10. **Feminism as an embodied politics of solidarity knows that different oppressions prop each other up.** The climate crisis reveals the conjoined exploitation of some humans and non-human nature. As Claire Jean Kim puts it: 'It may be that forms of domination – white supremacy, heteropatriarchy, human supremacy, mastery over nature and more – are so intricately woven together, so dependent on each other for sustenance, that they will stand or fall together.'[72] We require a feminism that explains the logic and practice of mutual exploitation, and offers alternatives to the binary 'Master model' that divides the world in service of hierarchy and instrumentalization.[73] As we write this book, genocidal violence continues in Gaza and elsewhere. We need a feminism that understands these violences as violence against people, against women, against queers, against animals, against trees, against Land, against water, against history and against the future. Our feminism sees these violences as connected, and approaches them as such.

When we fail to see interconnections between oppressions, we remain aligned to existing distributions of power (and shelter). An embodied politics of solidarity maintains that none of us is free until all of us are free.[74] Instead of building bunkers or launching life rafts, we need to ensure living land and breathing oceans for all. Noting the (literal and metaphorical) breath-taking aspect of the intersecting crises we are living, Blanche Verlie calls this kind of embodied solidarity an 'aspirational climate justice'.[75] This is different bodies dreaming, breathing, desiring, together as if all of our futures depend on it, because they do.

We hope this listicle also provokes a question, namely: can this capacious and non-linear feminism change what we mean by 'climate change'? Climate change is not only the climatological and existential threat facing earthly life; it must also be understood as a response to this same thing. *Some climates actually need changing*, and feminism has some good tools for getting down to business.[76] Weathering needs feminism because feminism is about transformation, and about calling and fighting for significant change.

Conclusion: Feminist theory is feminist practice

We have arrived at the kind of feminist theory we want by reading and writing about feminism for decades. But finding a feminist theory fit-for-purpose for climate change has also required practice. Sara Ahmed remarks that once you become skilled in theory's language, theory is actually pretty easy to do. What's hard, she says, is 'the empirical work, the world that exists'[77] – the practice. We agree, but we think making theory is also challenging when you ask it to hold all of the nuances, contradictions and feelings that subtend it. Making theory honest, where it matches (clarifies, distills) embodied experiences in the world is tricky, but it is the challenge we have set for ourselves in this book's four theory chapters.

In service of the aim to narrow the space between theory and embodied experience, we can turn to deliberate practices that can test, refine, and expand the theories we are working with. The Weathering Collective has developed specific practices that can try out and refine what an embodied politics of solidarity feels like. These practices toggle between imagining, desiring, speculating, on the one hand, and testing, enacting, feeling things out, on the other. 'Lucky dip' (Inset A) is one practice that helps us reimagine our relation to weather and climate change.

All the exercises outlined in the insets of this book play with the weather's openness in some way, but 'Lucky dip' is an entry-level activity. This exercise – versions of which we've facilitated with students, colleagues and community groups in many settings (classrooms, conferences, workshops, festivals) around the world – asks participants to select from a bowlful of envelopes. Each envelope includes a card with a question or prompt.

The cards comprise two different categories: the first is called 'Embodied Imagination', and suggests a thought experiment such as 'What is the weather on the last day of Earth?' or 'What is the smallest weather? Describe it.' These prompts also solicit reflections such as 'Is weather cultural?' or 'Is weather political?' The second category is called 'Imaginative Embodiment.' These cards engage participants in small embodied knowledge experiments. Examples include: 'Sit or lie down. Can you make the weather a blanket? Can you wrap it more tightly, or loosely, around your body?' or 'Close your eyes. Inhale and exhale deeply through your nose. What does the weather smell like?' Without telling our participants what weather is or can be, we invite them to stretch these possibilities via their own bodies and imaginations. Afterwards, participants report associations, connections and revelations that keep the question of 'weather' open – what, where and when it is, and for whom. As participants explore weather memories connected to strong emotions, or notice it in strange places (beneath a shoe sole, coating an eyeball), weather – and maybe the climate – begins to change.

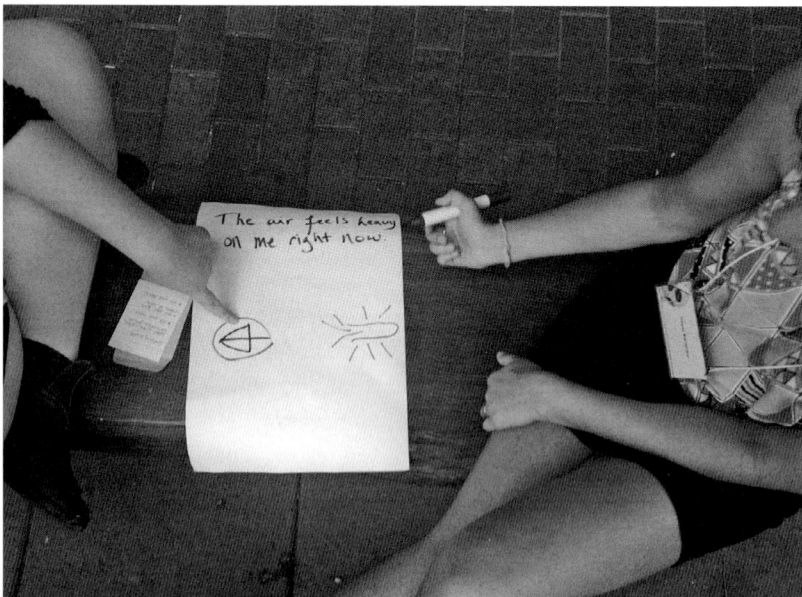

Figure 1.1 "Lucky Dip," or, Mapping the weather (Somatechnics Conference in Byron Bay, 2016). Photograph: Astrida Neimanis.

'Lucky dip' is a feminist practice because the feminism we describe above has prepared us for it. Feminism readies us to loosen any kind of weather 'essentialism' and be open to how our bodies might have a different story about the weather. We let the skin-shells of our bodies become thinner, finding a solidarity not only with air and soil, but with other times and other places, and with the bodies practising alongside us, who may be weathering in a very different way. In turn feminism changes through this practice, expanding to include an embodied solidarity with the planet so much bigger than us, and maybe with a changing climate, too.

'Lucky dip' validates the need for feminist ways of understanding climate change beyond rational, scientific analyses. In cracking open the idea of weather, this activity reveals the intimate connection between theory and practice, and words and worlds. Our bodily sensations spur our imaginations in new directions, while words-on-a-card shift how our bodies experience the world. This is not always neat, or rational, or free of contradiction. It is taken up by each body, in all of its difference, differently. Yet the emergent words and worlds implicate us all.

Feminism is a theory and practice of justice. In a climate-changing world, it may be impossible to comprehensively imagine all of the ways that justice will have to be practised, theorized and fought for. Instead, this justice must be sensed and felt, and moved towards, even as it is not fully known. But it *is* possible today to say what justice is not, namely: depriving others of shelter as you double down on your own.

And, whatever climate change is or will be, it is not 'out there', and beyond us. It is the very stuff of us. Climate change is in our bodies, and of our bodies. This is why we need our bodies – in all of their imaginative capacities – to change it. We are all climate changed; we are also all climate changers. Feminism – the kind we deploy in this book, the kind we need to weather better together – helps us figure out the 'how', changing itself in the process.

Notes

1. This wording comes from Thom van Dooren, *Flight Ways: Life and Loss at the Edge of Extinction* (New York, NY: Columbia University Press, 2014) and is indebted to the work of Deborah Bird Rose, among others.
2. The term 'multibeing' was coined by Susan Reid. We like it because it is more expansive than 'multispecies' (since air, water, rocks and sunshine are not all 'species') and less anthropocentric than 'non-human'. See Susan Reid, 'Ocean

Justice', *Cultural Politics* 19, no. 1 (March 1, 2023): 107–27, https://doi.org/10.1215/17432197-10232516.

3. Nancy Tuana, 'Viscous Porosity', in *Material Feminism*, ed. Stacy Alaimo and Susan Hekman (Bloomington, IN: Indiana University Press, 2008).
4. Eric Neumayer and Thomas Plümper, 'The Gendered Nature of Natural Disasters: The Impact of Catastrophic Events on the Gender Gap in Life Expectancy, 1981–2002', *Annals of the Association of American Geographers* 97, no. 3 (2007): 551–66.
5. Alvina Erman et al., *Gender Dimensions of Disaster Risk and Resilience: Existing Evidence* (Washington, DC: International Bank for Reconstruction and Development / The World Bank, 2021), https://wrd.unwomen.org/sites/default/files/2021-11/Gender-Dimensions-of-Disaster-Risk-and-Resilience-Existing-Evidence.pdf
6. Debra Parkinson and Claire Zara, 'The Hidden Disaster: Domestic Violence in the Aftermath of Natural Disaster', *The Australian Journal of Emergency Management* 28, no. 2 (1 April 2013): 28–35, https://search.informit.org/doi/10.3316/informit.364519372739042.
7. Sarah Deer and Elizabeth Kronk Warner, 'Raping Indian Country', *Columbia Journal of Gender & Law* 38 (2019): 31–95.
8. Sean Parson and Emily Ray, 'Drill Baby Drill: Labor, Accumulation, and the Sexualization of Resource Extraction', *Theory & Event* 23, no. 1 (2020): 248–70, https://doi.org/10.1353/tae.2020.0013.
9. Kim TallBear, 'Making Love and Relations beyond Settler Sex and Family', in *Making Kin Not Population*, ed. Adele E. Clarke and Donna Jeanne Haraway, Paradigm 56 (Chicago, IL: Prickly Paradigm Press, 2018), 145–66.
10. Elizabeth Kolbert, 'The Political Climate', *The New Yorker*, 22 August 2022.
11. bell hooks, *Feminism Is for Everybody: Passionate Politics*, 2nd edn (New York, NY: Routledge, 2015).
12. Françoise Vergès, *A Decolonial Feminism*, trans. Ashley J. Bohrer (London: Pluto Press, 2021).
13. We choose the word 'antifacist' knowing that the meaning of fascism is loose. This looseness is useful here, since the fascist feminisms we are describing are not unified according to a strict definition. Following Andrew Nikiforuk, we see fascism as referring not only to concrete beliefs and actions (e.g. that trans-women are not women, or that Indigenous women's rights are irrelevant in the context of clean energy production), but also to a general social mood (for example, where mentions of equity or pronouns are met with eyerolling or worse), supporting technology (such as social media platforms that funnel attention and reduce complexity to lowest common denominators) and context (such as our increasingly polarized political spheres.) At base, we understand fascism as an authoritarian refusal of other groups' humanity. Andrew Nikiforuk, 'What Is Facism?', *The Tyee*, 5 November 2024, https://thetyee.ca/Analysis/2024/11/05/What-Is-Fascism/.

14. Sophie Lewis, *Enemy Feminisms: TERFs, Policewomen, and Girlbosses Against Liberation* (Chicago, IL: Haymarket Books, 2025).
15. E.g. Jasbir Puar, 'Intersectionality, Anti-Imperialism, Anti-Semitism, and the Question of Palestine', in *The Routledge Companion to Intersectionalities*, ed. Jennifer Christine Nash and Samantha Pinto (London and New York: Routledge, 2023), 529–36.
16. Vergès, *A Decolonial Feminism*, 5–6.
17. Vergès, *A Decolonial Feminism*, 5.
18. Eve Vincent and Timothy Neale, *Unstable Relations: Indigenous People and Environmentalism in Contemporary Australia* (Crawley: UWA Publishing, 2017).
19. hooks, *Feminism Is for Everybody: Passionate Politics*, 110.
20. hooks acknowledges that there are many paths to feminism, but is clear about diversions that, even if they bring some change for some people, are not adequate to feminism's visionary, radical promise. She is particularly critical of 'reformist' feminists 'who really felt safer working for change solely within the existing social order'. hooks, *Feminism Is for Everybody*, 110.
21. Astrida Neimanis and Jennifer Hamilton, 'Falling Out Together', *Feral Feminisms*, no. 10 (Fall 2021): 114–31.
22. Vergès, *A Decolonial Feminism*, 5.
23. Françoise d'Eaubonne, *Feminism or Death: How the Women's Movement Can Save the Planet* (London and New York, NY: Verso, 2022).
24. 'Ecofeminism, N', *Oxford English Dictionary*, Oxford University Press, July 2023, https://doi.org/10.1093/OED/1314740230.
25. For example, Mary Daly's *Gyn/Ecology* doubled down on a supposed natural truth of both women's bodies and the natural world as a pathway to social and ecological liberation. Mary Daly, *Gyn/Ecology: The Metaethics of Radical Feminism* (Berkeley, CA: Beacon Press, 1978).
26. Charis Thompson and Sherilyn MacGregor, 'The Death of Nature' in *Routledge Handbook of Gender and Environment*, ed. Sherilyn MacGregor (London and New York, NY: Routledge, 2017): 48.
27. Judith Butler, *Gender Trouble: Feminism and the Subversion of Identity* (New York, NY: Routledge, 1990).
28. Julia Kuznetski (née Tofantšuk) and Stacy Alaimo, 'Transcorporeality: An Interview with Stacy Alaimo', *Ecozon@: European Journal of Literature, Culture and Environment* 11, no. 2 (September 20, 2020): 137–46, https://doi.org/10.37536/ECOZONA.2020.11.2.3478.
29. Examples of feminist new materialisms include: Stacy Alaimo and Susan Hekman, eds, *Material Feminisms* (Bloomington, IN: Indiana University Press, 2008), Karen Barad, *Meeting the Universe Halfway: Quantum Physics and the Entanglement of Matter and Meaning* (Durham, NC, and London: Duke

University Press, 2007), Vicki Kirby, ed., *What If Culture Was Nature All Along?*, New Materialisms (Edinburgh: Edinburgh University Press, 2017), Stacy Alaimo, *Bodily Natures: Science, Environment, and the Material Self* (Bloomington, IN: Indiana University Press, 2010). For feminist posthumanities, see Cecilia Åsberg and Rosi Braidotti, eds., *A Feminist Companion to the Posthumanities* (Cham, Switzerland: Springer, 2018) and Hasana Sharp and Chloë Taylor, *Feminist Philosophies of Life* (Montreal: McGill-Queen's University Press, 2016). For Feminist STS in this vein, see Annemarie Mol, *The Body Multiple: Ontology in Medical Practice*, Science and Cultural Theory (Durham, NC: Duke University Press, 2002).

30. Important critiques of some feminist new materialisms and posthumanisms include Zakiyyah Iman Jackson, *Becoming Human: Matter and Meaning in an Antiblack World* (New York, NY: New York University Press, 2020); Sara Ahmed, 'Open Forum Imaginary Prohibitions: Some Preliminary Remarks on the Founding Gestures of the 'New Materialism', *European Journal of Women's Studies* 15, no. 1 (2008): 23–39, https://doi.org/10.1177/1350506807084854; Zoe S. Todd, 'An Indigenous Feminist's Take on the Ontological Turn: "Ontology" Is Just Another Word for Colonialism', *Journal of Historical Sociology* 29, no. 1 (2016): 4–22, https://doi.org/10.1111/johs.12124. Black feminisms in particular have offered important alternative routes for thinking about our relationship to nature and matter. See e.g. Kathryn Yusoff, *A Billion Black Anthropocenes or None* (Minneapolis, MN: Minnesota University Press, 2018); Katherine McKittrick and Sylvia Wynter, *Sylvia Wynter: On Being Human as Praxis* (Durham, NC: Duke University Press, 2015); Katherine McKittrick, *Dear Science and Other Stories*, Errantries (Durham, NC, and London: Duke University Press, 2021); Alexis Pauline Gumbs, *Survival Is a Promise: The Eternal Life of Audre Lorde*, 1st edn (London and New York, NY: Allen Lane, 2024); Chelsea Mikail Frazier, 'Black Feminist Ecological Thought: A Manifesto', *Atmos*, 1 October 2020, https://atmos.earth/black-feminist-ecological-thought-essay/.

31. Jennifer Mae Hamilton, 'The Future of Housework: The Similarities and Differences Between Making Kin and Making Babies', *Australian Feminist Studies* 34, no. 102 (2 October 2019): 468–89, https://doi.org/10.1080/08164649.2019.1702874.

32. Sherilyn MacGregor, 'Reclaiming and Reframing Ecofeminist Politics in the Face of Continuous Global Crises' (Nature-Society Relations and the Global Environmental Crisis: Thinking on Climate Change and Sustainability from the Fields of Intersectional Theory and Transdisciplinary Gender Studies, Humboldt University, Berlin, 2023).

33. Lara Stevens, Peta Tait, and Denise Varney, eds., *Feminist Ecologies* (Cham, Switzerland: Springer International Publishing, 2018), https://doi.org/10.1007/978-3-319-64385-4.

34. See Catriona Sandilands' interest in 'the promise of ecofeminism' in expansive political terms, as well as Sherilyn MacGregor, 'Making matter great again?' and Greta Gaard, 'Toward a Queer Ecofeminism', among others. Ariel Salleh's 1997

Ecofeminism as Politics is also exemplary here for walking a really fine line between feminist Marxism, essentialist ecofeminism, postcolonialism and poststructuralism. We don't see the feminist poststructuralist debates as idealistic in the same way as Salleh, but Salleh's nuanced braiding of the different strands of feminism as ecofeminism gets at the layers of contradiction and complexity we're seeking. Catriona Sandilands, *Good-Natured Feminist: Ecofeminism and the Quest for Democracy* (Minneapolis, MN: University of Minnesota Press, 1999), xviii. Sherilyn MacGregor, 'Making matter great again? Ecofeminism, new materialism and the everyday turn in environmental politics', *Environmental Politics* 30, no. 1–2 (2021): 41–60. Greta Gaard, 'Toward a Queer Ecofeminism', *Hypatia* 12, no. 1 (1997): 114–37, https://doi.org/10.1111/j.1527-2001.1997.tb00174.x. Ariel Salleh, *Ecofeminism as Politics: Nature, Marx and the Postmodern* (London: Zed Books, 2017).

35. Thompson and MacGregor, 'The Death of Nature', 48.

36. Maria Mies and Vandana Shiva, *Ecofeminism*, 2nd edn (London: Zed Books, 2014).

37. Val Plumwood, *Feminism and the Mastery of Nature* (London: Routledge, 1993).

38. In her essay 'Sowing Worlds', Haraway critiques the way words have been used as weapons for denying the existence of some worlds, but also suggests that words can be enrolled to 'terraform' different worlds. Haraway's feminist politics are often overlooked in citations of this work. See Donna Haraway, 'Sowing Worlds: A Seed Bag for Terraforming with Earth Others', *Staying with the Trouble: Making Kin in the Chthulucene*, (Durham, NC: Duke University Press, 2016), 118–20.

39. Judith Butler, *Who's Afraid of Gender?* (New York, NY: Farrar, Straus and Giroux, 2024).

40. Butler, *Who's Afraid of Gender?*, 4.

41. There is an established tradition of examining the contested meanings of nature. See William Cronon, 'Introduction', in *Uncommon Ground: Rethinking the Human Place in Nature*, ed. William Cronon, 1st edn (New York: W. W. Norton & Company, Incorporated, 1996), 23–68.

42. The works of Elizabeth Wilson are examples of how poststructuralist feminist theory can inform new methods in biology and neurology. See Elizabeth A. Wilson, *Gut Feminism* (Durham, NC: Duke University Press, 2015), https://doi.org/10.1215/9780822375203, and Elizabeth A. Wilson, *Psychosomatic: Feminism and the Neurological Body* (Durham, NC: Duke University Press, 2004).

43. See also Jennifer Mae Hamilton and Astrida Neimanis, 'Composting Feminisms and Environmental Humanities', *Environmental Humanities* 10, no. 2 (Nov. 2018): 501–27, https://doi.org/10.1215/22011919-7156859, and 'Five Desires,

Five Demands'. *Australian Feminist Studies* 34, no. 102 (Oct. 2019): 385–97, https://doi.org/10.1080/08164649.2019.1702875.

44. Hamilton and Neimanis, 'Composting Feminisms and Environmental Humanities'.

45. 'Eileen Myles: To dig a hole in eternity', Eileen Myles in conversation with Annamarie Jagose at the 2018 Sydney Writer's Festival, https://omny.fm/shows/sydney-writers-festival/eileen-myles-to-dig-a-hole-in-eternity (accessed 29 October 2024).

46. Donna Haraway, 'Situated Knowledges: The Science Question in Feminism and the Privilege of Partial Perspective', *Feminist Studies* 14, no. 3 (1988): 575–99.

47. Adrienne Rich, 'Notes towards a Politics of Location (1984)' in *Blood, Bread, and Poetry: Selected Prose 1979–1985* (New York, NY: W. W. Norton & Company, 1994), 210–31.

48. Max Liboiron, *Pollution Is Colonialism* (Durham, NC, and London: Duke University Press, 2021).

49. Jennifer Hamilton and Gabrielle Briggs, 'Gabi Briggs: Long Version on the Vital Process of Centring Indigenous Sovereignty in Climate Action', Community Weathering Station: SoundCloud, 17 December 2021, https://soundcloud.com/weatheringstation.

50. Adam Dickinson, *Anatomic* (Toronto: Coach House Books, 2018); Cara Daggett, 'Petro-masculinity: Fossil Fuels and Authoritarian Desire', *Millennium: Journal of International Studies* 47, no. 1 (2018): 25–44; Stacy Alaimo, *Exposed: Environmental Politics and Pleasures in Posthuman Times* (Minneapolis, MN: University of Minnesota Press, 2016); Clifton Evers, 'Polluted Leisure', *Leisure Sciences* 41, no. 5 (2019): 423–40.

51. Val Plumwood, *Feminism and the Mastery of Nature* (London and New York, NY: Routledge, 2002).

52. hooks, *Feminism Is for Everybody*.

53. Gerald Vizenor, *Survivance: Narratives of Native Presence* (Lincoln, NE: University of Nebraska Press, 2008).

54. Audre Lorde, 'The Uses of Anger: Women Responding to Racism', *Sister Outsider: Essays and Speeches by Audre Lorde* (Berkeley, CA: Crossing Press, 2007), 124–33.

55. Audre Lorde. 'Uses of the Erotic: The Erotic as Power', *Sister Outsider: Essays and Speeches by Audre Lorde* (Berkeley, CA: Crossing Press, 2007), 53–9.

56. Kari Marie Norgaard. *Living in Denial: Climate Change, Emotions, and Everyday Life.* (Cambridge, MA: MIT Press, 2011), 3.

57. Aaron R. Brough et al., 'Is Eco-Friendly Unmanly? The Green-Feminine Stereotype and Its Effect on Sustainable Consumption', *Journal of Consumer Research* 43, no. 4 (Dec. 2016): 567–82, https://doi.org/10.1093/jcr/ucw044.

58. Kiju Jung et al., 'Female Hurricanes Are Deadlier than Male Hurricanes', *Proceedings of the National Academy of Sciences* 111, no. 24 (June 2014): 8782–7, https://doi.org/10.1073/pnas.1402786111.
59. See for example Elizabeth Stephens, 'Bad Feelings: An Affective Genealogy of Feminism', *Australian Feminist Studies* 30, no. 85 (July 2015): 273–82, https://doi.org/10.1080/08164649.2015.1113907 and Sara Ahmed, *The Promise of Happiness* (Durham, NC: Duke University Press, 2010).
60. Catriona Sandilands, 'Desiring Nature, Queering Ethics', *Environmental Ethics* 23, no. 2 (2001): 169–88.
61. Catriona Sandilands, ed., *Queer Ecologies: Sex, Nature, Politics, Desire*, Nachdr. (Bloomington, IN: Indiana University Press, 2011); Stacy Alaimo, 'Wanting All the Species to Be: Extinction, Environmental Visions, and Intimate Aesthetics', *Australian Feminist Studies* 34, no. 102 (2 October 2019): 398–412, https://doi.org/10.1080/08164649.2019.1698284.
62. Farhana Sultana, 'The Unbearable Heaviness of Climate Coloniality', *Political Geography* 99 (2022): 102638, https://doi.org/10.1016/j.polgeo.2022.102638.
63. adrienne maree brown, *Pleasure Activism: The Politics of Feeling Good* (Chico, CA, and Edinburgh: AK Press, 2019).
64. Sandilands, 'Desiring Nature, Queering Ethics'; Annie Sprinkle et al., *Assuming the Ecosexual Position: The Earth as Lover* (Minneapolis, MN, and London: University of Minnesota Press, 2021).
65. Eileen Myles and Maggie Nelson, 'Eileen Myles in Conversation with Maggie Nelson', *Women's Studies* 51, no. 8 (17 November 17 2022): 880–98, https://doi.org/10.1080/00497878.2022.2138029, 888.
66. Wendy Brown, 'Suffering Rights as Paradoxes', *Constellations* 7, no. 2 (2000): 208–29, https://doi.org/10.1111/1467-8675.00183.
67. Max Liboiron, "There's No Such Thing as 'We,'" *Discard Studies* (blog), October 12, 2020, https://discardstudies.com/2020/10/12/theres-no-such-thing-as-we/.
68. Robyn Wiegman, *Object Lessons.* (Durham, NC: Duke University Press, 2012), 13.
69. Alexis Pauline Gumbs, 'This Is What It Sounds like (an Ecological Approach)', *The Scholar & Feminist Online* 8, no. 3 (12 August 2010), https://sfonline.barnard.edu/this-is-what-it-sounds-likean-ecological-approach/. 17–18.
70. Myra J. Hird, 'Naturally Queer', *Feminist Theory* 5, no. 1 (2004): 85–9, https://doi.org/10.1177/1464700104040817; Joan Roughgarden, *Evolution's Rainbow: Diversity, Gender, and Sexuality in Nature and People* (Berkeley, CA: University of California Press, 2004).
71. Astrida Neimanis, 'Toxic Erotics and Bad Ecosex at Windermere Basin', *Environmental Humanities* 14, no. 3 (1 November 2022): 699–717.
72. Clare Jean Kim, "'Michael Vick, Race, and Animality' in *Ecofeminism: Feminist Intersections with Other Animals and the Earth*, ed. Carol J. Adams and Lori Gruen (New York, NY: Bloomsbury, 2022), 20.

73. Plumwood, *Feminism and the Mastery of Nature*.
74. This phrase has been articulated in a variety of forms by activists and writers across centuries, from Black American civil rights activist Fanny Lou Hamer, to Muri Elder Lilly Watson in Australia. For a discussion of this phrase's origins, see '. . . Until Everyone Is Free', *SURJ Toronto* (blog), n.d., https://www.surjtoronto.com/blog/-until-everyone-is-free.
75. Blanche Verlie, 'Climate Justice in More-than-Human Worlds', *Environmental Politics* 31, no. 2 (February 2022): 297–319, https://doi.org/10.1080/09644016.2021.1981081, 298; Blanche Verlie and Astrida Neimanis, 'Breathing Climate Crises: *Feminist Environmental Humanities and More-than-Human Witnessing*', *Angelaki* 28, no. 4 (July 4, 2023): 117–31, https://doi.org/10.1080/0969725X.2023.2233810.
76. Blanche Verlie, *Learning to Live with Climate Change: From Anxiety to Transformation* (New York, NY: Routledge, 2022), https://doi.org/10.4324/9780367441265.
77. Sara Ahmed, *Living a Feminist Life* (Durham, NC: Duke University Press: Durham, 2017).

INSET B: close meteorology

The meaning of weather is in flux. As the climate changes, we come to develop new and recognise old weather knowledges. In close meteorology, participants use the academic method of "close reading" (i.e. paying attention to what is backgrounded, marginalized, not taken into account, as part of the main story) to read how different bodies in the workshop space are "weathering". They then create a weathering report via a transversal poem-generator activity. These reports invite us to understand everyday atmospheres in creative, relational and surprising ways.

What you need

- Paper
- Writing implement × each participant

How to play

Part 1. (Close) reading the room

Move about this space and note: what marks of weathering show up? On which bodies? Which bodies are more permeable to weather? Which are more resilient? Why? Observe, and make notes all over your page.

Part 2. A weather transversal

Decide on a weather-related line (see → next page) to be your data-sorting tool, and draw it across your notes. A transversal is a line that links data points: it generates meaning from what is gathered. While this may seem random, connecting the words with a line drawn by weather (rain, shade, sunlight etc.) makes weather a co-author of the poem.

Part 3. Poem generator

On another piece of paper, make a list of words gathered by your transversal line. Then, generate a poem from those words. (Haikus are a place to start, but free verse, concrete poems or other simple formats also work). These poems will create unexpected connections between your observations. Themes or questions that emerged during note-taking will surface.

Part 4. Collective weathering report

Invite participants to share their poems! Finish by collating everyone's poems into a collaborative "weathering report" on the atmosphere of your workshop.

transversal poetics

c) shade/sun differential

PLACE YOUR PAGE IN THE PARTIAL SHADE. MAKE A LINE THAT MATCHES WHERE THE SHADOW IS CAST.

a) chance of precipitation

SPLASH WATER ON YOUR PAGE. MAKE A LINE THAT CONNECTS THE DOTS.

b) temperature

MAKE AS MANY CIRCLES ON YOUR PAGE AS IT IS DEGREES CELSIUS RIGHT NOW. DRAW A LINE CONNECTING THOSE CIRCLES.

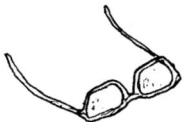

CHAPTER 2
Weather

Introduction: Stormy inheritance

Weather is thunder, lightning, wind, rain, sunshine, fog, clouds, hail. Weather is hot, cold, wet and dry. Weather is the relative presence and absence of these things depending on the qualities of the day. Weather is any kind of atmospheric disturbance, and the (barely noticed) lack of disturbance. Weather is all of this, but to develop our feminist practice for climate change, we tell a more expansive story about weather. Weather is the way the world touches us and becomes us, as well as the way we shape it in turn. We hope, by the end of this chapter, that readers will understand 'weather' to refer to something more than thunder, lightning, wind and rain.

To get there, we need to talk about language. As the linguist Ferdinand de Saussure taught us,[1] language is always an inherited product of historical forces. We subscribe to his theory of language where the meaning of a word does not exist in isolation from the world. At the same time, the relationship between word and world is complex.[2] This relationship is not fixed, since the meaning of a word relies on an inherited social contract about what it means and its difference from all other words. According to Saussure, this contract can be amended (language is mutable!), but making changes is sweaty work (language is – more or less – immutable!).

Thunder, for example, could be called anything, but most English speakers use 'thunder' because as children, we were taught that the clap after lightning is referred to as 'thunder', because that's the social contract that our parents inherited, and so on. Thunder's meaning also comes from its difference from other terms for weather (lightning, wind, rain), and other words that sound similar (blunder, chunder, wonder). In learning a word, we implicitly sign up to these agreements, so changing a word's meaning is not something we can do alone or overnight; any amendments require others to sign on. In addition, we are writing in English in the settler colonial states of Canada and Australia respectively. The English language is dominant in these places due to the history of shipbuilding and colonialism's crimes. So, words carry histories. We never just learn one word. All words are relational. They are products of intergenerational knowledges that exist beyond us.

Drawing on this socio-historical and systemic understanding of words, this chapter suggests an amendment to the social contract of what 'weather' means. We begin by describing how our received understanding of weather is colonial, and how we are in the process of unlearning that knowledge, acknowledging our own starting place within queer feminist humanities. We tell a historical story about the weather's role in our culture because it shows us how weather became backgrounded, and why its political, social and cultural dimensions have been downplayed. Bringing these dimensions out of the background, we argue, is crucial for a feminist practice of climate change. To do so, we show how an expanded view of metaphor and the changing meaning of weather reveal connections between meteorological and social worlds. We call this 'more-than-meteorological' weather. The final sections of the chapter then recount some of the creative and embodied practices that have encouraged us to develop an expanded understanding of weather. We situate our own experiments alongside the work of other writers and artists, to stretch what weather means in and beyond our bodies, other technologies, times and scales. The conclusion comes full circle, reminding us of the critical ongoing process of unlearning colonial weather. This is the only way to make the meaning of weather adequate to the demands or our changing climates.

Unlearning colonial weather

We began our weather research in the only way we knew how: as ourselves, a white non-Indigenous feminist philosopher based in Canada (Astrida) and a white non-Indigenous literary studies scholar in Australia (Jennifer), both interested in queer feminist theory and human–environmental relations. For the most part, the cultural research we were studying figured weather as no more than ambient backdrop to human dilemmas. This ambience intrigued us. From the position of our own similar and different inheritances, our research asked a shared question: how is the weather meaningful – culturally, philosophically, poetically, politically and sensorially – specifically as the climate is changing?

While cultural scholarship on weather is growing,[3] back then we both spent considerable time arguing for its importance to literary studies and philosophy.[4] We now see this was an inefficient place to begin. For more than a decade, we developed an idea that discrete weather events are always part of the dynamic process of *weathering* (durational, multiple, shared, varied, experienced, embodied, emotional, political and cultural) – only to learn that this is very close to diverse Indigenous ways of knowing weather as a fundamental part of culture. In other words, we came upon an answer to our question that is thousands of years old.

So why did we take the long way? Mununjali Yugambeh poet Ellen van Neerven describes how 'colonial misinformation whitewashes crimes of the past committed by settlers'.[5] As non-Indigenous people we benefit from such crimes – most obviously attempted genocide and systematic land theft. But the erasure of Indigenous weather knowledge is also a crime and colonization whitewashed our knowledge of weather, too. We learned colonial weather as members of the English language group, who were taught how to map weather onto the universal four seasons at school. All this was reinforced daily in the weather reports on TV and in the newspaper, which left little room for contemplating the relationship of this version of weather to frontier violence. As environmental historians O'Gorman, Beattie and Henry state bluntly, 'if colonization meant making weather knowledge, it also involved erasing alternatives'.[6]

Diverse Indigenous views of seasons and weather patterns are place-based, or grounded in what Mohawk and Anishinaabe scholar Vanessa Watts calls 'place-thought', where thinking and Land are inseparable.[7] Such weather knowledges emphasize cycles of light and temperature, plant expression, animal movement and human activity, which are all vital for survival.[8] This understanding now shows up in some settler weather services (like Australia's Bureau of Meteorology), but the subtleties of Indigenous weather knowledges, as connected to entire ways of living, do not dominate the nightly news. That's why we have to work against what non-Indigenous anthropologist Sarah Wright calls 'tendencies in mainstream work on weather and climate' that 'invisibilise prior Indigenous relations and theorisations'.[9]

We suspect that some readers of this book will be a bit like us: living in the wake of colonialism and Imperialism, trained to uniquely valorize Western science by an education system where learning is Anthropocentric and weather is background. You will likely be reading from a place impacted by colonialism, or a place that did the colonizing. Maybe you are well into a journey of unlearning how the colonial drive to domination shapes how you know what you know, or just at the beginning. Or, you might be Indigenous and, as Bundjalung writer Evelyn Araluen has described, struggling with this process too:

> It is hard to unlearn a language:
> to unspeak an empire,
> to teach my voice to rise and fall like landscape.[10]

Araluen elsewhere describes directly how Indigenous literacy programmes under settler colonialism educate Indigenous folks with whitewashed syllabi that perpetuate their own culture's erasure.[11] Within this colonial education context weather knowledge is generally separated from cultural knowledge, even as it is instrumentalized and controlled for specific cultural ends. In a colonial frame, weather – a vital and dynamic force of relation – is meant to be measured, predicted and mastered. The colonial way of knowing, thinking and being is insidious. Unlearning it is slow and painstaking work.

Settler artist and scholar Christine McFetridge develops unlearning as a methodology. Building on the work of others, she defines it as a 'process of critically working back through one's history, prejudices, and learned, but now seemingly instinctual, responses'.[12] While the aim is to get somewhere different, the process has to start from one's own intellectual and social contexts. For us, this was and is the feminism we discuss in Chapter 1. While starting here was inefficient, it was not without value. The tools we acquired allowed us to get this far. Feminist methods encourage us to pay attention to embodied experience, read for difference, and refuse violent universalisms. We are taught to question inherited categories and hierarchies, and dismantle pervasive and problematic nature/culture and human/non-human binaries. Feminism spurs us to think critically about power, and how it consolidates different forms of oppression. It gives us tools for dismantling and denaturalizing the logics of colonial, heteropatriarchal capitalism. It also warns us about master narratives, and encourages us to be open to what we don't know, and respect those intellectual labours we may arrive at belatedly. We are taught the value of finding connection, too.

Jen asked Anaiwan scholar and artist Gabi Briggs directly whether and, if so, how feminist and queer thinking by non-Indigenous scholars can connect with explicitly decolonial ways of addressing climate change. Gabi replied that it is possible, but is definitely not guaranteed:

> At the end of the day (queer and feminist focused climate action) needs to centre Indigenous sovereignty. I really feel that's what's gonna liberate us all ... feminism is important at this point, [but] feminism has to work towards Indigenous sovereignty; queer activism is important, but it needs to work towards Indigenous sovereignty.[13]

Queer feminist environmentalisms *can* potentially act like a stepping-stones towards allying with the project of Indigenous sovereignty, but they need to actually be oriented towards that goal. For example, as queer feminists we pay attention to place, embodiment and interconnection, alongside critiquing heteronormative family constructs to liberate all genders and create new forms of kinship. This thinking can help undo our indoctrination in the normative settler colonial situation. But, for Briggs, queer feminisms can lead non-Indigenous people towards Indigenous sovereignty only if they are genuinely taken up with the intention to act in solidarity with that project.

So the story we are writing here is about slowly coming to understand and support Indigenous weather knowledges, but also about using our own intellectual and cultural inheritances in service of the broader project that Briggs outlines. In Chapter 1, we detailed how feminist tools and concepts are helpful for thinking about climate change, weather and weathering. The rest of this chapter focuses on another key dimension of our feminist starting point – that is, as literary and cultural scholars, who think a lot about the power and possibilities of language.

The story of weather's erasure

Tracing a cultural history of weather-thought helps us better understand our trajectory of unlearning and relearning weather. We aren't the first to notice the strange narrowness of the meaning of 'weather' in English. For example, almost a century ago cultural critic Walter Benjamin suggested that weather-talk indicated 'boredom.'[14] Later in the twentieth century, literary critic Roland Barthes remarked that one speaks of the weather in order to say 'nothing.'[15] At a similar time, philosopher Michel Serres also noted 'the erasure of the meteors.'[16] Of course, he didn't mean the literal disappearance of rain and heat, nor man's successful control of the weather. He was referring to the changing cosmological conditions, whereby weather no longer had the cultural meanings and functions it used to, in England and other European traditions.

What kind of powerful force must take hold such that weather could be erased from cultural consciousness, reduced to nothingness or boredom by the 1900s? Serres pinned this period of erasure to the 1600s–1800s,[17] which maps directly onto British and European Imperialism and Enlightenment. To this we can add the Copernican revolution, secularization and scientific positivism (whereby the same measurement can be performed by anybody to get the same result, eliciting the same interpretation) – all of which conspire to minimize the view of the meteors as the heavens communicating with earth.[18] Where the meteors once delivered contentious messages from the gods, the natural world was now the object of scientific inquiry.

The ideal endgame of such a process is imagined in detail in Francis Bacon's seventeenth-century work *The New Atlantis* – a speculative fiction that presents the case for a 'perfect' island society (Bensalem), achieved through the 'prevention and remedy' of nature's problems, including 'tempests, earthquakes, great inundations, comets, temperature of the year, and divers [sic] other things' on account of a perfect scientific method.[19] Notably, Bacon's story shows how the study of nature is symbiotically related to a patriarchal and hierarchically gendered social order. There folks can 'imitate and demonstrate meteors' and control temperature (with 'furnaces of great diversities'), while at the same time tracking the 'deceits of the senses' to eliminate all potential for strangeness, transgression and cultural change. In short, in *The New Atlantis* the weather is studied to help maintain the status quo.

This myth of controlling nature to control culture speaks to an enduring real-world desire. It is central to the development of the modern sciences of meteorology where the desire to predict the weather accurately relates to its controlled functions within a capitalist system: seamless transport logistics, maximum agricultural yields, free economic flows and optimized civil engineering. It is moreover reinforced by dualistic thinking, where the body is subordinate to the mind, nature subordinate to culture, female to male, Black to white, emotion to reason and so on[20] – upholding not only the logic of scientific positivism, but also patriarchy, white supremacy and colonialism. In other words, Western imperialist ways of knowing weather 'erased' the ways that weather was connected to contentious cultural and political elements of the same period.

The story of the weather's erasure as part of the Western cultural worldview is not trivial. It shows how particular ways of knowing and attempting to control the weather, among other things, support modern power structures. But, tragically, ironically, or predictably, as the projects of Western Imperialism and modern industrialization started to dominate globally, the weather itself became increasingly difficult to control and background. Presently, climate change triggers record-breaking heat waves, storms rupture levees built for once-in-a-century floods, and droughts are so widespread that the rainforests of Gondwana have caught fire for the first time since the formation of planetary landmasses. Predictions have become less predictable. Meanwhile these phenomena are accompanied by other disruptions (regressive policies, global protests, diverted migrations, mass die-offs) and other atmospheres (anxiety, depression, doubt, anger, sadness, denial).

We hope this brief history demonstrates that even though weather was never fully erased, its neutralization and attempted containment entailed an acute narrowing of weather's meaning and relations. Our aim is to open weather back up. Indeed, a defining conclusion of our research is that *all* of this – the politics, the cultural imaginaries, the feelings, and more – can be understood as weather, too. If we erase meteorological weather's imbrication in social, cultural and political life, we are also erasing vital ways for learning how to weather together, better, amidst climate crisis. In the rest of the chapter, we develop this idea via the concept of 'more-than-meteorological' weather, first by turning back to language and specifically metaphor.

Metaphor and weather as 'more-than-meteorological'

The *Oxford English Dictionary* tells us that weather is 'the condition of the atmosphere (at a given place and time) with respect to heat or cold, quantity of sunshine, presence or absence of rain, hail, snow, thunder, fog, etc., violence or gentleness of the winds. Also, the condition of the atmosphere regarded as subject to vicissitudes'.[21] Vocabulary.com gives us a considerably vaguer definition: weather is 'anything else that is happening outside'.[22] We find this vagueness weirdly helpful. To say *all* of this is weather, we mean: yes, weather is sunshine, rain and wind; but it is also the social, cultural, and political atmosphere around us, conditioned by the ideas that we inherit, and that we pass on.

When we share this expanded understanding of weather, people often say, 'but aren't you just being metaphorical?' We agree that on first pass, it might seem like associating weather with a mood, for example, is 'just' a metaphor. The mood is not *literally* connected to 'the meteors'; the mood is just 'pathetic fallacy' according to the nineteenth-century critic John Ruskin.[23] We might say 'that was a stormy conversation!' even though outside, the sun is shining. The storminess is 'just' metaphorical because even though the mood resembles a kind of weather, it is not connected to the literal weather.

But, when we expand what weather can mean, its function as metaphor will also change.[24] It is useful here to recap what a metaphor is. According to George Lakoff, a traditional view of metaphor requires that the metaphor and the thing it is describing come from different domains. In the example above, since mood belongs to the domain of the personal or social, and a storm belongs to the domain of the natural or meteorological, describing a mood as stormy weather would be 'just' metaphorical. But we've already said the social contract of language *can* be amended. Lakoff points out that in a contemporary theory of metaphor, 'cross-domain mapping' – where words come to belong to more than one domain – is part of how language changes to represent our lived reality.[25] To take a different example: while your email inbox isn't actually a 3D box with a slot on top, we don't think about the word 'inbox' as 'just' a metaphor, even though it could be classified as one. Here, the word 'inbox' shows how the domain of physical material construction and the domain of digital software are 'crossed.' For us, the key point is that this contemporary theory of metaphor also has social and political implications. What social and political phenomena do these changes in metaphor alert us to? Using the inbox example: the domain-crossing might point to the replacement of physical infrastructures with digital ones, and ask us to consider the many social, economic and political implications of this.

Coming back to weather, cultural theorist Anita Girvan argues that in this time of 'heightened climatic and ecological instability', our inherited ways of making sense of the world are collapsing, and as a result, 'novel metaphors' emerge.[26] Or, in Lakoff's terms, different domains are 'cross-mapped' in new ways. We are interested in what these 'novel metaphors' and new associations signal. What are they telling us to pay attention to? If something is dismissed as 'just' a metaphor (where terms belong to two unrelated domains), what changes and connections might we fail to notice?

We are invested in what different domains can be thought together when we expand the definition of the word 'weather.' We understand (and concede) that our expanded use can be understood as metaphor, but we disagree that it is 'just' metaphor, as if that qualifier somehow diminishes its significance. We press the question: *what do we stand to lose when we say weather as social, cultural, interpersonal, infrastructural, etc, is 'just' metaphor*? What do we stand to lose by insisting that the natural world of the meteors and the social or political world of humans are securely distinct domains? For us, relearning weather is not about totally flattening these domains. We know that a rain cloud and a crappy day at work are not the *same* thing. Sometimes a metaphor is just a metaphor! Relearning weather, though, lets us notice and analyse connections between domains. And, to signal our desire to expand-but-not-flatten weather's place in the meteorological domain, we use the term 'more-than-meteorological'. This approach also creates space for knowledges that already recognize the interdependence of natural and cultural domains. As such, it is a useful stepping stone in our process of unlearning colonial weather.

Let's get more specific about how these domains are connected in ways that highlight this 'more-than'. While meteorology is now defined as 'the branch of science that deals with atmospheric phenomena and processes, esp. with a view to forecasting the weather',[27] forecasting has always had a more-than-meteorological function. For example, Australia's Bureau of Meteorology has legal obligations, as set out in the Meteorology Act 1955, to act in 'the public interest generally and in particular: (a) for the purposes of the Defence Force; and (b) for the purposes of navigation and shipping and of civil aviation; and (c) for the purpose of assisting persons and authorities engaged in primary production, industry, trade and commerce'.[28] This Act conflates the public interest of weather forecasting almost directly with the (colonial capitalist) state's, and meteorologists have a professional obligation to forecast in support of strategic military, transport and economic purposes.

As climate change accelerates, and the forecasting systems, infrastructures and evacuation plans designed to control and contain weather catastrophically fail, weather's 'more-than' dimensions are increasingly revealed. When Hurricane Katrina made landfall in August 2005 in New Orleans, this was most certainly a meteorological event. Category 5 (the highest category) winds and rains meant storm surges, ruptured levees and devastating floods. Trees were uprooted and roofs torn from houses. But as we all soon learned, this was not an 'equal opportunity' storm. It was a watershed moment for widespread awareness of just how unequal and deeply cultural storms can be. Far more Black people were killed and displaced than white. Far more women were killed and displaced than men (these data are available only in gender-binary terms). The poor suffered far more than the wealthy. Reporting on the devastation of Indigenous community lands was almost entirely absent from the news. Of course, this is not because wind gusts can sense skin colour or bank balances or chromosomal make-up. This is because the 'weather' that gathered and broke in New Orleans that summer was more-than-meteorological: weather was also the racism (and misogyny and colonialism and poverty and ableism) that structured everyday life in the lead-up to that storm, rendering a very unequally distributed vulnerability to it.[29]

The racialized harms from the Katrina disaster connect up with more recent Black feminist work that considers seemingly banal weather as related to the structural violence that shapes everyday existence. For example, Black Studies scholar Christina Sharpe suggests that 'weather' is antiblackness; Black bodies must endure 'the total climate'[30] that is antiblackness. She writes: 'In what I am calling the weather, antiblackness is pervasive as climate.'[31] Sharpe's chapter 'The Weather' from her 2016 book *In the Wake* specifically references the Middle Passage and Black slavery in the US, as well as its contemporary manifestations (such as Black deaths in custody and police killings of Black and other racialized people), but her point is that this climate cannot be reduced to an event or a set of events. Sharpe is concerned with 'the totality of the environments in which we struggle; the machines in which we live; what I am calling the weather'.[32]

In other words, weather swirls as atmosphere and context, both everywhere and unnoticed (by some). Again, some might think Sharpe is 'just being metaphorical' (where antiblackness is *like* bad weather). But racism and weather are deeply entangled, and the climate crisis has been long foreshadowed in our social systems and structures of power. In John Protevi's work on Hurricane Katrina, for example, he gives a big-picture analysis that directly relates the hunger of Empire for cotton and sugar that fuelled the Middle Passage to the changing environmental conditions of Louisiana and New Orleans (such as the destruction of wetlands that were a buffer between land and sea) that in part facilitated Katrina's devastation.[33] Protevi is not suggesting straightforward causality; it would be ludicrous to claim that Hurricane Katrina was 'caused by' the slave trade and leave it at that. But on account of the intensity and differentiated impacts of the same storm, the long histories of Empire and white supremacist structures cannot be disentangled from the disaster. Again we wonder: Whose interests does it serve to keep these 'domains' separate?

Fast forward fifteen years to the COVID pandemic, where again Black and Indigenous people in the US, and other racialized and poor people in other countries, are disproportionately dying. At the same time, George Floyd's murder by police in Minneapolis mid-pandemic accelerated the Black Lives Matter movement. On 22 June, 2020, a poem by Claudia Rankine appeared on the front page of the *New York Review of Books*. It was called 'Weather'. Here, Rankine draws together the 'droplets' of debilitating disease ('Six feet / under for underlying conditions. Black.') with Floyd's murder and the gathering force of protest ('We are here for the storm / that's storming because what's taken matters').[34]

As poet Ada Limon reminds us, poetry disturbs our human inclination to read for straightforward sense.[35] In a poem, we are instead 'working in the smallest units of sound and syllable and clause and line break' where straightforward meaning becomes ambivalent, overdetermined, partial, and at the same time more honest or true. In Limon's words, in these ways a poem 'makes more sense as the language for our human experience than, let's say, a news report'.[36] This is why in Rankine's poem, it 'makes sense' that antiblack police violence, and an antiblack official response to the COVID pandemic (both figured by Rankine as 'a form of governing that deals out death and names it living'), and the rising storm of protest, are all simultaneously lived and mutually implicated phenomena.

In both Rankine and Sharpe's work, the meteorological sense of weather (and climate change) takes a backseat to the more-than-meteorological sense that, we agree, can seem primarily anthropocentric and thus metaphorical. But the aim of this book is to insist on the connections between these domains, to pay attention to where and how the weather is involved in our meaning-making practices, even when it is not immediately recognizable as related to the environment. Lakoff's modern theory of metaphor gives us license to do this, but more importantly, we want to push our readers to think with us about what the changing meaning of weather signals. Climate crisis cannot in any sensical way be divorced from the systems of power that have thrown human relationships with the non-human world out of whack. The COVID-19 pandemic is connected to these unbalanced relationships, just as surely as is the brutal policing of Black bodies, directly related to a white supremacist ideology of private property and extraction. An expanded sense of 'weather' helps us hold these different domains together.

One final point before moving on: we also hope that this expanded sense of weather reveals that weather is not only made in the 'heavens'. Humans are weather-makers, too, via the systems we build and perpetuate. Climate change is anthropogenic (human-made), not only because of our carbon emissions, but because of human values, institutions and actions that support the exploitation of the earth and most of its inhabitants. Capitalism, heteropatriarchy, racism and colonialism are not (only) powerful ideas or ideologies; they are material phenomena that imprint on bodies (like all weather). So, as we develop and promote different ideas, we can in time create different weathers. This slow and ambivalent process is what we call *weathering*. We get into this in more detail in the next chapter.

Relearning weather through practice: Close meteorology

Relearning weather asks us to be curious about what else weather might be, beyond or athwart the colonial story. Claudia Rankine's poem is one example of how art can do this particularly adeptly: less beholden to language's social contract, creative practice can kickstart unlearning in helpful and startling ways. The remainder of this chapter turns to look more directly at other helpful examples of arts-led practices.

In Chapter 1, we introduced one of the 'entry-level' exercises developed in the context of the Weathering Collective. 'Lucky dip' (see Inset A) primes participants to observe weather in expanded and embodied ways. Via a set of simple instructions, this feminist practice invites participants to both imagine and experience weather beyond what colonial knowledge tells us it is. The objective here is to bring the large, abstracted idea of 'climate change' back to our bodies: we feel the weather in our hands, or beneath our shoe. We imagine weather beyond Earth, or deep in the ground.

'Close meteorology' (see Inset B) is a related activity for unlearning colonial weather knowledges. Riffing on the literary method of 'close reading'– observing the powerful structuring features of the world, as well as the possibilities for unmooring them, in the smallest parts of a text – 'Close meteorology' commits to observing and disrupting climate change in the most local of weathers. As explained in Inset B, 'Close meteorology' begins by asking participants to observe the weather of their immediate surroundings. Maybe participants are already thinking about weather as sweat, tears, air conditioning, colonial architecture; maybe they simply notice the sunlight coming in through a window. It doesn't matter. As they observe, participants record careful and detailed notes onto a physical piece of paper.

As a literary method, close reading also commits to a relationship between worlds and words, finding the far-away worldly domain in the close-by textual one. The next step of 'Close meteorology' makes this relationship explicit: participants invite meteorological weather as a direct and literal collaborator for analyzing their notes. By placing the paper in the dappled sunlight, or dripping puddle water over it, or recreating the day's temperature graph across the notebook page with a pencil line, the weather 'chooses' which observations will be in play.[37] Participants circle the words touched by the shade or the rain, or the temperature line. They then craft a simple poem from the circled words. This becomes their 'weathering report.'[38]

Using weather this way might seem like a gimmick, but we offer it as a method of data sorting similar to many others: parameters are set, and relevant data is selected. Weather is our collaborator! Get closer. Sense it. See where the practice takes you. Neither remove weather from the picture, nor devalue it. Notice how weather impacts your words – i.e., the way you make the world meaningful. In this exercise, the far-away meteors interact with our up-close observations, condensing them into surprising new combinations.

While the resulting poems may not be Claudia Rankine-level, the physical interruption of weather helps produce deeply honest 'weathering reports' that likewise jumpstart an expansion of what weather can mean.

Similar to the way contemporary metaphors engage in what Lakoff calls cross-domain mapping, 'Lucky dip' and 'Close meteorology' also play with scale. These activities disturb what we think weather is because they bring together dimensions that are usually opposite, distant or in tension: near and far, abstract and lived, planet and body, rainclouds and words, colonial inheritance and anticolonial desire.

Shrinking the distance between climate and weather: *Open-weather*

Our research continues to learn from other creative practices that bring different scales of experience together in order to dislodge our habits of understanding and see their connections. An obvious separation we seek to challenge is the one between climate and weather. The modern distinction between climate (long term averages, patterns) and weather (immediate or short-term events, randomness) can make it seem like climate and its change are happening somewhere else, to someone else (or, indeed, not at all). Bringing climate and weather together foregrounds how climate is not just abstract calculations but is being lived by us, right now, at a very human scale, too. In turn, weather is not without consequence: it can hang around long enough to form a pattern, or even a structure. Even if the modern climate/weather distinction is sometimes useful, a hard cut can lead to climate change denialism ('it's not climate change; we've always had the odd hot day in winter!'). Keeping both scales separate limits the opportunity to understand daily life as implicated in climate change.

Challenging this distinction is a key feature of *open-weather*, a long-term project led by researcher-designer Sophie Dyer and creative geographer Sasha Engelmann. One of their typical workshops might feature a group of people on a grassy hill, some of them kneeling down in front of laptops, the others standing with 4ft antennae in their hands, staring up into the sky. As part of this 'feminist artistic experiment',[39] participants learn to hack and read satellite data about large-scale weather events using DIY tools. These activities show us that the modern distance between 'weather' and 'climate' is at least in part due to the hegemony of certain kinds of expertise that discount embodied, localized and accessible knowledge-making. *Open-weather* offers

Figure 2.1 *When we image the earth, we imagine another*, 2022. Illustration by Golrokh Nafisi in collaboration with open-weather for *Ecoes #3*, a publication by Sonic Acts.

us ways to downscale climate science to our own bodies, not to valorize individualism[40] but to expose systems of power. As Engelmann and her co-authors explain, 'In the tradition of intersectional feminism, *open-weather* investigates the politics of location and interlocking oppressions that shape our capacities to observe, negotiate, and respond to the climate crisis'.[41]

Open-weather's constellation of participatory workshops, writings, transmissions and installations also point out that bodies that do the measuring also influence the measurement. In renouncing their role as mere consumers of weather information, participants at *open-weather* workshops become producers. As they put their own signal into the mix, their locations are read and interpreted by weather-readers elsewhere. Even something as big as atmospheric patterns can be measured by us, at the scale of our bodies. And even more wildly, by sending up our own signals, we are also making weather. Who we are and how we are situated influences the weather we make. The supposed gap between abstract climate change and localized weather again gets smaller.

Open-weather's research method of 'imaging' is complemented by 'imagining', where they draw on feminist speculative storytelling to bridge the distance between our situated bodies and the technoscientific modeling and prediction of climate science. In the story *When we image the earth, we imagine the other*, Engleman and Dyer describe a network of womXn called the Feminist Anti-Fascist Weather Front as part of the 'emancipatory possibilities of a network of amateur satellite signal decoders and earth-watchers'.[42] Here, weather 'forecasting' is applied to the whole future of the planet, as the authors use speculative fiction to prefigure a different kind of world into being. The story also asks us to notice the seeds of those more-than-meteorological weathers in the present, as alternative kinds of kinship, sexuality, community and care that can and do flourish, despite but also because of harsh meteorological conditions. The bridge between present and future is narrowed, too.

Bodyweather

Just like climate and weather are often understood as belonging to different scales or domains, so too are weather and bodies. This is classic feminist nature/culture binary stuff (see Chapter 3 for more of this). Treating humans as though they are not also nature, and nature as though it weren't thoroughly steeped in culture, is a separation that feminists have long criticized and which many Indigenous worldviews never bought into in the first place. Unlearning colonial weather is invested in reconnecting these domains.

Anthropologist Tim Ingold, for example, criticized meteorological models of climate as a total system that we stand outside of so that we can comprehend it. For Ingold, climate is more accurately described as a milieu, or a 'common immersion' of humans and other beings in the generative fluxes of the weather-world.[43] Experiencing heavy rainstorms, wild wind, intense sun or biting cold can easily verify this sense of immersion. While we need to shelter ourselves from some weathers, it is futile to think we could ever be entirely separate from it. But if we want this expanded sense of weather to serve the social justice goals of this book, we need to push further. Immersion is an intimate relation, but it still leaves intact the idea that bodies are somehow different and separate from the world ('nature' or 'weather' or whatever else). Ingold comes closer to this fundamental implication when he reminds us that 'to inhabit the open is to dwell within a weather-world in which every being is destined to combine wind, rain, sunshine, and earth in the continuation of its own existence'.[44] Shrinking the distance between climate and weather also shrinks the distance between climate, weather and our own bodies.

Again, embodied and creative practice helps us connect bodies and weather in ways that facilitate unlearning the colonial separation of these domains. Most iconically is 身体気象, or bodyweather, a performance training method started by Min Tanaka in Japan the 1980s.[45] Originating as a dance school, farm and commune that hosted events elaborating the Japanese dance art of Butoh for a collective agrarian setting, dance companies around the world now run regular bodyweather training sessions and performance events. Our own knowledge of this practice was significantly deepened through the work of Victoria Hunt, an artist and teacher who led a bodyweather session at our *Hacking the Anthropocene* symposium in Sydney in 2016.[46] Bodyweather performers are trained to sense their bodies as elemental and connected with the wider environment.

Astrida's early weathering research was anchored in similar embodied observational practices, which subsequently led to the development of many of our 'Lucky dip' prompts (see Inset A): If I stick my palm out flat, can I feel the weather resting on it? Can I wrap my hand around it and squish the weather into a ball? Can I open my mouth, pop the weather-ball in – and then swallow it? If I do, where does it go? What is the weather in my belly? Do I incorporate it – becoming the weather? Or do I send it back out into the world, transformed, and transforming the weather in turn? In Polish artist

Karolina Sobecka's work 'Thinking like a Cloud',[47] a contraption called a cloud collector collects water vapour from the atmosphere, converting it back to its liquid state. The artist examines the sample to see what other lives (bacterial? microbial?) might have been collected. She then swallows the sample. If the cloud is 'weather', is it still weather inside the contraption, and then inside Sobecka's belly? What about when she metabolizes it, pees it out, and sends it back out into the hydrological – also meteorological? – cycle, changed? Are the bacteria now part of her gut? This gives rise to further questions: how is weather also a multispecies affair? And, how is Sobecka thus implicated in climate change? Asking such questions through *practice* helps us reconnect the faraway abstraction of climate with the intimate here-ness of our own bodies.

The subtle connections between body and weather are also examined in Roni Horn's artwork 'you are the weather'.[48] In a series of photographs all of the same person, Horn invites the viewer to perceive the minute changes in their subject's face as an index of the (meteorological) weather that dominates the Icelandic landscape. Not really visible in the photographs which are tight, up-close headshots, weather is nonetheless recorded in small shifts of expression, eye sparkle, and so on. The work can be interpreted as a study of the subtle interface between atmospheric conditions and human beings, and suggests that the weathers inside and outside are not always distinct domains. Like *open-weather*'s feminist practices that insist that weather measurement need not rely on inaccessible high-tech, 'you are the weather' invites us to consider our own bodies as a measure of weather, climate and the world – and vice-versa.

In times of accelerating climate anxiety, (meteorological) weathers outside get turned into (affective, emotional) weathers inside our bodies; many of the salves we use (shopping, travel, drugs) return to the atmosphere, and change it. Weather moves from the outside in and inside out, in a feedback loop. Feminist researcher Blanche Verlie documents something like this in the case of bushfire smoke taken into our bodies not only in its material form (becoming asthma or other respiratory conditions), but also as anxiety, depression and other forms of unwellness and dis-ease.[49] Poet Alexis Pauline Gumbs has drawn similar connections between a heating planet, the levels of violence experienced by Black women, and their elevated heat-related menopausal symptoms. Playing with the scale of weather, Gumbs speculates whether 'the "climate anxiety" we are collectively experiencing is increasing cortisol levels, too'.[50] Maybe the planet is a body, she wonders, registering the weather that has been made by our human bodies. The title of Gumbs' essay, 'Heat is not a Metaphor', is an argument for how climate change heat is literal temperature, but also the heat of Black women's menopausal bodies, as well as the stress and oppression that gathers in those bodies and exacerbates their symptoms. Neither is 'just' metaphorical. The domains of the personal/bodily and planetary/meteorological are not separate.

This all leads us to consider: if I am the weather, is the weather also me? Just as Roni Horn's photographs register weather in the subject's face, we wonder how we might also register in the weather, or as weather. This is another way of thinking about anthropogenic climate change. We are weather-makers: our collective acts and affects become the weather-world that in turn becomes us. Again, this is both meteorological (as we burn fossil fuels that release carbon into the atmosphere) and more-than-meteorological (in the social atmospheres we precipitate and the structures of power we uphold, or tear down). We get much deeper into how our bodies make and are made by the weather in the next chapter.

Conclusion as full circle, from weather to weathering

To conclude, we share one more example of creative practice, 'Liberation of the Chinook Wind' by Secwépemc artist Tania Willard. This work references the Chinook Wind as an animate being in Secwépemc creation story, and invites the wind to be a collaborator in writing poetry. Willard worked with data scientists to develop a Python code that used the power and movement of the wind (held in windsocks) as a way to arrange fragments of text offered by Willard. In this way, the wind wrote poems four times a day.[51] These poems lean into the potentially polarizing tension between AI (artificial intelligence) and (what Willard calls) NI (natural intelligence), as the artwork's animating force. Invoking the planetary alongside the local, the traditional alongside the modern, and computational tech alongside Secwépemc dreaming, Willard's work also engages in startling 'cross-domain mapping'. Willard wonders, 'If the wind can write poetry, what is the wind saying to us at other times?'[52] She suggests that listening to the wind might help us learn an anticolonial story of the weather that is natural, cultural, multispecies, translocal, ancient and still alive.

'Liberation of the Chinook Wind' also brings this chapter full circle, back to Indigenous weather knowledges. In Western universities, our jobs are to ask big questions that address problems and provide meaningful solutions that will benefit the communities we serve. And so, when we find answers to the questions we generate, we must stand by the findings. Often, this means that Western scholars seek mastery, and overlook, appropriate, or deliberately ignore other knowledges that we need to address those big questions better. In her influential article 'An Indigenous Feminist's Take on the Ontological Turn', Zoe Todd voices a related concern about how Euro-Western audiences consume 'new' concepts (like Bruno Latour's 'Gaia theory' of climate change) 'without being aware of competing or similar discourses happening outside of the rock-star arenas of Euro-Western thought'.[53] The concern for us is how easy it is and for how long it can go on.

We arrived at an answer to our question – how is the weather meaningful culturally, philosophically, poetically, politically and sensorially? – by using our own knowledge systems to see if we could 'close read' the weather-world differently: that is, by noticing what was in the background, both in the texts we read and in the spaces we inhabit. We also found knowledge of weathers that seriously contravened the story of weather we'd inherited. To challenge our inheritance, this chapter has sought to push the definition of the English word 'weather' into deeply historical, cultural, political and decolonial terrain, because language is defined by how we use it, and why; language cannot change without this kind of work.

But it took us a long time to get here. Like people who belatedly arrive at the protest are told: the best time to get involved was yesterday, the second-best time is today. Luckily, our training in feminist humanities also encouraged us to resist the allure of mastery, while still acknowledging that we *do* know some things. We can welcome (with some authority) what feminist humanities methods revealed about weather in this expanded cultural sense, while firmly committing to the project Gabi Briggs speaks about in the beginning of this chapter: allowing Indigenous ways of knowing to intentionally reshape our understanding for decolonial ends and change our knowledge, like rain on an old leaky roof.

Indigenous weather knowledges always have and always will connect long-term climate averages to the short-term immediacy of bodies in place. Weather is always already weathering and weathering is always and already Country, Land, relations. These knowledges are not new. Weather is more than thunder, lightning, wind and rain. It is abstract and intimate, measured, embodied, political, shared, emotional. Weather binds us, even in our difference. We are all connected. We are all indoctrinated. We are all displaced. We are all disconnected. We are all trying to survive. We are all part of the weather and we are all always weathering, even as the erasure of knowledges means we all bear the marks of weather – in its most expansive sense – in very different ways. This book invites a way of thinking about and relating to climate change that can address this uneven distribution of exposure, and redistribute shelter, and this chapter has laboured to relearn weather to assist with this big task. In the next chapter, weathering – as the central tool for doing this work – becomes our focus.

Notes

1. Ferdinand de Saussure, *Course in General Linguistics* (London: Duckworth, 1983).
2. Ferdinand de Saussure's theory of language was developed by Jacques Derrida, and then picked up by poststructuralist feminists such as Vicki Kirby and Elizabeth Wilson. This theory of language is a cornerstone of the 'antiessentialist neo-ecofeminism' we jokingly propose in Chapter 1, but inherits a longstanding reckoning with the dynamic relationship between words and worlds in feminist poststructrualism.
3. See, for example, Janine Randerson, *Weather as Medium: Toward a Meteorological Art* (Cambridge, MA: The MIT Press, 2018), Kaya Barry, Maria Borovnik and Tim Edensor, eds., *Weather: Spaces, Mobilities and Affects* (London: Routledge, 2020), Christoph F. E. Holzhey and Arnd Wedemeyer, *Weathering: Ecologies of Exposure* (Berlin: ICI Berlin Press, 2020), and Sarah Wright, *Becoming Weather: Weather, Embodiment and Affect* (London: Taylor & Francis Group, 2024).
4. In the late 2000s, Astrida began delivering 'weather writing' workshops that explored weather's embodiedness. See Astrida Neimanis, 'Weather Writing (Out of the Classroom)', in *Teaching with Feminist Materialisms*, ed. Rachel Loewen Walker and Pat Treusch, AtGender Teaching With Series (Budapest: CEU Press, 2015). In 2009, just starting on her PhD research, Jen won the Best Paper Award at a transdisciplinary Climate Change and Sustainability Research showcase at UNSW for a short presentation proposing research into better understanding of how we tell stories about weather.
5. Ellen van Neerven, *Personal Score: Sport, Culture, Identity* (St Lucia: University of Queensland Press, 2023), 292.
6. Emily O'Gorman, James Beattie and Matthew Henry, 'Histories of climate, science, and colonization in Australia and New Zealand, 1800–1945', *WIREs Climate Change* 7, no. 6 (2016): 900.
7. Vanessa Watts, 'Indigenous Place-Thought & agency amongst Humans and Non-Humans (First woman and Sky Woman Go on a European World Tour!)', *Decolonization: Indigeneity, Education & Society* 2, no. 1 (2013): 20–34.
8. The Bawaka Country collective (a more-than-human, Indigenous and non-Indigenous research collective led by Bawaka Country in northeast

Arnhem Land, Australia) writes about Wukun, a Yolŋu songspiral that is 'an embodied and affective co-constitution of peoples, places, times and complex weatherings including clouds, winds, mists and seasons'. 'Co-constitution' here means a relation that is always in process. 'Wukun, rather, points to weather and climate as patterned, relational, affective and deeply situated; as co-becomings in, with and as Country. It also signals the need to nurture multi-temporal, more-than-human relationships of belonging and care.' Bawaka Country et. al. 'Gathering of the Clouds: Attending to Indigenous understandings of time and climate through songspirals'; See also Sarah Wright and Matalena Tofa, 'Weather Geographies: Talking about the Weather, Considering Diverse Sovereignties', *Progress in Human Geography* 45, no. 5 (October 2021): 1126–46, https://doi.org/10.1177/0309132520982949.

9. Wright, *Becoming Weather*, 9.
10. Evelyn Araluen, 'Learning Bundjalung on Tharawal' in *Dropbear* (St Lucia: University of Queensland Press), 8.
11. Evelyn Araluen, 'Snugglepot and Cuddlepie in the Ghost Gum', *Sydney Review of Books*, Writing and Society Research Centre, Western Sydney University, 11/2/19.
12. Christine McFetridge, 'An Inconvenient Curve: Unlearning Settler Colonial Representations of Birrarung' (PhD diss., RMIT University, Naarm/Melbourne, 2024): 16.
13. Jennifer Hamilton and Gabrielle Briggs, 'Gabi Briggs: Long Version on the Vital Process of Centring Indigenous Sovereignty in Climate Action', Community Weathering Station: SoundCloud, 17 December 2021, https://soundcloud.com/weatheringstation.
14. Walter Benjamin, *The Arcades Project*, trans. Rolf Tiederman (Washington, DC: Library of Congress 1999), 101.
15. Roland Barthes, 'Pierre Loti: Aziyade' in *New Critical Essays* (Los Angeles,CA: University of California Press, 1990), 81.
16. Michel Serres, *La Distribution* (Paris: Editions de Minuit, 1977), 229.
17. Serres, *La Distribution,* 229.
18. See, for example, Katharine Anderson, *Predicting the Weather: Victorians and the Science of Meteorology* (Chicago, IL: University of Chicago Press, 2005), Jan Golinski, *British Weather and the Climate of Enlightenment* (Chicago, IL: University of Chicago Press, 2010), and Craig Martin, *Renaissance Meteorology* (Baltimore, MD: Johns Hopkins University Press, 2011).
19. Francis Bacon, *The New Atlantis*. Project Gutenberg, 2008, https://www.gutenberg.org/files/2434/2434-h/2434-h.htm, n.p.
20. Val Plumwood, *Feminism and the Mastery of Nature* (London: Routledge, 1993).
21. 'Weather, N', *Oxford English Dictionary*, Oxford University Press, September 2024, https://doi.org/10.1093/OED/9362591585.

22. 'Weather', *Vocabulary.com Dictionary,* Vocabulary.com, https://www.vocabulary.com/dictionary/weather (accessed 30 September 2024).

23. John Ruskin, 'Of the Pathetic Fallacy' in *Modern Painters Volume 3,* https://www.gutenberg.org/cache/epub/38923/pg38923-images.html (accessed 30 October 2024).

24. For a method for reading and interpreting this shifting significance, see Jennifer Hamilton 'Meteorological Reading' in *This Contentious Storm,* 11–30.

25. George Lakoff, 'The Contemporary Theory of Metaphor', *Metaphor and Thought,* ed. Andrew Ortony (Cambridge: Cambridge University Press, 1993), 201.

26. Anita Girvan, *Carbon Footprints as Cultural-Ecological Metaphors* (London: Routledge, 2017), 3.

27. 'Meteorology, N', Oxford English Dictionary, Oxford University Press, March 2024, https://doi.org/10.1093/OED/4699985049.

28. 'METEOROLOGY ACT 1955', https://classic.austlii.edu.au/au/legis/cth/consol_act/ma1955160/s6.html (accessed 9 June 2024).

29. Detailed accounts and analyses of this can be found in Nancy Tuana ('Viscous porosity: Witnessing Katrina', in *Material Feminisms* 2008).

30. Christina Sharpe, *In the Wake: On Blackness and Being* (Durham, NC: Duke University Press, 2016), 104.

31. Sharpe, *In the Wake,* 106.

32. Sharpe, *In the Wake,* 111.

33. John Protevi, 'Katrina', *Symposium* 10, no. 1 (2006): 363–81.

34. Claudia Rankine, 'Weather', *The New York Times,* 15 June 2020, https://www.nytimes.com/2020/06/15/books/review/claudia-rankine-weather-poem-coronavirus.html.

35. Ada Limon, interview with Krista Tippett, *On Being with Krista Tippett* [podcast], 16 February 2023, https://onbeing.org/programs/ada-limon-to-be-made-whole/

36. Limon, interview with Krista Tippett.

37. This method was inspired by poet Natalie Rice, where she invites Land as a collaborator in her poetic practice. Natalie Rice, 'Without End', *FEELed Notes* (blog), 29 March 2023, https://thefeeledlab.ca/2023/03/29/without-end/.

38. James Gardiner, Hayley Singer, Jennifer Hamilton, Astrida Neimanis and Mindy Blaise, 'Reading Group as Method for Feminist Environmental Humanities', *Australian Feminist Studies* 37, no. 113 (2022): 296–316.

39. Sasha Engelmann et al., 'Open-weather: Speculative-feminist propositions for planetary images in an era of climate crisis', *Geoforum* 137 (2022): 237–47.

40. See Klein on the misalignment of 'feelings' and fact in Naomi Klein, *Doppelganger: A Trip into the Mirror World* (New York, NY: Farrar, Straus and Giroux, 2023).

41. Engelmann et al., 'Open-weather'.
42. Engelmann et al., 'Open-weather'.
43. Tim Ingold, *The Life of Lines* (London and New York, NY: Routledge, 2015), 115.
44. Ingold, *The Life of Lines*, 115. This literal incorporation of the 'wind, rain, sunshine, and earth' is also the basis of Astrida and Rachel Loewen Walker's argument in their 2014 article on Weathering. See Chapter 3.
45. 'Body Weather Laboratory', https://www.bodyweather.org/about
46. Victoria Hunt's bodyweather creative work is described in Rachael Swain, 'A Meeting of Nations: Trans-Indigenous and Intercultural Interventions in Contemporary Indigenous Dance', *Theatre Journal* 67, no. 3 (2015): 503–21.
47. Karolina Sobecka, *Thinking Like a Cloud*. Installation, 2014, https://karolinasobecka.com/thinking-like-a-cloud.
48. Roni Horn, *You Are the Weather*. (Scalo in collaboration with Fotomuseum Winterthur, 1997).
49. Blanche Verlie, *Learning to Live with Climate Change: From Anxiety to Transformation* (London: Routledge, 2022), https://doi.org/10.4324/9780367441265.
50. Alexis Pauline Gumbs, 'Heat Is Not a Metaphor', *Harper's Bazaar*, 2023, https://www.harpersbazaar.com/culture/features/a44819303/climate-crisis-maui/ (accessed 30 October 2024).
51. Tania Willard, 'Liberation of the Chinook Wind', https://www.blackwoodgallery.ca/projects/liberation-of-the-chinook-wind-lwc (accessed 30 October 2024), which was part of a large exhibition of works connected to similar themes – https://workofwind.ca/.
52. CBC Arts, 'What would the wind write if it could write poetry?: interview with Tania Willard', https://www.cbc.ca/arts/exhibitionists/what-would-the-wind-write-if-it-could-write-poetry-1.4892750. This artwork also implicates settler fish species management, and Indigenous legal claims around water that connect Willard's home territory and the lands of the Mississaugas of the New Credit, on whose Land the artwork was installed.
53. Zoe Todd, 'An Indigenous feminist's take on the ontological turn: "Ontology" is just another word for colonialism', *Journal of Historical Sociology* 29, no. 1 (2016): 4–22.

INSET C — weathering with & without

WINDOWS, DOORS, ROOFS, JACKETS, SOCKS, HOT WATER BOTTLES, SUNHATS, BEANIES, SINGLETS, FANS, OPEN FIRES, AIR-CONDITIONING, CARS, CUPS OF TEA, SPICY FOOD, ICED WATER... THIS EXERCISE INVOLVES LISTING THE OBJECTS AND TECHNOLOGIES WE USE TO MANAGE WEATHER. IT CAN OPEN UP DISCUSSION ABOUT HOW TO INCORPORATE A POLITICS OF REDISTRIBUTED SHELTER, COMFORT AND PLEASURE INTO FEMINIST, QUEER, AND ANTI-COLONIAL ENVIRONMENTALISM TODAY. THE TWO MIRROR VERSIONS OF THIS GAME STOKE THAT FIRE AND CHILL THAT ICE.

WHAT YOU NEED

basic
- A GROUP OF PEOPLE (IDEALLY 5-6) LESS IS OK
- PEN + PAPER × EACH PARTICIPANT

extra
- NICER DRAWING PAPER + PENS
- COLOUR — EG. PENCILS, TEXTAS, WATERCOLOURS

optional extension — DEHUMIDIFIER INGREDIENTS:
- "LID + BAND" PRESERVING JARS
- COFFEE FILTER PAPERS
- SCISSORS
- TWINE
- MUSLIN
- ROCK SALT

HOW TO PLAY

1. NOMINATE A TIMEKEEPER, DISTRIBUTE PAPER + PENS.

2. EACH PERSON TAKES 5 MINUTES TO MAKE A LIST OF ALL THE THINGS OR PRACTICES THEY USE TO MANAGE THE WEATHER.

3. DISCUSS AS A GROUP EVERYONE'S LISTS. (YOU CAN ADD ANY OVERLOOKED ITEMS HERE). SPEND 10 MINUTES ON THIS.

"without"

4. PASS YOUR LISTS AROUND THE CIRCLE, EACH PLAYER CROSSING ONE ITEM OFF EACH LIST BEFORE PASSING IT ON. CONTINUE UNTIL THEY FEEL DIMINISHED, BUT WITH SOME THINGS LEFT.

5. RETRIEVE YOUR LIST AND TAKE STOCK OF WHAT IS LEFT, ALSO HOW IT FELT TAKING AWAY FROM OTHERS.

"with"

4. PASS YOUR LISTS AROUND AS BEFORE. THIS TIME, EACH PLAYER "GIFTS" YOU AN ITEM FROM YOUR LIST, BY DRAWING IT ON THE OTHER SIDE OF YOUR PAGE. DO A SECOND ROUND IF NEEDED.

5. DISCUSS WHAT YOU'VE RECEIVED AND WHAT THAT MEANS FOR YOU IN TERMS OF WEATHERING.

6. **crafty option** — YOU CAN TURN YOUR DRAWN LIST INTO A D-I-Y DEHUMIDIFIER!

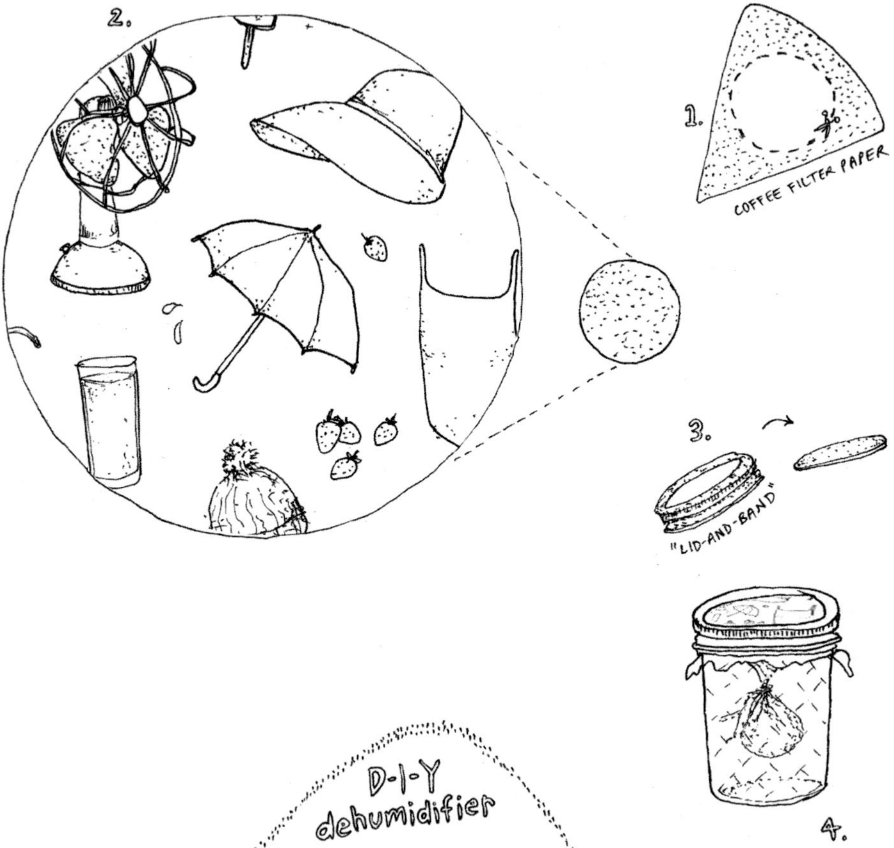

D-I-Y dehumidifier

1. CUT A CIRCLE OF COFFEE FILTER PAPER TO FIT YOUR JAR LID.
2. USE A WINDOW TO TRACE A PORTION OF YOUR "GIFTED ITEMS" DRAWING ONTO THE CIRCLE OF FILTER PAPER.
3. REPLACE METAL DISC IN YOUR JAR LID WITH THE CIRCLE OF FILTER PAPER.
4. WRAP A SPOONFUL OF ROCK SALT IN MUSLIN, TIE WITH TWINE AND SCREW ON YOUR LID SO THE SALT PARCEL HANGS SUSPENDED INSIDE.
5. USE YOUR DEHUMIDIFIER IN A DAMP, ENCLOSED SPACE. YOU MAY NEED TO PERIODICALLY EMPTY ANY WATER THAT HAS COLLECTED.

CHAPTER 3
Weathering

Introduction: Stones in the water

Over time, rocks become weathered by the forces of wind and water. This change usually occurs so slowly that it is imperceptible to an individual human. In June 2018, we (Jennifer and Astrida) spent a week on Coast Salish territory, at a writing retreat on Galiano Island in British Columbia's Pacific Northwest, writing beside the rocks at the edge of the ocean that stretches wide between the places each of us now lives.[1] We wrote about the sounds of the tiny archipelagic waves lapping relentlessly on the pebbly beach. We read about piddock clams who looked like inert features of the rock platform, but actually spend the best part of a decade moving about two centimeters as they live and then die burrowing small holes. We would finish our work most days by jumping into the cold and salty Salish Sea, our bodies creating ripples like those a stone makes when thrown in the water. During the conference the following week, we took a day trip to the Sooke Potholes for another swim. This geological feature – a chain of mountain freshwater ponds created over 15,000 years ago by water pressure from glacial melt – draws its name from the T'souke Nation. The rocks look pretty static but they have a long and dynamic history. To swim in these places, or in any place, is to immerse oneself in slow, deep time.

For over a decade, we have continued to think, write and act anew with the concept of weathering. This chapter elaborates how this concept adds the dimension of time to weather, an idea we unpack just below. In other words, weathering as a concept is our way to link the experience of weather to the vastness and duration of climate change. But the implications of 'adding time' (meaning thinking about weathering as an accumulation of weathers) is complex because our definition of weather, as outlined in Chapter 2, is broad. So, in addition to adding time to weather, this chapter provides the opportunity to recount our process of developing 'weathering' as a theory and practice – namely, how we've used it to build solidarity between feminist social justice and environmental justice questions, and to further erode our sticky inheritance of the nature/culture binary. Like a rock that becomes ever so slightly more weathered by each cold rainstorm or rough high tide, our concept continues to be gradually shaped, in response to its contexts. Weathering, like the feminist practice for climate change it undergirds, is a slow and careful process.

Weathering as a feminist concept for connecting weather and climate

Weathering is both a common word and a feminist concept for climate change. As a common English word, 'weathering' describes several things, including 'to change by exposure to weather' or 'subject to the beneficial action of wind and sun'.[2] Another definition of weathering relates to erosion which invokes weather's slow impact on rocks: 'the action of the atmospheric agencies or elements on substances exposed to its influence; the discoloration, disintegration, etc. resulting from this action.'[3] By adding the suffix 'ing' to the noun, weathering is a gerund that adds duration or time to the weather. Other languages such as French ('temps') and Spanish ('tiempo') don't need gerunds to underline the weather's relation to time. Still, weather events are mostly understood as short-lived and sometimes intense: a thunderstorm, a rain shower, a windy morning, a frosty night, a hot afternoon. Even weather that lasts weeks, or that is contained by what we classify as a 'season', is still short-term in the context of climate change and the deep time of planetary history. So 'weathering' in the first instance is a concept that helps us pay attention to the slow accumulation of weathers across place and time.

As a feminist concept for understanding climate change, weathering was introduced by Astrida and Rachel Loewen Walker in their 2014 article 'Weathering: Climate Change and the Thick Time of Transcorporeality'.[4] There, as here, the aim is to expand common definitions of weathering to include present day ecological concerns from a feminist perspective, primarily by thinking about weather across time. 'Matter is weathering in its making of temporality', they argue; 'the striations of rock that jut out over the sea not only mark time with their varied colors and lines, but make time through their encounters with the waves and wind.'[5] This weather is also archived in our bodies, marking them, such that our bodies are 'part and parcel of the making of time'.[6] The accumulation of hot summers and cold winters, or cold summers and hot winters, is weathering. Astrida and Rachel summarize this time–weather–body relationship, whereby 'the felt degrees of hotness and coldness, of speeds and slownesses, saturate this temporality with a sense of the material duration, or the thick time, of that weather or climate'.[7] It all sounds very philosophical (and it is), but it is also quite familiar, mundane and literal: watching freckles appear on your cheekbones; the excitement of returning to a favourite swimming spot when warm weather arrives; winter clothes packed away until next year.

Take a moment and, if it feels okay, sit with your memories of weather in relation to your body. Can you invoke some sense of those experiences, accumulated across time? For us, our movements around the world have helped us notice our own weathery accumulations: my hot summer, your warm winter, our extreme rainstorm, their protracted drought. Have you experienced nostalgia triggered by cold summer rain when you longed for a long warm sunset, or some similarly complex feeling or memory of weathers past, prompted by weather present? This strange triangulation between the weather now, a memory of different weather, and longing for some sensation other than what you are presently feeling is an example of the 'thick time' of weathering. I am always weathering. You are always weathering. We are always weathering.

We carry the accumulation of weather across time in our bodies, but weather can also accumulate in a specific place. For example, Wright's Lookout in the mountainous area between Gumbaynggirr and Anaiwan Country is a large rocky hill in the middle of a large valley. Walking in the valley you are surrounded by towering trees, ferns, epiphytes and all manner of climbing plants that together make up a subtropical and ancient Gondwana rainforest. The ground is soft, leafy and muddy. Although it only takes ten minutes to climb from the valley floor to the top of the lookout, once there you tower over short shrubs with spiky leaves. The ground is hard rock, and seems very dry. These plants, requiring very little soil, have evolved over time to withstand the windy dryness of the rocky outcrop. These two places side by side – the valley and the outcrop – are weathering very differently. Or to put it otherwise, they are weathering the same weather, differently. These places are differently exposed, and they embody different relationships to wind, rain, and biota.

These accumulated weathers – these weatherings – constitute our lives and can, if we let them, inform an embodied understanding of climate. As such, attuning to them becomes a unique method of sensing climate change and guiding adaptation. This is a specific feminist mode of adaptation, because of the value it places on bodily difference.

As we continued to develop the weathering concept, we noticed something parallel happening within other feminist work we were reading, where structural, embodied trauma was being referred to as 'weather'. Chapter 2 describes Christina Sharpe's 2016 book *In the Wake* as one example, where Sharpe explores the experience of being Black in the United States in the aftermath of slavery as the 'total climate of antiblackness' – a phenomenon she names 'the weather'. To incorporate Sharpe's ideas, and the work of others who bridge critical race and environmental justice studies, we needed to deepen our understanding of weathering to more directly address weathering as a structural effect within unjust societies.[8] We continued to notice this connection elsewhere. Public health professor Arline Geronimus, for example, has used the term 'weathering' for years to describe the cumulative impacts of racist hierarchies and economic oppression on people's physical health.[9]

This led us to ask: how does weathering as structural embodied harm intersect with a feminist understanding of weathering environmental crisis? Or more specifically, how does an accumulation of weathers over time in a body subject to structural disadvantage change how bodies accumulate the weathers of a specific place? Here, the experience of a heatwave in summer is weathered differently by the neighbour with aircon than by the neighbour without it, or by the neighbour who can rest versus the neighbour who cannot afford to. To access some of these nuances, one of the Weathering Collective's early projects was creating 'The Weathering Map of Microclimates and Approximate Water Bodies'.[10] Members described subtle microclimates that differentiated our experiences of living in the same city (and one offered a contrast of experience, as she was temporarily located halfway across the globe). In a similar vein, we have wondered how our feminist context could better accommodate insights from research in areas like urban heat mapping, that tries to describe the uneven distribution of access to 'coolth' in a city.[11] How does, could or should an accumulation of different weathers in our different bodies impact climate adaptation? We claim it should matter, and the question of how it should be remedied needs to be a focus of climate change adaptation strategies.

We have also *practised* thinking through these conceptual developments. For example, 'Weathering with and without' (Inset C) is a game we designed to reflect on having or not having infrastructures or technologies to help us weather. In playing it, we examine how we feel about these differences, both subtle and overt, at an interpersonal level. We all are always weathering, but some folks weather *with* relevant tools – secure housing, affordable heating, a warm hat – and other folks weather *without* them. Here, gender, sexuality, race, class, economics and ability all relate to how we weather the world and the world weathers us. To use the concept of weathering as a process-oriented tool for guiding feminist practice for climate change means starting to think slowly and carefully about how these different and intersecting social categories impact the more ecological ones. In this way, weathering both draws on and complements decades of work in the field of environmental justice, and the more recently emerging field of climate justice.

Weathering as an ambivalent and slow politics of solidarity and resistance

Figure 3.1 Stones in the river at the FEELed Lab on unceded syilx territory. Photograph: Astrida Neimanis.

We have come to understand weathering as an ambivalent concept to support slow eco-political work. Our ambivalence is not about the overarching ethical imperative of the project and the uneven distribution of shelter and vulnerability. We strongly and clearly feel this requires attention and remedy. Within this, however, the concept allows us to hold mixed feelings and uncertainty about climate change, our lives today and the best pathways for mixing adaptation with revolution, while also committing to doing the work. We invite you to snail your way through the next example to see how its little twists and turns can still amount to a politics of solidarity and resistance.

Astrida has been haunted for years by a single sentence in Audre Lorde's autobiographical novel, *Zami: A New Spelling of My Name*: 'In order to withstand the weather, we had to become stone, and now we bruise ourselves upon the other who is closest.'[12] Here, Lorde discusses weather as 'more-than-meteorological' (see Chapter 2) and in the sense Sharpe develops in *In the Wake*. The lesbophobic, antiblack and anti-poor atmospheres that Lorde describes in the novel are experienced like rain or hail: i.e., as bad weather. But in the context of climate crisis, in a world where colonial capitalist technofixes represent the most powerful kinds of responses, we need to add literal weather to this idea too. On one hand, the reference to becoming stone against the weather is clearly a fierce call to feminists to acknowledge the real difficulty of living under oppression, the need to work in solidarity across our differences, and a warning not to turn on each other in the process of liberatory struggle. On the other hand, if this weather is understood as more-than-meteorological *and* literal, what does it mean to have to become stone in relation to the elements? In this context weathering is thus both being vulnerable and exposed to something hard, and wanting to be sheltered from it, too. Nudging along our inquiry into Lorde's stoney stance is the critical geology of Kathryn Yusoff. They invite a curious engagement with geology as 'a mode of material expression that is already active within [social, sexual, political and labour] formations, yet often bracketed out, and its political potential as a dynamic power within socialities, underplayed.'[13] Holding hardness, softness, rocks, bodies, weather, time, sexuality, society and politics together at once requires slow and intentional work. Let's try!

To become stone against the weather contains a desire or longing to be soft, and not to have to harden. Sometimes exposure feels good, other times it feels terrible. Often it is a bit of both, or at least a fine balance. Elsewhere in *Zami*, Lorde admits to wanting to be both hard and soft: 'I have always wanted to be both man and woman . . . to be hot and hard and soft all at the same time in the cause of our loving'.[14] To be hard and soft as needed for love is a particular kind of politics where the endgame of being hard or soft is not fitting a social norm but feeling good, and responding to the world with the materiality of our bodies. We might liken painful or traumatic weathering to a rainstorm, but walking in cold rain can be invigorating, if the conditions are right. Importantly, the requirement to become stone in the face of unjust weathers is not (or never fully) a choice: hardening is necessary for survival. In other words, it is not the rain (weather) that is essentially good or bad; what makes it bad is the affordance of a body to withstand it, and the presence or absence of shelter. (See also Chapter 4, where we discuss something similar in terms of resilience politics.)

So being eroded is not always bad. Sometimes we come to accept this inevitability, like queer archaeologist Denis Byrne who develops a feeling for sandstone as he ages: 'I am disaggregating, and perhaps it is that which creates the conditions for me to feel an affinity for the stone'.[15] In Lorde's telling, stones can also be bruised. These stones aren't the static solid masses of impenetrability we typically take them for, but bodies that slowly change too. Sara Ahmed, who also notices Lorde's interest in stones, observes that although stones seem to 'embody what is passive', the hardening of the self into stone is responsive; to have to become stone should point to 'what made hardening seem necessary: that sense of being too soft, too receptive; too willing to receive an impression'.[16] Ahmed also describes shoreline pebbles shaped by the ocean, where we can feel the pebble's smoothness 'as a trace of where it has been'.[17] Again, the specific place (conditions) of weathering matters.

When we think about the activism of expressing solidarity with another's cause, or resisting unjust power, we often associate this with big and fast actions: speaking out for what we believe in when the moment is right, going to a protest, chaining oneself to a mining machine. Using weathering to guide such politics is different, but we hope complementary. It is a slower eco-politics that accompanies the slow process of unlearning colonial meteorology that we described in Chapter 2, or the cosmic weathering we describe in the Epilogue. Alongside more conventional political actions, it involves a slow and ambivalent weathering of one's identity and self-perception. In Chapter 2, we cite Bundjalung poet Evelyn Araluen who points out that unlearning is necessary not only for settlers, but also for Indigenous folks who have grown up and been educated in colonial systems. Our efforts to do this work are different to Araluen's. To 'unlearn a language', or worldviews of oppressors, for us means writing of another world in what is more or less the same language we inherited. We are weathered by the damage our culture causes in the name of progress, but we are nowhere near unmade enough just by reading once about an alternative way of knowing. We need to be gradually weathered by each poem we read, each letter we sign, each protest we attend, each stranger with whom we can make a connection, and each time we turn our face towards the wind to act as a windbreak for another.

This is what we mean by weathering as an ambivalent process. It is a process against seemingly unchanging rock; it is also a process against self which is sometimes good and sometimes bad. And it is always slow: in our case, rewiring our settler and white supremacist brains, upbringings and worldviews. This is again also why, as a concept for solidarity and resistance, weathering cannot stand alone; it needs a feminist, queer and anticolonial ethics to construct contexts for safe and pleasurable kinds of exposure, and more substantial shelter for those who are vulnerable. Weathering as an ambivalent and slow politics of embodied solidarity and resistance allows for the durational and detailed work that is needed to build a different kind of world.

Weathering as further eroding the nature/culture binary

We are living in a paradoxical moment. Many folks increasingly recognize that the hierarchical binaries underpinning Western thought are bad for people and planet alike, and support moves to challenge them. When rivers or animals receive recognition or legal status usually reserved for humans, the nature/culture binary erodes a bit further. When trans and non-binary folks insist on recognition for lives lived beyond the confines of binary sex and gender, the gender binary gets a bit looser. But the moment is paradoxical because powerful forces are also reasserting a hierarchical and binary perspective: that sex is binary, that women are subordinate, that trans and non-binary folk don't exist, and that some parts of nature should be destroyed for culture – in law, policy and everyday life practice.

When we teach our students about binary hierarchies today, they have new contexts for understanding how these binaries work – not only in cultural texts, but around their dinner tables, and in the mouths and actions of politicians and other powerful people. So while it sometimes feels baffling that such binaries still endure ('aren't we just so tired of taking down the nature/culture binary?!', our friend Sue recently asked us), our current moment brings home the need to continue the work of eroding hierarchical binary thinking. This erosion is slow work against relentless opposition.

Weathering as a concept works against the nature/culture binary in particular. Like the concept of queerness, weathering prioritizes change and difference over the fixed, oppositional and hierarchical way of thinking we've inherited from Eurocentric Christian colonial forefathers and mothers. This, of courses, is not the only way to understand the world. Consider that Indigenous scholars like Jeannette Armstrong tell us that there is no word for 'nature' in nsyilxcən (a language in the Salish language group, spoken by syilx people in British Columbia's interior) because human cultural and natural ecological worlds are not separate.[18] This syilx worldview aligns with many longstanding Indigenous knowledges that include sophisticated theories of animacy where culture is nature and nature is culture, and everything is storied and has a story.[19] So part of our commitment to unlearning colonial weather, as we outline in Chapter 2, requires a commitment to continue scratching away at this binary.

We don't have to look further than our breakfast table to spot the fiction of any clear separation between nature and culture: there is nothing both more natural and cultural than a loaf of white bread. Flour, water, sugar, yeast, salt, maybe lard. Add plastic bag wrapper, twisty tie. Pan out to fields of wheat (former grasslands, forests), fed by sun, watered by the rain or sprinkler, enhanced with chemical fertilizers. Notice the fertilizer- and chemical-rich water flowing into rivers, where algal blooms flourish from eutrophication, sapping the oxygen and killing the fish. Meanwhile, loaves are trucked across the country for your convenience. Just try to defend any clear distinction of nature from culture over a slice of toast![20]

But while easy to challenge in examples like this one, the nature/culture binary is resilient because it fortifies the status quo of power – as our current paradoxical moment shows us. This binary licenses us to conceptualize nature as outside and over there, rather than as something harnessed for profit inside the supermarket, for example, full of products derived from an unsustainable agri-food system that is one of the biggest drivers of climate change. Moreover, it is actually quite challenging to replace this binary with words or concepts that can still hold on to meaningful differences between humans, other living beings, earth materials and anthropogenic transformations. As one response, feminist biologist and theorist Donna Haraway suggests we replace the hierarchical binary with the concept of 'naturecultures'.[21] New materialist feminists like Vicki Kirby get around the problem by proposing that nature was culture all along.[22] This feminist work contributes to eroding the binary, but the word 'culture' (e.g. as human choice, intentionality, rationality, creativity, agency) still tussles with the word 'nature' (e.g. as inherent qualities, uncontrollable forces, chaos). The tenacity of these two words, nature and culture, means we need to learn to talk about them with care and nuance, rather than writing them off wholesale (can you imagine never being able to use either of these words in an sentence?).

In *Who's Afraid of Gender?*, queer feminist Judith Butler examines the nature/culture debate within feminism in relation to their own (decades-old) theory of gender's performativity, where the gender binary is a habit that Western culture (more or less) chooses. Butler addresses how performativity, as a theory that emphasizes agency, choice and changeability around gender, has been implicated in the rise of transphobia. Their argument now attends more explicitly to nature, in ecological terms. Bodies are inseparably nature *and* culture, they argue, 'formed through what is ingested, and the atmospheres to which one is exposed, the kinds of food available, the air that one breathes, the entire environmental infrastructure through which bodies are formed and sustained. They are not just outside the body, but the stuff from which it is made.'[23] This is still a rejection of the nature/culture hierarchized binary, but includes a more careful articulation of the role of what some might call 'nature'.

Arline Geronimus seeks a similarly nuanced view, but in the context of studies of human disease and illness. In her book *Weathering: The Extraordinary Stress of Ordinary Life in an Unjust Society*,[24] Geronimus also uses the word 'weathering' to describe the impacts of an unequal society and socio-economic precarity on bodies. In Geronimus's words, weathering 'encompasses the physiological effects of living in marginalized communities that bear the brunt of racial, ethnic, religious, and class discrimination'; weathering is 'about hopeful, hardworking, responsible, skilled, and resilient people dying from the physical toll of constant stress on their bodies, paying with their health because they live in a rigged, degrading, and exploitative system.'[25] There is nothing 'natural' (meaning 'inevitable') about these vulnerabilities, even though they manifest at a cellular level in the body, and at an epidemiological level in society. Socio-economic impacts of marginalization are brutally materialized when catalogued as poor health outcomes.

In other words, even as we erode the nature/culture binary, we still need ways to talk about materiality, or the raw state of things, as different from their representations, or from how they have been shaped by humans, even if 'nature' and 'culture' aren't quite the right words for doing so. Weathering offers careful, intentional and non-hierarchical ways to hold these differences. It helps us argue *against* a nature/culture binary that insists climate change is 'natural' (inevitable; nothing anthropogenic about it). At the same time, it can also still hold on to *material* difference that may be incidental, evolutionary, or not necessarily anthropogenic. The base dictionary definition of weathering tells us that granite does not weather the same way as clay. The three little pigs taught us that straw houses don't withstand the weather (human or wolf-created) the same way brick ones do. Nature – as material affordance – matters.

This brings us to the work of cultural theorists Yasmin Gunaratnam and Nigel Clark, whose 2012 essay on race and climate change explored the ways 'heat, drought, extreme weather events and other manifestations of climate change, will be impacting upon bodies whose life chances are already conditioned by race'.[26] This example helps us understand how weathering can work *alongside* the nature/culture distinction, accounting for its persistence and continuing to trouble it. Gunaratnam and Clark note that nearly all human societies and activities are 'influenced by the ambient climate'.[27] How one weathers depends very much on one's adaptation to heat, damp, and cold, as materially present circumstances – even before anthropogenic climate change started hitting some cultures harder than others. More provocatively (for reasons that will become clear), Gunaratnam and Clark point out that the materiality of bodies also matters. Here, they refer to 'differences both visible and invisible' such as 'how and where we store body fat; our efficiency in metabolising nutrients; the composition of our intestinal flora; our skeletomuscular proportions; our immunological resistance to pathogens' and 'even, or especially, that most historically fraught of visible markers, the colour of our skin'.[28] They refer to data showing how dark skin offered a strong evolutionary advantage in some climates. This observation is affirmed in more recent global health research, claiming that 'dark skin pigmentation, a phenotypic feature common among those who are racialised as Black, presents many advantages in this environment, including the protection of folate from photo-degradation'.[29] So Gunaratnam and Clark wonder how these differences 'will play out in a world whose average surface temperatures may be 2, 3, 4, 5, or 6 degrees warmer than at present'.[30] Pigmentation may be an important climate adaptation.

Gunaratnam and Clark recognize the danger in their suggestion; they are aware of 'discredited geographical or environmental determinisms' and 'crude racial climatologies' that have been handmaidens to white supremacy and settler colonialism.[31] In a feminist context, this can also sound a lot like a gender essentialism that claims women are 'naturally' caring, hysterical, passive or stupid, because of their biological or anatomical features. In their health research, Etti et al. also recognize the danger of invoking biology without looking at social circumstances. Even if dark skin might be advantageous in certain climates, healthcare and health research has done lots to mitigate this disadvantage for pale-skinned people. Meanwhile, 'the *social* threats to Black people's health' – as thoroughly documented by Geronimus, for instance – have not been mitigated to anywhere near the same degree. Etti et al. put it well when they say 'Both our physical and social environments determine our skin's strength and weaknesses'.[32] Weathering as a concept explicitly holds on to the interplay between materiality (like skin pigmentation, or the sun's intensity in a particular region) and social-cultural forces (like racism) to understand the complex ways that bodies weather.[33]

Against racist climatologies that associate tropical climates with backwardness, Gunaratnam and Clark argue that deep-time body morphologies also carry useful knowledges and 'complex chemistry memories of past environmental limitations they overcame'[34] – these are testimonies of survival in the physical archives of flesh. They continue: 'More useful than simply dissolving corporeal variation into cultural difference', we might view the 'range of human biological being [as] itself a socio-cultural achievement'. Through this innovation and problem-solving, biology, too, is 'cultural'. This cannot be a romanticized story of resilience. We know that vulnerability to weather is still vastly unequal. Weathering as a concept, though, helps us remain curious and agile in how we tell the stories of weathering through the materialization of difference.

This proposal also aligns with disability justice. We know that physical disability, for example, usually results in increased climate vulnerability; Mel Y. Chen, for example, documents the double whammy of wildfire smoke (close the windows!) and COVID-19 risk (open the windows!) for immunocompromised folks.[35] Thinking about materiality though, we note that even as the barriers that disadvantage disabled people are social and cultural, bodies are very real. As Eli Clare puts it, discussing his inability to complete a steep mountain hike, there is a difference between barriers due to social construction (e.g. trails not wide enough for mobility aids) and those due to bodily limitation – perhaps acquired, perhaps innate.[36] To overlook the fact of bodies, Clare tells us, is a failure to see disabled people as full people. Naming these two kinds of factors (natural/innate; social/constructed) enables us to work towards more equitable distribution of vulnerability and shelter, even if for Clare, there is 'no neat theoretical divide' between how such factors are experienced.[37]

And again, as Leah Lakshmi Piepzna-Samarasinha reminds us, vulnerability experienced by disabled people is also the source of important adaptation and knowledge in climate catastrophe. When catastrophic forest fires hit the West Coast of US and Canada in 2017, she tells us:

> it was sick and disabled folks – particularly folks with chemical injuries, environmental illness, asthma, and other autoimmune conditions who had been navigating unsafe air for years – sharing the knowledge that being sick and disabled had already taught us. We had comprehensive information about where to get masks and respirators and about the right herbs to take to detox after exposure to air pollutants. We knew to go to libraries and other airconditioned places to get an air break. We knew about HEPA filters and how you can make one with a furnace filter and a box fan. We knew it was normal to feel fatigue, confusion, and panic.[38]

Weathering does not erase all difference between nature (if by that we mean materiality, the stuff of the world, bodily limitations, etc) and culture (if by that we mean process, structure, politics, creative inclination, sociality, etc). Instead it insists that both the material and the social/cultural/structural *matter* in terms of how *any* body weathers. As Butler puts it, 'it turns out that what we call biology is always interacting with social and environmental forces'.[39] It matters if a house is brick or stone. It matters if a body's skin is melanated or not when exposed to the sun. It matters if immune systems are developing or mature when exposed to toxins. It matters if lungs are strong or weak when smoke fills the skies. These factors don't *determine* how we weather – there is far too much more-than-meteorological weather in play – and they certainly don't fully account for how those strengths or vulnerabilities came to be. Materiality is part of the story in complex ways. We acknowledge that a focus on materiality is ripe for exploitation by racist or ableist or other harmful ideologies. This is why we need more nuanced, creative, and careful ways to think against and alongside nature and culture as feminist practice for climate change.

Conclusion: Feminist infrastructure for better weathering

In 2020, we wrote an article called 'Feminist infrastructure for Better Weathering' with Tessa Zettel (who illustrated all the insets in this book).

Once we had developed the concept of weathering into something sufficiently expansive, we turned to infrastructure because we realized we needed more than theory to enact 'better' weathering. We needed the material supports to bring it together: tents, joists, hoists, tables, signage, websites, containers, platforms, composting bins, meeting rooms, raincoats, sunhats, houses.

But the question of 'better' was actually quite contentious between the two of us: are we saying that our proposed infrastructures were of 'superior character or quality' than other climate infrastructures? Who are we to make this claim? After all, we are talking about little pen-and-paper, pass-to-the-player-on-your-right type games, with a nice pot of tea to accompany them. Who are we to claim these little social infrastructures are better than a solar farm, a good piece of climate adaptation social policy, or even just a well-designed stormwater drain? Astrida trusted the project and had a deep faith in its mission. Jen was sceptical and felt she was betraying her scholarly principles by asserting any moral high-ground. (To be fair, on a different day we might have switched positions.)

But we recount this disagreement because the world is a bit of a mess and maybe it always has been. So while all of this is theoretically careful and nuanced and complex, we believe that it is also our obligation to put a stake in the ground to try and improve things. If we are always weathering, how can we do it better? We claim that feminist weathering, which seeks to account for the relevant complexities of different human experience as a part of adaptation, is better than other kinds of weathering. We don't equivocate on our core offering. In addition to connecting weather and climate through the arts of weathering, the weathering concept brings with it an ethical commitment to a more just world and the redistribution of vulnerability and shelter. We think that the rampant injustices and inequities of the world need to be addressed as part of any climate adaptation. This is not complicated.

Weathering as a concept supports that work by focusing on the mundane and material impacts of oppression – a leaky ceiling, heat sensitivity due to lifestyle disease because crappy food is cheaper than healthy alternatives – alongside the melting ice caps. But in developing the concept of weathering as both complexly nuanced and a non-negotiably simple way of slowing down and describing how the world impacts us, we also have become interested in weathering as a creative and material practice. Is weathering something we can actively do and do better together? In the next chapter we look more explicitly at feminist infrastructures as a means of intentionally remaking the world in the name of weathering.

Notes

1. Participants at this retreat included Catriona Sandilands, Susan Reid, Janine MacLeod, Emily McGiffin and us. One of our collaborative outcomes is: The Piddock Clam Collective, 'Wrack Writing (Selections)', *Feminist Review* 130, no. 1 (2022): 115–19, https://doi.org/10.1177/01417789211062208.
2. 'Weathering, *n*. Meanings, Etymology and More Oxford English Dictionary', https://www.oed.com/dictionary/weathering_n (accessed 7 June 2024).
3. Ibid.
4. Astrida Neimanis and Rachel Loewen Walker, '"Weathering": Climate Change and the "Thick Time" of Transcorporeality', *Hypatia* 29, no. 3 (2014): 558–75, https://www.jstor.org/stable/24542017.
5. Neimanis and Loewen Walker, 'Weathering', 569.
6. Neimanis and Loewen Walker, 'Weathering', 569.
7. Neimanis and Loewen Walker, 'Weathering', 569.
8. See Astrida Neimanis and Jennifer Mae Hamilton, 'Weathering', *Feminist Review* 118, no. 1 (2018): 80–4. Key references include Timothy Choy and Jerry Zee, 'Condition—Suspension', *Cultural Anthropology* 30, no. 2 (25 May 2015): 210–23; Kristen Simmons, 'Settler Atmospherics', https://culanth.org/fieldsights/settler-atmospherics (accessed 11 June 2019).
9. Arline T. Geronimus, 'The Weathering Hypothesis and the Health of African-American Women and Infants: Evidence and Speculations', *Ethnicity & Disease* 2, no. 3 (1992): 207–21.
10. The project was for Chart Collective's digital publishing project, Legend. Originally published at https://legend.chartcollective.org. At time of writing and proofing, the website was broken. For our own archive, please see 'The Weathering Map of Microclimates and Approximate Watery Bodies', https://weatheringstation.net/2017/12/18/the-weathering-map-of-microclimates-approximate-watery-bodies/ (accessed 30 October 2024).
11. Abby Mellick Lopes and Stephen Healy, 'Cultivating the Habits of Coolth', in *Assembling and Governing Habits* (London: Routledge, 2021).
12. Audre Lorde, *Zami: A New Spelling of My Name* (London: Sheba Feminist Publishers, 1984), 160.
13. Kathryn Yusoff, 'Queer Coal: Genealogies in/of the Blood', *philoSOPHIA* 5, no. 2 (2015): 204.
14. Lorde, *Zami: A New Spelling of My Name*, 7.
15. Denis Byrne, 'Weathering in Common', in *Feminist, Queer, Anticolonial Propositions for Hacking the Anthropocene: Archive*, ed. Jennifer Mae Hamilton et al. (London: Open Humanities Press, 2021), 106.
16. Sara Ahmed, 'Willful Stones', feministkilljoys, 29 January 2016, https://feministkilljoys.com/2016/01/29/willful-stones/.

17. Ahmed, 'Willful Stones'.
18. Jeannette Armstrong, 'Syilx-Led Climate Justice in a Global Context' (UBC Okanagan, 4 November 2024), https://climatejustice.ubc.ca/news/armstrong-klein-syilx-led-climate-justice-in-a-global-context/.
19. For example, Robin Wall Kimmerer, *Braiding Sweetgrass: Indigenous Wisdom, Scientific Knowledge, and the Teachings of Plants* (Minneapolis, MN: Milkweed Editions, 2013).
20. See also Butler, *Who's Afraid of Gender?*, 176–7.
21. Donna Haraway, *The Companion Species Manifesto: Dogs, People, and Significant Otherness*, 6th print, Paradigm 8 (Chicago, IL: Prickly Paradigm Press, 2012).
22. Kirby, as well as other feminist new materialist theorists such as Elizabeth A Wilson and Karen Barad, argue that non-human entities like birds, organs and viruses are engaged in all kinds of creativity, musicality, sociality and problem-solving, or what we might call 'cultural' practices, in ways that have importantly eroded the nature/culture binary. Karen Barad, *Meeting the Universe Halfway: Quantum Physics and the Entanglement of Matter and Meaning* (Durham, NC: Duke University Press, 2006); Vicki Kirby, *Quantum Anthropologies: Life at Large* (Durham, NC: Duke University Press, 2011); Elizabeth A. Wilson, *Gut Feminism* (Durham, NC: Duke University Press, 2015).
23. Butler, *Who's Afraid of Gender?*, 33.
24. Arline T. Geronimus, *Weathering: The Extraordinary Stress of Ordinary Life in an Unjust Society* (New York, NY, Boston, MA, and London: Little, Brown Spark, 2023).
25. Geronimus, *Weathering,* 10–11.
26. Yasmin Gunaratnam and Nigel Clark, 'Pre-Race Post-Race: Climate Change and Planetary Humanism', *Darkmatter* 9, no. 1 (2012), http://www.darkmatter101.org/site/2012/07/02/pre-race-post-race-climate-change-and-planetary-humanism/, n.p.
27. Gunaratnam and Clark, 'Pre-Race Post-Race'.
28. Gunaratnam and Clark, 'Pre-Race Post-Race'.
29. Melanie Etti, MyMai Yuan, and Jesse B. Bump, 'Sun, Skin and the Deadly Politics of Medical Racism', *BMJ Global Health* 8, no. 8 (2023): 1.
30. Gunaratnam and Clark, 'Pre-Race Post-Race'.
31. Gunaratnam and Clark, 'Pre-Race Post-Race'.
32. Etti et al., 'Sun, Skin and the Deadly Politics of Medical Racism', 2.
33. Feminist new materialisms, discussed in Chapter 1 and above in endnote 22, offer many useful analyses on a range of similar situations.
34. Gunaratnam and Clark, 'Pre-Race Post-Race'.
35. Mel Y. Chen, 'Feminisms in the Air', *Signs*, https://signsjournal.org/covid/chen/

36. Eli Clare, *Exile and Pride: Disability, Queerness, and Liberation* (Durham, NC: Duke University Press, 2015), https://doi.org/10.1215/9780822374879.
37. Clare, *Exile and Pride*, 8.
38. Leah Lakshni Piepzna-Samarasinha, *Care Work: Dreaming Disability Justice* (Vancouver: Arsenal Pulp Press, 2018), n.p.
39. Butler, *Who's Afraid of Gender?*, 176. Critical feminist investigations of biology abound, predating what is sometimes known as feminist new materialisms and the substantial contributions that this area made to eroding the nature/culture binary. See Stacy Alaimo and Susan J. Hekman, eds., *Material Feminisms* (Bloomington, IN: Indiana University Press, 2011) and Sara Ahmed, 'Open Forum Imaginary Prohibitions: Some Preliminary Remarks on the Founding Gestures of the 'New Materialism', *European Journal of Women's Studies* 15, no. 1 (2008): 23–39, https://doi.org/10.1177/1350506807084854.

INSET D — #haircuts for planetary survival

A haircut is a particular social infrastructure: between two people in a specific place for a set time. Haircuts invite vulnerability: conversation can be personal or intimate, while you place part of yourself (your hair!) in the hands of a relative stranger. This is a practice of risk and trust. Haircuts are usually transactional: money in exchange for services. Here, the transaction is a haircut in exchange for the chance to practice difficult conversations about climate change. The haircutter proposes: I'll cut (or style, or play with) your hair, if you help me learn to talk about polarizing topics, especially with people I care about. In other words, this haircut is an experiment in learning to have conversations about shelter and exposure, while also practicing these orientations.

What You Need

basic
- A semi-private space
- A chair with room to move around it
- Haircutting tools: scissors, razor cutter, clippers, comb, spray bottle, mirror, towel. Alternatively for styling or playing with someone's hair, you might need a brush, pins, elastics or clips.

optional
- A sign or blackboard to explain the activity while you are doing a haircut

How to Play

1. Advertise your salon. Be explicit about the terms of exchange. This includes a foundation of consent. The participant can opt out at any time: from the haircut, or from specific conversation topics!

2. Once you have a willing participant, agree on a time-frame (20 mins, 45 mins, 1 hour).

3. As you cut (or style) your participant's hair, feel out a conversation. Prompts might include the following...

4. A good conversation is reciprocal: respond to your participant's offerings and questions thoughtfully.

5. When you're done, ask your participant what they think of the cut and of the conversation! Maybe take a selfie together.

HAIRCUTS FOR PLANETARY SURVIVAL

Do you need a trim? A quick undobuzz? Something more daring?

I will cut (or style, braid, play with) your hair, and I would love to talk to you about the health of...

Maybe we can all be a bit brave and a bit vulnerable together.

Thank you for your trust ♡

- IS THERE ANYONE IN YOUR LIFE WHO IS DIFFICULT TO TALK TO, ESPECIALLY ABOUT CLIMATE CHANGE?
- HOW HAVE YOU APPROACHED SUCH CONVERSATIONS IN THE PAST?
- WHAT DO YOU WISH YOU COULD SAY TO THEM?
- CAN YOU IMAGINE ANOTHER WAY TO HAVE THIS CONVERSATION?
- HOW CAN YOU KEEP COMMUNICATION OPEN, ESPECIALLY IF YOU WANT TO KEEP THIS PERSON IN YOUR LIFE?

> This activity works well as a "side event" at a related workshop, festival, market stall or social gathering.

CHAPTER 4
Infrastructure (A bridge between theory and practice)

Introduction: Different bridges

When you hear the word 'bridge', what do you think? It might depend on whether you are playing a guitar or travelling by car. A bridge in music connects one part of a song to another, often shifting between moods. It is also a literal piece of infrastructure connecting two land masses divided by a waterway, a deep ravine, or anything else tricky to cross over. Bridges imply a social function, too: they bring things (bodies, times, places, feelings) together. If someone said to you 'name three bridges', you would likely privilege large-scale and iconic examples such as Vancouver's Lions Gate Bridge or Sydney Harbour Bridge. But bridges can be many things, built with many materials, facilitating different styles of crossing and different kinds of lifeways.

Juan Salazar's film *The Bamboo Bridge* (2019) traces the final year of a large 1.5 kilometre bamboo bridge across the Mekong River.[1] For generations it was (re)constructed annually to facilitate seasonal movement between Koh Paen and the city of Kampong Cham in Cambodia. In 2017 the government built a concrete bridge that allowed for the ongoing connection between the two places. This resulted in a rapid change to life on Koh Paen. While both of these bridges are weather management and mitigation devices, each enables different styles of weathering: one bridge gives itself over to the floods that wash it away and cut off the island for a season; the other defies the water and refuses to let the weather disrupt (some) human access to the island. Both bridges embody different ideas of connection.

The feminist infrastructure for weathering climate change we describe in this chapter emerges at a historical moment when most of the world's 'bamboo bridges' are being replaced by concrete ones. Or, to put it differently: when smaller-scale, seasonally attuned systems of care and connection have been interrupted, destroyed or devalued to prioritize flows of global capital in spite of people, place and planet. To weather the crisis called climate change, we need infrastructures of resistance for alternative collective ways of being and being together. Queer feminist theorist Lauren Berlant calls this 'managing the meanwhile within damaged life's perdurance'.[2] We parse this as: how can we keep on going in spite of it all? (We unpack this more later.)

The point is that specific infrastructure creates and supports specific social worlds. We need infrastructures that are both more and other than Big Infrastructure (such as concrete bridges) premised on a logic of neoliberal resilience. We offer feminist infrastructure as the support structure for resistance and transition: an alternative way of making and holding relations for a specific reason and duration. We see feminist infrastructure as a kind of bridge connecting the world as it is and the world as we'd like it to be, where differently sheltered and differently vulnerable bodies can relate, differently.

As a critical concept and physical set of pages, the infrastructure chapter of this book itself functions as a bridge between the theoretical work that has both guided and emerged from our weathering experiments, and the chapters that describe these practices for others to learn from and take up in their own ways. Following a public talk where we shared our weathering work in this same sequence, an audience member prefaced their question with: 'once you finished the boring theory part, I was interested in learning more about the practical examples.' This 'theory=boring/practice=interesting' equation has become a meme we keep coming back to while translating our work into book form – not because we want to rush towards our practical examples, but to remind ourselves to do the hard work of showing why the so-called boring theory is useful.

In humanities and social sciences, theory is a tool for explaining how and why something is operating in a particular way and how it might operate differently. If we need different infrastructures to support different social systems, theory is useful in three ways. First, theory can explain why certain infrastructures dominate (both in our imaginations and in practice). Second, theory helps us understand how these infrastructures silently guide our daily habits, sometimes detrimentally. Third, theory can propose how both the infrastructures and what they facilitate could be otherwise. Feminist theorist Elizabeth Grosz actually refers to concepts – the building blocks of theory – as 'moveable bridges': they are 'modes of connection', Grosz writes, between 'those forces that relentlessly impinge on us from the outside to form a problem' – such as capitalism or climate change – 'and those that we can muster within ourselves to address such problems'.[3] In other words: a theory doesn't solve anything alone, but it can create a bridge. That bridge is not a concrete one, but maybe a log across a river that could be placed here, or maybe there. Maybe we only need it seasonally. In any case, it helps get us from where we are to somewhere different.

But as long as there are living creatures on the planet, we will have to deal with the weather. We will need some ways of managing it, and perhaps mitigating it, because we are always weathering. Different infrastructures – like different bridges – facilitate different ways of weathering. This chapter begins with an overview of the kinds of infrastructures that dominate today and describes their connection to resilience thinking. The aim of this section is to think carefully about how present-day infrastructure supports weathering (or doesn't). We then propose weathering as a concept to guide infrastructure design, as an alternative to the bounce-back logic of resilience. We conclude the chapter by explaining our theory of feminist infrastructures, and show how, guided by weathering, they facilitate *better* weathering as feminist theory and practice for climate change.

There is a staggering difference in scale between what we propose here and the massive sea-walls and megadams of climate mitigation infrastructure. We know that the smaller, stranger and socially playful support systems we propose cannot do the work of holding the weight of water at bay. Feminist infrastructures are a method for helping us transition to a better world, where different infrastructural choices become more possible.

What is infrastructure?

Infrastructure is an industrial age and increasingly technocratic term for support structure. What we call 'infrastructure' today was called 'public works' yesterday: roads, dams, seawalls, sewage and drainage networks. Infrastructure has the dual purpose of managing people and non-human nature, but in ways that are never neutral. Anthropologists Hannah Knox and Evelina Gambino put it like this: 'Paying attention to infrastructure allows us to account for the everyday work that goes into making, breaking, and living with systems of power, control, possibility, and inequality.'[4] As designed entities, infrastructures channel and distribute these things, serving some people and purposes, while precluding (or stymying) other possibilities.

While once primarily a concern for civil engineers and planners, a more general 'infrastructural turn' has taken place within anthropology, sociology, media and communications studies, as well as humanities. Why has infrastructure all of a sudden become so interesting? There is no one answer, but we notice that this turn roughly coincides with other 'turns' in critical scholarship; turns to the more-than-human, to materiality, to concepts like entanglement and scale, are all part of an impulse to unpick the binary separation between 'nature' and 'culture'. This scholarship directly and indirectly asks questions about how humans and societies relate to non-humans and the earth. In turn, this work is related to a more general (love it or hate it) Anthropocenomania: all aboard the Age of Man! Infrastructure, as connective tissue, helps us understand relationships between near and far, big and small, before and after, as we rethink ourselves in planetary terms.

But most importantly, infrastructure is social *support*. Infrastructure is a substructure, meaning it is the stuff that makes social worlds – getting to work, getting home, throwing a party, taking a bath – possible for living human animals (and some of their more-than-human kin). As the Infrastructural Inequalities collective puts it: 'Infrastructure is one answer to the question: on what does this action, that endeavor, or that capacity depend?'[5] Like a lot of reproductive labour, infrastructural labour is often obscured. This is why it is also a feminist question. Some infrastructures are subterranean and physically invisible, but more generally, what is invisible is the extent to which infrastructure influences our lives. According to Susan Leigh Star,[6] we only see infrastructure when it breaks. Star has a point. If we're stuck in traffic trying to leave a city to take a holiday elsewhere, for example, we might express a frustration: 'I hate traffic! Who designed this bridge?' Transportation infrastructure shows itself when it is not functioning as it is supposed to.

That said, to become aware of infrastructure because you're frustrated by traffic does not sufficiently explain all the ways infrastructure is central to forms of life, environment and society. This is why Brian Larkin takes issue with Star's blanket characterization. For Larkin, 'The point' is 'to examine how (in)visibility is mobilized and why'.[7] Ample knowledge, technology, resources and skills are invested in designing, building and maintaining infrastructures, and their approval processes can be protracted and contentious. But once built, these infrastructures are taken for granted: we can't imagine life without their specifically established form (a car-snarled, bitumen-surfaced bridge, for example). Especially if it helps us get to the beach! This points to the second way that infrastructure is invisible, namely via the everyday practices they enable (driving, but also flying, shopping, consuming, washing, drinking, exercising and so on). In contrast to behaviouralist theories that focus on individual change, Elizabeth Shove's social practice theory helps us to see how infrastructural choices are also an overarching prioritization of certain practices (e.g. road expansion that supports more driving).[8] We are particularly interested in how infrastructure design relates to social practices, as a key inroad to answering the question of the book: *how to weather together?* We get to this in the second half of the chapter.

But specifically in terms of climate change, the cornerstone of many infrastructure projects is managing the variations, flows and excesses of the non-human world for the purposes of human development. Take, for example, the Sydenham stormwater pit and pumping station in inner city Sydney. Built to enable the extension of the southern rail line that connects the eastern Australian cities of Sydney and Wollongong, as well as industrial development in the Sydney suburbs of Sydenham and Marrickville, this pit and pump were also about minimizing the influence of the Gumbramorra Swamp on human development. As terminal lakes without outlets for drainage, swamps fill up with every rain. They are damp places. The Sydenham stormwater pit thus manages these inner city swamp waters that would otherwise thwart the outward sprawl of urban development. Now, water drains to a concrete holding pond instead of to the swamp, and is then pumped to a nearby estuary and out to sea.

An analogous example, just inland from Vancouver BC, is the Sumas Valley, which hosts a meaningful proportion of the province's commercial agriculture.[9] This is thanks to a years-long campaign begun a century ago to install dykes, canals, and pumps to divert the shallow lake waters that seasonally flood the valley bottom into the Sumas River.[10] Here again, non-human nature (water) is managed by infrastructure. This benefits some people and ways of life (settler-farmers in a system of commercial agriculture), but the infrastructure is invisibilized by all the everyday habits it enables. This place is now called the Sumas Prairie. Meanwhile, other lives and ways of life (for the Stó:lō people, for example) are displaced and disrupted.[11]

One key environmental issue with big infrastructure like stormwater pits and pumping stations is the environmental damage produced as side-effects of their functionality. In the twentieth century, turning urban waterways into concrete channels, pumps and diversions was considered normal to support a particular kind of urban growth and mobility. It was not until the 1990s that this practice of covering cities in 'impervious surfaces' was acknowledged in engineering circles as environmentally problematic.[12] We can also see the results of this along Goolay'yari (also called the Cooks River) – an urban waterway that was also the site of many of our early weathering research experiments. While this river used to end in a swampy estuary, it has since been channelled and diverted, not least to make way for

Sydney's international airport terminal. As such, it exemplifies civil engineering processes that created ways to promote human developments near rivers and estuaries, but degraded local ecosystems, biodiversity and water quality in the process.

Moreover, climate change and changing meteorological norms mean that a lot of infrastructure is no longer fit for purpose: airports are at risk of flooding from rising sea levels; rainfall extremes put pressure on stormwater networks; dam levels fluctuate far more widely than anticipated. Going back to the example of the Sumas Prairie, we note that the Stó:lō people don't call this place a 'prairie'. It is Semá:th X_ó:tsa. Before massive infrastructural incursion, Semá:th X_ó:tsa was a seasonal lake: sometimes water, sometimes land. While 'prairie' implies only grassland, the Stó:lō place name accommodates both wet and the dry forms; the colonial name, reinforced by big infrastructure to deny the water, does not. When a major atmospheric river event blew through Sumas in November 2021, Semá:th X_ó:tsa reemerged in its undeniable lake form, cutting off the Lower Mainland of BC from the rest of the country for weeks. All the engineering in the world couldn't keep the weather at bay.

Making cities more porous again, bringing life back to coastal littoral zones and reengaging wetlands are all examples of how we might help human communities weather differently. More often, though, infrastructural tweaks only mean increased fortification to maintain and grow the status quo. In response to the 2021 Sumas Valley flood, the BC government invested about 80 million Canadian to upgrade the Barrowtown Pump Station with a new six-metre flood wall, intended to mitigate any repeat.[13] Despite the anticipation of future atmospheric river events, it was inconceivable that Semá:th X_ó:tsa would be allowed to continue in its hybrid and seasonal form, where it might serve as a different kind of bridge, holding and facilitating other kinds of connection across knowledges and times. As Deb Cowen and Winona LaDuke suggest, settler infrastructures entrench and harden 'the very means of settler economy and sociality into tangible material structures'.[14] Big infrastructure remains a hard habit to break, also because it has the violent power of the settler colonial-capitalist state behind it.

All that said, we are not advocating blowing up dams or pipelines, or pumping stations. For now, we are interested in attending to the 'terms of transition' and 'managing the meanwhile',[15] to use Berlant's powerful phrases. This means asking questions like: how are these sites of major infrastructural impact – like the hydroengineering of Semá:th X_ó:tsa or Goolay'yari – home to different kinds of eco-social relations? What infrastructure is

Infrastructure (A Bridge Between Theory and Practice)

needed to support those relations and better human and non-human living? If you've walked along the Goolay'yari lately, did you notice the footbridge over the river just east of Wardell Road? Sure, it is made from steel and bitumen, but you get to occupy parts of the golf course as pedestrian space to use it. You might get your shoes muddy, but you can walk right next to the mangroves. If you go at night, you won't have the benefit of streetlights, but along with the dogwalkers, you might see the flying foxes lifting up from their Wolli Creek home to head out over the darkened suburb. Or you could delight in 20-metre-tall strings of fairy lights that animate one of the backyards on the Undercliff side of the river, and even chat to the folks sitting around their firepit. If you were there in January 2021, you might have even seen the mobile feminist infrastructure led by Aunty Rhonda Dixon-Grovenor, in the form of an all-day slow-moving walk that followed the pace of the outgoing estuary tide, and asked participants to pay attention to Country, persistent in spite of these colonial infrastructural incursions. You might have noticed twenty people paused on the Princes Highway bridge, resting, laughing, sharing tastes of the wild fennel picked along the way, and looking out past the airport to where the river becomes the sea.

Figure 4.1 On the Princes Highway bridge over Goolay'yari. *The River Ends as the Ocean: Walk the tide out.* Aunty Rhonda Dixon-Grovenor, Clare Britton and Astrida Neimanis. Shanghai Biennale *Bodies of Water.* Sydney, 2021. Photo Lucy Parakhina.

(You can read more about this walk and other mobile infrastructures in Chapter 9.)

These social infrastructures disrupt colonial and capitalist infrastructure development norms, and enable different kinds of weathering. Before describing such feminist weathering infrastructures in more detail, we first tackle the dominance of resilience thinking in relation to climate adaptation, to understand how it has made a monoculture of different infrastructural possibilities.

From resilience to weathering

There is no version of climate change that doesn't involve crises. Accordingly, we need concepts that can account for storm, fire, flood, heatwave, drought and pandemic as well as more mundane weathers. Herein lies the appeal of resilience. Resilience implies that there is a norm that has been disrupted or damaged, and offers a way to restore that norm when a crisis hits. How nice! Something (a city, an ecology, an infrastructure, a community) is afflicted by disaster, trauma or crisis, but recovers, unscathed and stronger than ever!

Resilience is a ubiquitous concept guiding climate change adaptation, focussing on a 'bounce-back' logic that champions a quick and strong return to business-as-usual.[16] Although it is a word, it is also a politics with material consequences that include divestment from government and social services meant to support those who need these in times of disaster or crisis. Instead of focusing on specific emissions reduction targets or slowing average temperature increases, large-scale climate change adaptation projects protect the socio-economic status quo for elites, or those who can adapt to the social and economic modes of using the metaphoric concrete bridge. For example, projects like the World Bank's 'Green Structural Adjustment' will further deregulate developing economies and create new kinds of national debt and private investment opportunities.[17] This top–down social experimentation is occurring with limited community control or civic input into design.[18] A neoliberal resilience framework cannot imagine that the metaphorical bamboo bridge might offer a mode of crossing over the water, as it is outside the values of strength, speed or purported permanence. Nor can this mode be seen as desirable, not in spite of but because of the shared and unprofitable differences it can temporarily hold together.

A feminist alternative to these logics begins by paying attention to the diversity of bodies and environments that infrastructures have to manage.[19]

Infrastructure (A Bridge Between Theory and Practice)

Under resilience logics, we have to fortify ourselves against our own bodily needs; we are not permitted to be diversely vulnerable.[20] This one-size-fits-all system, focussing on strength, pays almost no attention to the different ways and different degrees to which our bodies are resilient. It also fails to heed the most basic lesson of weathering (see Chapter 3) – that some materials erode quickly, while others take years, or centuries. We all weather differently, due to both desirable and imposed differences.

Under neoliberal resilience, difference is only permissible, or indeed possible, if it lets us strongly bounce back to some unquestioned norm, and triumph against the odds. Our feminist critique of this draws on disability justice work that warns us against 'cures' and quick fixes.[21] Instead of trying to shove everyone into the structures on offer, either 'fixing' or abandoning those who don't fit, disability justice teaches us to accept and support different vulnerabilities. For example, a bridge built not only for cars and trucks, but for bicycles, pedestrians, prams and mobility scooters, recognizes both imposed and desirable bodily differences.

Paying attention to alternative definitions of resilience is helpful here. After all, resilience – the material quality, not the neoliberal concept – is not a bad thing. In its most physical sense, resilience indexes the potential 'elasticity' of a material or, more specifically, '[t]he energy per unit volume absorbed by a material when it is subjected to strain; the value of this at the elastic limit'.[22] This definition simply describes material differences in response to strain: any material might be more or less resilient, more or less elastic, than another. In other words, resilience does not necessarily have an imperative to underpin a corporate agenda. It could instead describe a diversity of responses, by different kinds of bodies, to a changing situation. Here, being 'less resilient' would be neither better nor worse; it would just need different kinds of attention and support. We would realize that it is the system and the values that undergird it that need 'fixing', and not the bodies that don't adhere to those norms.

The less heroic use of the term is closer to what we call *weathering*. Unlike neoliberal resilience, weathering gets us to think about enduring a crisis, but without insisting on fortifying an unsustainable and unjust system. Weathering acknowledges experience and inheritance. If, for example, the strongest and most elastic, most resilient, person on earth is subject to extreme stress over and over again, weathering can account for their decreased elasticity, decreased resilience. Weathering is a theory of adaptation that entails transformation: it is making it through the storm of a crisis, but being materially changed by it (for better or worse). Weathering recognizes

107

that different bodies will always withstand the storm differently, and those differences can not, and should not, be planned away. Against resilience's appeal of a perfect bounce-back, weathering is less bouncy, working instead towards transformative justice in sunshine and in rain.

Infrastructures for managing the meanwhile

As geographer Deb Cowen puts it: 'Alternative worlds require alternative infrastructures – systems that allow for sustenance and reproduction.'[23] Yet there are fewer and fewer non-commodified, non-criminalized opportunities for relative strangers within (or across) communities to engage in experimentation in how to weather our current storms differently, in ways that will expose us but where this exposure is not fatal. At the same time, on account of the climate emergency, advocating for anything other than 'resilience infrastructure' seems almost impossible. Real cultural change seems too hard and will take too long. We disagree. But we do need ways to actually adapt to climate change while changing the world at the same time. We need infrastructure that will help us get to where we want to go, both carefully and incrementally and radically and transformatively.

At the beginning of this chapter, we noted that all infrastructure has a social function; bridges, for example, bring things (bodies, times, places, feelings) together. But different bridges support different social worlds. The Bamboo Bridge in Salazar's film enables crossing over, but it also supports social relationships: from the bamboo growers inheriting their vocation from their ancestors, to small vendors who serve refreshments to bridge-crossers, to the bridge-builders who barter their labour for free tolls. The bridge is also a cultural repository of the province's unique traditional craft, bridging past and future. It is a literal support not only for cars and trucks but motorcycles, bicycles, pedestrians, dogs and fishermen who launch their nets from the bridge. Can a bamboo bridge be a lesson in weathering together, rather than resilience? The last master bridge-builder discusses bamboo's advantages over concrete: 'Even if [bamboo] breaks', he says, 'it stays together'. While this may sound like romantic nostalgia, it is a real response to the technical and political question of what kind of weathering the new concrete bridge actually affords, versus the bamboo one. As one local vendor explains, 'only car owners prefer the concrete bridge'.[24] So what modes of crossing over are prioritized, and what modes are disrupted and displaced?

Or consider an example more familiar to us. When the q̓awsitkw (Okanagan River), south of Astrida's home in Kelowna, was channelized as one such project in the 1950s, the salmon that journeyed upriver to spawn no longer had any nooks or crannies for rest. Exhausted, they didn't do well. So the syilx people of the Okanagan Nation began a programme to restore the k'əmcnitkw floodplain, including a slow, riparian resting habitat along one stretch of the river. It is not yet clear what effect it is having on the salmon population, but it is clear that this small-scale intervention has re-engaged all kinds of other social events: visiting bears, osprey and turtles, milkweed and butterflies, more wild rose habitat for the the yellow-breasted chat at the end of its long migration. Humans can slow down too. Cyclists and pedestrians on the river path stop to find out more, while shovel-wielding volunteers plant riparian species grown at the En'owkin nursery, just down the track on the other side of the makeshift plank bridge that crosses over a smaller creek. It wasn't easy to cross (back) over to other eco-social relations. But nor was it impossible.[25]

Alternatives to concrete bridges are either not perceived as sufficiently scalable to solve the big problems of the world, or are not imaginable as 'infrastructure'. But what if we *did* imagine them as infrastructure? Such alternatives could include not only bamboo bridges (which can be readily understood as infrastructure) but also Indigenous-led riparian restoration, protest movements, grassroots campaigns, community initiatives or social enterprises, feminist classrooms, decolonization, queer joy, and in more disruptive cases, crimes and/or (eco) terrorist acts (which are less readily imagined as such). For whom or what are these substructures crucial? What kinds of shelter and vulnerability can they support? How, and what, will they help us cross over?

In building specifically feminist alternatives, we want to think carefully about infrastructure's social functions. Here, the work of queer feminist cultural theorist, Lauren Berlant, has been particularly instructive. Perhaps this is because Berlant's background is *not* in social policy or other traditional 'infrastructural' disciplines, but rather in how to think through the mess of social experience under late capitalism. Berlant calls infrastructure 'the living mediation of what organizes life: the lifeworld of structure'.[26] This includes many supports that fall outside of capitalist economies (care, support, material assistance, recognition, respect). You don't need steel and concrete to have infrastructure.

Instead of focusing on the end goal – some kind of utopian commons where everyone will agree and live in harmony – Berlant encourages us to attend carefully to the 'terms of transition'. We see this as a method, a practice, and an outcome in itself. By 'managing the meanwhile', as Berlant calls it, we undertake the slow and transformative work that is a prerequisite for living together differently. As she puts it, this 'is less an end [. . .] than a technical political heuristic that allows for ambivalence, distraction, antagonism and inattention not to destroy collective existence'.[27] In plainer words, this means that the real work happens on the bridge, so to speak: in the phase between where we are now, and wherever we're going to end up. This work has to be able to hold tension and conflict; its usefulness lies in a carefully held process, not in a predetermined outcome.

The experiments we propose in this book's illustrated insets, as well as our 'reports from the field' in Chapters 5 to 9, may not seem very infrastructural, either. Initially, we thought these activities were ways to spark our thinking *about* infrastructures that support different kinds of weathering – which they have! Take 'Weathering with or without' (Inset C), for example. It asks participants to make a list of all of the things that help them mitigate the weather – from space heaters to sun hats to houses. We have played two different versions: in the first, you pass your list around the table, and others are asked to cross items off your list at random. When everyone gets their own redacted list back, we discuss what it feels like when others make these decisions for you. We also talk about how it feels to increase someone else's vulnerability or discomfort (this can be ambivalent, noting that limiting aircon in private homes, for example, might be positive or negative). In the second version, participants are asked to choose one of the items on someone else's list and make a drawing of it. Each drawing is circulated, and grows as everyone draws additional shelter-items. It is then gifted back to the list-maker. This version practises the communal creation and redistribution of vulnerability and shelter.

But after thinking alongside Berlant about infrastructures, we started to see these activities themselves as feminist climate change mitigation infrastructures – holding spaces where bodies can rest, reenergize and actually experiment with the redistribution of both shelter and vulnerability. They are about building new and different kinds of infrastructures for weathering these storms together. Our proposal, then, is to theorize infrastructure differently – to include not only dams or even (literal) moveable bridges, but all of those phenomena that support the 'terms of transition'. Characterizing our low-stakes weathering practices in this book as infrastructures allows us to see how they are both *like* things like concrete bridges (in providing a way to weather the world), but also *unlike* them, in terms of their attention to a diversity of bodily vulnerability, scalability (including scaling *down*), and the fringe benefits they offer.

The remaining chapters of this book provide details of possible models for this work – things we have done, and that you might do, differently, in response to your own situation. This chapter aims to provide more of the theoretical backstory that helped us figure out what we've been doing. As a bridge to those chapters, the last section explains what we mean by feminist infrastructure for better weathering in more detail.

Why and what is *feminist* infrastructure?

Above, we claim that feminist infrastructure becomes necessary when most of the world's bamboo bridges have been replaced by concrete ones. What do we mean by 'feminist infrastructure'? Feminism can mean many things to different folks. In Chapter 1, we specified the kind of feminism we think is necessary to support weathering better together. One way we describe this feminism is as *an embodied politics of solidarity*. This means valuing and supporting difference as we live it in and as bodies. While feminism sometimes starts from gender-related differences, an inclusive feminism also considers differences or divisions sedimented by colonial, white supremacist and capitalist structures of power, as well as factors such as age and disability. Our feminism also challenges any simple understanding of the nature/culture divide, which means we are committed to embodied solidarity with non-human natures as well. Moreover, we understand embodied differences as a complicated interplay of both material or physical factors (what we might call 'nature'), and systems of power that cause bodies to weather differently (what we might call 'culture'). Because feminism entails not only analysis but action, it should also offer ways of connecting across differences, especially when our differences are exploited to uphold the status quo. This is where feminist infrastructures come in.

As feminists attentive to what it means to live in feeling, animal, desiring and vulnerable bodies that all relate differently to each other and weather, we have identified some core elements of eco-social life that are minimized under the current regime of concrete bridges. First and foremost, the non-human world is marginalized by design to keep the weather and the vermin out, and *certain* humans in. But the exclusively human domain includes other critical marginalizations. As noted above, in a world of concrete bridges, minimal support is provided for the development of meaningful, non-commercial relations and intimate exchanges with human and non-human strangers. The stranger might be someone who lives next door who we don't know yet, or the undocumented migrant living in the margins under a life-threatening regime of militarized borders and xenophobia; the stranger could be the creek redirected beneath our backyard, or the creature that cannot access food because of all the backyard fences.[28] We don't underestimate the power of finding new ways of relating to others in these times where dissent is criminalized, and borders are fortified. Since our feminism (as we describe in Chapter 1) seeks connection across polarization, while also taking a stand against the rise of fascist exclusions and dehumanization, these stranger forms of connection, seeded in nascent and small-scale ways, are central to our feminist practices for climate change. These practices are feminist infrastructures because they are support structures that can subtend a form of embodied solidarity.

When we think of the world today, dominant infrastructure supports the privatization, commercialization and uniformity of social connection. Moving between socially sanctioned relations/practices (the family home, shop and workplaces) in socially sanctioned ways (in a car at the speed limit), possession of property and proprietorial relations of family comprise the ultimate goal – one that we are all supposed to want. But the feminist solidarity we support does not mean sameness, nor even sharing the same interests or priorities. Nor is this solidarity about possession. It means being together, recognizing difference, valuing it and working towards redistributing shelter and vulnerability in ways that are attentive to different needs and desires.

Berlant's idea of 'stranger intimacy' has been particularly helpful in thinking through what this kind of being together entails.[29] 'Stranger intimacy'[30] accurately acknowledges the ways that (not only human) bodies affect one another when we find ourselves in a common situation. But, as Berlant puts it, 'just because we are in a room together does not mean that we belong to the room or to each other'.[31] We share a common situation, rather than a common identity. We need these relations to be possible even without a sense of deep connection, ownership, or possession. Berlant's theory of the commons reminds us that what we share in climate crisis is not necessarily belief, desire or future hopes, but the fact that we must all manage a weather-world that may or may not accommodate us equitably. Climate change is a situation that *cannot* rely on a common identity. Instead, we need to find ways to hold difference in common, with care. For this, we need different infrastructures.

This need is nothing new. Lauren Berlant and Michael Warner's landmark 1998 queer theory essay 'Sex in Public' examines how the gentrification of Times Square in late twentieth-century Manhattan required shrinking public space for self-expression outside capitalist consumerist or nuclear family norms. Planners and lawmakers exploited moral panic around sexuality to green-light the building of infrastructure that restricted queer practices that fell outside the norm, while proliferating practices that supported consumerism, property development, and nuclear family-making. Berlant's most recent (and last) book continues the line of thinking, calling for a sense of commons that can hold and allow for the unfolding of the queer messiness of our lives. This would be a social space that in Berlant's words is 'null, delightfully animated, stressful, intimate, alien, and uncanny'.[32]

Queer feminist ecocritic Sarah Ensor adds to this way of thinking about ethical relations without long-term commitment or belonging. In her environmentally attuned reading of Samuel Delaney's writing on cruising (again starting with the example of Times Square in the late twentieth century), Ensor highlights social encounters that are brief, or accidental.[33] Her examples include ephemeral sexual encounters, but also meeting others on a walk through a neighbourhood, or passing by plants in a forest.[34] Ensor argues that non-committal relations can still build robust social ecologies, when practiced with an 'ethos of care'. These ephemeral social infrastructures produce 'queer fallout'. Ensor contrasts this fallout of fleeting connection with nuclear fallout. Instead of poisoning things, queer fallout can sustain and reshape a social scene or an ecology for the better. The absence of close or long-term relations between individuals is not a threat to community, but the loose weave of fabric that actually keeps it together.[35]

It is not coincidental that Berlant, Warner and Ensor all look to queer sociality for models of different social infrastructures. While their examples are rooted in sexual identity and practices, they also all suggest that queer ways of life are much broader than that. As Marianne Liljeström notes, 'sexuality can mean affect, kinship, social reproduction, the transmission of property, the division between public and private, and the construction of gender, race and nationality'[36] and more – not least because sexuality is about how we are together, in the world, and how our forms of relating to each other are supported, or not. Colonialism, and its violent negation of Indigenous intimacies and kinship relations, as Lakota scholar Kim TallBear points out, also underpins infrastructures (e.g. single-family patriarchally governed homesteads) that enable theft of Indigenous land.[37] In other words, sex and intimacy have always been sites of both oppression and resistance.

This is why for us, feminist infrastructure for better weathering is also queer infrastructure. We want infrastructures that support queer ways of life – forms of being together, across difference, that the metaphoric concrete bridge will not accommodate.

Queer feminist infrastructures also challenge the ideas that significant infrastructure must be large-scale. Just as J.K. Gibson-Graham insists that diverse economies are vital for feminist praxis,[38] we argue that differently scaled infrastructures need to be taken more seriously as an alternative to the neoliberal model of climate adaptation. Feminist infrastructures can be built in everyday, quasi-domestic spaces of a social-but-not-mutual commons, where politics manifest through mundane stranger intimacies with friends and strangers, humans and non-humans. This is how they adapt to climate change by changing the colonial heteropatriarchal climate.

#Haircutsforplanetarysurvival as a strange mobile hair salon is an example of one such infrastructure from our practice. Astrida started this project in 2020 as part of the 'Weathering Everything' symposium that Jen organized in Armidale, NSW (see Inset D). In this art project, consenting participants agreed to let Astrida cut their hair; in exchange, she would ask them about difficult climate change conversations they've had. These little pop-up salons sit at the intersection of fleeting stranger intimacies, that are temporary yet potentially transformative, and feminized labours, that subtend and make possible many other day-to-day, quasi-domestic forms of sociality. We are interested in exploring both dimensions in our weathering work. Moving away from a resilience-based approach to climate change, the salon provides an opportunity to experiment in social forms that explicitly invite conversations about risk and vulnerability, while also practising these orientations together: Astrida, a practiced but amateur cutter, feels differently vulnerable than the participant, who sits with very sharp scissors very close to their ears. Both people share the risk of undesirable outcome.

The climate change conversations add another layer to this vulnerability. Astrida and her participants have shared personal stories of family relationships that have broken because of climate change denial. And together, they have shared tactics for how, instead of winning an argument, we might learn to stay in relation, even when it's difficult. These salons are rehearsals in managing the meanwhile. They are not abstract or ready-made utopias. A defining quality of infrastructures (including and maybe especially feminist ones) is that they require maintenance. As Ruth Gilmore reminds us, 'even solidarity needs to be remade and remade and remade, it never just is'.[39] This means grappling with tensions that are always part of the 'meanwhile', and supporting the key queer feminist ambit of a critical form of repair/reparation[40] as part of everyday life. Relationships (also bridges) need care and repair.

Experimenting in feminist infrastructure as climate change mitigation has also foregrounded the need to navigate between the collective grunt labour (some of which will always be unglamorous, like sweeping floors or sending email reminders) and hospitality (where there is an expectation of support for the needs and vulnerabilities of the group). In other words, this infrastructural work, like all work, involves a measure of housework – which is another important feminist aspect of weathering work (see Inset H). For the Weathering Collective, this has included maintenance of our website (that was not updated for about four years) and other practicalities, as well as careful tending to the relationships between us. In a description of the 'collective effort required, to keep a social infrastructure well maintained',[41] the Infrastructural Inequalities collective points out that figuring out this labour is also how we learn about the phenomenon we are trying to understand, i.e. infrastructure. In the case of that Collective, it meant reconsidering how shelter and vulnerability could be differently distributed between academics in secure jobs, precarious workers, students, artists and community.

Feminist infrastructures can support many things, but they cannot control them.[42] In other words, the outcomes of these infrastructures are not determined by us; if a haircut conversation or a workshop activity is to be transformative, we need to loosen our grip and be open to being changed. We are not going to pretend this is easy, or even always pleasurable (but often is)! Committing to this kind of community can be challenging. After all, the title of Berlant's book on all of this is *The Inconvenience of Other People*! This inconvenience is more than a 'doing the dishes' question of community housework; it's about the equally mundane challenge of just being together. This is why we theorize these spaces as training grounds. We follow Harney and Moten, who understand rehearsal as study or practice, i.e. 'what you do with other people. It's talking and walking around with other people, working, dancing, suffering, some irreducible convergence of all three, held under the name of speculative practice'.[43] Or maybe it can be giving a haircut while practising a tough conversation. Can this be how we build muscles for the more significant kinds of redistribution that climate change calls us to? When we disturb 'what threatens and what comforts', Berlant says, we're 'training in collaboration'.[44]

And we need this training, as things really start heating up. While our participant-audiences are always diverse, they tend towards middle-class and educated folks familiar with (if also critical of) capitalist-colonial ways of being. In our activities, we aim to tenderly push our participants – and ourselves – into questioning what we think is secure. If we're living under seamless climate-controlled conditions, we need to practise being less afraid of exposure. In Berlant's words, 'to be exposed to one's exposure is not equal to being destroyed by it'.[45] A bad haircut won't kill you, but the queer fallout of risking community connection might be what saves us.

Conclusion: Don't call the cops

What would we like our infrastructures to do? How sheltered do we want to be? How sheltered do we *need* to be? How much more (or less) sheltered do others need to be? We can't just prioritize expedience (the 'no time, this is an emergency' logic of resilience), but nor can we sit around waiting for perfectly pre-formed, problem-free politics. We can be practical radicals and grounded utopians. We don't need to call the cops on the climate emergency. We can allow for the time needed to participate and make ends meet in the current economy, while also opening up space for practices that bring alternative collective ways of being into view.

We do not have to be only pure, orthodox, relentless, ameliorative or singly-focussed to change the world. We can play. We can pause. We can take breaks. We can lose sight of the ball. We can lose our grounding and have to come back to the breath. And as we do this, we will get older, we will get sick, we will feel the cold, we will have to sleep. And we will do this variously, at different times and to different extents. So there's a pragmatism in using weathering as our key term of transition. Weathering means finding infrastructures that can redistribute both shelter and vulnerability.

Our shared lifeways depend on the seemingly paradoxical activity of stopping anthropogenic climate change that is destroying life on earth, while simultaneously changing other kinds of climates. We propose that feminist practice for climate change can become the substrate of a changed social order over time, because it reckons with this specific paradox. The feminist infrastructures we propose are a methodology for bringing people together (in more-than-human contexts and specific places) to do new things, engage in new practices, test new selves – and also to change the climate of colonial capitalist cisheteropatriarchy. We need infrastructure to adapt to and mitigate climate change, but we need to change the terms of both infrastructure and climate change, too.

Infrastructure (A Bridge Between Theory and Practice)

We hope that the examples in this book can be useful. We hope they will provide ideas but also partial maps for how to meet similar objectives in the meanwhile you currently inhabit. At the same time, we often feel like we are just at the beginning of this project; our experiments are all provisional and partial and still-unfolding, as well as morphing and sometimes now hibernating or even expiring. That is also why we are offering this chapter on theory as a moveable bridge: we hope that when you take it and extend it between the gathering storm and what might come after, different and even new possibilities will open.

Notes

1. Juan Salazar, *The Bamboo Bridge* (Matadora Films, 2019).
2. Lauren Berlant, 'The Commons: Infrastructures for Troubling Times*', *Environment and Planning D: Society and Space* 34, no. 3 (2016): 393–419.
3. Elizabeth Grosz, 'The Future of Feminist Theory: Dreams for New Knowledges', in *Undutiful Daughters: New Directions in Feminist Thought and Practice*, ed. H. Gunkel, C. Nigianni, and F. Soderback (Durham, NC: Duke University Press, 2012), 14.
4. Hannah Knox and Evelina Gambino, 'Infrastructure', in *Cambridge Encyclopedia of Anthropology* (2023), http://doi.org/10.29164/23infrastructure
5. Liam Grealy, Andrew Brooks, Astrid Lorange, Christen Cornell and Tess Lea, 'Introduction: Tending a Social Infrastructure', *Infrastructural Inequalities* 1 (2019).
6. Susan Leigh Star, 'The Ethnography of Infrastructure', *American Behavioral Scientist* 43, no. 3 (1999): 377–91.
7. Brian Larkin, 'The Politics and Poetics of Infrastructure', *Annual Review of Anthropology* 42, no. 1 (2013): 327–43.
8. Elizabeth Shove, 'Infrastructures and Practices: Networks beyond the City', *Beyond the Networked City: Infrastructure Reconfigurations and Urban Change in the North and South*, ed. Olivier Coutard and Jonathan Rutherford (London: Routledge, 2015), 242–58.
9. 'Agricultural Land Use Survey in the Sumas River Watershed Report' (BC Environment, 1994), https://publications.gc.ca/collections/collection_2015/ec/En83-6-1994-21-eng.pdf.
10. Laura Cameron, *Openings: A Meditation on History, Method, and Sumas Lake* (Montreal & Kingston, London, Buffalo: University of British Columbia, Academic Women's Association ; McGill-Queen's University Press, 1997).
11. Madeline Donald and Astrida Neimanis, 'Sema:Th X'otsa: Fringe Natures as Decolonial Feminist-Queer-Trans Water Imaginaries', in *Routledge Handbook of Gender and Water Governance* (London: Routledge, 2024); Chad Reimer, *Before*

We Lost the Lake: A Natural and Human History of Sumas Valley (Halfmoon Bay, BC: Caitlin Press, 2018).

12. Chester L. Arnold Jnr and C. James Gibbons, 'Impervious Surface Coverage: The Emergence of a Key Environmental Indicator', *Journal of the American Planning Association* 62, no. 2 (1996): 243–58.

13. Michele Brunoro, '"We Can't Wait": B.C. Spending 76.6M on Pump Station to Protect Sumas Prairie from Future Flooding', *CTV News*, 14 February 2024, https://bc.ctvnews.ca/we-can-t-wait-b-c-spending-76-6m-on-pump-station-to-protect-sumas-prairie-from-future-flooding-1.6769137.

14. Winona LaDuke and Deborah Cowen, 'Beyond Wiindigo Infrastructure', *South Atlantic Quarterly* 119, no. 2 (1 April 2020): 243–68, https://doi.org/10.1215/00382876-8177747, 244. For an account of the relationship between settler colonialism, policy worlds and Indigenous dispossession in Australia, see also Tess Lea, *Wild Policy: Indigeneity and the Unruly Logics of Intervention*, Anthropology of Policy (Stanford, CA: Stanford University Press, 2020).

15. Berlant, 'The Commons', 394.

16. For critiques of resilience logic, see: Jeremy Walker and Melinda Cooper, 'Genealogies of Resilience: From Systems Ecology to the Political Economy of Crisis Adaptation', *Security Dialogue* 42, no. 2 (2011): 143–60; Ashley Dawson, *Extreme Cities: The Peril and Promise of Urban Life in the Age of Climate Change* (London and New York, NY: Verso Books, 2017).

17. The scale is mind-boggling. The UN is using 'Green Structural Adjustment' to inform all environmental policy, http://www.unepfi.org/psi/global-resilience-project/, and so is the World Bank http://www.worldbank.org/en/topic/environment/publication/environment-strategy-toward-clean-green-resilient-world.

18. Patrick Bigger and Sophie Webber, 'Green Structural Adjustment in the World Bank's Resilient City', *Annals of the American Association of Geographers* 111, no. 1 (2021): 37.

19. This claim likely overlaps with the logic of 'diverse economies' (J.K. Gibson-Graham and Kelly Dombroski, eds, *The Handbook of Diverse Economies* (Cheltenham: Edward Elgar Publishing, 2020)), but not all bodily practices, habits or even relations are economic exchanges with a surplus able to be distributed. A project exploring the overlaps and divergences in these different diversities would be really interesting!

20. For an analysis of how resilience policies seek to manage and regulate diverse vulnerabilities, see Sarah Bracke, 'Bouncing back: vulnerability and resistance in times of resilience', in *Vulnerability in resistance*, ed. Judith Butler et al. (Durham, NC: Duke University Press, 2016)

21. Leah Lakshmi Piepzna-Samarasinha, *Care Work: Dreaming Disability Justice* (Vancouver, BC: Arsenal Pulp Press, 2021); Eli Clare, 'Meditations on Natural Worlds, Disabled Bodies, and a Politics of Cure', in *Material Ecocriticism*, ed.

Serenella Iovino and Serpil Oppermann (Bloomington: Indiana University Press, 2014).

22. 'Resilience, n.', *OED Online*, Oxford University Press, https://www.oed.com/view/Entry/163619 (accessed 19 August 2020).

23. Deb Cowen in Shiri Pasternak et al., 'Infrastructure, Jurisdiction, Extractivism: Keywords for Decolonizing Geographies', *Political Geography* 101 (1 March 2023): 102763, https://doi.org/10.1016/j.polgeo.2022.102763.

24. Salazar, *The Bamboo Bridge*.

25. For more information, see Okanagan Nation Alliance, 'Okanagan River Restoration', https://enowkincentre.ca/departments-ecommunity.html (accessed 27 October 2024). See also Maria Correia, Sarah Alexis and Aleksandra Dulic, 'Bringing the Salmon Home: A Study of Cross-Cultural Collaboration in the Syilx Okanagan Territory of British Columbia', *Ecology and Society* 29, no. 1 (2024): art15, https://doi.org/10.5751/ES-14831-290115.

26. Berlant, 'The Commons', 393.

27. Berlant, 'The Commons', 394.

28. See Laura McLauchlan, *Hedgehogs, Killing, and Kindness: The Contradictions of Care in Conservation Practice* (Cambridge, MA: The MIT Press, 2024).

29. Berlant, 'The Commons', 398.

30. Berlant, 'The Commons', 398.

31. Berlant, 'The Commons', 395.

32. Berlant, 'The Commons', 399.

33. Sarah Ensor, 'Queer Fallout: Samuel R. Delany and the Ecology of Cruising', *Environmental Humanities* 9, no. 1 (2017): 160.

34. Sarah Ensor, 'The Ecopoetics of Contact: Touching, Cruising, Gleaning', *ISLE: Interdisciplinary Studies in Literature and Environment* 25, no. 1 (2018): 154.

35. Writing about participatory taste workshops held online during the COVID-19 pandemic, Lindsay Kelley describes trying to collaborate on this work as a 'battle for together'. Also citing Berlant, she argues we cannot take togetherness for granted anymore; we have to fight for it. We can also try to set different terms of togetherness. Lindsay Kelley, 'Kitchen Futures: Participatory Taste Workshops and the Battle for Together', *Australian Feminist Studies* 38, no. 115–16 (3 April 2023): 85–102, https://doi.org/10.1080/08164649.2024.2338793.

36. Marianne Liljeström, 'Feminism and Queer Temporal Complexities', *SQS– Suomen Queer-Tutkimuksen Seuran* 13, no. 1–2 (2019): 31.

37. Kim TallBear, 'Making Love and Relations Beyond Settler Sex and Family', in *Make Kin, Not Population* (Chicago, IL: Prickly Paradigm Press, 2018).

38. J.K. Gibson-Graham, 'Waiting for the revolution', in *The End of Capitalism As We Knew It: A Feminist Critique of Political Economy* (Minneapolis,MN: University of Minnesota Press, 1996).

39. Ruth Gilmore, *Geographies of Racial Capitalism*, 2020. https://www.youtube.com/watch?v=2CS627aKrJI.
40. Eve Kosofsky Sedgwick, *Touching Feeling: Affect, Pedagogy, Performativity*, Series Q (Durham, NC: Duke University Press, 2003).
41. Grealy et al., 'Introduction: Tending a Social Infrastructure'.
42. Berlant describes infrastructures as wormholes. You have to let the worm move, and see what direction it will take. Lauren Berlant, *On the Inconvenience of Other People* (Durham, NC: Duke University Press, 2022), 93.
43. Stephano Harney and Fred Moten, *The Undercommons: Fugitive Planning and Black Study* (Brooklyn, NY: Minor Compositions, 2013), 110.
44. Berlant, 'The Commons', 108.
45. Berlant, 'The Commons', 101.

INSET E: reading & listening groups

There is a lot to read online and in print these days. Add to that all there is to listen to. Listening (to conversation, audio book, interview or song) is a form of reading too. Reading and listening diversely and widely enables different kinds of knowledge to become part of the body. Reading and/or listening collectively is an opportunity for that knowledge to be shared and discussed between bodies. Books are sometimes banned or burnt because some knowledge is risky; some knowledge challenges unjust power structures.

Reading groups can be a cornerstone feminist practice for climate change. They keep genealogies of counter-hegemonic knowledge alive. In sharing the knowledge they generate, reading groups also build fairer, safer, less hierarchical, more inclusive and diverse worlds. When choosing readings on environmental crisis, ask: how do queer, Black, feminist, trans-inclusive and anti-colonial readings merge with multibeing justice to produce knowledge for the future? Poems, songs and fictions welcome.

WHAT YOU NEED

- A group of interested people (any size)
- A reading or listening list (someone can create it or it can be co-designed).

HOW TO PLAY

- Plan how you will read together (eg. pre-read and discuss; read out loud in collaboration)
- Plan how you will meet (IRL or online or hybrid or asynchronous with a blog).
- What is the format of the meeting? (introductions, note-taking/doodling, facilitation style etc).
- Plan a calendar and set times in advance to build momentum.
- Nominate someone to send out reminders.

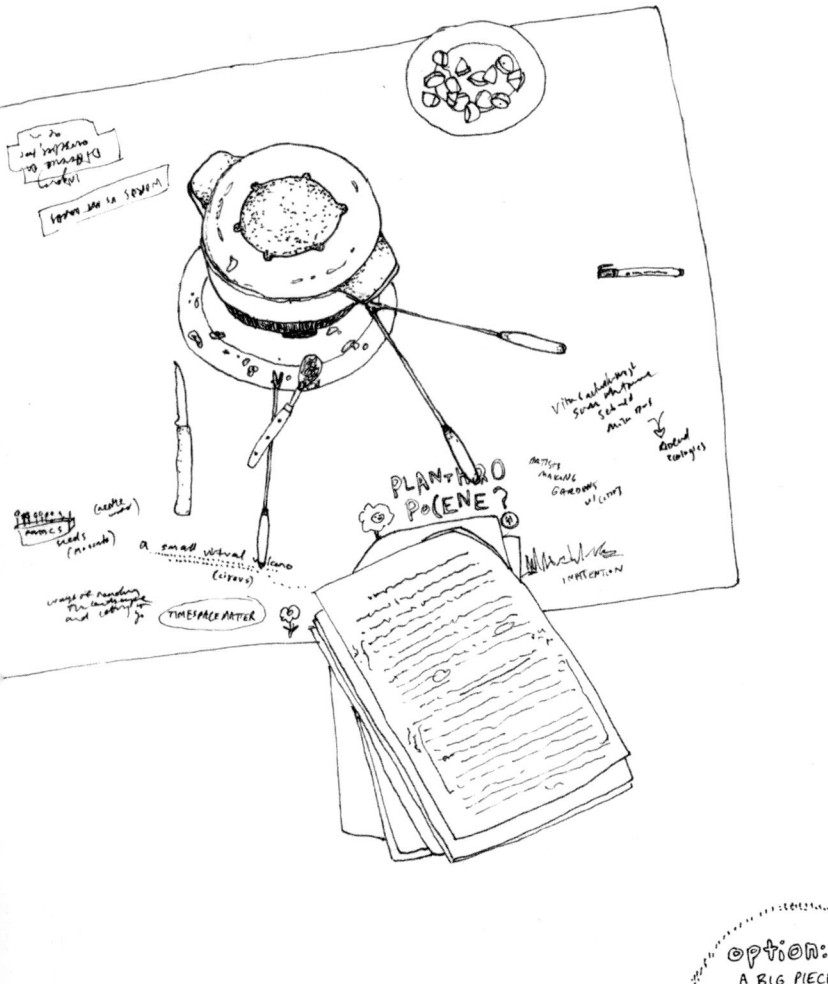

option: use a big piece of butcher's paper as a tablecloth and collaborative notebook!

CHAPTER 5
Field report: Weathering the university

Introduction: Breakfast at the lake

Our first report from the field comes to you from our place of work: the university. We are university workers employed to research and teach in feminist environmental humanities, gender studies and literary studies. Although we hope the ideas from this book can make their way beyond scholarly articles and classroom activities, our weathering work started as research and teaching.

Universities are sprawling and political workplaces. On one hand, they hold the promise of the future, as they prepare students for their lives in theory and practice; on the other, a contest for what that future looks like plays out in subtle and overt ways inside the institution. The status quo is resisted through radical pedagogy and student protest, while business deals between high-paid university management and corporate leaders further entrench it. When it comes to climate change, the university is similarly ambivalent – giving lip service to climate justice, while taking donations from major polluters and changing little in terms of its own practices. We subscribe to the view that climate change 'changes everything'.[1] In response, research, teaching and the institution itself need to radically change, too. This report outlines the ways we aim to seed that change within our work in the university.

'Weathering Everything' was a university research symposium a week to the day before the Coronavirus outbreak was declared a world-wide pandemic by the WHO.[2] Organized by Jennifer at the University of New England (UNE) in Armidale, NSW, it was our last academic gathering of the pre-pandemic era. The program contained many of the practices that we outline in this book – such as speed-zining, #haircutsforplanetarysurvival, community housework and cosmic weathering. A cornerstone of the programme was an open breakfast at 'Lake Madgwick'. We chose the site for the breakfast because it is a stormwater drainage pool: a human-made body of water that manages the university's weather and also bears the name of the first Vice Chancellor of the University of New England in Australia,

Sir Robert Madgwick. On paper it is a proud memorial lake in a very colonial-sounding establishment.

But the lake is far from monumental. At 40 m x 25 m it is more like a large pond. Students reportedly refer to it as 'Lake Sludgewick'. Its diminutive size and functional yet drab concrete inlet humorously subvert the idea of the water body as a commemoration for a founding father of a colonial institution. Our repurposing of the lake on that March morning represents the kind of work we aim to do as academics weathering the university: questioning the institution and finding ways to navigate it that do not simply support it as edifice of colonial capitalist control.

In conceptualizing the university as a technology for building certain kinds of worlds instead of others, cultural and educational theorist la paperson helps us think carefully about how to approach this work: 'Figure out how technologies operate', he advises us. 'Use a wrench. Technologies can be disrupted and reorganized';[3] 'Use these technologies to bend the fabric of power to suit your decolonial desires.'[4] We want to use such wrenches to hack the university, changing or taking apart the colonial university as much as we can. We do this in full awareness that the idealism of our stance is fundamentally compromised by our privileged position inside, or, put otherwise, knowing that our activism and world-making is enabled by our privileged position inside. (We get to this double valence below.)

Although Lake Madgwick represents the way that the university manages weather and water by way of a network of connected stormwater lakes, the lake is alive in its own right and exceeds the total control of the establishment. The lake has its own weather and is home to many beings.[5] The persistent liveliness of unceded Anaiwan Country thrums in and through it. When we started planning the breakfast in late 2019, it was towards the end of Armidale's worst drought on record and before the rain began again; the lake was dry. Six months later, after the drought broke and the rain started, the lake was a lovely place to gather again – a body of water rather than a bowl of dust. Even as weather effects are tightly controlled by the engineering of the stormwater lake, the weather has incredible transformative power in this place.

The stormwater lake – its name, its location, its function, its liveliness and changeability, the pond bed we cannot see and the banks that support our breakfast – animates a constellation of questions that interest us in the context of weathering the university: what is the material relationship of universities to place and their environs (land, water, sky)? Can we work within the establishment to change how it operates as an infrastructure, and

Field Report: Weathering the University

Figure 5.1 Lake Madgwick and the Community Weathering Station Stall and Breakfast for the 'Weathering Everything' Symposium University of New England campus, Anaiwan Country, Armidale, February 4 2020. Photograph: Astrida Neimanis.

if so, how? How can we create events inside the university that do not just describe weathering in theory, but activate it for participants through thoughtful and feelful embodied practices?

We also see the lakeside breakfast example as providing you energy for the reading journey ahead. This chapter is our first 'field report' as we pivot to look more directly at how we have activated our theories of weathering in practice. You may also be in or adjacent to a university. What are your own ideas and hopes for addressing climate change in that context? Do our practices spark ideas for other kinds of feminist engagements? The practices we outline throughout this book are sometimes presented as blueprints (literally in the form of the insets), but these chapters are mostly gentle suggestions for how you too might proceed.

We need to add that we loved 'Weathering Everything'. It was work, but also joyous, creative, informative, community-building and a bit risky, pushing us beyond our comfort zones. Which is also to say: despite the problems of the university, we are still able to find ways within it to model caring and attentive connection to the world and each other. This chapter critiques the university in relation to weather, but we are not letting go of the university as a place of potential transformation. This chapter describes how we understand our work within the institution and hopefully against it; the institution supports our work, even though we are critical of the institution. We acknowledge that we are both academics who make our living teaching, researching, and (literally) 'serving' the institution, as defined in our contractual obligations. In suggesting specific ways to weather the university as a climate change tactic, we do so as both weather-makers and weatherers.

Below, we begin by describing the university's role in weather and climate change research. Turning then to practices that do the doubling work of critique and transformation, we elaborate the activity outlined in Inset E: a feminist environmental humanities reading group. The chapter ends with five accountabilities that underpin our methodology for weathering the university, and revisits the student encampments protesting the genocide in Gaza as a pressing example of the doubled university.

The university's various weather fronts

The university (as discrete institution or as globally networked sector) has several different approaches to meteorological research. Since we cannot escape the weather, weather research even in its most 'blue sky' form (meaning experimental or without immediate use-value) has clear application: we seek to understand the weather's variability in order to meet our basic needs, from what we wear to whether or not food will grow. Different kinds of weather research are distinguished by the nature of their endgames: will the application of this weather knowledge respond to, design and/or dominate the world?

As we pointed out in Chapter 2, modern meteorological science is intimately connected to national security, the military and the colonial-capitalist nation state. This relationship is written into national laws, such as Australia's Meteorology Act 1955. The desire for accurate forecasting associated with modern meteorology is a cornerstone of knowledge for national defence and economic growth. The language matches this. A 'weather front' and its representation on maps as a line mirrors the military metaphor that conceptualizes atmospheric movements in and as frontlines on a battlefield. This way of understanding weather as military force is not a metaphor. It is quite literal.

Modern Western meteorology in direct support of military proliferation is often developed through university, or university-adjacent, research. Joseph Masco's work on Cold War science is a particularly potent historical example.[6] Masco unearthed how fears about the radioactive fallout from nuclear bombs produced research questions to help inform Cold War strategy (e.g. 'if we were to bomb enemy X in location Y, how far will the fallout travel and in what direction? Who will it affect / harm?'). This in turn revealed the global nature of weather patterns, where the role and large-scale movement of winds meant that nuclear fallout would move everywhere and impact everyone.[7] Even though Indigenous ontologies already understood Land or Country as a whole earth system, it was only once that system was mapped via the technologies of modern meteorology that these relations were recognised by nation states and their militaries. Even then, the aim was not (for example) to return Indigenous lands and recentre Indigenous knowledges, but to find ways of pursuing military proliferation and national security. Indeed, most modern nations see the development of more sophisticated meteorological technologies, in particular forecasting techniques, as part of defense strategy.

The ultimate dream, of course, is controlling the weather as one controls a border or even a citizen. As Masco points out, the US military sees the 'weather as a "force multiplier"'; 'the value of weather modification as not unlike "splitting the atom"'.[8] And, even where university research on weather and national security dovetail around a concern about climate change, this is not necessarily liberatory. Take research into 'low-carbon warfare', for instance, that presents 'a valuable starting point for conceptualizing how militaries are beginning to address their "carbon bootprints"'.[9] Same militarism, just greener.[10]

But university research into weather can and does work towards different ends. Most obviously, we owe much of what we know about the science of climate change to dedicated university researchers. Other subversive knowledges have managed to grow, too. In her 1985 'Cyborg Manifesto,'[11] Donna Haraway influentially explored the purpose of research into nature and technology. She noted that feminists have long sought to articulate language and methods for rejecting the militarized agenda of this research. Haraway did this through feminist hacking of the cyborg figure. This move rejected any 'seductions to organic wholeness'[12] of a pre-modern nature before the destructive onset of the military-industrial complex; instead, it embraced the 'illegitimate promise' of the cyborg, whose Star Wars destiny would be subverted in the process.[13]

Today, this promise has been again reconfigured by scholar-activist la paperson, who instructs us that dismantling the colonial university demands becoming 'scyborg'. Scyborging means 'hotwiring' colonial technologies – such as the research machine – by transforming them for anticolonial and revolutionary purposes. Extending Haraway's cyborg figure, paperson adds an 's' to remind us that the agency of the scyborg comes from being part of the system;[14] it is the system (in this case, the colonial university) that makes the scyborg's mischief possible in the first place! In paperson's words, 'the cyborg is a machined person, technologically enhanced by legitimated knowledge, and stamped with the university's brand'.[15]

This mischief-within interests us. We think that weathering is part of the move from cyborg to scyborg.[16] Despite sustained and powerful attempts to defund and therefore diminish research with agendas different to the capitalist, colonialist and nationalistic one, there still remains space inside the university for weather-knowledge for a different world. Our weathering research works against the use of knowledge of weather as a defence of arbitrary colonial borders, capitalist growth and an unjust status quo, but it draws on the university's resources to do so. Again: double trouble! We do this alongside others who are part of what *open-weather* researchers Englemann and Dyer have named a 'feminist anti-fascist weather front'.[17] With others, we want to be part of the barometric pressure change.

In addition to the university as a place that researches and teaches different, and sometimes, contradictory kinds of weather-knowledge, the university is also a workplace that is weathered by those who work there. In 'Endless Study, Infinite Debt: On study inside and outside the university classroom', Astrid Lorange and Andrew Brooks affirm that 'the university is not a monolith, nor is it the same kind of worksite for the teacher, the administrator, the cleaner, or the casualised employee . . . when we speak of the university we speak about both the institution as a place that constrains, even prohibits study as well as the university as a social world in which study is made against the odds'.[18] Lauren Berlant's provisional distinction between institution and infrastructure similarly counters the idea of university as just one thing. For Berlant, while institutions 'enclose and congeal power, resources and interest' and 'represent their legitimacy as something solid and enduring', infrastructures refer to the 'the patterns, habits, norms and scenes of assemblage and use'.[19] Of course, institutions and infrastructures overlap. As an institution, the university is simultaneously weather front and weather-master; as an infrastructure, it provides different kinds of mitigation for bodies that are weathered by it.

The everyday weather of the university workplace is varied. There is an unequal distribution of shelter and vulnerability in terms of those who work within it. Different kinds of academic employment contracts, for example, often translate to a host of different kinds of accommodations, or lack thereof (from desk space and library access to sick leave and retirement benefits, to access to secure and even insecure housing). The university union in Australia (NTEU) refers to ongoing academic jobs as 'life-changing jobs' because the socio-economic security of a permanent contract can change one's life and economic circumstances in fundamental ways. But even with the various forms of shelter and security provided by an ongoing job, there are other forces to weather inside the establishment. Enduring colonialism, racism, misogyny, ableism, classism and queer- and transphobia determine not only who gets to show up, but how one will weather things (or not) once here. Importantly, while some of this is empirically documented, much of this bad weathering is invisible, insidious and difficult to name or call out. Addressing it is a double bind where, in the words of Sara Ahmed, to name the problem is to become the problem.[20] And it is difficult to say how many never chose this path because they didn't imagine themselves here.

Many universities have taken formal policy measures to change this weather, largely through what have come to be known as EDI (equity, diversity, and inclusion) initiatives: targeted hires, trainings, curriculum initiatives and more. These policies have enjoyed some success. At the same time, if an *institution* must have 'solid and enduring' legitimacy,[21] then unsurprisingly, EDI initiatives have also become an alibi for *not* making meaningful changes.[22] These measures have also been accompanied by countermeasures, such as the US Supreme Court's 2023 ruling that limits consideration of race in college applications. And, so-called austerity measures mean that shelter in and by the university is increasingly scarce for many.

Our own experiences of the university testify to some of these varied weather effects. As middle-class students, we were drawn in by the liberatory promises of feminist theories. There is a special kind of internal good weather that comes from learning feminist theory as an undergrad student. Becoming literate in ways of thinking and being that validate your sense of self and inform how you can contribute to changing the weather is world-opening. Sara Ahmed asks us to reflect on these rays of sunshine: 'Where did we find feminism, or where did feminism find us?'[23] We agree with Ahmed that 'feminism can begin with a body, a body in touch with a world, a body that is not at ease in a world'.[24] If the shape of our bodies was the source of our oppression (and unearned privilege), how can we still love our bodies and fight for liberation? The sunshine of feminist theory usually comes after the rain. Predisposed to challenging the status quo thanks to our upbringings, at university we found a vocabulary for the paradoxes and seeming dead-ends. Words and things come together in the feminist archive. The dizziness and excitement of being able to think through seemingly intractable problems, alongside others similarly basking in this sunshine, is liberatory in itself.

But the reality of the institution sometimes contradicts that sunny experience of learning feminist theory and finding feminist community. Ahmed's own career is a case in point. Although she was involved in creating a Centre for Feminist Research, which she describes as a 'lifeline and a shelter' from the world but also the university, she resigned 'in protest against the failure to address the problem of sexual harassment' throughout the wider university.[25] Our own experiences with navigating the university's paradox are neither the same as Ahmed's, nor as each other's, but all are shaped by the possibility of feminist shelters (finding them, building them, defending them). We see Ahmed's refusal and (literal) resignation as an important defence tactic. For the time being, though, we choose the tactic of seeking to change the nature of the work – our work, and the work of everyone here.

Shifting what the university makes possible – and bearable – is also one step along the way to the ultimate goal of our weather work, which is Indigenous-led climate justice. The environmental theories and philosophies non-Indigenous folks like us are developing involve an investment in the kind of holistic non-binary thinking that is the marker of many Indigenous knowledges. At the same time, Métis scholar Zoe Todd (among others) has cautioned against Western scholarship that does not take the time or care to learn from Indigenous thinking about interconnected ecological systems. Todd asserts that without institutional recognition of Indigenous ways of knowing what Western and settler theories are now 'discovering', the knowledge is appropriative, impoverished, and inaccurate.[26] As settler feminists writing 'new' cultural theories of weather from inside the establishment, it is our responsibility to keep these risks of appropriation and impoverishment front-and-centre. As paperson says, decolonization is 'a rematriation of land, the regeneration of relations, and the forwarding of Indigenous and Black and queer futures: a process that requires countering what power seems to be up to'.[27] Learning from folks like Anaiwan artist-scholar Gabi Briggs who reckons that feminism and queer activism can be used as 'stepping stones . . . towards Indigenous Sovereignty' if the theories are taken up with that intention,[28] we position our non-Indigenous queer feminist weathering research in support of this aim. In response to syilx scholar Jeannette Armstrong, who calls on researchers at UBC Okanagan to recognize that syilx people are the 'best protectors of [their] syilx lands, waters and *timix^w*, and [they] need everyone who lives here on [syilx] territory to feel and act that way',[29] we know that weathering the university must also demand more shelter for Indigenous scholars and their crucial work. We turn to the 'how' of this commitment later in this chapter, and in the chapters that follow.

Reading group as Infrastructure

In Chapter 4, we summarized Berlant's understanding of infrastructure. For her, infrastructure shapes and guides how we endure life; infrastructure is not the water moving through a pipe, but it guides how and where the water will go. Berlant focuses on the social dimension of infrastructures as a way to understand how we are in common; social infrastructures guide how and where we can exist together. While the neoliberal university is an infrastructure that seeks to channel our energies towards outputs and those outputs towards 'the national interest' (this is a real criterion for grants funded by the Australian Research Council), we can make microinfrastructures within. These can be harbours and havens for redistributing shelter and vulnerability among those within and adjacent to the university who experience it in different ways for different reasons.

As we have recounted elsewhere,[30] we (Jennifer and Astrida) met at an informal environmental humanities retreat in 2015. We were both weathering the university in different but related ways: Jennifer had just had a baby and was trying to make a go of academia through various kinds of insecure labour; Astrida had temporarily left her partner and three kids to move to the literal other side of the earth to take up the only permanent or tenure-track job that had been offered to her in six years of applications. (Academia can do wild things to family, relations and place-belonging.) We shared common research interests but also a desire to spread some feminist sunshine. We decided to start a reading group.

The practice of creating reading groups is simple, central to university study and yet potentially transformative. In Inset E, we recount one of the key purposes of feminist reading groups, namely to dismantle, interrupt and rebuild knowledge, in collective ways. Reading a book can be a wrench; reading and sharing questions and insights with others can be a whole toolbox. But while the texts are important, the space of the reading group itself is significant. As a micro-infrastructure inside a mega-infrastructure, reading groups can be that mobile and mutable space that in Berlant's words, helps us 'manage the meanwhile'.

When we initiated *Composting Feminisms and the Environmental Humanities* (hereafter *Composting*), our research goal was to probe some of the feminist elisions and silences within an otherwise robust and growing environmental humanities community in Australia. Taking a lead from Haraway's 'compostist' declarations and Eve Sedgwick's definition of 'we' as a rogue and promiscuous pronoun for gathering diverse people, our group's initial intention was to read classic feminist texts alongside environmental humanities ones, in order to trace how the feminist ideas were 'composted' in more recent texts (or not).[31] We wanted to map an often unnamed feminist foundation for the emerging field of environmental humanities, and we wanted to do this with others.[32]

Inspired by the work of Fred Moten and Stefano Harney, The Infrastructural Inequalities collective has described something like what we were aiming for, finding shelter 'inside of, and in spite of, existing infrastructures and institutions'. They continue:

> The gestures of the undercommons to create alternative models of value can be major or minor: they can include, for example, staking out a few hours to come together and plan, to read and write, to share and collaborate, or to celebrate. We have tried to move against the logics of performance evaluation and research metrics that structure contemporary universities to instead carve out some space for collective study, foregrounding the sociality of thinking.[33]

From the beginning, *Composting* was in the business of building stealth pipes to direct university resources for different kinds of world-building. Commandeering University of Sydney meeting space (and tea kettles, washroom facilities, white boards and digital infrastructures, particularly in the reading group's last years as it moved partially and then entirely onto Zoom), we assembled a shifting group of scholars, artists, activists and community members and met approximately monthly from 2015 to 2021. A (non-university-hosted) website and newsletter announced the meetings, each with a 'Lead Composter' who chose a theme, a limited set of primary readings (usually around twenty pages, and sometimes including audio or visual texts), and a more robust set of supplementary readings. In-person meetings featured a long piece of butcher's paper on which participants would make notes and doodles as a meeting archive, and which also served as a tablecloth for tea and snacks; each announcement included detailed instructions for accessing the meeting room, and an invitation to BYOM (bring your own mug).

Our practice included habits that emerged over time, which we came to recognize as important protocols. Each meeting began with introductions around the table (and later, around the Zoom room). Since there was no registration requirement and meetings were advertised openly, these introductions meant we would know something about the people we were sharing ideas with. Meetings were never recorded, but we made a photograph of whiteboard notes (and later a Zoom chat transcript) available to those who showed up. We offered food and hot drinks. A small grant from the University of Sydney in 2016 funded a 'Compost Mixer' for two years to update the website and send out a monthly newsletter, but we mostly got by with a potluck and DIY, or DIT (Do-it-Together),[34] ethos. Particularly as we became more established, we resisted including this work within the University's formal research structures (i.e. on corporate research pages or as a part of departmental or faculty business). As a result, this research did not 'count' in the same way as traditional outputs such as papers or conferences.

When Jen left Sydney in 2018 for UNE in Armidale, a virtual group ran parallel to the in-person one in Sydney. This felt novel until COVID sent us all online in 2020. For a while, both groups merged into one Zoom-based monthly meeting until we decided to rest the compost pile indefinitely in 2021. Participation ranged from five composters to over fifty on a few occasions. While *Composting* had a shifting group of regular participants, each meeting always brought at least one new composter to the table. Our micro-infrastructure also went on the road a few times, convening field trips, walkshops and even a trainshop! (See Chapter 9.) We put together side events with other community groups, artists, and galleries. We hosted panels and talks as part of a number of academic conferences. When Astrida left Sydney as well in 2021, a few more Zoom sessions were hosted before we decided that *Composting* had served its function for the time being. Committed to lifecycle rhythms and intentional endings, we sent an email to mailing list subscribers, thanking them for their contributions and informing them we were letting the compost pile rest for the indefinite future.

Composting sessions explicitly worked towards a different kind of meteorological research: we insisted on contextualizing climate change and environmental change more generally within broader questions of colonialism, cisheteropatriarchy, capitalism and white supremacy. But for us, at that time, this group was also a life-line in the way that Ahmed says feminist academic work can be.[35] Was it experienced in this way by others? As *Composting* wound down, we invited our colleagues James Gardiner, Hayley Singer and Mindy Blaise (who have organized similarly politicized reading groups) to collaborate on research about our groups to find out.[36]

Survey responses that explained why people participated in *Composting* varied, but they touched upon ideas about weathering that we're developing in this book. For example, one noted that the group provides 'community and solidarity in the midst of deeply challenging working conditions in universities'; another appreciated the principles of 'equity that are built into the meeting. It ensures everyone gets a voice and that that voice is listened to without unwarranted critical interpretation.' Others wrote: 'That structural set up of going around introducing oneself and a question is a banger. Such a good way to bring everybody at the table to the table'; 'I always found the tone and the moderation of the meetings really useful/helpful in allowing myself to be challenged without the stress/shame of being called out or pulled up in more aggressive ways'; 'It's an inclusive space and the organizers are thoughtful about how to create space. I have learned a lot about pedagogy and creating inclusive spaces from the culture of these meetings'; 'It encouraged me to start another feminist reading group within my discipline. It helped me to activate a more deliberate and intentional feminist-focused way of doing research leadership'; 'It was great to see people who were attached to universities in precarious ways, sessional teaching, students, former students feel like they belonged.'

On face this sounds like a big pat on our own backs for our amazing efforts: yay, us! But we share these responses to show how with the very simple infrastructure of the reading group, a bit of intentionality around its practices, and a sense of accountability to each other and the bigger implications of the project, *Composting* brought some real scyborg-witchcraft to university spaces. Just like the stormy academic weather fronts we describe in the first half of this chapter, good weather can be hard to empirically measure, and is often unnoticed by the institution (which is part of its power). Above all we recount our experience as an invitation to you to try it yourself. Be the wrench!

Five accountabilities as methodology for weathering the university

Since *Composting*, both of us have gone on to form and be part of other reading groups as ways to continue weathering the university.[37] We also recognize *Composting* as formative for our broader thinking about scyborg methodology. We have attempted to boil this down to five accountabilities (kind of like principles, but where actions accompany our intentions). These accountabilities underpin our thinking and our approach to research and learning design, as well as our 'service' in the university. These accountabilities help centre weathering as both a concept and an ethical and applied practice. We have practised bringing this accountability to our classrooms,[38] but also to our overarching research programmes, such as CoWS (see Chapter 7) and the FEELed Lab (see Chapter 6). These accountabilities are a lens through which we invite you to read all of the practices we share in this book.

1. **Approach climate change as primarily a symptom, not the cause, of planetary crises.** This seemingly subtle shift in standpoint significantly alters how we understand our work's relation to climate crisis. For us, that work involves designing research questions, undertaking literature reviews, setting readings, writing lectures, moderating seminar discussions and organizing assessments. But this shift in standpoint is relevant for anyone doing anything, as it reorients one's endgame and motivation. This standpoint also helps move away from framing climate change as an 'emergency'. In describing the crisis as symptom, we can resist granting the military and police exceptional powers to continue to further exploit and harm those already vulnerable.

2. **Decentre colonial knowledge as the only form of meteorology, and in particular recognize Indigenous weather knowledges.** In their essay on why Indigenous weather knowledges are crucial for responding to climate change, Mununjali writer Ellen van Neerven tells us: 'The country is like the body. You say your ankles are sore and stiff, but it originates in your hips and starts to affect your back and knees.'[39] Taking seriously this basic level of ecological connectivity and consequence changes everything about research and climate action. For us, decentring and unlearning colonial weather (see Chapter 2) is an ongoing process that is slowly changing our literature reviews and ostensible 'canons', our

citational practices, our methodologies and the habits of our own feeling body-minds to move, in solidarity, conscientiously towards something else.

3. **Develop responses to the problem of the uneven distribution of shelter and vulnerability.** Building on 1 and 2, we think the wicked problem is not climate change *per se* but the unequal distribution of shelter and vulnerability as a perverse structural principle of cisheteropatriarchal colonial capitalism. If we attend only to climate change as the primary problem, the unequal distribution of exposure (physical and existential) remains unaddressed. Our weathering research, germinating in the broader terrain of feminist environmental humanities, holds that 'weathering better' must include noticing these specific unequal distributions, and then finding ways to weather differently.

4. **Refuse scalability as a cornerstone of project design (in research and elsewhere).** This accountability relates to local projects, site specificity, social practice, and community. The FEELed Lab and Community Weathering Station are site specific. They cannot be replicated in a straightforward way because they relate to place.[40] They may be mobile, tentacular and networked with others (see Chapters 6 and 9), but they cannot just be rolled out or scaled up like a chain store. Multispecies ethnographer Anna Tsing refers to this as 'non-scalability'.[41] 'Scalable projects', Tsing says, 'are those that can expand without changing.' As a result, scalability often means that biological and cultural diversity have to be 'banished', she explains.[42] We commit to diversity and transformative relationships, which requires (non-scalable) specificity.

5. **Redefine work collaborations and partnerships.** There are so many possible people to collaborate and partner with, but often the most glamorous partners come with the most strings attached. Thinking about partnerships requires thinking about the kind of world you want to build. This is not a facile warning against 'selling out', which is a bit of an old-fashioned, purist concept. What we're talking about is intentionally minimizing your level of compromise and complicity, and directing energies into building the world you actually want to see. This is not to say building more ethical collaborations is quick or easy. Many settler researchers rush to Indigenous communities seeking 'partnership'. Where this can be

done meaningfully, it can be valuable. In many cases, though, it is another burden on Indigenous communities and does not necessarily redress material vulnerability and power imbalances. Many Indigenous weather knowledges are publicly accessible in various forms. As settler academics we need to begin by carefully learning from what is already generously offered. We have to think carefully, read well and wide, and understand how to stay ethically grounded in collaboration.

Conclusion: The people's university is everywhere

As we began writing this chapter in April 2024, students had established protest encampments in support of Palestine at over 100 universities around the world, with daily or weekly gatherings and events at countless others. While their demands varied from place to place, students were united in their solidarity with Palestinian struggle for freedom and in their protest against the investments by their (our) institutions in the genocide in Palestine and elsewhere.[43] This is also to say: over the course of drafting a chapter on how we weather the university, all the universities in Gaza were physically destroyed by the Israel Defense Forces (IDF). Even if you are unwilling to witness this horror, or if you still don't really know what is happening in Gaza because it isn't being reported adequately by the mainstream media, please know that there are no physical universities left in Gaza. The IDF systematically destroyed twelve universities.

Many student encampments responded by demanding that their universities disclose and divest financial ties to the State of Israel. In doing so, these students take up lessons on human rights, international law, and global justice that they are studying in their classrooms—lessons that are informed by the reports, rulings and statements issued by internationally recognized governmental and legal bodies.[44] In most cases, student encampments are also fulfilling the goals of their (our) universities' own stated policies and strategic 'vision' statements, in their drive to inspire 'ideas and actions for a better world . . . to foster global citizenship and advance a sustainable and just society'.[45] The encampments are therefore in some ways as much of the university as they are against it. They recognize the value of universities as sites of the rigorous contestation about what 'a sustainable and just society' means, and how these values contribute to world-building and culture-making.

Both the student intifada and the IDF want to destroy the university. But while the infitada seeks to 'wreck, scavenge, retool, and reassemble the colonizing university'[46] as part of a wider project of justice and freedom for all, the IDF's apartheid regime and colonial expansionist project seeks to destroy the 'decolonizing desire'[47] that universities can also nurture.

As this chapter hopefully makes clear, as university workers, we are interested in these kinds of doublings. The liberatory promise of learning and the university as an actual vehicle for liberation that these students are fighting for is what encouraged us to pursue academic work in the first place. There is no doubt the encampments are extensions of classroom teachings and (stated) commitments of the universities themselves. Yet, these same students have been variously suspended, charged, beaten, harassed, policed, ignored, surveilled and dispersed by institutional representatives who are salaried by the fees of the students they arraign. While universities may officially tout themselves as places of world-changing ideas and actions, the student intifada lays bare the staggering hypocrisy of the neoliberal university. But in a complex way, the intifada – materialized as structures and actions on campuses that have achieved a number of significant gains, and as a movement that decries the obliteration of universities in Gaza – also affirms that universities can be places that foment transformation after all.

Set against the lived realities of student protestors and more critically, the people of Gaza and other besieged lands, our weathering experiments feel very insignificant. We didn't know how to write this chapter without writing about scholasticide in Gaza, but we also didn't know how to readily articulate our own work that valorizes mundane being-together in the context of the life-or-death violence of those events. How can our weathering practices engage in feminist climate change research while acknowledging carefully and intentionally the horror of this moment in history (at the time of writing: scholasticide, ecocide, the murder of tens of thousands of children and over 100 journalists, cops arresting students who are protesting a genocide)? How, we wonder, can our piddly little weathering games (Lucky dip, Close meteorology, Weathering with and without, Walkshops, Cosmic weathering, and so on) possibly relate to the brutal intensity of the moment, and also to climate change?

As we drafted this chapter we also visited student encampments, joined in, tabled motions and signed letters calling for universities to divest from genocidal violence, walked out of graduation ceremonies, taught campers how to cut their own hair, supported our colleagues who are being silenced, organized, donated to and attended fundraisers, made zines, and continued the weathering work learned via *Composting* of diverting resources to redistribute the shelter and vulnerability manufactured by the university. We agree with Pankaj Mishra and others who are looking at this moment as a 'profound rupture . . . in the moral history of the world since the ground zero

Figure 5.2 Jen's Community Weathering Station 'Drought-Friendly Hairstyles' zine makes an appearance at the People's University for Gaza on UBCO campus. Photograph: Astrida Neimanis.

of 1945',[48] but we also agree with adrienne maree brown who argues that 'things are not getting worse, they are getting uncovered. We must hold each other tight and continue to pull back the veil'.[49]

Over the course of co-writing this book, the two of us have also spent hundreds of hours on Zoom. Writing together is also about being in relationship with each other. We talk about our kids, our partners, our health and our jobs, including the latest bad weather in our academic networks: programme cuts in arts and humanities; sexual predators who get promoted; racialized colleagues who feel no choice but to leave; students in crisis. Jen has begun training as a shiatsu practitioner and is learning how to move heat and cold around the body's system through gentle finger pressure. Astrida still contemplates a full-time gig as the People's Haircutter. But for now, we are staying in our jobs.

Possibly, this chapter is our attempt to help ourselves feel better about being part of this colonial machine. It is sometimes hard to tell the difference between propping up something unreformable, and doing the work of staying with practical and ideological trouble. Leanne Betasamosake Simpson has written about a commitment to one's Land that has been injured or broken, noting 'this idea that you abandon it when something has been damaged is something we can't afford to do'.[50] The university is nothing like the Anishinabe lands that Simpson specifically references; to care for land is very different than caring for a colonial institution! But there are lessons for us in Simpson's words about the 'fertility of alternatives' and the responsibility one has to share one's vision, and 'bring that vision forth into reality'.[51]

So for now, we conclude that there is value in scyborging: wrecking, scavenging and retooling. These efforts can change the weather for those within this infrastructure. These practices can change the directions and habits of what is and can be held here, nested within the trouble, including the composty tendrils that violate this institution's boundaries, snaking in and out and back again. These efforts can be part of, as paperson says, 'the process that requires countering what power seems to be up to'.[52] Maybe this reverberates, emboldens and multiplies. Maybe these efforts remind us the university is not just institution but infrastructure, where being in common begins with a *desire* for being in common.[53] Maybe this 'training in collaboration,' as Berlant says, will be mobilized elsewhere.[54]

When the People's University for Gaza UBCO decamped at Astrida's university on 29 June 2024, the campers read out a statement. While they will now focus their efforts on other tactics, they affirm that 'the existence of this encampment has made an irreversible mark on this campus and the community'. Their statement ends: 'The People's University for Gaza is everywhere.'

Notes

1. Naomi Klein, *This Changes Everything: Capitalism vs the Climate* (New York, NY: Simon & Schuster, 2015).
2. Australian Government Department of Health and Aged Care, 'About Coronavirus Disease 2019 (COVID-19)', https://www.health.gov.au/topics/covid-19/about (accessed 28 October 2024).
3. la paperson, *A Third University Is Possible*, vol. 19, Forerunners (Minneapolis, MN: University of Minnesota Press, 2017), https://doi.org/10.5749/9781452958460, 24.
4. paperson, *A Third University*, 59.
5. Our creative and critical attention to stormwater infrastructure began alongside other academics in Sydney, on Gadigal Country. See *Mapping Edges*, in particular 'Green Square Water Stories', by Alexandra Crosby and Ilaria Vanni; and Taylor Coyne's work on underground waterways in Sydney. Alexandra Crosby and Ilaria Vanni, 'Green Square Water Stories (2021–2023)', Mapping Edges, https://www.mappingedges.org/projects/water-stories-activating-water-civic-ecologies-in-green-square/ (accessed 15 January 2025). Taylor Coyne, 'Listen Deep to Subterranean Kinfrastructures', *Swamphen: A Journal of Cultural Ecology (ASLEC-ANZ)* 9 (2023). 'Listen to deep subterranean kinfrastructures', *Swamphen* 9 (2023).
6. Joseph Masco, 'Bad Weather: On Planetary Crisis', *Social Studies of Science* 40, no. 1 (2010): 7–40, https://doi.org/10.1177/0306312709341598.
7. Masco, 'Bad Weather', 16.
8. Masco, 'Bad Weather', 171.
9. Duncan Depledge, 'Low-carbon warfare: climate change, net zero and military operations', *International Affairs* 99, no. 2 (2023): 667–85, https://doi.org/10.1093/ia/iiad001.
10. In addition to national military interests, universities also sponsor research with 'the appearance of credibility and neutrality given by the university' in support of the interests of multinational fossil fuel corporations, such as Shell Oil. See Geoffrey Supran, 'The Fossil Fuel Industry's Invisible Colonization of Academia', *The Guardian*, 13 March 2017, https://www.theguardian.com/environment/climate-consensus-97-per-cent/2017/mar/13/the-fossil-fuel-industrys-invisible-colonization-of-academia.
11. Donna J. Haraway, *Manifestly Haraway* (Minneapolis, MN: University of Minnesota Press, 2016), https://doi.org/10.5749/minnesota/9780816650477.001.0001.

12. Haraway, *Manifestly Haraway*, 8.
13. Haraway, *Manifestly Haraway*, 8.
14. paperson, *A Third University is Possible*, 61.
15. paperson, *A Third University is Possible*, 55–6.
16. Jennifer Hamilton and Astrida Neimanis, 'Nature / Culture – Fields of Difference – Composting', in *Informatics of Domination*, ed. Zach Blas, Melody Jue and Jennifer Rhee (Durham, NC: Duke University Press, 2025). Here, we argue for a more holistic shift from cyborg to composting as a guide to politics.
17. Sophie Dyer and Sasha Engelmann, 'When I Image the Earth, I Imagine Another', *Ecoes* #3 (10 August 2022), https://sonicacts.com/archive/engelmann-dyer-when-i-imagine-the-earth.
18. Astrid Lorange and Andrew Brooks, 'Endless Study, Infinite Debt: On Study Inside and Outside the University Classroom', *Critical Studies in Teaching and Learning* 10, no. 1 (2022): 1–20.
19. Lauren Berlant, *On the Inconvenience of Other People* (Durham, NC: Duke University Press, 2022), 95.
20. Sara Ahmed, 'Introduction: Sexism – A Problem With a Name', *New Formations* 86, no. 86 (15 December 2015): 5–13, https://doi.org/10.3898/NEWF.86.INTRODUCTION.2015.
21. Berlant, *On the Inconvenience of Other People*, 95.
22. Sara Ahmed, 'The Nonperformativity of Antiracism', *Meridians* 7, no. 1 (2006): 104–26, https://www.jstor.org/stable/40338719.
23. Sara Ahmed, *Living a Feminist Life* (Durham, NC: Duke University Press, 2017), https://doi.org/10.1215/9780822373377, 3.
24. Ahmed, *Living a Feminist Life*, 21.
25. Sara Ahmed, 'Resignation', feministkilljoys (blog), 30 May 2016, https://feministkilljoys.com/2016/05/30/resignation/.
26. Zoe S. Todd, 'An Indigenous Feminist's Take on the Ontological Turn: "Ontology" Is Just Another Word for Colonialism', *Journal of Historical Sociology* 29, no. 1 (2016): 4–22, https://doi.org/10.1111/johs.12124.
27. paperson, *A Third University*, xv.
28. Jennifer Hamilton and Gabrielle Briggs, 'Gabi Briggs: Long Version on the Vital Process of Centring Indigenous Sovereignty in Climate Action', SoundCloud, 17 December 2021, https://soundcloud.com/weatheringstation.
29. Jeannette Armstrong, 'Syilx-Led Climate Justice in a Global Context' (UBC Okanagan, 4 November 2024), https://climatejustice.ubc.ca/news/armstrong-klein-syilx-led-climate-justice-in-a-global-context/.
30. Jennifer Mae Hamilton and Astrida Neimanis, 'Five Desires, Five Demands', *Australian Feminist Studies* 34, no. 102 (2 October 2019): 385–97, https://doi.org/10.1080/08164649.2019.1702875.

31. Eve Kosofsky Sedgwick, *A Dialogue on Love* (Boston, MA: Beacon Press, 1999); Donna Haraway, *Staying with the Trouble: Making Kin in the Chthulucene* (Durham, NC, and London: Duke University Press, 2016).

32. Jennifer Mae Hamilton and Astrida Neimanis, 'Composting Feminisms and Environmental Humanities', *Environmental Humanities* 10, no. 2 (1 November 2018): 501–27, https://doi.org/10.1215/22011919-7156859.

33. Liam Grealy et al., 'Introduction: Tending a Social Infrastructure', *Infrastructural Inequalities*, no. 1 (2019), https://infrastructuralinequalities.net/issue-1/introduction/.

34. Hayley Singer et al., 'Do-It-Together (DIT): Collective Action in and Against the Anthropocene', *Feral Feminisms*, no. 10 (Fall 2021): 7–21, https://feralfeminisms.com/wp-content/uploads/2022/03/1-2-FF-ISSUE10-front_and_intro.pdf.

35. Ahmed, *Living a Feminist Life.*.

36. These results are detailed in James Gardiner et al., 'Reading Group as Method for Feminist Environmental Humanities', *Australian Feminist Studies* 37, no. 113 (3 July 2022): 296–316, https://doi.org/10.1080/08164649.2023.2267759.

37. At UBC Okanagan, one of the first infrastructures Astrida established in collaboration with Madeline Donald was an online reading group called 'Littoral Listening'. Again, protocols were important for creating an infrastructure that was simultaneously a shelter and a site of low-stakes vulnerability. Read more about it in Madeline Donald's blog post,' Littoral Listening 2021–2022 in Practice: An Archive', *FEELed Notes* (blog), 30 August 2022, https://thefeeledlab.ca/2022/08/30/littoral-listening-2021-2022-in-practice-an-archive/.

38. Astrida Neimanis and Laura McLauchlan, 'Composting (in) the Gender Studies Classroom: Growing Feminisms for Climate Changing Pedagogies', *Curriculum Inquiry* 52, no. 2 (15 March 2022): 218–34, https://doi.org/10.1080/03626784.2022.2041982.

39. Ellen Van Neerven, 'The Country Is Like a Body', *Right Now: Human Rights in Australia*, 26 October 2015, https://rightnow.org.au/creative-works/the-country-is-like-a-body/.

40. For example, when Astrida began the FEELed Lab at UBC, she was encouraged to apply for a major infrastructure grant. When the work requires the slow labour of building relationships to place and to other people, how does becoming a mostly full-time accountant and project manager make sense? Who does 'scaling up' benefit? Refusal includes a refusal of academic impact metrics, if we are sheltered enough to take this risk.

41. Anna Lowenhaupt Tsing, 'On Non-Scalability', *Common Knowledge* 18, no. 3 (2012): 505–24.

42. Tsing, 'On Non-Scalability', 507.

43. See Maya Wind, *Towers of Ivory and Steel: How Israeli Universities Deny Palestinian Freedom* (London and New York, NY: Verso, 2024).

44. European Centre for Consitutional and Human Rights, 'Gaza and the Matter of Genocide: Q&A on the Law and Recent Developments', December 2024, https://www.ecchr.eu/fileadmin/Q_As/ECCHR_Q_A__Gaza_and_Genocide_20241210.pdf.
45. The University of British Columbia, 'UBC Vision, Purpose and Values', https://www.ubc.ca/about/vision-values.html (accessed 28 October 2024).
46. paperson, *A Third University is Possible*, xiii.
47. paperson, *A Third University is Possible*, xiii.
48. Pankaj Mishra, 'The Shoah After Gaza' in *The London Review of Books*, 46.6, 21 March 2024, accessed 1 November 2024, https://www.lrb.co.uk/the-paper/v46/n06/pankaj-mishra/the-shoah-after-gaza
49. adrienne maree brown, 'Living through the Unveiling', https://adriennemareebrown.net/2017/02/03/living-through-the-unveiling/ (accessed 1 November 2024).
50. Naomi Klein, 'Dancing the World into Being: A Conversation with Idle No More's Leanne Simpson', *Yes! Magazine*, 6 March 2013, https://www.yesmagazine.org/social-justice/2013/03/06/dancing-the-world-into-being-a-conversation-with-idle-no-more-leanne-simpson.
51. Klein, 'Dancing the World Into Being'.
52. paperson, *A Third University is Possible*, xv.
53. Berlant, *On the Inconvenience of Other People*, 93.
54. Berlant, *On the Inconvenience of Other People*, 108.

INSET F: speed-zining

Speed-zining is a way to practice weathering together. Zines communicate in short-hand, open-ended ways, our spontaneously-scribbled musings standing in for larger and more complex questions. This collaborative zine-making activity can be done in ten minutes or less. Participants respond quickly and creatively to climate-related prompts, questions, dreams or images suggested by others. How do we interpret the same questions, differently? How can we extend, deepen and diversify each other's visions? When these responses are gathered in a personal, handmade, rough-and-ready, easily shareable zine format, we collectively imagine other worlds through, and not in spite of, our differences.

What You Need

- 1 piece of paper per participant (any kind, but printer paper is easiest for reproduction)
- Scissors
- At least one writing implement (pencil, pen) per person.

How to Play

1. Teach everyone how to make a simple 8-page zine (see next pages).

2. Decide on a theme or a general question, for example...
   - The title of a short story about weather.
   - Your favourite kind of weather.
   - A newspaper headline about climate change.
   - A memorable weather event.
   - Etc.

3. Decide how long each round will be (eg. 1, 2 or 3 minutes). An 8-page zine needs 8 rounds.

4. Start the timer for the first round. Everyone makes their own cover page based on the theme/question.

5. Time's up! Pass your zine to the person on your left.

6. Start the timer. Looking at the zine in your hands, create the next page.

7. Time's up! Pass the zine again to the left. Continue until 8 rounds (and all 8 pages) are complete.

8. Now you have a set of collaboratively made zines on the topic. Discuss, display, reproduce (with a photocopier), share!

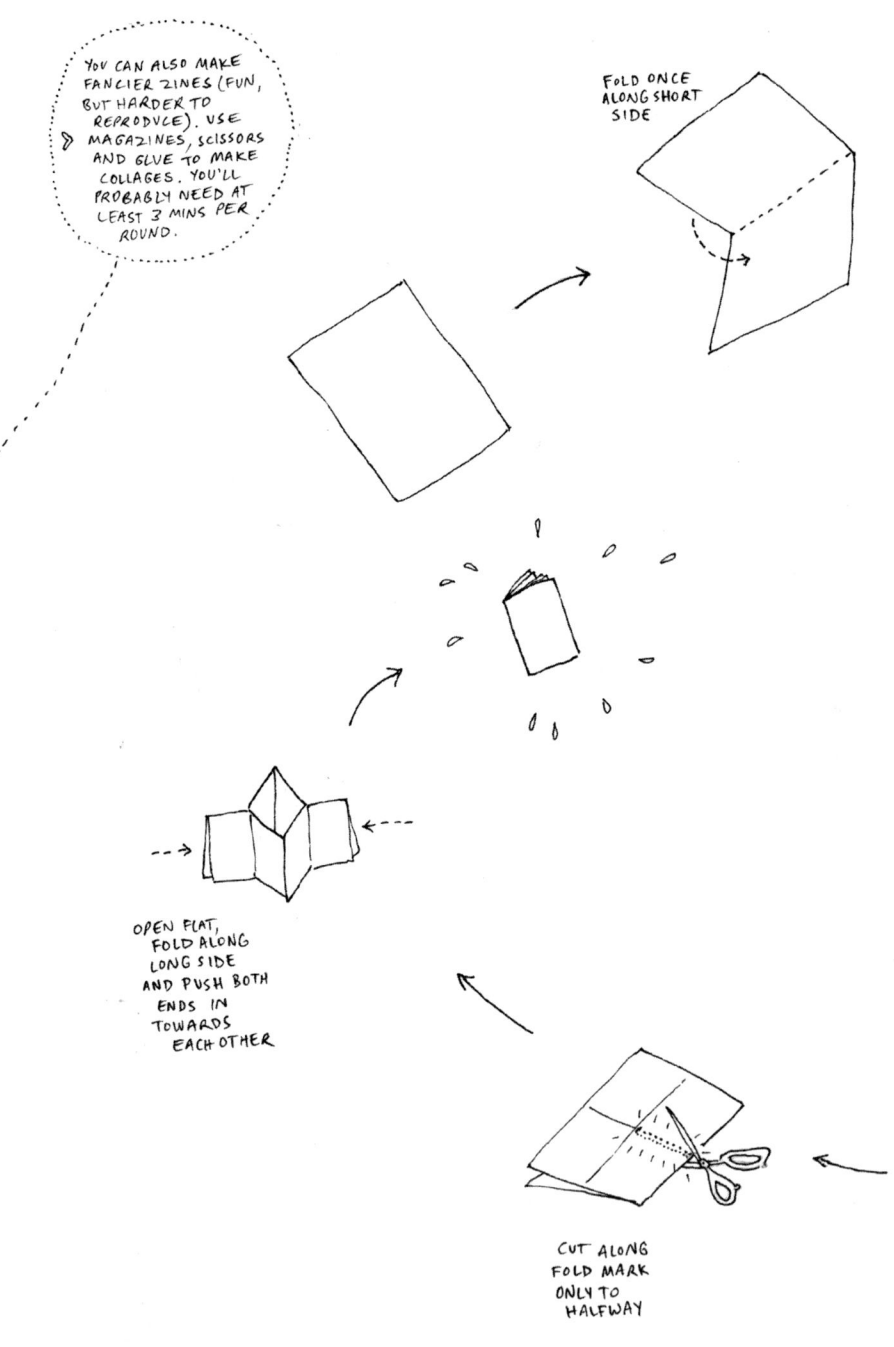

Plate 1 Earthenware bowl from *The River Ends as the Ocean: Walk the tide out*. Aunty Rhonda Dixon-Grovenor, Clare Britton and Astrida Neimanis. Shanghai Biennale *Bodies of Water*. Sydney, 2021. Credit: Victoria Hunt.

Plate 2 Bridge over Goolay'yari. Credit: Astrida Neimanis.

Plate 3 Reflected clouds in Goolay'yari. Credit: Astrida Neimanis.

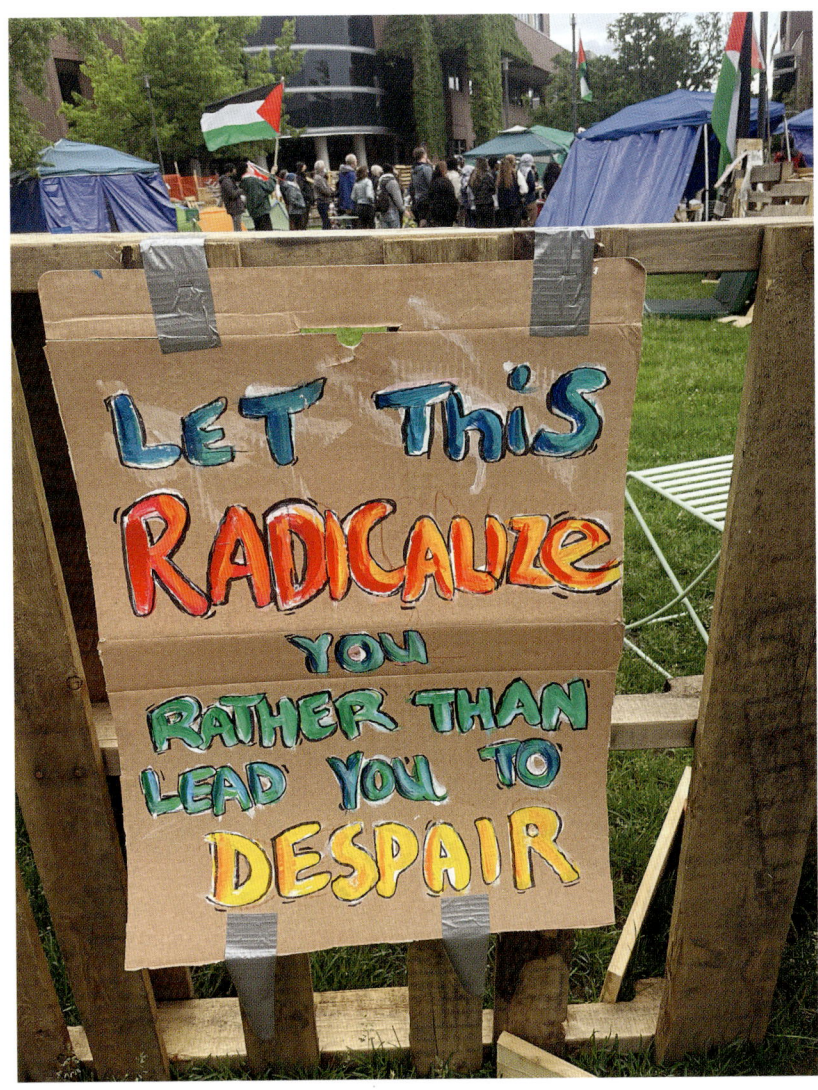

Plate 4 Protest sign at the People's University for Gaza UBCO student encampment. Credit: Astrida Neimanis.

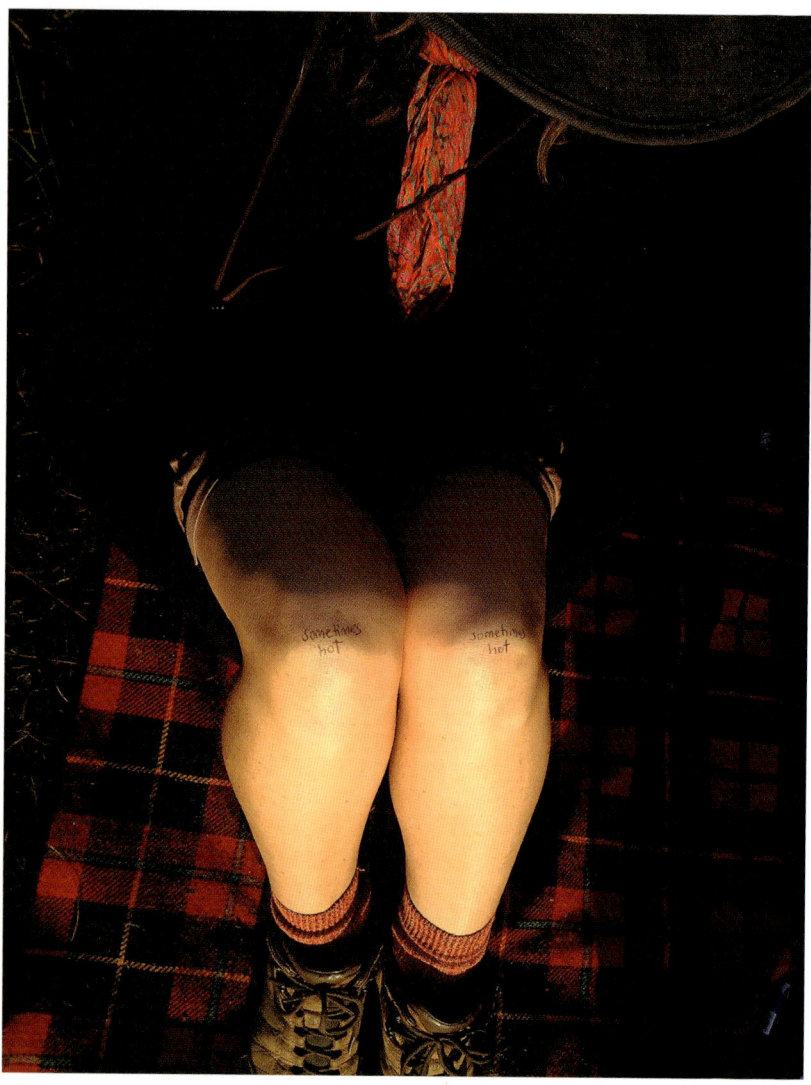

Plate 5 "Sometimes hot" knees at a retreat of the Weathering Collective, 2016. Credit: Astrida Neimanis.

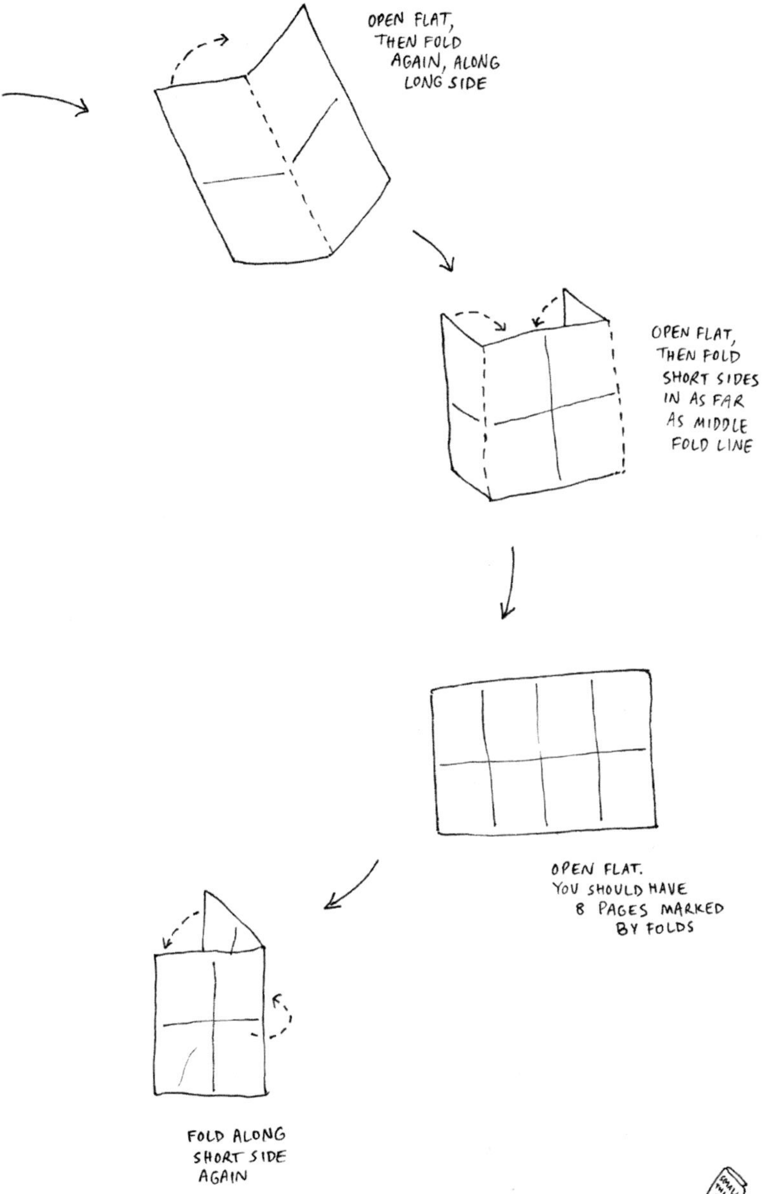

OPEN FLAT,
THEN FOLD
AGAIN, ALONG
LONG SIDE

OPEN FLAT,
THEN FOLD
SHORT SIDES
IN AS FAR
AS MIDDLE
FOLD LINE

OPEN FLAT.
YOU SHOULD HAVE
8 PAGES MARKED
BY FOLDS

FOLD ALONG
SHORT SIDE
AGAIN

CHAPTER 6
Field report: Feeling research (Astrida)

THE FEELED LAB

Introduction: 'A certain feeling . . .'

Many smart and compassionate people have written usefully about climate feelings: anxiety, grief, anger and more.[1] As many note, not feeling is not really an option these days, and feeling in the company of others is recommended. When queer ecologist Cleo Wölfle Hazard speaks to climate scientists about their grief, which has no outlet for expression, he wonders: 'Like living a closeted life, does this private lament cause psychic harm?'[2] For Wölfle Hazard, this risk should move us not only towards sharing our feelings with colleagues and other human publics, but towards feeling with the land, animals, water, and other beings who are all feeling things, too: 'Feeling for one another, we gain energy to recommit to struggle with a long horizon.'[3]

Taking my experience with the FEELed Lab at UBC Okanagan as an example, this chapter explores feelings as a part of feminist climate justice research and practice. As our former FEELed Lab Administrator, Dani Pierson, phrased it in a collaborative zine we compiled after our first year of operations: 'Members, participants and FEELed friends have described a certain feeling that cocoons our time together.' While FEELed Lab events are not unique in their generation of 'a certain feeling', I am sure this feeling is what keeps many feminist and social justice-oriented scholars tethered to the oftentimes 'cruel optimism'[4] of universities (or other institutions) that don't necessarily care for us. So this feeling is no small thing. It is actually quite powerful. As Audre Lorde reminds us, feeling *is* power.[5]

So what happens when, despite dominant Western epistemologies and research methodologies that we are trained in, and whose values of rational detachment and objectivity we have absorbed, we nonetheless insist that this feeling, or feeling in general, can be an anchor for what we do? Below, I address this question in two ways: first, by describing the FEELed Lab – a feminist environmental humanities field lab at UBC Okanagan – as one kind of social infrastructure for better weathering; and second, by taking feelings seriously as part of climate change research. While these two dimensions don't have to be connected, this chapter describes how each supports the other.

But before proceeding I want to begin with an important lesson I have learned from this work. When I was trying to get the Lab going, I put a lot of effort into making space for gathering community: convening workshops, symposia, reading groups, walks, work space and lunchtime conversations. My assumption was that this is what I had to do as a *preamble* to future FEELed Lab research; I thought this is how I would identify and assemble potential collaborators and participants. After two years, though, I realized I was wrong: this gathering, social infrastructure work is not 'research prep'. This *is* the research – creative, practice-led research on the possibility of bringing people together across difference, in relation to Land and place, and in a context of explicit commitments to feminist, queer and anticolonial perspectives, in order to change the climate as the climate changes us.

A cabin in the woods (on unceded syilx territory)

When I arrived in Kelowna – a small city nestled between two mountain ranges in Western Canada – in January 2021, I came with a lot of personal grief and difficult feelings. The heavy feelings of sadness I had about leaving behind a beloved place and very dear people in Sydney were augmented by grief and stress in relation to my family situation; my dad was ill and dying (the primary reason for coming back to Canada), and the move away from Sydney was very difficult for my kids. Because we had arrived in the middle of the early pandemic, no one was around. We couldn't make friends, join clubs, go to other people's homes for dinner or invite anyone over. Even if we could, lockdown was also psychological: few people had a capacity to open themselves to strangers.

I was also feeling climate change very heavily in my heart. When we left Sydney, it had only been around 200 days since the last bushfires of Australia's devastating 2019–20 Black Summer had been extinguished. They had burned for eleven months. Less than 100 days after our arrival in BC, this country caught fire too: the town of Lytton, less than three hours northwest of Kelowna, literally burned down overnight, but less dramatic fire was extensive, and seemingly endless. I went for daily swims in Lake Okanagan beneath a piss-yellow sky and a glowing fuchsia orb sun. It was beautiful, terrifying, still and silent. It felt like bad weather was following me everywhere. I finally felt, viscerally and fully, the truth that there really was no 'elsewhere'.

I was also finding it increasingly impossible to keep the personal and professional aspects of living in a climate-changed world separate. And I was not alone. Geographer Farhana Sultana, for example, details the 'heaviness' of climate feelings both in herself and in the communities she visited, long before she felt she could write about it in the pages of her published climate change research.[6] Naomi Klein and geographer Judee Burr explored something similar in a graduate class called 'Ecological Affect', that Klein taught and Burr attended in 2022. Klein describes noticing young researchers, many of them still students, being called upon 'as undertakers for many different kinds of life being lost to the climate crisis' while at the same time, 'the academic world in which they're being trained' doesn't recognize or give room for these feelings.[7] And as Wölfle Hazard again notes, feelings for the beings and places studied by climate scientists and ecologists subtends the work they do, even if it is masked in the 'objective' results they publish.[8] While institutional denial of these powerful feelings is another kind of 'weathering the university' (see Chapter 5), or 'greenhouse gaslighting',[9] as Blanche Verlie aptly calls it, the question remains: what are we to do with these feelings? What kinds of research infrastructures *can* support them?

Enter the FEELed Lab.

One spring morning about four months after I arrived in Kelowna, I was invited by my new Dean to a place in the southern part of the city. I had offered to help clean up an apartment to prepare for the impending arrival of an artist-in-residence. Not knowing where I was going, I rode my bike through an upper middle-class suburb with many cul-de-sacs that abutted a tree-lined ridge, then down a narrow gravel road between the ponderosa pines and Douglas firs, to a small forested clearing with several outbuildings around the perimeter of a circular drive: a large house, a couple of cabins and a shed. This was Woodhaven Eco Culture Centre.

I learned it had been a venue for eco-poetry readings and some small literary festivals, and that my new colleagues had staged an eco-art project there some years ago. This plot was part of the neighbouring Woodhaven Regional Park, managed by the regional government, but this small corner was now leased to my faculty. The university covered the costs of upkeep by renting out the upper and lower floors of the main house as graduate student housing. The main building also included a one-room live-in studio for short-term rental. A smaller outbuilding (with electricity but no heating) could host small readings or gatherings. Bellevue Creek ran along the southern edge of the property. As we cleaned the downstairs apartment, I asked about the empty upper suite. It couldn't be rented anymore, I was told – something to do with zoning. Basically unused, it included a living room, a small bedroom, a large eat-in kitchen and a bathroom, all furnished with retro furniture and an outdated cottagey vibe.

Years before, when Jen and I were running the *Composting Feminisms* reading and research group at the University of Sydney (see Chapter 5) in the prime real-estate centre of Australia's largest city, Jen had once mused: 'Imagine if we could commandeer or build a little cottage on campus here somewhere? We could have a garden, and actually compost,' she enthused, 'really integrating the theory and the practice!' I nodded, but I was eye-rolling on the inside. Things like that just don't happen at big rich university campuses! Guerilla gardens might thrive temporarily, but eventually they get razed in favour of engineering buildings and parking lots. Field labs, where they exist, need budgets only the sciences can muster.

Yet there I was, standing in a cottage in the woods, that was leased by my university, with about 80 square metres looking for a use. Can you believe it? About one year on, you would find me in the top floor suite, helping craft the zine I mention in the introduction to this chapter. The year in-between was the birth of the FEELed Lab: from idea, to pop-up event lab, to situated-in-place community.

The FEELed Lab hatched from an impossible dream that started in Sydney, but it also hatched from a research proposal. When I applied for this job, I had proposed setting up a feminist environmental humanities research lab. I had imagined it as a physical, and/or online, and/or ephemeral place for faculty, students and community who wanted to do environmental research that centred feminist, queer, anticolonial and antiracist perspectives. I had imagined it as a hub for research projects, training and mentoring, a base for visiting artists or activists or scholars, and a place where collaborative work could be concocted. All of this could be an interface between universities and communities they serve, and between humans and the more-than-human lands that hold us. But here's the rub: I had been tasked with imagining all of this, in proposal form, despite never having been to Kelowna. I had no connection to this place. How was I to propose a research programme in *this* place and with *this* community? A common, albeit problematic, assumption in academia is that 'community' just appears for you to work with, when you arrive somewhere new.

Of course, community has to be found, earned and cultivated. While my Dean supported my plan to turn the upper suite at Woodhaven Eco culture Centre into my research lab, in the meanwhile I had to find community. I hired a student, Kyla Morris, to help me build a website, believing if you build it, they will come. I started conversations with environmental humanities graduate student, Madeline Donald, who had been at UBC Okanagan for two years already. With Madeline's help and enthusiasm, we started thinking about small events and activities that could bring people together (again, building leading to coming), before the Lab as a physical space became a thing. These included the first Fringe Natures walkshop near campus that I describe in Chapter 9, and the online Littoral Listening reading group mentioned in Chapter 5. We adopted the motto: 'The FEELed Lab is where the FEELed lab does.'

But to activate the physical space of Woodhaven, we had to seriously consider this weird situation: me, a researcher, given a free pass to inhabit a beautiful forested space, leased to the University by the Regional District, who 'controlled' this land nestled on the edge of a wealthy suburb ... but all of this, of course, on occupied syilx lands. An early action was therefore to arrange a morning walk through Woodhaven with a Band Councillor from Westbank First Nation and some of his colleagues. We discussed what the nsyilxcən name of the creek might be and how, prior to colonial displacement, these lands would have been seasonal wetlands, full of food and medicines. Now the park was in drought, since French drains and water diversions had been installed, lest the affluent homes on its perimeters experience (unlikely) flooding. The cedars were parched, and the cottonwoods no longer had any streams to grow alongside. We discussed other lands in the region that had since been returned to First Nations communities. Since that meeting, the FEELed Lab has continued the long and slow work of building this relationship with syilx community, most recently in the form of an emergent, collaborative project with a community group called IndigenEYEZ, using arts-based, embodied and participatory methods to reimagine climate justice from a syilx-led perspective. The Lab also collaborates with the neighbourhood 'Friends of Woodhaven' society, whose members worry about the drought, too.

So all of our work here is grounded in the specificity of this place. This includes noticing tree species and seasonal changes in the creek's levels, but also being curious about how to respond to what this place wants.[10] This shows up directly in projects like the FEELed Library instigated by poet Natalie Rice, where we buried a book of poetry about syilx land, and asked the earth to read it for six months. (The earth's review is still forthcoming.) Or in an anthotype printing workshop run by artist and PhD student Tara Nicholson, where natural materials – grasses, berries, barks – helped expose and develop images we created. Sometimes the land participates in less obvious ways: at an outdoor dance party where we rhyme our bodies to the shadows cast by the trees, or as the soundscape to outdoor potluck lunches.

Figure 6.1 Caolan Leander reads from his draft manuscript *Bad Weather* at the FEELed Lab's Welcome the Dark gathering, on unceded syilx territory, December 2022. Photograph: Astrida Neimanis.

Field Report: Feeling Research

Committing to specificity also means exploring our own feeling-ful relationships. These feelings are not neutral. Feeling is gendered and raced, and how our feelings are understood is also a product of cultural contexts and structures of power.[11] When felt by Black bodies, Indigenous bodies, feminine bodies or disabled bodies, feeling is often dismissed as not real, or at least not as important as facts: *nothing to see here*. We know that climate feelings vary among these groups. In climate change research more generally, important differences are noted, for example, in how Black and Indigenous youth versus white youth feel about climate emergency, and their hopes for the future.[12] These differences also subtend the way we feel about place. Social scientists like Ashlee Cunsolo describe how Indigenous people in the Arctic mourn the present and future loss of so much that defines them as people: weather patterns, the cold, ecological relations.[13] These feelings are not easily comparable to the climate grief of settlers, who may have a more fungible relationship to where they live, even if they love it deeply. In this sense, feeling is part of the unequal distribution of shelter and vulnerability that this book explores as the basis of the weathering concept. As queer feminist scholar Ann Cvetkovich suggests, 'we are a sensitive interface with the world' and 'we are carrying historical residues, collective residues',[14] but these residues are not uniformly felt, or archived.

The FEELed Lab's obligation to approach climate change and related issues from feminist, anticolonial, queer, antiracist and accessible perspectives means that we refuse to flatten these differences. At our research events, some settlers might feel joy or calm, and some might feel shame and guilt (sometimes at the same time.) Others might feel discomfort, since 'the forest' is not a comforting and safe-feeling place for bodies weathered by antiblack racism, as we learned in one of our workshops. Indigenous folks might feel suspicion, or wariness, or respite, or something else. The FEELed Lab aims to be a place where these differences can be acknowledged, and somehow (even awkwardly) held. For example, instigated by FEELed Lab Research Associate Rina Garcia Chua, two *Fire + Water / Water + Fire* symposia have been convened as a way to expressly centre syilx, other Indigenous and racialized perspectives on watersheds and wildfire. Or, in her 'Rest as Resistance' workshop series, inaugural FEELed Lab administrator Dani Pierson foregrounded the uneven distribution of opportunities to rest in colonial, capitalist societies, and invited participants to learn about rest from a Métis perspective.[15]

We often experience feeling as an intensely personal phenomenon; when I arrived in Kelowna I felt very isolated in my grief. But feelings can also be communal. Cultural theorist Raymond Williams describes a 'structure of feeling' as a class-based affect or mood that takes hold at a certain time and location.[16] Riffing on Williams, Lauren Berlant describes an *infra*structure of feeling as the networks of feeling that move into and out of this 'common' feeling-structure: past feelings feed into the common structure, perforating it, while future possibilities for feeling open up out of it.[17] Hence structures of feeling shift and change. Cvetkovich also describes how these communal feelings can be stored in what she calls 'archives of feeling'. While sometimes these 'archives' are very material (such as a box of posters, banners, and buttons that archive the communal feeling of an activist movement), they are often 'more ephemeral',[18] writes Cvetkovich, found in feelings that sustain group belonging, or friendship. Feelings connect presumably discrete minds and bodies,[19] but they also connect different bodies to each other. Feeling 'is ecological by nature',[20] moving in and out of, and between bodies. As Verlie suggests, 'Just like air, affects swirl, waft, interpermeate and exude from human and non-human bodies and practices, and in so doing, they effect change in the world'.[21] The FEELed Lab as a social infrastructure aims to make a deliberate place for these feelings to circulate.

Craft-a-strophe! and other Feelings

When I drafted my job application research proposal, I didn't have a good name for the imagined lab. But after learning that this work could actually happen 'in the field', the choice seemed obvious. In the first place, The FEELed Lab is a *field* lab. There is a strong tradition in the sciences of doing research in (what we short-hand as) 'nature'. Where such research is long term and well funded, field labs and field stations become outposts not only for gathering data; as social infrastructures, they also present possibilities for building community.

At the same time, scientific field labs have reputations as places most safe for white, cis-male, non-disabled researchers, where relations to place are not always in respectful collaboration with Traditional Owners. Both Max Liboiron and Cleo Wölfle Hazard, however, write insightfully about models of scientific ecological fieldwork undertaken by Indigenous, queer, trans and disabled researchers, where anticolonial obligations are taken seriously.[22] Environmental humanities scholars have also been looking to science models to develop more practically engaged, hands-on ways of doing research. Under the name of 'field philosophy', for example, environmental

Field Report: Feeling Research

philosophers Brett Buchanan, Matt Chrulew and Michelle Bastian describe a mode of 'exploring relations within and between human communities, nonhuman animals, plants, fungi, forests, microbes, minerals, spirits, and scientific practices'[23] that requires work *in the field*. Jen's work at The Community Weathering Station (CoWS) is another version of this (see Chapter 7). The FEELed Lab looks to these models.

But *this* field lab would also be a feel-ed lab: i.e. an infrastructure for feeling-ful work, that would also be a place where feeling is taken seriously as climate change research. Feeling is an interesting notion because it moves in several directions. On the one hand, feeling is often used as a loose synonym for emotions ('You hurt my feelings'), or to indicate a general attitude or orientation ('How do you feel about that?'). How something 'feels' might refer to a kind of . . . vibe. Feeling, in this sense, can be vague, ephemeral and difficult to name. On the other hand, feeling also invokes materials, touch and tactility; how something 'feels' could also be taken in a very concrete sense: rough, smooth, scratchy, damp. In this way, feeling is also specific, emplaced and gets your hands dirty. Feeling can move in both directions at once. So feeling is double-edged: material and abstract; particular and fungible. And, as ecocritic Heather Houser reminds us, feeling 'can carry us from the micro-scale of the individual to the macro-scale of institutions, nations, and the planet'.[24] Feeling is personal and communal. Like weathering, feeling is also a gerund – a verb and a noun. We have it and we do it. It is a promiscuous and hard-to-pin-down word; the *Oxford English Dictionary* suggests twenty-two different meanings! And still, feeling can be a transformative 'lifeforce' and 'creative energy',[25] connected to 'our deepest and nonrational knowledge',[26] as Audre Lorde describes. While inchoate and often ineffable, feeling is absolutely real.

So in choosing the name FEELed Lab, I welcomed feeling's ambiguity and uncertainty. I wanted a word-bag that could hold all the stuff that Western epistemologies and masculinist certainty tell us doesn't matter, or matter much, to real research. I was interested in feelings as these hugely significant things that we don't really categorize, count and measure, precisely because they are hard to categorize, count and measure. Ambiguity and uncertainty can be uncomfortable, but also spacious. When you are unsure about something, or trying to figure it out, you are open to being moved in one way or another. As Berlant says, 'feeling becomes a way of feeling things out'.[27] I leaned into this invitation to curiosity and experimentation.

The FEELed Lab's work thus keeps feeling at the centre of our research. While climate feelings can certainly be the object of research,[28] feeling can also be a way of *doing* research. Feeling is a way of knowing the world: asking questions, exploring answers, and generating data. Bladow and Ladino, drawing on Houser's work, observe that feeling can also be a connector across difference. 'Looking for micro-moments of affective intersection and building from them', they suggest, 'may be one small way forward in a political atmosphere of bubbles, divides, and seemingly entrenched polarization'.[29] In other words, feeling can be a method for antipolarization work, and thinking through difference, together. Trying things out means trying out collectivity. In the first zine our Lab made collectively as part of a DIY research methods conference, one contributor characterizes our work as 'an ongoing practice or mode of feeling out and embodying ways to be with and open to each other and the places we inhabit'; another describes lab gatherings as 'different from a solitary hike or camping with friends. The reciprocity that emerges is between me, the collective, and the process of our interactions with the environment. The collective is only loosely connected.'[30]

Another research event, funded in part by UBC's Centre for Climate Justice, and organized by students Erin Delfs, Sierra Lammi, Lola Melchior and Dani Pierson, was convened not long before the People's University for Gaza on UBCO campus set up camp in the spring of 2024. Supported by BFA student Claude Angelo, we used art-making as a method for countering the dissonance many who work at a university feel, when stated commitments to decolonization run alongside a failure to address complicity in global colonial violence, such as in the genocide in Gaza and elsewhere. People who had never been to the FEELed Lab, and Palestinian and international students in particular, attended.

This workshop and others included speed-zining as a method of feeling and making together (see Inset F). Loosely modelled on 'exquisite corpse', the Weathering Collective first experimented with speed-zines at a symposium in Armidale in 2020 (see Chapter 7). The method looks approximately like this: following a lesson on how to make a simple eight-page zine, each participant offers a key phrase, question, or proposition that compels us, excites us, or troubles us. We write that on a card and put in the middle of the table. Then, everyone selects someone else's card. The phrase or question you select becomes the title of a zine that you initiate, by crafting a title page in just three minutes. When time is up, you pass your zine to someone else (who also passes on the one they just initiated), who has three minutes to contemplate your title, and add page two to the zine. The zine is passed again, and someone new makes page three, and so on, until all eight pages are complete. Both the time limit (a constraint, but not an overly hectic one), as well as the openness of the zine genre (where a few words, a diagram, a scribble, a short dialogue or a brief essay are all equally acceptable), mean that feelings erupt, get recorded and are then collaboratively augmented as the zines make the rounds.

Speed-zining affirms the algebra of '*Craft-a-strophe*': *crafting* (or art-making) + *poetics* (strophe is another word for 'stanza') = *methods for thinking about or working through catastrophe*. This is the name we gave to a series of workshops we launched in March 2023 when I was headed to the Alberta Tar Sands on a field trip (FEELed trip?) with two visiting artist-scholars, Therese Keogh and Rebecca Macklin. This first *Craft-a-strophe!* session included silk-screening and cyanotype printing of FEELed Lab shirts and cards, as gifts for the people we would meet there. But as part of our preparation to be visitors on Cree, Dene and Métis lands, we also read poetry about the Tar Sands and extraction out loud to each other while crafting. This session extended in time and space to Northern Alberta, where we collected objects near the Tar Sands extraction sites, and printed cyanotypes by the side of the road, using some of the printed poetry pages and the energy of the Alberta sun. Some months later, the next *Craft-a-strophe!* session was themed 'Cooling Down'. To slide into the autumn season, we made micro-poetry with a button maker, using printed pages from poems, essays and policy documents on climate change, thermal regulation, and feelings, in various combinations, rooted in and on syilx lands. In another session, we sewed tote bags from thrifted curtains and silkscreened FEELed Lab logos, while reading poetry about water, or *siwɬkʷ* in nsyilxcən, to prepare for our second *Water + Fire* symposium.

To some readers, these practices may read as non-serious or somehow separate from the 'real work' of researching climate change mitigation and adaptation strategies. But as climate researchers we know that if rational empirical data was all we needed to successfully address climate crisis, we could have sorted it decades ago. As Natasha Myers reminds us, creative practice as research method can 'support the creation of knowledge forms that can help us to contest constrained regimes of evidence, unsettle ideas about what modes of attention, objects, methods and data forms are proper to the sciences, and disrupt assumptions about whose knowledge counts'.[31] Like Myers, FEELed Lab research does not discount the importance of science in learning to live with climate change. But alongside Myers, we want to 'invest our efforts in generating robust forms of knowing (and not knowing) that can stand both alongside and athwart science'.[32]

While many FEELed Lab events involve arts-based and practice-led methods, not all fly under the *Craft-a-Strophe!* flag: queer ecogothic portraiture with PhD student and artist Tara Nicholson, a soundwalk with visiting artist Anne Bourne; an outdoor winter dance party around the fire with guest artist Hanna Sybille Mueller; a multispecies drag workshop with visiting anthropologist and drag king Laura McLauchlan. Still on the horizon is a Kelowna edition of #haircutsforplanetarysurvival (see Chapter 4). But all of these are linked by an expanded version of the *Craft-a-Strophe!* formula: arts-led making/doing + climate change thematic + people + specific place or context = learning to live with climate change. I borrow the phrase 'learning to live-with climate change' from Blanche Verlie, since it closely resonates with weathering's mandate to practice the redistribution of shelter and vulnerability. Building feminist infrastructures, where we can drop out of our 'heads' and into our fully present bodies, is a way to cultivate tactics – ones that concern relationships, trust, solidarity, support and risk-taking – that support this redistribution. It is worth noting that our events have been sought out not only by artists and pedagogues, but also geographers, anthropologists, conservation biologists, hydrologists and more. Everyone feels climate change.

Feeling matters if we want to create social change in the face of climate change. Feelings are necessary for trying out weathering together, differently. They are inextricably tangled up in how we act, who we form alliances with, and what ideas or policies we throw our weight behind. Feeling can be a powerful override switch. But just because feeling as method can exist alongside and athwart climate science, its meaning is not necessarily self-evident or necessarily 'proof' of what a feeling purports. If I feel scared, it may or may not be true that my person is under imminent threat; if I feel sad, it may or may not mean that things are shit. In her book *Doppelganger*, Naomi Klein describes far-right forces that propagate various conspiracies, including climate change denialism, as getting the facts wrong but the feelings right.[33] So feeling is powerful in this regard, too. Feelings such as fragility, discomfort and even audacity can be manipulative or problematic, particularly when felt by white settlers or other privileged people in spaces where they are asking things of Indigenous folks and people of colour.[34]

Even in these cases feelings are still useful data, because they indicate something that we *must* be curious about, if our research objectives include policy change, behaviour change, better relations, new environmental imaginaries or anything else that involves humans being in the world differently. Writer Maggie Nelson reminds us that feelings are 'diagnostic'.[35] A headache might mean you are dehydrated, or need new glasses or many other things besides. So in this sense, this sensation is the start of an inquiry. Similarly, feelings signal to us: *pay attention to what's happening here*. When we relegate climate change solely to the realm of rationality, logic and objective fact, we miss out on a huge part of the way we, as humans, are weatherers and weather-makers. A feeling is not a fact, but it is an indicator of an obstacle. Or an opening.

Conclusion: Unfinished protocols for FEELed work

1. FEELed work is always in the field (in the FEELed). Land is always a participant, to whom we have specific obligations.

2. FEELed work is for whoever shows up. We remain curious about who might be part of our temporary collective. That's why introductions are important, and often the main point.

4. FEELed work is a matter of choice. We deliberately and specifically centre anticolonial, feminist, queer and antiracist perspectives, foregrounding questions of access and inclusion, even and especially when we fail at living up to our obligations.

5. FEELed work is a matter of chance. We make room for whatever comes up. If we are grounded in accountability, we can responsively pivot as needed.

5. FEELed work is housework. This means everyone does the dishes. Equally important is creating atmospheres of comfort and conviviality. (See Inset H).

6. FEELed work is practice.

Practically speaking, the FEELed Lab has been a confluence of timing, the specificity of my job, the weird coincidence of Woodhaven Eco Culture Centre's empty upper suite, a supportive Dean, eager student collaborators and a fantastic group of helpful staff in the faculty offices. Even more practically, since my job is (at time of writing) funded through the Canada Research Chairs scheme, I have had access to modest annual research funds, which I treat as seed money for our small-scale and low-stakes events: honoraria for student organizers or syilx Elders, modest supplies (like two tea thermoses, notebooks and clipboards), and the like. Small grants are frequently sought and successful enough to keep us going. The FEELed Lab has always been a recycler with a strong Do-It-Together ethos.

This also relates to the research: we rescale and try out ideas that come from elsewhere, which become something different when tended in this place. The FEELed Lab exists because other humanities research centres, labs and ephemeral collaborative infrastructures (summer schools, field schools) exist. Other examples allow us to think: 'I can do that too, but differently.' We help each other imagine ourselves into being!

Another important ingredient in all of this is me. I am an ambivert who has ADHD. I am a compulsive pollinator and instigator of collaborative doings. I say 'compulsive' because often, I truly can't help myself, and organizing so much is not always good for my health and my relationships. Despite this, I get immense joy and satisfaction from this work; I have honed a skillset and a personality that suits it, and I have learned that this is one way I can work on my obligations to this place. If you don't enjoy this kind of work, I wouldn't recommend it. There are other kinds of work that need to be done. Weathering together, and building different kinds of worlds, needs all of us, with all of our different skills, talents and feelings.

Back at the FEELed Lab, traces of our research remain piled on our bookshelves and affixed to the lab's walls as protocols, poems and posters. This lab, too, becomes an archive of feeling, where *practice* is again primary, mostly in the sense of 'working on something in order to get better at it' or 'skilling up'. But practice also means choosing a habit and trusting it (see Prologue). Practice-led, creative methods, especially when done together, produce useful research, with (as our higher-ups like to say) 'real-world impact'. We are skilling up for apocalypses that are already here.

Notes

1. Naomi Klein, *Doppelganger: A Trip into the Mirror World*, 1st edn (New York, NY: Farrar, Straus and Giroux, 2023); Rebecca Solnit, Thelma Young Lutunatabua, and David Solnit, eds., *Not Too Late: Changing the Climate Story from Despair to Possibility* (Chicago, IL: Haymarket Books, 2023); Kari Marie Norgaard, *Living in Denial: Climate Change, Emotions, and Everyday Life* (Cambridge, MA: MIT Press, 2011); Sarah Jaquette Ray, *A Field Guide to Climate Anxiety: How to Keep Your Cool on a Warming Planet* (Oakland, CA: University of California Press, 2020); Jade Sasser, *Climate Anxiety and the Kid Question: Deciding Whether to Have Children in an Uncertain Future* (Oakland, CA: University of California Press, 2024); Blanche Verlie, *Learning to Live with Climate Change: From Anxiety to Transformation* (New York, NY: Routledge, 2022).

2. Cleo Wölfle Hazard, *Underflows: Queer Trans Ecologies and River Justice* (Seattle, WA: University of Washington Press, 2022), 90.
3. Wölfle Hazard, *Underflows,* 92.
4. Lauren Berlant, *Cruel Optimism* (Durham, NC: Duke University Press, 2011).
5. Audre Lorde, *Sister Outsider: Essays and Speeches*, The Crossing Press Feminist Series (Trumansburg, NY: Crossing Press, 1984), 53.
6. Farhana Sultana, 'The Unbearable Heaviness of Climate Coloniality', *Political Geography* 99 (2022).
7. Naomi Klein and Judith Burr, *The Right to Feel*, podcast, Future Ecologies, 2024, https://www.futureecologies.net/listen/the-right-to-feel.
8. Wölfle Hazard, *Underflows*.
9. Blanche Verlie, 'Feeling climate injustice: Affective climate violence, greenhouse gaslighting and the whiteness of climate anxiety', *Environment and Planning E: Nature and Space* 7, no. 4 (2024): 1601–19.
10. Amer Kanngieser, 'Listening as Taking Leave', *The Seed Box* (blog), 15 January 2021, https://theseedbox.mistraprograms.org/blog/listening-as-taking-leave/.
11. Sianne Ngai, *Ugly Feelings*, 1st paperback edn (Cambridge, MA, and London: Harvard University Press, 2007); Sara Ahmed, *The Cultural Politics of Emotion* (Edinburgh: Edinburgh University Press, 2014); Bettina Judd, *Feelin: Creative Practice, Pleasure, and Black Feminist Thought* (Evanston, IL: Northwestern University Press, 2023).
12. Sasser, *Climate Anxiety and the Kid Question*, 6; Tara J. Crandon et al., 'A Social–Ecological Perspective on Climate Anxiety in Children and Adolescents', *Nature Climate Change* 12, no. 2 (2022): 28.
13. Ashlee Cunsolo et al., 'Ecological Grief and Anxiety: the Start of a Healthy Response to Climate Change?', *The Lancet Planetary Health* 4, no. 7 (2020): e261–e263.
14. Ann Cvetkovich et al., 'Cruising the Archive with Ann Cvetkovich', *Recaps Magazine*, 2011, http://recapsmagazine.com/rethink/cruising-the-archive-with-ann-cvetkovich.
15. All of these research events are recounted on the FEELed Lab's research blog, FEELed Notes: https://thefeeledlab.ca/feeled-notes/
16. Raymond L. Williams, *Marxism and Literature*, repr, Marxist Introductions (Oxford: Oxford University Press, 2009).
17. Lauren Berlant, *On the Inconvenience of Other People* (Durham, NC: Duke University Press, 2022), 20.
18. Ann Cvetkovich, *An Archive of Feelings: Trauma, Sexuality, and Lesbian Public Cultures* (Durham, NC: Duke University Press, 2003), 159.
19. As ecocritics Bladow and Ladino note, 'reading the news is never the task of a disembodied mind', citing neuroscientific research that shows how processing

stories is a whole-of-body experience.' Kyle A. Bladow and Jennifer K. Ladino, eds., *Affective Ecocriticsm: Emotion, Embodiment, Environment* (Lincoln, NE: University of Nebraska Press, 2018), 2.

20. Bladow and Ladino, *Affective Ecocriticism*.
21. Verlie, *Learning to Live with Climate Change*, 24.
22. Wölfle Hazard, *Underflows*; Max Liboiron, *Pollution Is Colonialism* (Durham, NC: Duke University Press, 2021).
23. Brett Buchanan, Michelle Bastian and Matthew Chrulew, 'Introduction: Field Philosophy and Other Experiments', *Parallax* 24, no. 4 (2 October 2018): 383.
24. Heather Houser, *Ecosickness in Contemporary U.S. Fiction: Environment and Affect* (New York, NY: Columbia University Press, 2014), 223.
25. Lorde, *Sister Outsider*, 55.
26. Lorde, *Sister Outsider*, 53.
27. Berlant, *On the Inconvenience of Other People*, 97.
28. This research is very interdisciplinary, spanning ecocriticism to psychology to planetary health. See, for example, Cunsolo et al., *Ecological Grief and Anxiety*.
29. Bladow and Ladino, *Affective Ecocriticsm*, 3.
30. Yazdan Gordanpour, one of our original 'friends of the FEELed Lab', had shared an opportunity with our loose collective to make a zine as part of an unconventional conference on Low-Carbon Research Methods (https://diymethods.net/). We held another open day at the lab later that year to read the conference zines, and participate in the Twitter conference. You can find our zine at https://thefeeledlab.ca/projects-2/project-3/.
31. Natasha Myers, 'Ungrid-able Ecologies: Decolonizing the Ecological Sensorium in a 10,000 year-old NaturalCultural Happening', *Catalyst* 3, no. 2 (2017): 3.
32. Myers, 'Ungrid-able Ecologies', 2.
33. Klein, *Doppelganger*.
34. As feminist scholar Kyla Schuller notes, 'White feelings' can be 'the fertile products of racialized vulnerability, disposability, and death'. Kyla Schuller, *The Biopolitics of Feeling: Race, Sex, and Science in the Nineteenth Century* (Durham, NC: Duke University Press, 2018), 2. See also Verlie, 'Feeling Climate Injustice'; Natasha Abhayawickrama et al., 'White Audacity and Student Climate Justice Activism', in *Planetary Justice: Stories and Studies of Action, Resistance and Solidarity*, ed. Michelle Lobo, Eva Mayes and Laura Bedford (Bristol: Bristol University Press, 2024).
35. Maggie Nelson, *On Freedom: Four Songs of Care and Constraint* (Minneapolis, MN: Graywolf Press, 2021), 201.

INSET G — market stall

A market stall is a low-cost infrastructure that can be used by anyone to do almost anything. It can be a gazebo that models a queer, feminist, anti-colonial & community economy, and shares methods for ecological care and the redistribution of surplus shelter and vulnerability. It does not necessarily need to make money. A market stall is open-access. While different markets and stall types will attract different cultural, socio-economic and political classes, the ideas, goods and services on offer at the stall can reach a new audience.

What You Need

basic
- 1 × market stall gazebo
- stools/chairs as needed
- 1 × project title sign
- 1 × noticeboard or chalkboard showing any activities or workshop times
- facilitators (at least one! more if possible)
- a table

extra
- so many possibilities! see overleaf

How To Play

1. Devise the purpose of the stall in relation to your project.
2. Identify a market day/s (could be at a regular community market or as part of a festival or special event).
3. Contact market managers and book a space.
4. Consider larger project objectives and gather any items that might assist you.
5. Run the market stall.
6. If you are journalling or blogging the process, be sure to take pictures & notes, and document the event and any interesting things that come of it.

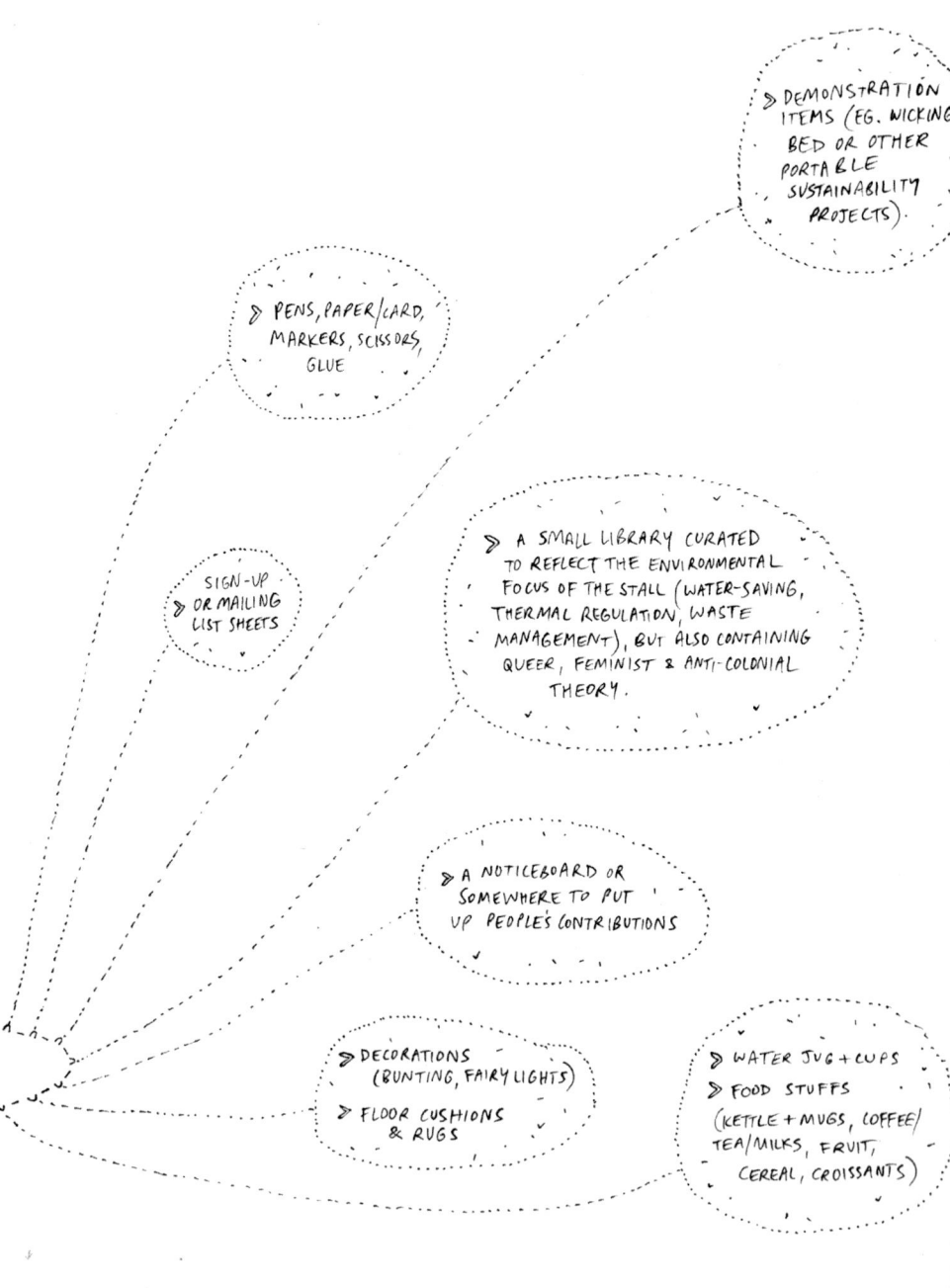

CHAPTER 7
Field report: Finding community (Jennifer)

THE COMMUNITY WEATHERING STATION (COWS)

Introduction: Leaving the city

When I moved out of the city to take up a job at a regional university, the relationship between the different people in The Weathering Collective changed. We continued to collaborate long-distance, but I also felt like I wanted to ground myself in my new place and start weathering work there. Given the place-based nature of weathering activities I started to ask what else the weathering work could become in Armidale. This chapter shares how I answered that question by devising the Community Weathering Station (CoWS) during a drought, and how it continues today.

More personally, the chapter tells a story of working with and through the risks and uncertainties presented by one's own self-identity and politics in a new community. It sometimes feels tricky being a queer feminist environmentalist academic in a small regional community that on paper might be suspicious and non-accepting of such folks (that is: queers, feminists, environmentalists and academics) and their politics. Straight-passing and white privilege gives me a substantial leg-up, but my queer non-binary femme self-identity and anticolonial environmental feminist political beliefs are working towards a different world to the cisheteropatriarchal colonial capitalist one in which we live.

Living and working outside the inner-urban context changes the nature of some community-oriented academic and artistic work; in the big city you can most likely find some like-minded people and there's safety in numbers, even if sometimes your work sparks controversy and is dragged by the right-wing media.[1] Though the make-up of community is different in a smaller and regional place, the gradual work of CoWS over the years in Armidale has allowed for me to proceed in gentle confidence that work grounded in feminist, queer and anticolonial environmental ethics is beneficial in and for the whole community and that there are lots of folks receptive to this work;

doing the work is worth the risk of being turned into a pariah for radical or anti-normative beliefs.

The drought that created CoWS

At the time of writing, the global cow population is estimated to be somewhere between 1 billion and 1.5 billion.[2] There are more sheep than cows in Australia, but the way cows chew and stare is captivating for me.[3] With so many of them grazing on deforested grassland paddocks or in enclosed feedlots, it is easy to make cows environmental villains: they burp too much, they impact soil, they take too many antibiotics, they trample the banks of rivers, creeks and lakes. Where they are, other things are now not: native grasslands, forests, topsoil and wild animals, or even just 'biodiversity'. Cows are the enemy! In addition, cows and livestock more generally (sheep, pigs, horses) are often characterized as willing accomplices in the colonization in Australia.[4] But cows can be viewed as both colonial agents and environmental enemies only if our approach to environmental crisis is anthropocentric and we do not even try to, on one hand, think about the bigger systems the cows are part of and, on the other, account for the cows' place in the world that we share.

Thinking seriously about the cows helped me find a path into the project. When I moved to Anaiwan Country, the settler colonial agricultural region known as The New England, I was shocked to learn that the health of all the creeks and waterways was compromised because of beef cattle farming. This was naïve. But I was operating under some latent pastoral fantasy. The cows were living in every single river and stream catchment, including human drinking-water reservoirs. Where cows hadn't found a way through gaps in fences and across grids, some agricultural run-off found its way into every stream. I had been unconsciously trained in thinking about environmental harms in relation to the cows, rather than to the colonial agrifood system they are caught up in (if not coercively born and bred into service). At some point during a drought, I was looking at all the emaciated cows exposed to blistering heat on the dusty, dry and treeless landscape, and I felt compelled to pause and try to understand it all differently. Cows are not the enemy! Cows are not responsible for the poor water quality on the tablelands and the difficulty of finding a safe place to swim on a warm day: humans are responsible. I am more complicit than the cows in this settler colonial horror story. It is definitely not the cows' fault.

CoWS is a market stall and feminist practice for climate change (INSET G) that seeks to create space for exploring big challenges on a mundane scale and create alternative ways to respond to wicked ecological problems and contentious environmental challenges. The name CoWS is explicitly irreverent, hoping to mobilize some of the possibilities in what Nicole Seymour terms 'bad environmentalism', or work that is premised on a refusal of 'purity politics – and, subsequently, on an embrace of contradiction, imperfection, and ambiguity – as well as an opposition to antiprogressive modes such as racism and homophobia, modes that often go hand in hand with mainstream environmental campaigns. These works find nothing sacred – and, in fact, find sacredness to be part of the problem when it comes to environment and animals'.[5] Some gentle irreverence towards the dominant culture of Armidale, small-town environmentalism and my own status as a queer environmental feminist researcher in this context felt like the only viable way to design the stall.

Though the work of the CoWS stall has a politicized vision for climate adaptation (low-fi, collective, grassroots, fun), the guiding principle is an affectively ambivalent one: the belief that strong feelings about climate change do not necessarily lead to concrete actions. Stemming from this principle, which contrasts with the rhetoric that we need folks to 'care' about the issues in order to do anything, CoWS is a facilitation infrastructure rather than an agent for a particular environmental cause. The specific cause that CoWS comes to support is planetary health, but the details of this commitment will be explored in the next chapter.

The CoWS market stall practice developed into a feminist practice for climate change during my first couple of years living and working on unceded Anaiwan Country, also known as Armidale, New South Wales. These years coincided with what is (at the time of writing) the worst drought on record. Although some might argue that cows create droughts, this drought created CoWS. We moved to this part of the world on 26 January 2018 on a hot and very dry day. In Australia, 26 January is better known as 'Invasion Day' or 'Survival Day', or both. It is officially a national holiday, 'Australia Day', which to our shame is a celebration that coincides with the establishment of the first colonial settlement of Sydney. On that day, the Armidale Aboriginal Community Garden was having a survival gathering and protest event.[6] It was our very first time in Armidale and our first stop. We got out of the car and the intensity and dryness of the heat struck me. I was surprised because I had read on websites promoting regional growth that Armidale was a cool and humid city, likely insulated from the effects of

Figure 7.1 Community Weathering Station Breakfast Stall at the Compassions, 'A Timely Feeling' Conference at UNE October 26, 2019. The picture includes Jen's partner (Craig) and son (Stan) who were helping out that morning. Photograph: Jennifer Hamilton.

climate change and thus a good place to move to. That day we asked people where to go to swim and were told of various good waterholes that in the coming weeks we found stagnated, if not dried out. It turns out that although no official announcements had been made yet, that January was unusually hot and dry: by May 2018 the whole state of NSW would be declared in drought and by mid-2019 it looked like Armidale could run out of water altogether. The drought did not break until early 2020, and not before the Black Summer bushfires that took the lives of hundreds of humans (thirty-three directly in the fires, and 450 due to smoke inhalation), millions of hectares of bush (including never-before burnt Gondwana rainforests) and a billion animals.[7]

At the same time that I was seeking a new way into weathering work, I was also becoming aware how many people were feeling very unsettled, afraid and hopeless about the drought in ways that the Weathering Collective's work addressed. As the drought escalated, so too did the discussions and debates about how to respond, via social media forums, in the local paper,[8] podcasts,[9] informally at water coolers and officially at town hall meetings.[10] It started to feel important to directly contribute to the public discussion about the unfolding crisis and devise a way to allow for the Weathering Collective's work to inform the community of Armidale's response to the drought. A town hall meeting in a small town alongside the mayor, farmers and infrastructure managers isn't your usual place for a queer feminist, but that's where I found myself.

The solutions proposed by government and business leaders did not address the way people felt about the problem. Most people recognized that the primary solution for this drought was beyond everyone's control: rain. In the absence of rain, attention was given to what was in our control in the present. As such, the solutions were imagined on two separate scales, which suits the neoliberal framing of most problems: one at the personal use level and the private domestic home, and the other at the large-scale infrastructure level of the municipal dam. The small-scale solution was for private citizens to change their water practices and reduce consumption. We were encouraged to reduce water use through restrictions and modified habits.[11] The large-scale one was the domain of politicians and business-people, who discussed seeking multi-million dollar grants for a big infrastructure project to raise the dam wall to try to store more water during future boom times.

These solutions had some material and affective benefits, and also drawbacks. Individualistic solutions were effective in slowing the community's collective consumption and conserving water. We were encouraged to save water through restrictions and the threat of fines (by washing less and letting gardens die). But these solutions also led to resentment around perceived double standards. In particular, the tomato farm in Guyra, which exported tomatoes out of the region, was effectively blamed for draining the local supply.[12]

Meanwhile, politicians were proposing very expensive, large in scale infrastructural solutions, designed to show how they were in control of the situation and to support business as usual. They offered no short-term respite, but the message was clear: if we survive this drought as a town, then we *might* get a larger dam at some point. At time of writing, politicians have promised a 27 million dollar grant to raise the wall 6.5 metres but the money appears more of a promise than a reality, and work has not commenced.

Though granular details of the community's response were not officially documented, research conducted elsewhere shows how water restrictions can cultivate a stronger sense of communal accountability and responsibility.[13] My informal observations noted that people in Armidale responded similarly.

For example, efforts to save old trees in local parks by getting residents to walk their greywater down the street to water to the trees were so successful that it was reported in national media.[14]

What was missing from the public discourse was climate change and how changing practices relating to water and weather during drought could also be connected to climate adaptation. Although Armidale had never come close to this level of water scarcity before (it wasn't even thought to be a place vulnerable to drought), the drought was not being treated as a climate change event. There was a sense that when the drought breaks, our resilient community will bounce back stronger than ever, the bigger dam will support the status quo, and that will be that. The drought has broken and we have had years of plentiful rain, and we have all reverted back. But it started to seem like a missed moment for a more substantial or enduring kind of response to climate change.

I captured some of my own feelings of despair in a reflection on the very first CoWS stall. Here, I describe a drive west from Anaiwan Country (Armidale) to Gamilaraay Country to the Groundswell festival in Bingara. It was early September 2019, and so dry. There was a dust storm, and the bushfires that would gradually envelope the whole eastern seaboard of the continent over the coming months, had just started east of Armidale on the last day of winter:[15]

> Driving to [Bingara] last weekend felt like I was in a disaster movie or the end times. Maybe both. A hot and powerful westerly blew like nothing I'd ever witnessed before. Dust was blocking out the sun and masking the road like a thick dirty fog, moving chaotically in every direction. We were slowed by heavy trucks hauling water to the next tank that's run dry. All the while my phone was beeping: 'how are you in the fires?' and 'It will be a miracle if her house doesn't burn'. The one comfort of driving through in the over-cleared, over-grazed, bare, dusty, dry land is that the risk of fire is negligible because there is nothing left to burn.[16]

The world was bleak and dry and getting dryer. We needed rain. But as Lauren Berlant says, we also need to 'forge an imaginary for managing the meanwhile within damaged life's perdurance'.[17] In other words, sometimes life goes on even when it feels like it might be so bad it could end. And so we need to find a way to live in this zone. My feelings about the severity of the situation and lack of attention to this drought as climate change, had started to form as questions: How can we respond to the drought in a way that also addresses climate change? How can people address the drought differently, without sublimating the fear and terror of the dryness and fire? Could this include imagining their response as not just an endurance test until the rain comes, but also as an adaptation to climate change? How can my weathering work very concretely and directly be involved in Armidale's drought response?

Market stall as community-scaled response

My response to these questions was to set up CoWS as a market stall at local community markets and fair days. As a specific response to the drought, I thought it could offer people ways of thinking and acting in the scale *between* the small (bucketing water)[18] and the large (raising the dam wall). The collective activity was not just about saving water so we could survive the drought, but collectively starting to think a bit about how we could use this moment to collectively adapt to climate change. This is the zone outside the private domestic space and before (and hopefully in lieu of) the literal construction of the future 'drought-proof' high-tech mega dam.

In this sense, CoWS is an example of the feminist infrastructures for better weathering that we discuss in Chapter 4. In a more traditional political and economic sense, CoWS connects up with the philosophies of 'community' and 'diverse economies' developed by J.K. Gibson-Graham in *The End of Capitalism (As We Knew It): A Feminist Critique of Political Economy* (1996).[19] They describe the problem of doing anti-capitalist work as hampered by the privileging of the large scale as the most powerful and impactful: 'Most theories of scale are dominated by a vertical ontology that presumes a hierarchy of scales from the global to local, mapped onto a hierarchy of power.' But, they continue, 'this worldview demands that local initiatives "scale up" before they can be seen as transformative.'[20] Gibson-Graham build on classical feminist political economy to argue that 'household and community conditions are important constituents of industrial development'.[21] But rather than just using the details of domestic and community life to better describe the global economy, they also want to understand how these practices might themselves contain examples of revolution we seek, already existing inside the economy, just in smaller-scale form. Their hope is to create the conditions under which 'socialist or other non-capitalist constructions become a 'realistic' present activity rather than a ludicrous or utopian future goal'.[22] So through the lens of J.K. Gibson-Graham's work, CoWS can be seen as modelling an ideal vision of the world that is not just a fantasy proposition, but a material mini-transition economy in a playful market stall setting.

The first iteration of the market stall set up was Bingara's Living Classroom in September 2019 at the aforementioned Groundswell festival. Groundswell was run by the Kandos School of Cultural Adaptation (KSCA), a group of artists who work out of the small town of Kandos and propose creative ways of approaching climate adaptation. The Living Classroom is a publicly owned and operated outdoor regenerative agriculture demonstration farm and conference centre; Groundswell was focussed on fostering a conversation between regenerative agriculturalists, scientists and farmers.

For this first iteration I was assisted by Imogen Semmler, Kade Smith and Lauren Moss. Imo is a friend and artist from Sydney, who moved to the region to study soil ecology at UNE and was a founding member of KSCA. She connected me with two off-grid homesteaders, Kade and Lauren, who also supported me on this inaugural CoWS day. Kade created the CoWS title sign, recycled corflute signs illustrating how the wicking beds work, and made a massive sandwich board with prompts for the little weathering exercises in relation to water. In addition, she made a small demonstration wicking bed out of an old fish tank and a large A-frame blackboard for displaying the results of the weathering activities. Lauren went shopping for watercolours, paper, pencils and pens to create space for creative reflection. I did not know them very well at the time but due to the dusty windstorm, their tent at the festival collapsed and they ended up sleeping on the floor of our motel room as short-term climate refugees: a new way to forge a friendship! They ferried my gazebo, trestle tables, water jug and chairs in their big van. I brought a small library of books and zines to complement the wicking bed and activities.

The stall was intended to prompt people to reflect on how they were feeling about the drought, offer tools for gardening in a dry climate, and create ways for thinking about how the drought connected up with hetero-colonial-patriarchal capitalism. There was no expectation that every participant would join all the dots between the watery reflections and the bigger social political concepts; it was just a suggestion. The festival was not a niche eco-arts festival, but rather a general community and farmer-adjacent one. Visitors at the first iteration of the stall ranged from artists, scientists and farmers to unaffiliated local community members from Bingara and other neighbouring towns. Folks engaged in different ways:

reading books, picking up zines, photographing the wicking bed instructions and participating in the tasks.

Two reflection prompts accompanied the activities: 'who needs water?' and 'how do you feel about water?' These were designed to give rise to different kinds of thoughts about the drought, to open space for reflection that was not only about anxieties about running out of water but about something more. Participants reflected on these prompts creatively. Hopefully, this would inject some non-anthropocentric and community-scaled thinking into drought debates which were, as mentioned above, very focussed on a set of colonial and proprietorial assumptions about domestic living standards and big infrastructure. The responses ranged from 'I don't know how I feel about water' to 'despair' to 'I love to be out in the rain as it can feel really cleansing',[23] and lots of ideas and impressions in between. I felt nervous about the vagueness of the task in times when people were so anxious and wanting clear solutions, but the success of this task was in its ability to cut across the existing debates and access different thoughts, feelings and practices.

When combined with the general reflective prompts, the library and the zines were what really connected the wicking bed demonstration – as exemplar of a method for drought-tolerant and possibly community-scaled agriculture – and the larger-scale drought itself to ideas of weathering, decolonization, queer kinship and inclusive feminisms. I brought a complement of my own zines ('A Field Guide for Weathering' and 'Drought-Friendly Hairstyles') and a small library (including the work of Charmaine Papertalk Green and John Kinsella,[24] Judith Wright,[25] Alison Whittaker,[26] Astrida Neimanis,[27] Gabi Briggs and Callum Clayton-Dixon for the Anaiwan Language Revival Program[28] and bell hooks,[29] alongside *Do it yourself 12-volt Solar Power*[30] and *Permaculture One*[31]).

The library was carefully curated to make explicit some of the ideas that I felt were implicit within the stall. bell hooks' *Feminism is for Everybody: Passionate Politics* felt like an appropriate book in the library because the argument of hooks' book is a touchstone of our feminist theory for climate change, but also the title is self-explanatory in a useful way when just browsing the shelf. In addition to feminist texts, it was important to seed thinking on drought as a symptom of colonization. *Mugun and Gun: Resisting the New England (Frontier Wars – Edition One)* was self-published by the Anaiwan Language Revival Program, with all proceeds going to their anticolonial work. The zine serves as a dictionary of words and yarns to prove that the land in the area was not just empty or passively surrendered, but that it was contested. (A more comprehensive argumentation about frontier wars in the region is outlined in Callum Clayton Dixon's book *Surviving New England: A History of Aboriginal Resistance and Resilience Through the First Forty Years of Colonial Apocalypse*,[32] which was added to the library when it came out in December 2019.) Other texts included the environmental prose of poet Judith Wright, who grew up in the region on a cattle station, and books by Charmaine Papertalk Green and Alison Whittaker, who write fierce anticolonial verse. As a whole, the library prompts people to provisionally think about their wicking beds in the context of settler colonialism and the unceded status of the land and water.

The stall was set up several more times in this format across late 2019 before the drought broke: at the Black Gully Festival of environment and arts, the UNE Compassions Conference, the Armidale Community Farmer's Market. I collected lots of drawings and reflections, got people talking about wicking beds, and kept developing the library. The community started to gather and share ideas for how we could build something more permanent in this space but the smoke from Black Summer bushfires meant it was unsafe to be outside for long periods of time. I travelled over the summer and when I returned to Armidale in early 2020, the fires were out and the skies had opened. At this point I began chatting to a local doctor about how to develop CoWS into a larger-scale and less pop-up community facility which eventually became the Armidale Climate and Health Project that I discuss in Chapter 8. We also started to develop CoWS activities for different situations, such as the CoWS Breakfast as part of the 'Weathering Everything Symposium', which we discussed in Chapter 5.

CoWS as a place for uncertain and ambiguous feelings

Moving to Armidale forced me to wrestle with some assumptions I had about living in the 'country' and to find ways of sharing what I knew, regardless of it feeling initially like I could become a outsider in the context. New England is a geographically large electoral district that encompasses many different small cities and towns; it takes in parts of Anaiwan, Gumbaynggirr, Gamilaraay Dunghutti and Biripi Country. It covers over 66,394 km^2.[33] It is a politically interesting place because each town's demographic alone is not enough to win an election. To illustrate what I mean by comparison: in an inner-city district, the identity of the suburb will usually express something about the identity of their political representatives and vice versa. Though Armidale is usually represented by a conservative politician in the National Party (a white Australian, still very masculine, rural and regional conservative group) on account of the University, there are some progressive folks here.

When moving here I did not realize the levels of nuance in the place historically, geographically and politically. I did not say the quiet part loud but I felt like I might be one of the most progressive people in the village. This was so arrogant and wrong, and definitely a stereotypical point of view that urbanites have of the 'country' that I am ashamed to admit I also held. At the same time, even though I approached the move with significant hubris, fortunately I was also embarrassed about it and this helped me apply the brakes. I did not want to be like a FIFO ('fly in, fly out') intellectual, proselytizing to the community with my good ideas. I was genuinely interested in the place: what was unique about it? What was its history? Who was already here and what were they thinking, feeling and doing in relation to climate change? Although in terms of electoral politics it signals as a very conservative place, CoWS was set up in a spirit of curiosity. Surely people are more complex than they seem. When we first started chatting, people seemed hungry to talk about the drought in terms of bigger political issues and were open to seeing it differently. One day on the CoWS stall, a farming couple came by and the wife shared how she had never believed in climate change, but is now reflecting on how her otherwise intolerable hippy sister-in-law might be onto something with this whole climate change thing. These kinds of conversations happened alongside heaps of folks who just accepted the fact the drought was part of climate change and participated in the tasks from that perspective.

As feminist practice for climate change, CoWS is a method for sharing skills and ideas, but also a place for different kinds of feelings to co-exist. While a stall that is championing a cause might lead with grief around loss and fear of further destruction to mobilize community engagement, CoWS is not trying to prefigure community responses. In Chapter 4, we argued that some of our practices support 'stranger intimacy' or connection between people who would not ordinarily hang out.[34] In CoWS, anyone is allowed into the stall and everyone is welcome to read the books and participate in the activities. This allows for the possibility of different, ambiguous and ambivalent feelings about climate change. For some, it might be the first time they've dropped their defences and opened up to even thinking about it; for others, it could be a chance for humour. Some of the reflections on 'how do you feel about water?' certainly reflect both poles.

Armidale is in a geopolitical context where there is some polarization on the issue of climate change. At the time of writing, strong governance on climate change remains to be seen, but a fairly visible activist sustainability community that is not entirely marginal; students and staff at the uni are not monolithic: some believe in climate change and others do not. It is not at the centre of the worst of the polarized culture wars, but it is not the most progressive place in the world either. Finding new ways of reckoning with political differences feels possible but also tricky in this context. While it is common to believe that political positions are separate to feelings, I hold the standpoint that political positions are complex and non-uniform articulations of feeling. CoWS seeks to hold space for the process: like a kind of mediation, but also just a demonstration of connection across difference.

This work of demonstrating a different way of exploring feelings feels important, because feelings do not prescribe responses. Responses are learned. Following the work of Silvan Tomkins as interpreted by feminist psychologist Elizabeth Wilson and queer literary historian Adam Frank, I believe that conflicts over how to respond to our feelings 'generate much of the complexity of human experience and become the hidden ground for ethical, religious and political debates about how life should be lived'.[35] If fear of the other manifests as contempt and hatred, rather than self-reflection, curiosity and compassion, the material outcome will be very different.

Similarly considering how our feelings connect to our politics, Samantha Pinson Wrisley introduced me to an unfortunate barrier to doing this slow emotional work: the twinned concept of 'ambiguity tolerance and intolerance'.[36] Wrisley found the concept described what she was seeing in her research on misogyny, the feeling of hatred, and online communities: a growing intolerance of ambiguity and uncertainty, combined with an increasingly polarized political debate as a result.[37] Climate change is a process that creates high levels of uncertainty: we have a sense that the stability of the planet is under threat but only best guesses (a lot of which look like worst case scenarios) as to what this might look like in future. And we are seeing widespread denial as a way of mitigating fear of uncertainty.

While the psychological data suggests that there are always some folks who can tolerate ambiguity and uncertainty alongside others that can't, Wrisley claims that the conditions for people to tolerate ambiguity right now are at an all-time low.[38] She explains that in these situations, many people reach for simple stories full of unambiguous certainties (black-and-white tales of goodies and baddies, of 'everything is fine' climate denialism or fantasies of total human control). These help us 'reestablish some order onto the chaos' we are contending with.[39] In contrast, CoWS aims to create a space to explore ambiguity together. By practising the arts of weathering, the stall suggests that in this lively world of mortal beings, low-stakes vulnerability is as good as it gets. Caringly sheltering together and creating feelings of security despite vulnerability is the goal. No human is 100 per cent invulnerable, immortal or secure; our earthly condition is naturally precarious, and finding an ethics and politics that can work with that material truth as a cornerstone is key.[40]

But what will it take for folks to be receptive to the idea that a simple low-tech proposition of living well in communities larger than a family but smaller than the planet can be a solution to climate change? There are economic and political barriers, but work is being done on this in terms of proposals around degrowth and food sovereignty.[41] What CoWS seeks to do is to bring together the hard work of building community alongside these more pragmatic propositions: the political farming books sit beside space for sharing feelings. There is emotional work involved in building sustained and enduring local connections. It is very hard if you're not used to it. In a settler colony, this will involve processing unresolved historical trauma as well as present-day interpersonal dynamics.

Berlant writes about the subtle difficulties of sharing the world with others, which is relevant here: 'When it comes to living in proximity [with others], there is no such thing as passivity. Adjustment is a constant action: the grinding of the wheels of awkwardness and the bargaining with life's infrastructures.' We are always weathering! It is constant work to connect with others and remain connected. But Berlant takes this further by saying that right now, these difficulties feel negative because of how challenging it is. From my own experience living in a smaller town, this is so true. The levels of accountability are ratcheted up; if you have a conflict with someone, you better at least figure something out or you will run into them for sure several times in the next week. For Berlant, 'people try to resolve the difficulty of being inconvenienced by the world by becoming depleted, cynical or dramatic fonts of blame'.[42] Think, for example, about times where you have a slight disagreement, but it feels like an affront to oneself and integrity, instead of, for example, the normal ambivalent ebb and flow of connection. Though she doesn't call it this, Berlant is encouraging us to settle into weathering and find ways to 'be there and repair what's overwhelming'. The CoWS market stall wants to make space for that difficult, awkward and slow work of being there and seeking to repair what's damaged in relation to our economy and political systems, but also between each other.

Notes

1. The 'Christmas Climate Change Variety Hour' (CCCVH) was co-produced by Jen, Craig Johnson and Lisa Mumford. The event was funded by an $AUD10,000 local council grant that allowed the curators to pay artists for the development and performance of the short works. Someone notified the Murdoch press, which turned it into a political football for the upcoming election ('Hey, NSW: You Spent 10K On A Variety Show Blaming Xmas For Global Warming', 2015; 'The Christmas Climate Change Variety Hour?', 2015). The curators and artists involved supported each other joyfully through the scandal, with Maria White and Emma McManus naming their performance group 'Too Rude' inspired by one of the graphics the newspaper used to sensationalize their reporting on the event.

2. 'Data Page: Number of cattle', part of the following publication: Hannah Ritchie, Pablo Rosado and Max Roser (2023), 'Agricultural Production'. Data adapted from Food and Agriculture Organization of the United Nations. Retrieved from https://ourworldindata.org/grapher/cattle-livestock-count-heads [online resource]

3. The importance of looking carefully at animal experience arguably defines the field of multispecies studies. In *When Species Meet* (Minneapolis, MN: University of Minnesota Press, 2008), Donna Haraway critiques Derrida's inability to really look at his cat in a way that clears space for the larger project: 'with his cat, Derrida failed a simple obligation of companion species; he did not become curious about what the cat might actually be doing, feeling, thinking, or perhaps making available to him in looking back' (19).

4. Fiona Probyn-Rapsey and Lynette Russell, 'Tools, Troops or Escapees? Cattle Trafficking in the Early Years of the Colony of New South Wales, Australia', *Environment and History* (17 October 2024): 1–22, https://doi.org/10.3828/whpeh.63861480327329.

5. Nicole Seymour, *Bad Environmentalism: Irony and Irreverence in the Ecological Age* (Minneapolis, MN: University of Minnesota Press, 2018), 232.

6. 'Survival Day Exhibition', retrieved from *Armidale Aboriginal Community Garden* [online resource], https://armidalecommunitygarden.org/exhibitions-and-public-events/survival-day-2018-exhibition/ (accessed 28 September 2024).

7. Garry Cook et. al., 'Australia's Black Summer of fire was not normal – and we can prove it', retrieved from *CSIRO* [online resource], https://www.csiro.au/en/news/all/articles/2021/november/bushfires-linked-climate-change (accessed 12 August 2024).

8. Steve Green, 'Day Zero for Armidale Water Supply Now Known', *The Armidale Express*, 17 July 2019, https://www.armidaleexpress.com.au/story/6279056/day-zero-for-armidale-water-supply-now-known/.

9. The 'Water Pressure' Podcast archives are not available online anymore, but it was a regional media-driven podcast created by two journalists from the *Northern Daily Leader*.

10. Sustainable Living Armidale (SLA) ran a 'Public Water Forum' at Town Hall, with the Mayor, the city's General Manager, facilities managers from the University and others, including myself as a representative of the Community Weathering Station. See: https://slarmidale.org/2020/02/15370

11. Different levels of water restrictions guide different kinds of household reduction strategies. At the time of writing, in Armidale, they are based on a very generous allocation of 200L of water per person per day and down to 145L in drought, https://www.armidaleregional.nsw.gov.au/environment/water-usage-and-supply/water-conservation.

12. See 'Untreated Water for Tomato Farm', *Guyra Gazette,* https://www.guyragazette.com.au/news/untreated-water-for-tomato-farm.php (accessed 24 September 2024).

13. Fiona Allon and Zoë Sofoulis, 'Everyday Water: Culture in Transition', *Australian Geographer* 37, no. 1 (2006): 51, https://www.tandfonline.com/doi/full/10.1080/00049180500511962#d1e399.

14. Peter McCutcheon, 'Residents Donate Water to Save Trees in Heritage-Listed Park as Drought Continues', *ABC News,* 4 November 2019, https://www.abc.net.au/news/2019-11-04/armidale-residents-donate-water-to-save-trees-in-drought/11661872.

15. The Bees Nest fire east of Armidale started a week before the festival on 'the last day of winter' 2019, and would burn through over a 113,000 hectares of bush before it was finally extinguished in November. *Bushfire Bulletin* 42, no. 1 (2020): 6, http://www.rfs.nsw.gov.au/__data/assets/pdf_file/0007/174823/Bush-Fire-Bulletin-Vol-42-No1.pdf (accessed 2 May 2024).

16. Jennifer Mae Hamilton, 'On Bucketing Water – and a Response to Jonathan Franzen', *Overland Literary Journal,* 13 September 2019, https://overland.org.au/2019/09/on-bucketing-water-and-a-response-to-jonathan-franzen/ (accessed 24 September 2024).

17. Lauren Berlant, *On the Inconvenience of Other People* (Durham, NC: Duke University Press, 2022).

18. 'Bucketing water' refers to the water-saving practice of hand-collecting grey water that ordinarily would have gone down a drain into buckets, and diverting it to other uses to save water, for example, catching shower water in a bucket and flushing the toilet with it or catching dishwater in a bucket and watering the plants.

19. Independently of each other, Declan Kuch and Nicolette Larder suggested that my work aligns with the theory and methods of community economies. During the period of this work, Dec and Nikki nominated me to join the Community Economies Research Network and I also attended the 2022 Community Economies Winter School led by Jenny Cameron to learn how to make these connections directly.

20. J.K. Gibson-Graham, *The End of Capitalism (As We Knew It)* (Minneapolis, MN: University of Minnesota Press, 1996) xxvi.

21. Gibson-Graham, *The End of Capitalism (As We Knew It)*, 236.
22. Gibson-Graham, *The End of Capitalism (As We Knew It)*, 263.
23. The archive of images is available at www.communityweatheringstation.net.
24. Charmaine Papertalk Green and John Kinsella, *False Claims of Colonial Thieves* (Broome: Magabala Books, 2018).
25. Judith Wright, *The Coral Battleground* (Sydney: Harper Collins, 1977).
26. Alison Whittaker, *Blakwork* (Broome: Magabala Books, 2018).
27. Astrida Neimanis, *Bodies of Water: Posthuman Feminist Phenomenology* (London: Bloomsbury, 2017).
28. Gabi Briggs and Callum Clayton-Dixon, *Mugun & Gun: Resisting New England – Frontier Wars (Edition One)* (Anaiwan Country: Anaiwan Language Revival Program, 2018).
29. bell hooks, *Feminism Is for Everybody: Passionate Politics*, 2nd edn (New York, NY: Routledge, 2015).
30. Michel Daniek, *Do It Yourself 12-volt Solar Power*, 3rd edn. (East Meon: Permanent Publications, 2016).
31. David Holmgren and Bill Mollison, *Permaculture One: A Perennial Agriculture for Human Settlements* (Hepburn: Melliodora Publishing, 2021).
32. Callum Clayton Dixon, *Surviving New England: A History of Aboriginal Resistance and Resilience Through the First Forty Years of Colonial Apocalypse* (Anaiwan Country: Newara Aboriginal Corporation, 2019).
33. Inner-city districts in Australia are – on account of their population density – on average less than 60 km^2.
34. Jennifer Mae Hamilton, Tessa Zettel and Astrida Neimanis, 'Feminist Infrastructure for Better Weathering', *Australian Feminist Studies* 36, no. 109 (July 2021): 237–59, https://doi.org/10.1080/08164649.2021.1969739.
35. Adam J. Frank and Elizabeth A. Wilson, 'Images' in *A Silvan Tomkins Handbook: Foundations for Affect Theory*. (Minneapolis, MN: University of Minnesota Press, 2020), np.
36. Else Frenkel-Brunswik, 'Intolerance of Ambiguity as an Emotional and Perceptual Personality Variable', *Journal of Personality* 18, no. 1 (1949): 108–43.
37. Not all of this work is published yet. We discuss it in the podcast referenced below, but see also Samantha Pinson Wrisley, 'Heteropessimism and the Pleasure of Saying No', *Capacious Journal* 3, no. 2 (2024), https://doi.org/https://doi.org/10.22387/CAP2024.78.
38. The full discussion is available to listen to at Jennifer Hamilton in conversation with Samantha Pinson Wrisley, 'Volume 1: Coda – Misogyny and the anesthetic affect', Daz Chandler (editor), *The Heteropessimists*, https://www.theheteropessimists.com/podcast/episode/780c468a/volume-1-coda-misogyny-and-the-anesthetic-affect (accessed 24 September 2024).

39. Hamilton and Wrisley, 2022.
40. Elsewhere I write about how this idea intersects with problematic expressions of masculinity, specifically regarding the lack of political space for the expression of vulnerability. Jennifer Hamilton, 'Tears, Rain, and Shame: King Lear, Masculine Vulnerability, and Environmental Crisis', *Water and Cognition in Early Modern English Literature*, ed. Nicolas Helms and Steve Mentz (Amsterdam: Amsterdam University Press, 2024), 157–76.
41. See Jason Hickel, *Less Is More: How Degrowth Will Save the World* (New York, NY: Random House, 2020). See also *Community Economies Research Network, Australian Food Sovereignty Alliance* and Jennifer Hamilton and Nicolette Larder 'Making Time to Care Differently for Food: The Case for the Armidale Food School', *Critical Studies in Teaching and Learning* (10, SI), 2022.
42. Berlant, *On the Inconvenience of Other People*, 9.

INSET H — community housework

Community housework is the practice of intentionally creating safe and hospitable atmospheres for gatherings of all sizes. It is linked to the diverse Black, queer, crip and socialist feminist traditions of pleasure, accessibility, care and wages for housework. Often a feminist project is framed around the refusal of this work, but femme-adjacent housework can be revalued instead. Building the world we want through acts of communal multi-being care is a key part of the climate adaptation process. The work is material, so it needs to be well-planned. And like at home, there are class differences: if you can't afford fancy catering, can you ask people to bring a plate? If you can afford either comfy seating or freshly squeezed juice, what do you choose and why?

What you need

- An event that could be done differently
- A sense of how you want it to change (eg. more collective/sustainable/slow/outdoors)
- Methods for enacting the change (eg. reusable plates, integrating clean-up into the program, different styles of event facilitation, humble outcomes, music, rest breaks).
- A willingness to trial and error new things

How to play

plan — Community housework begins at the planning stage and needs a budget. If you don't have these skills, build a relationship with a collaborator who does. They can be any gender. Make sure they're paid.

do it! / be responsive to conditions — A lot of unsustainable practices are time-efficient, so community housework during climate change all adds extra labour. Build time into your events so participants can take it in (live music, lush meals, rest breaks etc.)

clean up — The question of who does the dishes is always thorny and can make or break household dynamics. We all need to do our share of the dishes. Dishes are quite fun to do together.

reflect — Make time for reflecting on the event, looking over any documentation, accounting for feedback, noting what could have been done differently and better (or worse!).

CHAPTER 8
Field report: Downscaling planetary health (Jennifer)

THE ARMIDALE CLIMATE AND HEALTH PROJECT (ACHP)

Introduction: Downscaling planetary health

After I had been living and working on Anaiwan Country in Armidale for a couple of years, the Community Weathering Station (CoWS) spawned the Armidale Climate and Health Project (ACHP). CoWS is a market stall that is looking at changing what Lauren Berlant calls the 'terms of transition'[1] of living with climate crisis, without a clear and specific environmental or political goal in mind. CoWS is a temporary shelter and a way-station. ACHP is different. ACHP is committed to the specific outcomes of improving human health, and responding to climate change while centring Indigenous knowledge. Using weathering as a lens guiding climate adaptation (aiming for the redistribution of vulnerability and shelter, refusing resilience and emergency logics, unlearning colonial meteorology, centring climate justice, adding the body's mundane experiences of weather to climate change adaptation plans), this chapter shares a story of building a specific community project around this concept. It is a tale about collaborating and engaging in feminist practice for climate change in community as a way of downscaling planetary health, guided by weathering.

The term 'planetary health' is similar to the term 'One Health'. Both concepts encourage the research and development of solutions to environmental problems by focusing on the interconnections between human health, animal health and the broader environment, and the mutual dependencies between all things for good health.[2] These concepts have been circulating for some time, but it is only recently that scholars have observed how similar they are to Indigenous concepts of Land and Country.[3] In Australia, the idea of Country and the importance of healing Country for healing people is as old as time. It is heartening to see that research using ideas of planetary health and One Health is starting to recognize and learn from Indigenous knowledges. But the lack of essential connection between One Health, planetary health and any specific politics – anticolonial or otherwise – means both concepts are a bit vague and ripe for co-optation for the normative ends of capitalist growth. In asking 'What does One Health want?', Van Patter et al. point out that 'One Health addresses linkages between animal, human, and environmental health' but that 'Aside from this core characteristic, it is challenging to define'.[4] I agree with Van Patter et al., but for me this challenge also presents an opportunity for making claims about what One Health or planetary health actually is beyond received or normative definitions of health. There is a chance here to understand and move towards supporting holistic health outcomes. When I started collaborating with Astrida on weathering, I was not thinking about climate through a health lens, but this chapter explores the development of weathering as a concept to support work in the planetary and One Health areas, via the ACHP.

It started in theory and practice

The potential connection between our weathering work and planetary health was seeded early in the collaboration, while Astrida and I were both working at the University of Sydney. We were invited into planetary health conversations in 2017 and 2018 by Professor Anthony Capon, who started the Planetary Health Initiative there.[5] The discussions and workshops were exciting and I was also exposed to two really thought-provoking ideas. One is a simple comparison: that the difference between a clinical health concern and epidemiological studies of illness and health is analogous to the difference between weather and climate. So if weathering is useful for bridging the gap between weather and climate, it's also potentially useful for bridging the gap between individual and public and environmental health. The second was more complex. I was exposed to a memorable example of how normative thinking – i.e., thinking that the only and best world possible is the world as it currently is – can impact climate adaptation strategies in relation to health research. This also helped me to start reflecting on what it would take to apply the principles of weathering (eroding normativity, adding weather to community practice, remaking the world while adapting to climate change) critically in a planetary health project.

The example that seized my attention was Ollie Jay's 'Heat and Health Research Incubator', which at the time was investigating how different bodies respond to different temperatures in the workplace.[6] Thermoregulatory physiology is a branch of health sciences that studies how bodies respond to and regulate temperature. This health discipline struck me as uniquely relevant to the weathering work because of its focus on the details of the relationship between the body and the world in terms of weather. The aim of Jay's research was to mitigate heat stress, and reduce energy use, in order to maintain productivity, maximize profit and also lower carbon emissions. In its most basic sense, the health research is about understanding the uneven physiological impacts of climate change-induced heat and trying to fix it. The work is implicitly attentive to environmental justice concerns because it is examining the health risks of extreme heat on functioning of the body and understands that neither everyone weathers heat in the same way, nor has the same access to effective cooling technologies. This framing shows recognition that there are sustainability concerns around effective cooling (e.g. energy use in air conditioning) and socio-economic barriers to accessing effective cooling. There is no doubt that thermoregulatory physiology is urgent work because of the increasing severity of heat waves in climate change; heatwaves are already amongst the deadliest of natural disasters, and the death toll from heat stress is forecast to rise.[7] Knowing how to keep people safely cool is important for building a just and sustainable future.[8]

But Jay's research is applied, and it is the details of its application that triggered my critical interests. The work is not ultimately aimed towards the holistic pursuit of environmental justice but rather productivity in the office. The stated goal is that 'any cooling solutions in occupational settings should not interfere with the optimal completion of work tasks or exacerbate other health risks'.[9] In other words, it is important that work continues to get done and that workplaces are healthy and safe for all workers. On one hand, it is hard to argue with this; all workers need to earn wages because we need money to survive in the economy. But what is accepted as the fixed point in this equation is wage labour, not the need to slow down when the weather is hot. This is a large part of the problem: the drive to progress whatever the weather. Arguably, even though the extreme heat of climate change is not natural, slowing down in the heat to assist in healthy thermoregulation is a more natural response than pushing through and feeling sweaty, light headed, tired or sick at a desk just to maintain a capitalist value system. What is not normal is the idea productivity should never be compromised by weather, as if the body and the planet were machines in the service of economic growth. You can see my concern here is not with thermoregulatory physiology as a branch of science or even the research of the Heat and Health

Lab in general. Rather, it is with the specific framework that by definition excludes slowing down and compromising productivity as one way of mitigating heat stress.

What would it take economically, socially and politically to resist productivity being the central goal of such research? What would the research look like if productivity were not the central goal? Could we even go so far as to use knowledge from thermoregulatory physiology and apply it differently, to support the development of queer feminist and anticolonial environmental futures? Jay's research is about how heat stress can lead to medical emergencies in the present, and thus cooling people in the world in which we live is the goal. There is a vital duty of care built into this work. But it feels important to challenge the application of all this research as optimal completion of tasks and to offer building a better, fairer and more just world as an alternative application.[10] I value the knowledge generated by thermoregulatory physiology, but I really want to put health-centric knowledge to work for a less individualistic and capitalist definition of personal and planetary health.

It is not just the drive to productivity that is a barrier to this kind of goal, but also how we measure and define good health. There is a wealth of critical research that explores how discourses of health and healthy bodies often align with ideas of normativity and averages, especially by Indigenous, trans and crip research scholars and collectives.[11] Eli Clare's work *Brilliant Imperfection: Grappling with Cure* is a touchstone for me on this topic. Clare warns us of what can happen when we think about health in relation to the fantasy of a simple cure: 'as an ideology seeped into every corner of Western thought and culture, cure rides on the back of *normal* and *natural*. Insidious and pervasive, it impacts many, many bodies. In response we need a politics of cure.' But, they continue, cure is problematically defined 'as "the restoration of health". In developing a politics of cure based on this definition, it would be too easy to get mired in an argument about health trying to determine who's healthy and who's not, as if there's one objective standard'.[12] Following Clare's cautionary tale, we need to think about planetary health – as the interconnection between environmental health, human health, health of water ways, air ways, flight ways and so on – holistically and critically in terms of the full eco-socio-political mess we are in. Being healthy can and should mean much more than just being a productive neoliberal employee.

In the context of understanding the body's healthy boundaries in relation to weather via thermoregulatory physiology and rethinking health from Clare's provocation, the concept of weathering can help guide planetary health research and community development design in several ways. Firstly, given erosion is an entropic process, this can be thought of as an analogy to being alive, growing up and aging; weathering recognizes bodily growth, change and decline, sickness and health, scars, neurodiversities, transitions in identity through mind and body; in this regard, understanding health as the collective practice of weathering well, or better, together is neither an edenic fantasy of paradise restored nor a dream of immortality, but something that connects us to trying to improve our experience of life's variations, the messy liveliness of being animal.[13] Second, weathering allows us to comprehend the fact that ecological harms, from the planet's polar ice caps melting to cellular mutations in a single body, might not be curable in absolute terms. We can slow warming, and try to reverse cell damage. We can, for more examples, remediate damaged landscapes, regenerate bushland and, restore riverine health, to some extent. We can heal certain illnesses with medicines, diet, rest and exercise. But some things we just cannot fix. The presence of radioactive isotopes, 'forever chemicals' and microplastics cannot be undone; we will not be able to re-freeze the missing ice from the polar winters any time soon. While some injuries and illnesses are reversible, others are irreversible, degenerative or terminal. The scars of modernity are deep into the planet; they will remain in us and in the earth forever. This is what we refer to as the Anthropocene.[14] So how can we accept the limits of what we can achieve in terms of healing, while also holistically improving human and environmental health? Beyond understanding genetic predispositions and engaging in lifestyle hacks, what are the eco-political and economic causes of good and bad human health?

Weathering is a useful concept to guide this kind of systems thinking too because it is focussed on varied and durational processes of how weather and bodies relate. As we showed in Chapter 3, Black feminists Audre Lorde, Claudia Rankine, Christina Sharpe and Sara Ahmed all use 'weather' in distinct ways to describe the embodied experience of racism and socio-political marginalization; public health scholar Arline Geronimus has already undertaken extensive epidemiological research into the long-term socio-economic causes of poor human health and described it as a kind of 'weathering'.[15] There are also other established traditions of healthcare that are focussed on connections between bodies and ecosocial systems, including holistic Indigenous healthcare services, the Black feminist 'healing justice' tradition and Traditional Chinese Medicine (TCM). Given the context of all this established work focussing on health, weather, weathering, environmental systems and social justice, connecting the goal of our project (the redistribution of shelter and vulnerability) to weathering-informed climate and health work is actually a relatively minor next step.

That said, to pursue environmental health-related research questions that did not just reinforce the status quo, I needed to be careful about how I approached the work inside the university context as well. I could not just try to apply for a grant from a pharmaceutical company to advise them how to reduce their carbon footprint! I needed to become a scyborg, or 'reorganizer of institutional machinery'. The scyborg is 'lopsided bot [with a] queer gear'.[16] According to la paperson in *A Third University is Possible*, though we try to reorganize the machinery of the university for decolonial desires, 'scyborgs are not inherently decolonial';[17] we are not perfect or pure. Our positions of power are gifted by the colonial institution, but our work can be directed or reorganized to guide us towards true freedom and liberation. As a result, paperson suggests, 'scyborg dreams become blueprints'[18] for other ways of being. In this context, weathering acts as an ethical anchor point for this scyborg work in relation to planetary health. And the Armidale Climate and Health Project was an attempt to do that work guided by weathering.

ACHP as blueprint for small-scale planetary health work

About a year after moving to Armidale, I met Dr Sujata Allan. Allan is a doctor of medicine who works at the local Aboriginal health service, as well as a musician. She is also a climate activist, and at the time we met was a leader in the national advocacy group Doctors for Environment Australia (DEA). Allan attended the first CoWS stall (see Chapter 7) at Groundswell Festival and also the 'Weathering Everything' symposium (see Chapter 5) a few months later. Soon after that, the then Dean of Medicine and Health at my university, Professor Rod McClure, approached Allan, who was also lecturing and tutoring in the medical training programme, for ideas for local community health projects; Allan had seen my weathering work and approached me with Professor McClure's request. We started to collaborate and develop something together. We started out with huge and bold dreams for a fully sustainable and equitable environmental community centre and extreme weather shelter, but we had to wind it back into something more manageable for us both given we were already working full time.

I negotiated to use 'weathering' as a concept to help orient and guide our project design and we co-created the ACHP. Weathering was a logical lens for this work because it is a conceptual bridge between everyday embodied weather and big scale planetary climate change. It is an ideal concept to guide planetary health work on a local level because it helps hold focus on the particularities of people and place, while also being aware of the bigger picture. To do climate and health work guided by weathering meant we could not forget that we were living, breathing bodies, and the location of our bodies was on stolen Anaiwan Country. Rather than focussing on the effects of climate change alone (that we're negatively weathered by something), we can describe other ways we weather together too. We were freed from the need to think about heat stress and productivity at work, and could instead (if we wanted to) assess heat stress as a holistic issue: related to acute and chronic illness, precarious housing, intergenerational trauma, regional planning decisions, the nature of how the economy tries to manage and control humans, animals, plants, soil and water. We decided that instead of prefiguring the focus of the project for the community, we could structure the project around asking the community to join us in this process by asking a big question: how can we improve community health, respond to climate change, and centre Indigenous knowledge?

To start us off, Allan and I applied for AUD25,000 in funding from the NSW Government for the pilot. We won an 'Increasing Resilience to Climate Change Community Grant'. We were told informally at the time that it was the first climate change grant of its kind in the state to be given to a health-focussed project.[19] We proposed six workshops and a small festival to test out the ideas, build relationships, consult and educate community to seed a bigger project. We were awarded the grant in early 2020, and the pandemic radically changed the nature of the project. We pivoted from planning full day in-person workshops and began having a lot of informal one-on-one and small group conversations with local stakeholders (Indigenous leaders, sustainability advocates, academics) to build relationships and see what it was folks in the town wanted.

In spite of COVID, we also managed to hold a range of small events, before and between lockdowns; these helped seed information about climate change and health in the community. We held a project launch with speakers from the community. Uncle Steve Widders did a Welcome to Country, Callum Clayton-Dixon, co-founder of the Anaiwan language revival project, read a chapter about livestock and colonisation from his book *Surviving New England*[20] and a programme of local music acts, curated by Jhana Allan, provided atmosphere and tunes.[21] One of the first steps following the launch was to support local treaty negotiations to help provide Indigenous folks with access to Country for ceremonial and cultural healing work. A collective of Anaiwan folks decided to move the idea a step beyond treaty and initiated a Landback fundraising campaign. It was a huge success and a collective purchased 600 acres of Country for community use. We supported this through advocacy and amplification in the small ways we could considering it intimately connected with the Armidale Climate and Health Project.[22] In lieu of a specific climate and health festival, we facilitated Sustainable Living Armidale's established event 'the Home Grown Garden Tour'. We did this in 2022 and 2024. In 2022 it included a Welcome to Country and the local Indigenous community garden for the first time. In a more day-to-day and business-oriented sense, Sujata held a workshop on how to run a sustainable healthcare practice (including information about the health impacts of climate change that are starting to show up in the clinic and best clinical practices to reduce power use and medical waste). We held a creek walk to coincide with the COP26 summit, which was structured around Indigenous water sovereignty and climate adaptation. This event included a symbolic 'water back' activity where each participant filled a jar full of water from the University's large irrigation dam, Lake Zot, and returned it to the creek to allow it flow through Country again. Our biggest event was an 'Open Day' at the Aboriginal Cultural Centre and Keeping Place. The event's main goal was awareness raising, relationship building and knowledge sharing. We provided a free lunch, music, walks around the creeklands and community gardens, and talks to seed thinking in the community about the connections between climate adaptation, human health and Indigenous knowledge.

The design of all the in-person events was guided by the ethos of 'Community Housework' (outlined in Inset H), where we were trying to create the kind of community conviviality that we think could contribute to better health for people and planet. This meant providing simple healthy food, minimizing waste, offering music and outdoor activities, while creating a safe and inclusive atmosphere that allowed for togetherness in difference, alongside any information dissemination or exchange. Although the whole project was supposed to be done and dusted in twelve months, it spilled out over three years because of COVID.

In organizing all these formal and informal conversations and events around the central question (as noted above: how can we improve community health, respond to climate change, and centre Indigenous knowledge?), we were slowly led towards understanding that the nature of land and water was central to both human and planetary health. In an agricultural region, this largely relates to how food is produced, and the question of how we could

Field Report: Downscaling Planetary Health

Figure 8.1 The Armidale Climate and Health Project Open Day at the Aboriginal Cultural Centre and Keeping Place, Anaiwan Country, May 15, 2021. The Creek Walk was led by Uncle Steve Widders. Photograph: Stephen Tafra.

produce and consume food in a different way for the health of people and planet. The responses we got from Indigenous folks and non-Indigenous folks were in some ways complementary, albeit different in nuanced and politically complicated ways.

In chatting informally to Indigenous Elders, emerging leaders and reading around on the topic of planetary health in relation to Indigenous communities, a repeated message emerged: to heal people and planet, Indigenous people needed free access to Country. In the colony, property law dominates the governance of land and waterways, which in and around Armidale are mostly fenced off, as discussed in Chapter 7, for the farming of cows and other agribusinesses. In a podcast yarn with local Anaiwan Elder Uncle Steve Widders,[23] he describes the reciprocal and intergenerational relationships between people and place as central to Indigenous ways of being; it thus follows that the increased ability to heal places through accessing different parts of Country currently fenced off for colonial enterprises, would also in time heal people. He reminded us that 'Heal Country Heal People' was also the theme of the national Indigenous week-long survival celebration 'NAIDOC week' in 2021; this message was neither secret nor hidden, but it was just difficult to enact against the colonial laws that enclose and exploit the land and water and do not have an ethos of respect and reciprocity.

Conversations with non-Indigenous folks on the same question unfolded along slightly different lines, but with similar implications and important differences. With human geographer Dr Nicolette Larder, I undertook some research we called 'Unearthing Armidale's Diverse Food Economy'[24] as part of the ACHP. The aim was to get a snapshot of what small-scale food growing and provision practices were happening in the area and link it to the primary question of the ACHP project. In the focus groups, non-Indigenous people told us that local food-growing networks and community gardening can help foster grassroots planetary health: community gardens are sites where people are outside, hands in the soil, making the planet healthier while their own physical and mental health benefits from both the active lifestyle and fresh food, for example.

The difference between my yarn with Uncle Steve and the conversations in these focus groups was the relation with settler colonialism and perspectives on Land or Country. We asked participants in the non-Indigenous focus groups about whether they address the Indigenous history of place in their various community gardening, soil health, food advocacy or small-scale agriculture/food provisioning practices and enterprises. The answers mostly revealed a lack of strong and intentional connection between non-Indigenous local growing and anticolonial politics,[25] but once we had asked the question there was an active and open-ended interest in trying to learn about how to make these connections stronger to repair colonial harms to people and place in their work.[26] Though the responses from Uncle Steve and the focus groups are different in political and material ways, especially when it comes to anticolonial politics, they share a strong desire to do community work that is actively involved in healing people and planet simultaneously and on a small community scale.

One of the challenges of seeing health as *planetary* is the fact that we most commonly think about health in relation to the individual; or if we think about environmental health it seems too vast to be relevant to an individual. But solutions to problems require simultaneous action on different scales. The powers that be (international organizations, non-governmental organizations and nations) cannot solve the planet's health problems at the scale of large institutions and associated policies. Nor can we solve all of Armidale's health problems locally because we are part of a global system. But we can and need to contribute to the effort by attending to the specificities of a place and its people and thinking about how we could contribute something small to improving the health of the community. A policy or strategy made at an international level by the UN or a big multinational corporation would be hard (if not undesirable) to implement in a place like Armidale, because self-determination and local forms of agency are important. What the ACHP seeks to instil in the community is that reconnecting with the specifics of place and caring for it and each other is vital for cultivating both human and environmental health. Recognizing the centrality of human connection to place for planetary health offers a way to address planetary health issues at a community scale in the short term. How to do this and also centre Indigenous knowledge? That final aspect of our question remains very much a work in progress.

Conclusions: Guiding planetary health work towards queer, feminist and anticolonial futures

In the memoir *Personal Score,* Indigenous writer Ellen van Neerven fantasizes about their dream healthcare service. They say this: 'queer health services – often white by design – sit awkwardly next to heteronormative Aboriginal health services. There is potential between these two to have the magical, culturally informed, queer AF care that we don't have yet in this country.'[27] The ACHP is not so rigorously culturally informed such that it always does anticolonial work well, nor is the project exactly 'queer AF'. But van Neerven's dream touches on the more ambitious intentions of the ACHP that were not necessarily realized, but remain open-ended possibilities, stemming from the project. Is there real potential for weathering to guide queer, feminist and anticolonial work in the planetary health space? What if in future we pushed this work further towards something really impactful and grounded in anticolonial and queer feminist principles because of how weathering draws attention to the specificity and complexity of how people weather together in place and over time? How far could we go, as non-Indigenous people, and where would we be able to go in and for the Armidale community? And how could this inform work elsewhere? It is possible to imagine such things: for example, community dinners using sustainably grown produce remake kith and kinship structures and proceeds could go to 'paying the rent'[28] and supporting queer AF Indigenous health services.

We can also look to other kinds of initiatives to assist in building more alliances along these lines. The annual Winter Blooming Festival at the New England Regional Art Museum (NERAM) provides a provisional model for responding to these questions, even if it doesn't really address the environmental health piece. It brings together First Nations, queer and multicultural community in one space. The festival even contributed a little bit of money to the ACHP launch event in 2021 because the project was in the spirit of the festival (and that year the festival had to be cancelled due to COVID). Led by curators Dr Christina Kenny and Rachel Parsons, the festival provides a model for how to build new intersectional alliances through careful curatorial practice. The curators have held an exhibition on queering the museum's archive, combined with workshops on sexual health, alongside a panel with the anticolonial spoken word poets Omar Sakr and Rob Waters, painting demonstrations by queer portrait painter Kim Leutwyler, and followed by a panel of queer Pacifika folks, Amao Leota Lu, Ella Ganza and Leki discussing what it means to make queer of colour community inside and against white Australia. This was all followed by a panel on gender-affirming healthcare. There is usually a queer prom and variety show event where drag performance sits alongside poetry readings with work produced during workshops at the festival, with songs shared from local folk bands where some members are queer and others are not. This festival provides a model for how to build queer feminist anticolonial alliances inside a particular community. The festival is a model for bringing health into discussions of identity, decoloniality, pleasure and play.

A model for anticolonial health care can also be found in local Aboriginal health services. When we started the ACHP, Sujata and I discussed Armajun Aboriginal Health Service's mission with the CEO and we learned that written into its plan is the desire for the clinics to be fully integrated and holistic. In practice, holistic healthcare that connects up clinical practice with caring for Country is hard to enact. In Australia one of the best examples of this kind of clinic is Waminda in Nowra, about two hours south of Sydney, which blends Western medicine with a range of cultural practices including yarning circles and decolonization workshops.[29]

In thinking about the future of all this work, I shared van Neerven's quote about the dream of decolonized and queer AF healthcare with Sujata. She understood what they were talking about – that heteronormative values that dominate the Indigenous community, alongside the Western medical model of gender-affirming care sanctioned in clinics is such because that is the world in which we live. That said, although the perfect system might not have been realized, at least in a clinic founded on holistic care principles, all the balls are up in the air. The hardest step of all really is to connect all these things and keep all the balls up in the air – the desire for queer AF healthcare, the urgency of some health conditions and the need for decolonization – alongside the larger scale, slower, longer term ecological work.

But it is all the process, it is all weathering. We are always weathering. If we can't finish this work today, we can keep doing it tomorrow. During the space, time and intentionality created by the ACHP project phase one, other temporalities started to open up. Some community workers were inspired to think outside the box about how rehab programs could blend caring for Country in ways that contribute to human and environmental health with some support workers at least floating ideas of native bush regeneration projects for those trying to heal from addiction. So many possibilities emerge when a little time and space is given for thinking things through differently. Often community health services are under-resourced and need more people to do the work, so designing and seeking grants for targeted programs that activate planetary healthcare guided by feminist, queer and anticolonial principles is surely one way forward. The main thing is setting the intention of the planetary health project in a way that the project design moves *towards* the world you want to build – a queer feminist and anticolonial one – rather than away from it.

Notes

1. Lauren Berlant, 'The Commons: Infrastructures for Troubling Times*', *Environment and Planning D: Society and Space* 34, no. 3 (2016): 393–419, https://doi.org/10.1177/0263775816645989, 394.

2. Castañeda et al. trace the genealogy of the two terms: 'The One Health approach, historically focused on zoonoses, initiated and led by the veterinary and disease ecology communities', while 'Planetary health is a younger concept proposed in 2015 by The Rockefeller Foundation–*Lancet* Commission, coinciding with the launch of the UN Sustainable Development Goals'. Rafael Ruiz de Castañeda et al., 'One Health and Planetary Health Research: Leveraging Differences to Grow Together', *The Lancet Planetary Health* 7, no. 2 (1 February 2023): 109–11.

3. Dawn Hoogeveen et al., 'On The Possibility of Decolonising Planetary Health: Exploring New Geographies for Collaboration', *The Lancet Planetary Health* 7, no. 2 (2023): e179–e183; Nicole Redvers et al., 'The Determinants of Planetary Health: An Indigenous Consensus Perspective', *The Lancet Planetary Health* 6, no. 2 (2022): e156–e163.

4. Lauren E. Van Patter et al., 'What does One Health want? Feminist, posthuman, and anticolonial possibilities', *One Health Outlook* 5, no. 1 (2023): 4.

5. There were two key events: A Sydney Ideas Panel 'Hot in the City: Climate and Health in Urban Environments' in April 2017 and a one-day workshop at the Charles Perkins Centre 'Hot in the City: A systems approach to thermal stress, energy and health in our urban environments' in July 2018.

6. Ollie Jay et al., 'Fanning as an Alternative to Air Conditioning – A Sustainable Solution for Reducing Indoor Occupational Heat Stress', *Energy and Buildings* 193 (2019), 92–8; Ollie Jay et al. 'Reducing the Health Effects of Hot Weather and Heat Extremes: From Personal Cooling Strategies to Green Cities', *The Lancet* 398.10301 (2021): 709–24, https://doi.org/10.1016/S0140-6736(21)01209-5.

7. Eric Klinenberg, *Heat Wave: A Social Autopsy of Disaster in Chicago* (Chicago, IL: University of Chicago Press, 2015).

8. Other research that explores this point is Sam Bloch, 'Shade', *Places Journal* (2019); Abby Mellick Lopes et al., *Cooling the Commons: Pilot Research Report* (2016).

9. Ollie Jay et al., 'Fanning as an Alternative to Air Conditioning – A Sustainable Solution for Reducing Indoor Occupational Heat Stress', 716.

10. At time of writing, the West Australian Council of Social Services has a 'Heat Vulnerability Project' that maps exposures and seeks to develop programmes to mitigate heat stress in a more holistic sense. For emerging research on this, see Petra Tschakert and Krishna Karthikeyan, 'Embodied Thermal Insecurity and Counter-Hegemonic Heat Mapping', *Antipode* 57, no. 1 (2025): 433–54, https://doi.org/10.1111/anti.13113.

11. See, for example, Terri-Leigh Aldred et al., 'Mining Sick: Creatively Unsettling Normative Narratives about Industry, Environment, Extraction, and the Health Geographies of Rural, Remote, Northern, and Indigenous Communities in British Columbia', *Canadian Geographies* 65, no. 1 (2021): 82–96; Pasley et al., 'Transnormativities: Reterritorializing Perceptions and Practice', *Rethinking Transgender Identities*, ed. Petra L. Doan and Lynda Johnston (London: Routledge, 2022); Sarah Jaquette Ray and Jay Sibara, *Disability Studies and the Environmental Humanities: Toward an Eco-Crip Theory* (Lincoln, NE: University of Nebraska Press, 2017); and Aimi Hamraie, '(Ir)resistible Stairs: Public Health, Desiring Practices, and Material-Symbolic Ableism', *Journal of Architectural Education* 76, no. 1 (2023): 49–59.

12. Eli Clare, *Brilliant Imperfection: Grappling with Cure* (Durham, NC: Duke University Press, 2017), 206.

13. There is a lot of work to be done to open up to this idea emotionally as well. For an interrogation of the affective challenges of opening to life and death, see Jennifer Hamilton, 'Affect Theory and Breast Cancer Memoirs: Rescripting Fears of Death and Dying in the Anthropocene', *Body & Society* 27, no. 4 (2021): 3–29.

14. The public lecture given by Jan Zalasiewicz, 'The Anthropocene as a potential new unit of the Geological Time Scale' (2014), at the inaugural Sydney Environment Institute symposium is a very clear description of the materiality

15. Arline T. Geronimus, *Weathering: The Extraordinary Stress of Ordinary Life in an Unjust Society*, 1st edn (New York: Little, Brown Spark, 2023).
16. la paperson. *A Third University Is Possible* (Minneapolis, MN: University of Minnesota Press, 2020), https://manifold.umn.edu/projects/a-third-university-is-possible, 55.
17. paperson, *A Third University Is Possible*, 70.
18. paperson, *A Third University Is Possible*, 70.
19. For our summative reflections on the project for the grant provider, see 'Home Grown Climate Resilience', https://www.climatechange.environment.nsw.gov.au/stories-and-case-studies/home-grown-climate-resilience (accessed 3 November 2024); we are not at a place where the term 'weathering' can replace resilience in a government grant context just yet.
20. Callum Clayton-Dixon, *Surviving New England: A History of Aboriginal Resistance and Resilience Through the First Forty Years of the Colonial Apocalypse*. (Anaiwan Country: Newara Aboriginal Corporation, 2019).
21. The project and all the events and the ongoing developments are archived at https://armidaleclimateandhealth.com.au/.
22. We wrote about our support for landback as part of the ACHP for *Overland* (see Sujata Allan and Jennifer Hamilton, 'On Property Prices, Colonisation and Climate Change', *Overland literary journal*, 30 March 2022, https://overland.org.au/2022/03/on-property-prices-colonisation-and-climate-change/). But the project was so much bigger and reached the national news; see Tom Plevey, '"On Our Own Terms": Anaiwan People Look to Buy 240 Hectares of Bushland to Reclaim Country', *The Guardian*, 22 February 2022, sec. Australia news, https://www.theguardian.com/australia-news/2022/feb/23/on-our-own-terms-anaiwan-people-look-to-buy-240-hectares-of-bushland-to-reclaim-country.
23. Uncle Steve Widders and Jennifer Hamilton, 'Anaiwan Elder Uncle Steve Widders chats about climate change and colonisation', Nicole Curby (audio editor), https://soundcloud.com/weatheringstation/steve-widders-and-jen-hamilton (accessed 31 October 2024).
24. Research approved by the Human Research Ethics Committee at the University of New England, HR21-128.
25. This aligns with the findings in Christopher Mayes' *Unsettling Food Politics: Agriculture, Dispossession and Sovereignty in Australia* (London: Rowman & Littlefield Publishing, 2018); but organizations like the Australian Food Sovereignty Alliance are seeking to change this. See https://afsa.org.au/.
26. Focus group responses led to Nicolette and myself devising 'Food School', which is a pedagogical method for thinking about making time to grow food in the current economy while also learning about and integrating anticolonial

practices into sustainable food growing. Jennifer Mae Hamilton and Nicolette Larder, 'Making Time to Care Differently for Food: The Case for the Armidale Food School', *Critical Studies in Teaching and Learning* 10, no. SI (2022), https://doi.org/10.14426/cristal.v10iSI.1806.

27. Ellen van Neerven, *Personal Score: Sport, Culture, Identity* (St Lucia: University of Queensland Press, 2023), 206.

28. 'Pay the Rent' is a concept in wide circulation in Australia. It is an official charity name but also it is a collection of diverse and informal economic practices that involve non-Indigenous people paying financial reparations to Indigenous people for living on Country. The official 'Pay the Rent' charity (https://paytherent.net.au/) can take tax-deductible donations and has an Indigenous-led process of grant-making; some organizations, individuals and businesses will design their own 'paying the rent' strategy, from one-off donations, to a percentage of profits or sales, to something more like a tithe. These might be to different Indigenous organizations and causes. An individual might think of private donations to Indigenous organizations and causes as a practice of paying the rent.

29. Waminda's website is https://waminda.org.au/ (accessed 24 October 2024).

walkshop

INSET I

A walkshop is a mobile workshop, as bodies move through time and space together. Riffing on Ursula Le Guin, the whole event is like a carrier bag: it holds things, and holds things in relation. Your main task as the organizer, is to hold things together well, as a way to redistribute vulnerability and shelter. How can you provide an opportunity for participants to be in relation to themselves, each other, and the place? Walkshopping is weathering together! When you care for your participants' comfort, you support them through small moments of discomfort: they can open to new relations, new ideas, new journeys.

How to play

1. Whose land are you walking on? How will you honour and acknowledge that?

2. What do different bodies need? Support comfort with information and preparation.

3. Decide whether this walkshop will be:

loose & open-ended:
> People gather at a specific place at a specific time and are given a simple instruction (see below for examples). Close the walkshop at a specific time and place with collective conversation and refreshments.

or

a durational participatory & multiply-facilitated event:
> Each stop is activated with low-stakes tasks by a guest facilitator.
(examples overleaf)

- Slow your body down to the pace of the flowing river: walk the tide out.
- Notice what surprising forms of shelter are revealed along the way: who or what provides shelter for whom?
- Follow the clouds.

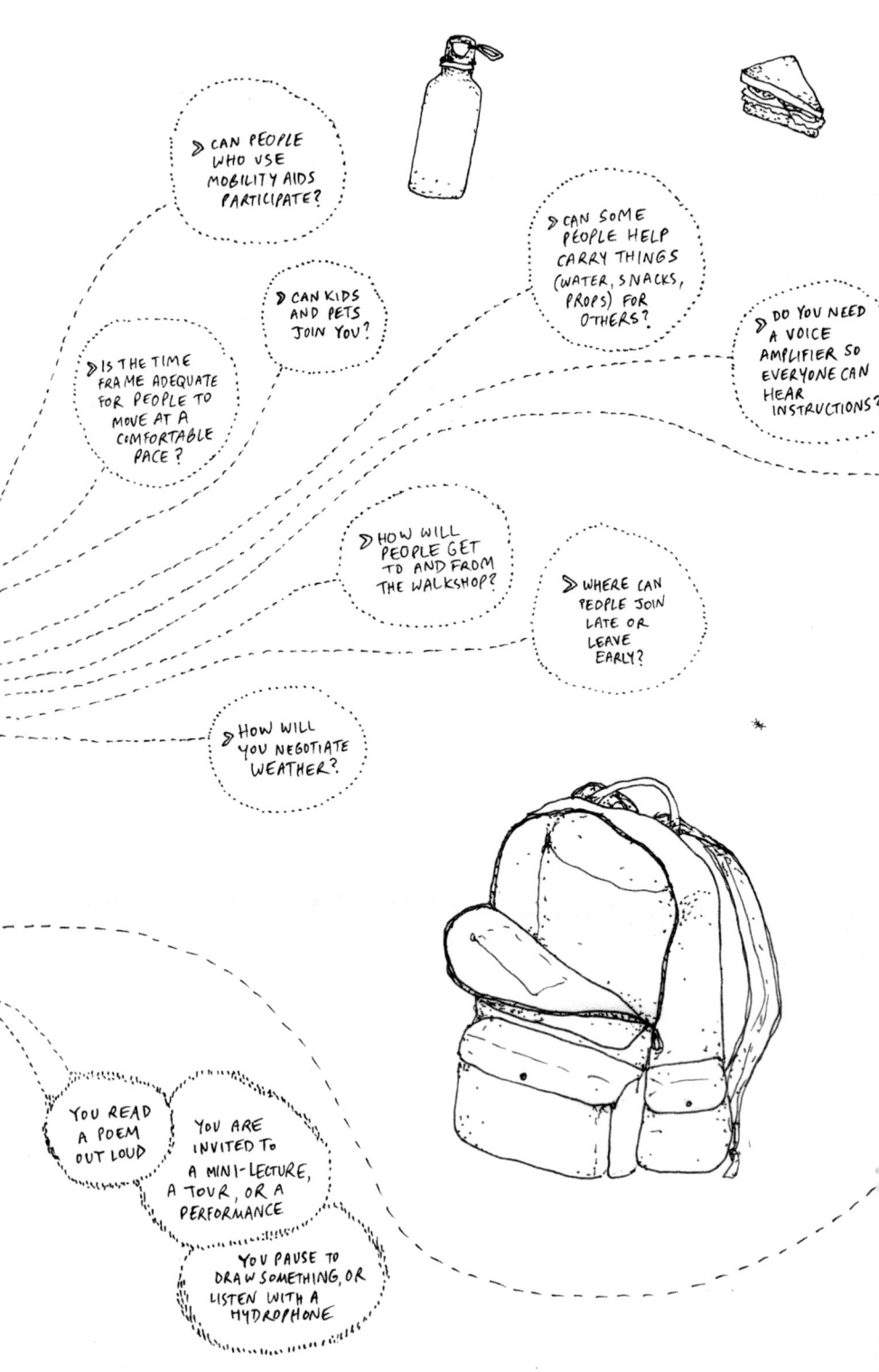

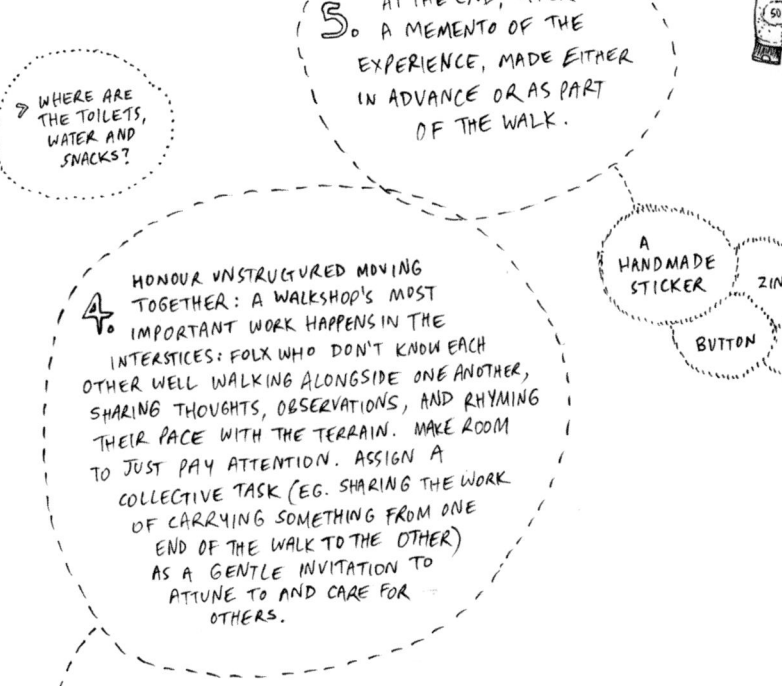

CHAPTER 9
Field report: Walking in the fringes (Astrida)

Introduction: Weather fronts and fringe natures

A weather front is the dividing line between air masses of varying densities, temperatures, or humidity contents. When these air masses meet, unstable weather emerges in the contact zone. Cold fronts might bring thunderstorms, and warm fronts can bring fog. Other fronts bring a palpable shift in the wind.

Something like this is described by Walpiri Elder Professor Wanta Patrick as 'Milpirri', where 'the hot air rising and cold air falling [...] makes the thunderhead or ceremony cloud so full of rage and lightning thrashing; a cumulonimbus cloud that is full of fury'. Wanta Patrick further describes Milpirri as 'really a metaphor for bringing Kardiya [Aboriginal people, human beings] and Yapa [non-Aboriginal people] together'. It is:

> ... the moment where these two different knowledges clash: 'how can you understand me, you are so different?' These two, the cold air and the hot air, are trying to adjust to each other, and it isn't easy. When the hot air rises, and cold air falls, it's about adjusting to one another; a disagreement then an agreement after. But after the big storm, when the hot air and cold air meet, after it settles down, that's when it gives birth to this cloud called Milpirri. Then we can recognise the ground-up duty of care, a responsibility for the country's knowledge.[1]

Elder Wanta Patrick offers many opportunities – in film, talks and writings, but primarily through cultural festivals – for us 'Yapa' to learn about Milpirri. Our knowledge of Milpirri is just nascent, barely born in fact. But Elder Wanta Patrick's discussion of weather fronts catches my attention: a moving line, where different weathers meet, and something changes. This is a way to understand weather as always part of Country expressing itself, and a way to think about weathering difference.

Things happen along edges and moving lines, where different bodies assemble. Things happen at the edges. A weather front is like an ecotone (the transitional area between two different ecological communities) and also like a littoral zone (the zone of freshwater closest to the lakeshore or riverbank, or the intertidal zone that buffers land and sea). The edgiest part of the littoral zone – where water and land socialize and have to come to terms with one another – is sometimes called the fringe.

This chapter is about what happens along moving lines, like weather fronts, in fringey zones where difference moves and mingles. It is specifically about the weathering methodology called walkshopping, and describes some of the walkshops that we've organized as part of our weathering work (not always under the auspices of the Weathering Collective). I have come to understand walkshops – like a workshop, but on the move – as a kind of moving line and contact zone. In the fringes and along the margins, walkshops activate a border, and are themselves a border zone: a mobile infrastructure as opportunity for careful contact and exchange. Walkshops as moving lines are sticky; they collect things and hold them for a while, hanging on the line, until things move again. Something different emerges from these ephemeral rearrangings.

There is a long tradition of walking as a way of understanding Country, or Land, or the more-than-human places we are a part of, from the since-time-immemorial songlines of Aboriginal people, to contemporary artists who use walking as methodology.[2] Walking is sensory and participatory, and can activate a meditative or reflective way of being: bodies take on a rhythm, and respond to what they encounter. Collectively, bodies attune to place. We briefly describe walkshopping in Inset I as a mobile workshop. Bodies move through time and space together, held temporarily by the route.

Walkshops take many forms: students walk through campus as a way of noticing architectures and ecologies that tell stories about who belongs here and who doesn't; or neighbours move across bushland, looking for traces of geologic strata as a way of feeling the land's timescale beyond human history. Walkshops can be a kind of dérive – a concept coined by situationist Guy Debord that means drifting, yourself be pulled by whatever grabs your attention.[3] Or they can be tightly planned and choreographed – for example, unfolding along a set route where Elders, artists, scientists and engineers offer activities or teachings at different stops along the way. In all of these examples, ephemeral groups of people are held together along and as a moving line, and place is an active participant. Riffing on feminist speculative fiction writer Ursula Le Guin's concept of the carrier bag that she describes as 'holding things in relation',[4] I think a moving line can be a kind of carrier bag. For a specific time, it holds bodies and Country in relation. Walkshopping is weathering together.

As weathering methodology, walkshops are holding containers. First, they are a kind of micro-commons, or a social infrastructure for (in Lauren Berlant's words) 'managing the meanwhile'. Infrastructures, according to Berlant, are 'relational and ecological processes of sustaining worlds'[5] determined by movement. Infrastructures, of course, are not just pipes and wires; they are social forms of being in the world. The folks held together temporarily by the walk's structure may not have anything in common but the time and space they are sharing. Jen and I are curious about what can happen when people arrive, in all of their difference, and are given the opportunity to bump up against each other for a while. Stranger intimacy, as Berlant teaches us, can be a bit awkward and 'glitchy', but walkshops can serve as a 'training' in glitchy ambivalence.[6]

One of the great things about walkshops is the way mobility – moving through space together – lets that awkward glitchiness work itself out, at least partially. A walkshop is a moving line but it is never a precise and perfect one. It is a bit mumbled and jumbled. One body slows down, and others bunch up in the back. A couple of bodies veer off to pet a cat, or use the toilet, and rejoin in a new formation. This pattern without predictability (like weather) means that moving alongside others is mostly about giving yourself over to the agency of the moving line itself.

Moreover, as a social infrastructure that rearranges difference into a new relation, walkshopping is specifically in place. We walk with each other but also with the gravel and the drainage ditch and the pelicans and the traffic and the pollen in the air. Elder Wanta Patrick's teaching on Milpirri is powerful because not only does it remind us that difference becomes something else, even temporarily, along the line, but also because Milpirri is always about how Country – the relationships between everything – shows itself. Both a walkshop and a weather front are about working things out in *emplaced* relation. Our bodies meet at and as weather fronts, moving along, moving through, and moving with Country (Land) in all of its present manifestations and challenges (human and non-human creatures, stories, rocks and waterways, but also social atmospheres, pollution and garbage, concrete structures, and so on).

When we pay attention to the specificity of place, we note that fringes are the frayed edges of what is categorizable or securely knowable (where does land end and water begin?). Fringey zones sometimes require that we change our habits and learn something new. Think about the littoral zone of a lake or river, between water and land. Neither is 'contained by its shoreline', and the shorelines themselves 'seep around underground, hidden or revealed through relations to other entities'.[7] This inherent border curiosity of watery bodies is repressed when settler imaginaries insist that these bodies be securely contained and separated. In the context of climate change, infrastructural restrictions like dykes and levees that try to enforce the binarization of land and water, increasingly cease to perform the function for which they were engineered: they seep and break, as containment mechanisms fail to contain. (We discuss this kind of climate change mitigation 'big infrastructure' in Chapter 4).

Ecologically speaking, ecotones and littoral fringes have high levels of biodiversity. These transitional spaces are lively, always pushing boundaries a bit this way or that. Fringes in littoral zones are also characterized by 'submerged, floating, or emergent vegetation'.[8] These place-specifics resonate in a particular way with queer feminist sensibility, as I am also interested in what happens in the fringe, or in the margins. Fringe natures inspire us to ask about which voices are submerged or marginalized, but also emergent. This is like what Macarena Gomez-Barris calls the 'submerged perspectives' of the colonial Anthropocene.[9] Queer feminism (and the field of queer ecologies) is also interested in practices that play with and within these contact zones, challenging the fixities of borders, and opening to new habits that can be learned within the churn.

As a queer feminist, I am also increasingly learning from trans ecologies about how to live in the transition times and spaces of climate change. Think about the round goby, a fish who changes gender in response to polluted and climate-changed waters. Many other species change genders because of changes in their environments: male ginkgo trees learn to make fruits when urban planners take away the messy and leaky female trees; four-wing saltbush plants change gender after stressful weather events, like cold temperatures and drought.[10] Learning with and from trans experience, trans feminisms open up the possibility of gender abundance as a climate change mitigation strategy. This insight also reminds us that climate change and rising anti-2SLGBTQ climates can and should be thought (and acted on) together. Trans ecologies also incite the curiosity to ask: How can feminism transition in response to climate change?

I am also learning a lot from trans studies about mobility within and as transition zones. Susan Stryker points out that 'trans' means 'movement across' rather than 'any particular destination'.[11] Transitioning, or transing, means being curious about borders – not necessarily rejecting them. Trans ecological research shows that non-human worlds are and have always been home to transitioning – moving, changing, shifting. Transing is not pathological, but entirely common, and 'natural'.[12] It always happens in relation to other bodies, and in ways that reconfigure how those bodies fit together, in place and in time. Cleo Wölfle Hazard cites the work of another trans ecological theorist, Eva Hayward, who asserts that there is a 'vertiginous joy at being unable either to turn back or to continue as before; new ways, transways, transselves are required of us here'.[13] In Hayward's words, 'to be *trans-* is to be transcending or surpassing particular impositions' (italics in original).[14] Trans ecologies teach us about moving differently.

This all helps us think about walkshops as this kind of fringey movement. Even if a walkshop proceeds through the dead-centre of a town, field or park, our bodies enact a fringe by cleaving two sides or two aspects of any place or time: a walkshop's movement is always what trans feminist theorist Karen Barad would call 'cutting-together'.[15] Cleaving, similarly, is a transy kind of word that means both drawing together and pulling apart.

FEELed Lab's Fringe Natures

These conceptual frames – mobile and emplaced social infrastructures that activate transitional fringes – may sound rather clever, as though I've always had this grand theory about what walking together through place might mean as a weathering methodology. But in reality, the theory has emerged mostly after organizing many walkshops. The practice came first, and then continued to unfurl alongside the concepts. The practice taught me that weathering together can be practised by clumping around a moving line and finding a way through.

When the FEELed Lab started to emerge as an idea in 2021, one of the first things I did was organize a walkshop. First of all, it was still mid-pandemic, and walking together outside is COVID-safer. It meant many of us could literally breathe more easily, as the virus still floated around us. Walking also removed some of the awkwardness that goes along with sitting in a room together, where unfamiliarity can make us insecure, avoiding eye contact, staying quiet or (alternatively) babbling a lot. All of this is fine, of course, but a walkshop can take the edge off. Moving side by side, we can risk saying something more personal, or more tentative (this is also the technique I use for having awkward conversations with my kids! A car ride is another great micro-infrastructure in this respect.)

In conversation with FEELed Lab Research Associate, Madeline Donald, we came up with the idea to call our first walkshop 'Fringe Natures'. As described above, this is a play on the littoral space that we would be walking along. Indeed, many of the places we work in Kelowna exist at the interface of very dry, drought-prone land, its precious creeks and wetlands, and the glacial river system that cleaves these lands right down the middle as kłúsx̌nítkʷ, or Lake Okanagan. 'Fringe Natures' then became the name of the Lab's outdoor event series that takes place in literal littoral zones and other transition times and spaces: marking seasonal change, or the transition from night to day. But the name 'Fringe Natures' was also a nod to my own position as a queer feminist environmental researcher in an unfamiliar city known for its conservatism (see also Jen's description of her arrival in Armidale in Chapter 7). I have learned it is good to work in the margins. You can do weird things under the radar. But the fringes can be lonely, and I was looking for some company.

This first walkshop was super low-stakes. I printed out parts of a poem by Alexis Pauline Gumbs called 'In Case You Wanted to Save the Planet' onto a series of index cards, and collated them into a packet for each participant. About ten of us met (mostly for the first time) on a drizzly afternoon near campus, and walked a brief distance along the paved bike path north from Carney Pond. At periodic stops, one of us read out part of the poem, using my portable amplifier to make sure everyone could hear clearly. Between readings, we walked and chatted. We offered thermoses of hot tea and snacks at the end. That was it! This was the beginning of the FEELed Lab. A number of participants at that walk continued to frequent FEELed Lab events, and one participant, Dani, became our FEELed Lab Administrator – a role she kept for two and half years.

These simple ingredients – fresh air, low-stakes, attention to mobility access, simple activity that allows space and time for conversation, refreshments – are all key elements of walkshops that Jen and I had been participating in and organizing for many years. In the rest of this chapter, I describe some additional walkshops we've developed in the past decade, together and apart. Each example offers specific practices and lessons that are transferable elsewhere.

'Going Underground'

One of the first significant walkshops I organized, together with Perth-based artist Perdita (Perdy) Phillips, was mostly a 'trainshop'. We were joined by thirty-five artists, academics, scientists and activists (including Jen) in

December 2017 at Central Station in Sydney to board a train to Lithgow, three hours due west. Once in Lithgow, we continued by foot to the State Mine Heritage Park and Railway four kilometres away, before retracing our tracks. This event is a good example of how some of our weathering concepts emerged in practice.

The event was called 'Going Underground' because we were exploring our own implication in extraction (mining) and groundwater issues.[16] We began by travelling fast, thanks to fossil fuel, into the heart of coal country. After disembarking in Lithgow, we walked to a nearby park to join Wiradjuri Elder Aunty Helen Riley and learn more about her Country before and since the Lithgow coal seam came to dominate the region's economy and culture. We then continued on to 'Blast Furnace Park', past a two-storey-high slag heap and the now-decommissioned coal furnace for which the park is named. At the park's far end, we stopped at Lake Pillans, an engineered and now contaminated lake that once provided cooling technology for the blast furnace. We noticed that the lake nonetheless still offers respite for fish, birds and algae. Guided by visual artist Louise Boscacci, we did some lakeside sketching using text fragments to help us attune to place. Leaving Lake Pillans, we walked silently, as instructed by Perdy, to the State Mine and Heritage Park museum, trying to pay attention to what we could hear, and what we could not.

Walkshops often use these kinds of practice-led weathering methods to bring climate change and environmental degradation down to the scale of embodied experience. But groundwater, filtering through karst systems and layers of shale, exists mostly beyond our direct sensory experience. We cannot walk through it, or with it, in any conventional way. This is where the weathering tactic of 'embodied extrospection' comes in: we speculate about what we *don't* know by tapping into what we *can* know, and extend our (sensory, embodied, storied) selves via processes of rigorous imagination[17] as a kind of practice-led hypothesizing (we discuss this more in the Epilogue: Cosmic Weathering). For example, we wondered: if we can hear the water in the creek under the bridge, can we also attune to all the water we cannot see? Or, can we connect the thirst of our bodies walking through this water-poor regional town on a hot summer's day to the thirst of the subterranean realm, as aquifer levels fall lower and lower because of extraction?

To assist our imaginations to become more rigorous – extending beyond what our bodies can directly sense – our trainshop began with three mini-lectures. Settling into our purple upholstered seats as we headed up to the Blue Mountains, we learned about subterranean watery geographies and dreams, coal-affected communities in regional NSW, and stygofauna – endearingly described by Dr Bill Humphreys as 'blind white cockroaches which get in the way of mines'.[18] Each talk gave us access to groundwater in a different way, thus activating and extending our sensory attunement as we walked through coal country.

Being social with strangers is an exposure. Stranger intimacy is potentially transformative; it might encourage us to reach more readily towards others. But it is also risky; we might feel vulnerable and want to withdraw. This is why walkshopping takes seriously Berlant's point that queer feminist infrastructures, like walkshops, can also be a way to 'hold' this vulnerability.[19] As walkshop organizers, we take on this holding function – holding the line, so to speak. Over the years, we have come to realize that most of the work of walkshops is (like groundwater) all the stuff you cannot see but that you absolutely rely on. For example, on the trainshop, we provided train fare for everyone to ensure the event was accessible. We brought pastries, fruit and other breakfast items onto the train to ensure that everyone was fed. We supplied readings related to the train seminars in advance, but reserved the first hour of the train ride as 'quiet reading time' so everyone would feel prepared to participate in the conversation. Once in Lithgow, we stopped to fill water bottles and walked at a speed dictated by the most gently-paced body. We arranged for a coffee truck to meet us at the museum.

If we pay attention to what bodies need – nourishment, rest, time – bodies can pay more attention to walkshop things. But holding the line is also about conviviality and joy. On the return train journey, we launched into an impromptu sing-along of miners' and other labour ballads. Not all train riders (trains are still a kind of public space) wanted to hear our lectures in the morning or our songs in the afternoon, but we offered them pastries and bananas, too. Some joined in the singing! Animating these spaces with respectful-of-our-neighbours queer feminist collective learning-making-singing together is another kind of practising the redistribution of shelter and vulnerability at the heart of feminist weathering practice.

Walkshopping as weathering methodology also helps us learn to move with contradictions and ambivalences that are part of fringey and transy zones, where knowledge isn't stable, and where binaries blur. For example, an awkward moment surfaced when our knowledgeable and very helpful tour guides at the mining museum realized we weren't mining enthusiasts, but environmental feminists. (Him: 'Wait . . . you're not greenies, are you?' Us: sheepish smiles.) Nor is our relationship to groundwater without contradiction. Environmental assessments teach us that groundwater biodiversity is endangered, but these assessments are done essentially to facilitate mining![20] The things we want to protect and the things we want to protest are tangled up in uncomfortable ways. Other tensions are banal: the perimeter of the old blast furnace was closed off; we couldn't get close to it. The coffee truck didn't arrive on time. The walk took longer than expected.

Lauren Berlant refers to this as 'glitchfrastructure' – tensions that are part of any social infrastructure. But their persistence does not mean that our social infrastructure 'failed.' The commons is never an easy 'good life fantasy' of togetherness.[21] As we've discussed already in Chapter 4, Berlant is interested in a concept of commons that is 'derived from scenes of ambivalence,'[22] where glitchy and awkward tensions are part of the scene. Our scene was the past and present and future of Wiradjuri Country since settlers learned how the coal seam could be exploited. While difficult, we have to try not to turn away from this scene, or 'homogenize the world as disaster.'[23] Instead, we have to figure out what being together in the mess might push us to become, and how it might push us to relate. This is weathering!

This also brings us back to weather fronts: Elder Wanta Patrick's idea of Milpirri is a tense contact zone, but it also makes new relations. Change can emerge from this mess of things, where different weathers meet. Walkshopping as weathering brings us, ephemerally and temporarily, together with those with whom we don't always align, and those against whose views and practices we might even struggle. Staying apart in order to avoid these tensions is, as Berlant says, 'even more ridiculous and deadly.'[24]

The specific public gathered by the mobile line of the walkshop cannot be sustained. At the end of the day, we return to our niches (the university office, the art studio, the protest march, the mine). The line extends in many ways beyond the walkshop – in the postcard art that Perdy and I designed afterwards, in the new collaborations that emerged from the time on the train together, perhaps even in the conversations that the mining museum staff had with each other when 'the greenies' left. These extending lines can never be fully knowable, either. For the ephemeral timespace of the walkshop, though, we tasted what it meant to be 'moving towards each other to make new forms of approach from difference and distance.'[25]

Care for the Stranded: A Shoreline Walkshop

Between Sydney, where the Weathering Collective emerged, and Western Canada, where I have landed, stretches the maw of the Pacific Ocean. This watery line joining places and times is also a holding space for other multibeing worlds. In September 2022, I organized 'Care for the Stranded: A Shoreline Walkshop' with my collaborators LA-based artist Patty Chang, and my sister, Aleksija Neimanis, a marine biologist and veterinary pathologist. We had been working together for almost two years on a project called *Learning Endings*, about scientists who provide end-of-life and death care to stranded marine mammals. The Henry Art Gallery in Seattle had just purchased one of Patty's artworks, and had approached her about a collaboration. In response we proposed a walkshop as a community-engaged performance art event that could invite the public into this research. Seattle is a port city, and many marine mammals have stranded and died on its shores. Our walk took place in one of the city's littoral zones: Lincoln Park in West Seattle, adjacent to Fauntleroy Ferry Terminal, which was the site of a humpback stranding and death in 2016.

We met participants at the edge of the park's forest on the escarpment above the sea. Ken Workman, a member of the Duwamish Tribal Council, offered us an extended welcome, reminding us that there are many ways to be stranded. Before we began walking, we gave the group three buckets full of sea water, and asked them to distribute the labour of carrying the water as we walked. The buckets were a bit heavy and awkward, but together we figured it out.

Our line stretched along a dirt path winding through the blackberries and the cedars. Maybe some of us were thinking about Ken's words while we walked, maybe some of us were thinking about the Fauntleroy humpback. Following a simple instruction inspired by Deep Listening practitioner Pauline Oliveros, we walked through one section 'as though our feet were ears'.[26] We stopped in a clearing that looked naturally like a classroom, where Aleksija and marine biologist Jessie Huggins shared a public conversation. Jessie was one of the first responders on site when the humpback stranded at the ferry terminal in 2016. 'We stayed there next to the whale putting water on it,' she told us. 'It was very calm. The breathing just sort of slowed. And then it stopped. I think it wasn't stressed because there were only a couple of us in the water. I think they know when you're trying to help.' She paused. 'I think it is calming for them. It looked at me a few times [. . .]. And it was very peaceful, and it just sort of stopped breathing.'

Carrying this story, we followed the path behind Aleksija and Jessie to where the trees parted to reveal the ocean. We arrived at a kind of portal – a wooden archway at the top of a forested trail that led down to the ocean. Two of us held the buckets as the participants passed through, dipping their hands in the seawater before descending down the path. Once on the beach, we listened to cellist Anne Bourne's hands and bow tune into the sounds of the ocean, the gulls and the wind. We placed the three buckets, along with three cloths, two cups and a few pieces of kelp, in front of the driftwood logs. As everyone settled into the scene, my sister and I knelt beside the buckets. She poured the water over my hands and washed them – not unlike the way she washes the stranded and dead marine mammals that she takes care of in her lab. Then I washed the hands of another participant, Jamie. Someone else came over, and Jamie washed their hands. We had no expectations for how this would go. Everyone was mostly silent, and attentive. Someone sitting at the back asked for one of the buckets to be brought closer to them, so they could avoid walking on the unstable pebble beach. Soon all three buckets were in use. Meanwhile, a ferry hummed aggressively as it pulled through the water across the sound, towards the Fauntleroy terminal.

This walkshop was more complex and well-funded than many others I've organized. It involved a large budget, support from the Henry Art Gallery, student assistants and two (funded) site visits to plan for an event on land that we were not familiar with. A key lesson of this walkshop concerned the redistribution of shelter and vulnerability. The holding work of walkshop

Figure 9.1 *Care for the Stranded: A Shoreline Walkshop*, 2022. Photograph: Jonathan Vanderweit, courtesy of the Henry Art Gallery.

organizers is also distributed: carrying the bucket, carrying the stories, caring for each other, caring for the Land, caring for the dead. After everyone's hands had been washed, three people took the buckets to the edge of the sea to rematriate the water.

Open Mic Creek Walks

Meanwhile, Jen has been developing Open Mic Creek Walks as weathering practice on Anaiwan County. These began by simply walking along creeks because, as described in the CoWS chapter, experiencing a catastrophic drought in inland high country with no large body of water above or below ground insists you think anew about water. Initially, the creek walks were more like curated walkshops where different folks were invited to talk about place and environment: Anaiwan Elder Uncle Steve Widders spoke about water as the live blood of Country; local land care bush regenerators talked about a chain of ponds they created while reforesting a gully creekland to improve the area's biodiversity. Another time, participants returned water from one of the university's stormwater ponds (Lake Zot) to the creek and discussed what decolonizing waterways would look like.

But in the spirit of CoWS, Jen wanted to make space for what other participants were thinking and feeling, too. In response, Open Mic Creek Walks enabled her to co-create the event with the community. She first tried the format at the Winter Blooming Festival: a queer, Indigenous and multicultural arts festival at the local museum in Armidale. As an experiment in form, it fused the careful planning of an organized walk with the ad hoc randomness of an Open Mic Night. Lacking the social lubrication of alcohol or night's protective darkness, it was unclear whether people in the (very) broad light of that first walk would be willing to share anything. It took a slow walk down one side of the creek to get the process started. On the return, lots of people opened up to sharing: favourite poems by others, original works, improvised pieces responding to the moment and song.

The Open Mic Creek Walk is an activity that it is grounded in place and proximate to water. It's healing and lovely to be outside in a group. But in a settler colonial country, place is complicated. This walk format creates a way to both enjoy watery places together and be aware of their materiality and history. For those who opt in, this includes thinking about how the environment and layers of historical violence intersect.

Field Report: Walking in the Fringes

Conclusion: The River Ends as the Ocean

This chapter is called 'Walking in the Fringes' because our walks often take place in littoral zones, along shorelines and creeks. They also consider transitions from one kind of system to another, for example, as the heyday of coal mining in Lithgow transitioned to something else. This final example is also about transition, endings and beginnings. It is also another bridge – a bridge back to the beginning of this book, to the banks of Goolay'yari. And it is a bridge to whatever comes next.

This walk took place in January 2021 and was called 'The River Ends as the Ocean'. It traced the Cooks River's literal end, as it flowed into the Pacific Ocean, as well as its anticipated end as 'the Cooks': this river was transitioning back to its name Goolay'yari. The walk coincided with the end of the year, and arrived at the end of the toughest period of COVID-19 lockdowns in Australia so far (although the pandemic was certainly not over). It also marked the end of my time in Sydney, a place I had fallen deeply in love with while living there for six years. I had taken another job in BC, mostly to be closer to my dying father. But I didn't know how to leave.

This walk was commissioned by the Shanghai Art Biennale, that year named *Bodies of Water*, (riffing on the title of my 2017 book). I organized it in close collaboration with my friend and artist-colleague Clare Britton, and her friend and collaborator, Aunty Rhonda Dixon-Grovenor, who is an artist and Gadigal, Bidjigal & Yuin Elder. Goolay'yari cuts through Gadigal, Wangal and Bidjigal Country. This is Aunty Rhonda's Country. While we had all sorts of ideas (well-funded walkshops can be elaborate creatures!), in the end we chose a simple proposition: *walk the tide out*. Participants were asked to rhyme their own bodies to the temporality of this tidal river's own journey back out to sea.[27]

The response to the walk was almost overwhelming. Almost 100 people signed up. We actually did the walk several times: first as a trial run, so we could ensure that there were places to fill water bottles, rest in the shade, and take our time, as needed. Clare and I were joined by a few friends and neighbours who would not be able to join on the planned day. The second time was a not-walkshop, since we cancelled it due to rising levels of COVID-19 infection, and we didn't want to put anyone at risk, even though we were outside. Those who couldn't make the rescheduled time still received the walk as a proposition.

The third time happened on a hot day in January. The walk was almost 14 kilometres and took all day. This walkshop was also a rest-shop, a connect-shop, an attune-shop. We provided plenty of advance information about transportation, toilet locations, parking, and opportunities to join or leave as necessary. After gathering by a golf course in Sydney's inner west, near to where this river makes its first aboveground appearance as an urban drainage ditch, the day began with an extended Welcome from Aunty Rhonda. Aunty Rhonda's proposition was that if participants could experience her Country in this way – up close, slowly, with others – they would fall in love, too. They would have no option but to care better for this place.

Our line soon stretched for a couple of kilometres, top to tail. Clusters of walkers gathered and reconfigured. We stopped for lunch at the park where our first Weathering Collective meeting was held five years earlier. At one point, we walked past the backyard of the house I had been renting with my family, butting up against the mangroves. I was moving out in a matter of days. Walks are about transitioning, and ambivalence.

After crossing the highway and skirting the international airport (whose construction forced a major rerouting of the river decades ago), we reached the river's mouth. As if by magic, we were at the ocean. My partner delivered dinner to us all. Some of us went for a swim, others sat on the sand. Aunty Rhonda moved around the inner perimeter of the circle we had formed on the beach. From a clay vessel held by her granddaughter, she poured water over each of our hands, and said a prayer.

Like the other walks described above, our main preparatory work was to provide a good holding container, as Berlant says. But while well planned and well executed, this walk was also something more. Jen and I can provide tips and instructions and lessons for all of our weathering methods, but every infrastructure has its own affordances, character and feelings.

Weather can be forecast, but it is ultimately unpredictable, and uncontrollable. I cited Eva Hayward above, who writes that transways imply 'being unable either to turn back or to continue as before'.[28] This was a good lesson to contemplate that day, as we walked with Aunty Rhonda's dramatically altered Country. Time is also like Milpirri – a weather front, where past and future continually clash. How do we keep walking? I was also thinking a lot about a sentence I had recently read in Cree poet Billy-Ray Belcourt's book, *A History of My Brief Body*: 'A mouth is no longer a mouth when it twists language into something without and against form. A mouth is no longer a mouth when it can't hold back what is inside it'.[29] The end of a river, where it joins the sea and becomes something else, is, I suppose, another kind of weather front. It is also called the mouth.

Notes

1. Wanta Steve Jampijinpa Patrick, 'Pulya-ranyi: Winds of Change', *Cultural Studies Review* 21, no. 1 (2015): 122.
2. See, for example, Clare Qualmann and Claire Hind, *Ways to Wander* (Axminster: Triarchy Press, 2015); Perdita Phillips, 'Walk 'til You Run Out of Water', *Performance Research* 17, no. 2 (2012): 97–109; Stephanie Springgay and Sarah E. Truman, *Walking Methodologies in a More-than-human World: WalkingLab* (Milton Park and New York, NY: Routledge, 2018); Sarah E. Truman, *Feminist Speculations and the Practice of Research-Creation: Writing Pedagogies and Intertextual Affects* (London: Routledge, 2021).
3. Guy Debord, 'Theory of the Dérive', trans. Ken Knabb, *Les Lèvres Nues* 9 (November 1956).
4. Ursula K. Le Guin, *Dancing at the Edge of the World: Thoughts on Words, Women, Places* (New York, NY: Grove Press, 1989).
5. Lauren Berlant, 'The Commons: Infrastructures for Troubling Times*', *Environment and Planning D: Society and Space* 34, no. 3 (2016): 393–419, https://doi.org/10.1177/0263775816645989, 402.
6. Berlant, 'The Commons'.
7. C. Wölfle-Erskine and J. Cole, 'Transfiguring the Anthropocene: Stochastic Reimaginings of Human–Beaver Worlds', *TSQ: Transgender Studies Quarterly* 2, no. 2 (2015), 304.
8. 'Littoral Zone', Environmental Encyclopedia, https://www.encyclopedia.com/earth-and-environment/geology-and-oceanography/geology-and-oceanography/littoral-zone#3404800887 (accessed 10 October 2024).
9. Macarena Gómez-Barris, *The Extractive Zone: Social Ecologies and Decolonial Perspectives* (Durham, NC, and London: Duke University Press, 2017).
10. D. C. Freeman et al., 'The Adaptive Significance of Sexual Lability in Plants Using Atriplex canescens as a Principal Example', *Annals of the Missouri Botanical Garden* 71, no. 1 (1984): 265.
11. Susan Stryker, *Transgender History: The Roots of Today's Revolution*, 2nd edn (Berkeley, CA: Seal Press, 2017), 1.
12. See also Douglas A. Vakoch, *Transecology: Transgender Perspectives on Environment and Nature* (London and New York, NY: Routledge, 2020); Wölfle Hazard, *Underflows*.
13. Hayward cited in Wölfle Hazard, *Underflows*, 105.
14. Eva Hayward, 'More Lessons from a Starfish: Prefixial Flesh and Transspeciated Selves', *WSQ: Women's Studies Quarterly* 36, no. 3–4 (2008): 68.
15. Karen Michelle Barad, *Meeting the Universe Halfway: Quantum Physics and the Entanglement of Matter and Meaning* (Durham, NC: Duke University Press, 2007).

16. Perdita Phillips and Astrida Neimanis, 'Postcards from the Underground', *Journal of Public Pedagogies*, no. 4 (2019): 127–39.
17. Susan Reid, 'Solwara 1 and the Sessile Ones', in *Blue Legalities: The Life and Laws of the Sea*, ed. Irus Braverman and Elizabeth R. Johnson (Durham, NC: Duke University Press, 2020).
18. Personal communication. See also William F. Humphreys, 'Diversity Patterns in Australia', in Encyclopedia of Caves, ed. B. White and D. Culver, *Encyclopedia of Caves* (Chennai: Academic Press, 2012), 203–19.
19. Berlant, 'The Commons', 404.
20. Astrida Neimanis, 'Stygofaunal Worlds', *Cultural Politics* 19, no. 1 (2023): 18–38.
21. Berlant, 'The Commons', 396.
22. Berlant, 'The Commons', 395.
23. Berlant, 'The Commons', 406.
24. Berlant, 'The Commons', 407.
25. Berlant, 'The Commons', 408.
26. This instruction was suggested by musician and walkshop team member Anne Bourne, a former student of Oliveros's.
27. Find documentation of this walk at http://clarebritton.net/a-week-on-the-river
28. Hayward, 'More Lessons from a Starfish'.
29. Billy-Ray Belcourt, *A History of My Brief Body* (Toronto: Penguin Canada, 2021), 34.

INSET J

Cosmic Weathering

Can we sit and cultivate a more conscious weathering practice? Drawing on traditions of guided meditation, cosmic weathering combines attention to the body 'in situ' with awareness of what usually feels distant. Participants will approach the practice with different experiences and skills, but at heart it is like a breath: an opening outward in a specific situation to connections beyond it – inhale – and a grounding, breathing, sinking back into the body – exhale. Cosmic weathering is an exercise in embodied extrospection.

What You Need

- At least two people: one to lead, one to participate.
- A written script adapted to your circumstances.
- A set duration (eg. 10, 20, 30, 60 mins), communicated in advance and accounted for in the script.

How to Play

Weatherers find a comfortable position, lying down, seated or standing, with eyes closed, listening (give permission for bodies to shift slowly and intentionally to remain comfortable during the practice). The reader/s position themselves where they can be easily heard by the weatherer/s, and slowly read out the script. When you are done, you might discuss the experiences, sensations and thoughts that arose during the session. This may also be an exercise in private introspective debrief via journalling.

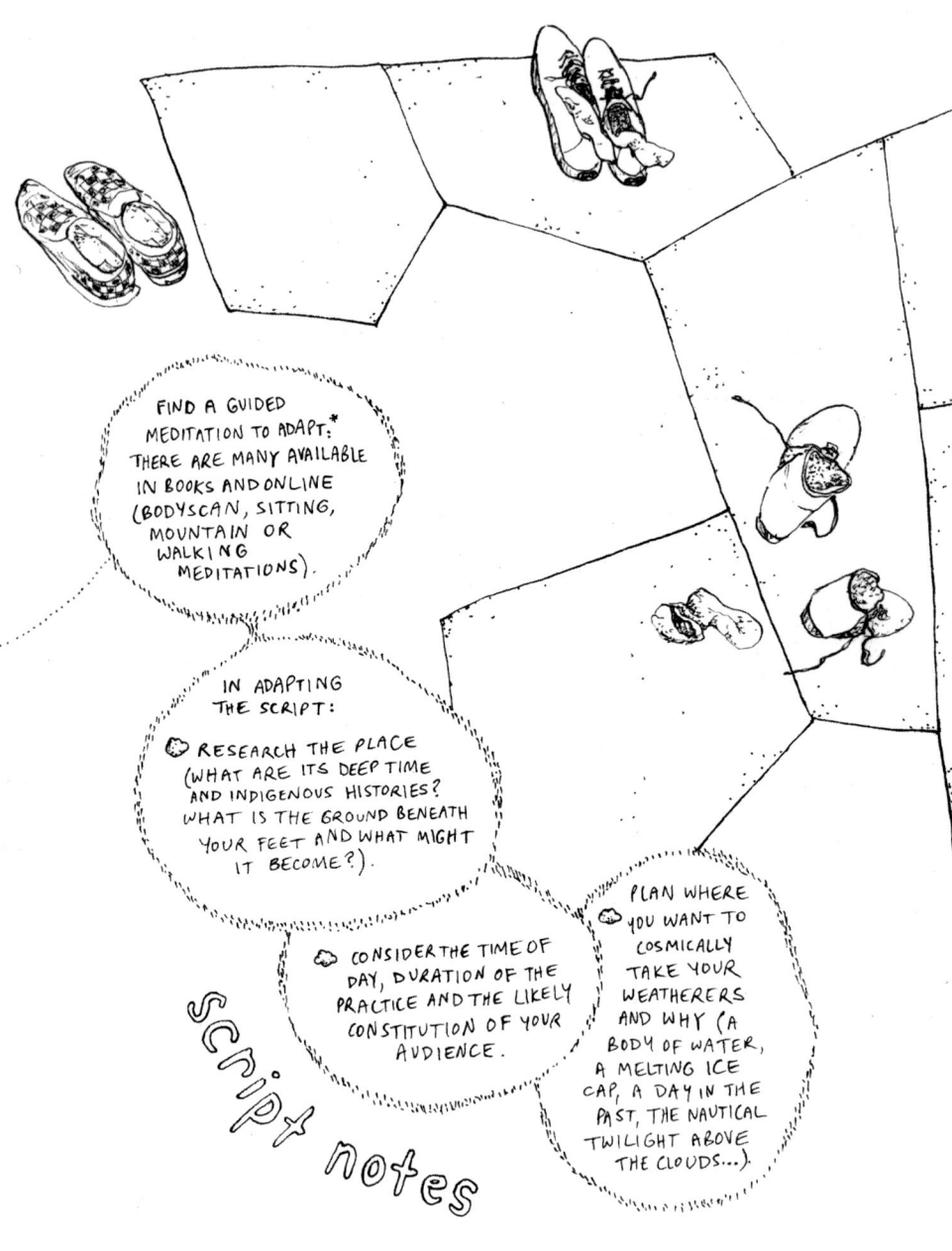

THE SCRIPT SHOULD AIM TO BALANCE A JOURNEY ELSEWHERE WITH THE PRINCIPLE OF COMING BACK TO THE WEATHER OR THE DAY AND THE WEATHERERS' FLESHY BODIES AND GENTLE BREATHS.

Epilogue: Cosmic weathering

How to Weather Together shares how we have developed weathering as a concept in theory and practice. Weathering means we have to withstand the weather: we bear the marks of weather. Weathering is making it through, together. Weathering also means we are weather-makers: we weather other bodies through the atmospheres we create. Weathering as a concept means recognizing our own bodily vulnerabilities and working towards more equitable shelter for bodies, human and not. Weathering is an urgent and slow process of changing ourselves as part of a changing climate.

Weathering is poetic and playful and grounded and practical; it could also inform a viable and just response to climate change, if we wanted it to. But as academic researchers in this field, we know there are real limits to creative and scholarly work under heteropatriarchal settler colonial capitalism. Academic research is harder to fund when it doesn't have an obvious commercial application, or isn't offering a technophilic and scalable solution of interest to venture capitalists. It's even less viable if it is explicitly feminist. Though our proposal doesn't add value to the economy in normative ways, we are not just critiquing normative responses to climate change. We are proposing a different mode of mitigation and adaptation.

As we describe in Chapter 5, although we work for colonial institutions funded by big polluting corporations and weapons manufacturers, we try to write towards queer feminist anticolonial futures. In committing to weathering, we are moved beyond the obvious limits of our work as academics and side-dabblings as artists and curators, dreaming of a new world. While both of us have been lucky to work with supervisors or funders who sometimes encourage this work (or at least happily let it fly under the radar), our larger institutional context reminds us to stay in our lane: such critical academic work is belittled, if not actively derided, by those committed to the current world order. We are always weathering.

Because practices of queer feminist anticolonial theory do not promise a capitalist solution to the world's problems, being committed to this work is also a commitment to the inefficiencies of nature, poetry and love. As Alexis

Pauline Gumbs says of *tūpoupou*, a dolphin that has been studied for centuries by Maori meteorologists for what their movements can tell us about the weather, 'I offer my days to your urgent instruction. The weather is changing. Yes. I understand.'[1] What is Gumbs' understanding about the dolphin? '[Y]our play and your thrash are prophetic.'[2] What can this teach us about weathering?

Does relating to the weather mean making sure planes land on time, or does it instead mean finding ways of sheltering well and communing otherwise? Wiradjuri poet Jazz Money asks 'where does the wind begin and how to make my body fit into the spaces left in the hollowed trees'.[3] The lack of the question mark suggests to us that this is a question that *has* to be asked; it functions more like a statement: where does the wind begin. But unlike a rhetorical question with an implied answer, this one has none. The process of searching for where the wind begins and how to fit in the hollows of the world around us is just life. We wonder about this too. This book documents our commitment, and our wonder, as we turn towards the weather and its everyday questions.

As a practice, weathering can be pleasurable, mundane or terrifying. Many different activities, feelings, and relations can occur in its name. Feminist practice for climate change, guided by weathering as a concept, is an intention to: 1) make careful observations about our shared world as it is; 2) cultivate attention to all eco-social weathers; and 3) work towards creating newly livable climates, in the tricky space between antipolarization (finding ways to meet each other across difference) and antifascism (taking a stand for some worlds and not others). It may be a climate emergency but this process cannot be rushed. We want to record the temperature, warm or cool our bodies, and seek shelter, differently. As Toni Cade Bambara said of the Black feminist revolution decades ago:

> We've got time. That of course is an unpopular utterance these days. Instant coffee is the hallmark of current rhetoric. But we do have time. We'd better take the time to fashion revolutionary selves, revolutionary lives, revolutionary relationships ... arguing that instant-coffee-ten-minutes-to-midnight alibi to justify hasty-headed dealings with your mate is shit. Ain't no such animal as an instant guerrilla.[4]

Weathering as feminist practice for climate change is a life practice, and a commitment to a life of certain practices. These practices are the specific, lo-fi, quaint and playful practices we describe in the book, but taken further,

Epilogue: Cosmic Weathering

weathering promises serious, large-scale, long-term change: a total revolution by bodies and slowness. Remember, as we noted in the Prologue to this book: practice is a habit you choose. Take a moment to sit with this idea. You might get curious about the final illustrated inset we offer in this book under the name of 'Cosmic Weathering':

/////////////////////

[A Template Script for Cosmic Weathering; modify as needed]

Find a comfortable place either lying down, sitting or standing.
Take a deep breath in and out.
To whatever extent it feels safe for you, start to pay attention to your body.
Close your eyes.
Feel yourself grounded and in your body.
Take a few deep breaths.

[Establish the meditation for as long as necessary, breathing in and out]

Notice what part of your body is in contact with the ground or floor. Sense the ground beneath your feet, sit bone, or back. Feel yourself supported by this connection.

You are supported by the ground and the planet beneath you.

[LONG PAUSE to allow everyone to sense the planet beneath]

Now come back into your body grounded in this place.

[As the person offering this exercise, you will have done your homework: what actually is the earth beneath? Whose Land is this? What was here 100, 1,000 or 100,000 years ago? What remains? What will you find in the soil – which plants, bugs, tree roots? What physical infrastructures support you? Where have their building materials been sourced from? What else has travelled here? Gently share some of these details, guiding your participants to fall deeper into the matter, the memories, and the time of this place. The ground beneath you is specific, even as it is connected to the whole cosmos. These details can be interspersed throughout the meditation as appropriate.]

Now we turn our attention to the weather of this place.
Notice the weather. What is the weather today?
What senses help you know the weather? How are you sensing the weather?

Where is the weather? Can you sense it on your body? How and where is it touching you? (Is it in your hair? Is it in your hands? Is it in your gut? Your feet?)
What does it feel like? (Is it hot? Is it cold? Is it moving? Is it dry? Is it damp?)
How does it come to be part of your body?
Notice how your body feels: does it correspond in any way with the weather?

Notice the weather on, and in, your body.

How is this weather you?

[LONG PAUSE *for sensing where the weather is and how it is you*]

Return to where you are grounded in your body (your back, sit bone, feet).

Attend to the connection between the weather in your body and the ground. Notice how the weather falls into deep earth. . .

[*note details of what the weather might be falling through: what kind of materials, organic matter, strata?*]

. . . into deep time.

What is the weather of deep time? (Where is the weather of deep time? Is it planetary? Is it cosmic? Is it real? Is it imagined?)

We're going to stay in this deep time weather for a while. Breathe in. Breathe out.

[PAUSE]

Return to your body again. Notice this deep time weather in your body.

[LONG PAUSE to allow participants to sense this]

Come back to the place that you are sharing with all these people. Breathe in and breathe out. Become aware of all that is around you and that is you.

Consider the feeling in your body. Are you warmer or colder than when we began? Notice if you feel the weather differently to when we began. Have your own conditions changed?

When you are ready, open your eyes.

////////////

We first developed this practice when working with a group of educators in Sweden. Like many academic workshops, the schedule was packed with discussions, talks and activities, including pilot versions of 'Lucky dip' and 'Weathering with and without' that you encountered earlier in this book. Expending energy to negotiate shared sleeping quarters and social interactions with people we'd never met, as well as jetlag from overseas travel and the long June days, all contributed to our fatigue. We wondered: what kind of weathering practice could also be about slowing down, and really sinking into our wondrous location – an island in the Stockholm archipelago – wrapped in the dusky midsummer's night air and the barely salty breath of the Baltic Sea? How could the more immediate work of weathering as climate change pedagogy also connect to a scale of weather that greatly exceeded us, but could still be somehow accessed or felt by us? We invited the participants to sit in a circle on a small jetty jutting out into the sea, the water lolling beneath us, as we guided them through a script something like the one you read above.

In this sample script, you probably recognize the genre of a guided meditation. Maybe this makes you a bit uncomfortable. These days mindfulness practices are tainted by a drive for quick-fix feel-good regimes that mostly just line the pockets of the privileged, and sometimes enable them (us) to have a spa day. So we think it is important to say that this weathering practice grew out of practices we had both been learning for some time.

How to Weather Together

Figure 10.1 Jen and Astrida leading the first Cosmic Weathering activity at the Common Worlds Weathering Early Childhood Education Workshop on Rindö, Sweden, 2017. Photograph: Affrica Taylor.

After Jen got sick with cancer in 2016, she did not cope well with the diagnosis and fell into anxiety-fuelled health hypervigilance. A leading professor in her field suggested that instead of applying for a massive research grant that would take many stressful months to write, Jen should try an eight-week meditation course. The recommended course was the MBSR, or mindfulness-based stress reduction course. Jen was sceptical about mindfulness for exactly the reasons you might be too. She didn't want to find ways to 'do more with less' or 'be more resilient' (although the instinct to apply for a big research grant shortly after a bilateral mastectomy belies the ways it is so hard to extricate ourselves from these mindsets). But she gave it a go. It was the best career advice ever. What she learned was that you have to confront whatever is present in the body. It can't be rushed. It is not a quick fix. Of course this is easier said than done – accepting what is here. But acceptance is not passive. Jen did not breathe her way to happiness and a cure; she accepted the diagnosis, still felt a lot of hard things, had a great deal of hospital treatment, and is not immune to recurrence. But feeling present with the situation of her bodymind helped her a build a very different pathway out of the crisis. Jen learned that this process takes time and practice.[5]

She also learned that health anxiety, or fear that something might go terribly wrong in the body, cannot actually prevent something from going wrong. She learned it is possible to experience the same material present – and importantly be reflective and even critical of that present – where fear is part of an experience, but not its only dimension. We talk about climate anxiety and health anxiety as though they are categorically different, but the feeling of anxiety is perhaps quite uniform. We could say that Jen's starting point connects the practice of cosmic weathering to climate feeling. Having climate anxiety does not stop climate change. But what if cosmic weathering could help us experience this same situation in ways that contextualize that anxiety, and open to a deeper understanding of what is bigger than ourselves?[6]

Astrida's starting point for this practice is a bit different, and ties back to the first meeting of the Weathering Collective on the banks of Goolay'yari, described in this book's Prologue. At that gathering we wondered: since all matter is somehow connected to all other matter in the world (for example, through the circulation of weather) does this mean we are able to experience things that are long ago or very distant?[7] Our friend Rebecca Giggs suggested that this might relate to literary critic Laurence Buell's description of environmental writing as 'disciplined extrospection'.[8] This is a term for writing that seeks to move humans out of the spotlight, and centre the more-than-human world. Instead of digging deeper into ourselves (introspecting) we are trying to dig deeper *beyond* ourselves.

This idea piqued Astrida's interest. For many years, she had been honing something her former philosophy professor Sam Mallin called 'body hermeneutics' – a phenomenological research method that offers a disciplined (that word again) attunement to worldly phenomena through our embodied affordances: sensation, feeling, movement, cognition, viscerality. Astrida had worked with this extensively in the research for her book *Bodies of Water*.[9] This entailed an exploration of how the statement *we are all bodies of water, connected to each other within a more-than-human hydrological cycle,* could be explicitly practised (that word again.) Bringing this together with Rebecca's nod towards Buell's work, might the Weathering Collective experiment with something like 'embodied extrospection'?

A lot of nature writing – especially written by white settlers – teeters on anthropocentrism, i.e. bringing everything back to the human. Buell suggests that extrospection, especially when disciplined (attentive, careful) might be the best we can do to counter this risk. For us, the 'disciplined' part was particularly important (our friend Sue Reid has also written about something similar, which she calls 'rigorous imagination').[10] This is not just a willy-nilly 'imagine yourself as a cloud' kind of exercise. It is actually really hard. Embodied extrospection is a bit of a paradox because we are trying to access the outside of the self by locating the 'extro' inside our bodies. So it requires rigorously calling in all of the ways of knowing we are slowly learning, from climatology to stratigraphy, to physiology and anatomy, to Indigenous cosmologies and sciences. We use these resources to stretch the muscle of our imaginations in ways that might dislodge the (colonial, settled, human-scaled) habits of how our bodies engage and know the world. Like all practices, this different way of knowing has to be a habit we choose. Cosmic weathering thus became a way to meaningfully extrospect an experience of climate change via our slowing, sinking, weathering bodies.

Subsequent Cosmic Weathering scripts also changed to reflect our experiences in facilitating guided embodied environmental activities (sometimes called 'the arts of noticing' or attunement, in reference to Anna Tsing's work[11]) in other contexts. We usually begin these workshops with an extended discussion about colonial dispossession of the Land that the workshop is taking place on, and other important histories of the place. At the start of one workshop on the edge of a lake, Astrida's participants discussed how histories of race riots and police crackdown on LGBTQ people had in more recent times layered onto the settler colonial land grab of the shoreline. They discussed how the environmental history of that lakeshore also included a literal archive of capitalist colonial detritus; the spit we could see across a small inlet was evidence of land reclamation via toxic dump, and that toxicity was leaking into the non-human bodies that still made that place home.[12]

But when the group then turned to the bodily attunement exercise (closely modelled on 'Lucky dip'), the observations were primarily localized in the participants' embodied present, sometimes slightly extended into their own personal memories: *I can feel the breath of the lake rustling in my hair. My toes in the shallow water are recalling a grey-skied summertime with my nan, who is no longer with me.* While these perspectives offered openings for thinking about weather and place as intimately related to our own bodies, the deeper histories – often related to colonial injustice – burrowed back down between the cigarette butts and microplastics in the sand. Poof! Disappeared again.[13]

So we reworked cosmic weathering so it could more directly choose the habit of un-disappearing these deep (and still resonating) histories. As you sink through the dirt, whose shell middens are you passing through? As you slip into the subterranean waters, can you also feel sovereign belonging to land and clean water, from the river to sea? As you drift up into the sky, can you imagine beyond the light pollution that interrupts the relations between Sky Country and their terrestrial kin? Meditation taught Jen that you can't turn away from what is in your body. What if all the weathers that have ever been, or will ever be, are in there too? Paying attention, rigorously, doesn't take the anxiety away, but it becomes differently available to us, as a touchstone and a tool. As writer and artist Caolan Leander recently suggested to Astrida, 'what if our anxiety could be a collective energy?'[14]

As anticolonial feminists, we must honour the Land we occupy, and as environmentalists, we are told we should focus on the local. But climate change is clearly a massive, translocal, planetary, multiscalar, deep time, deep future phenomenon. So in a way, this Epilogue returns us to our starting point – that we need an embodied, everyday way to think about the abstractness and hugeness of climate change – but flips it back outwards: how can we approach the planetary, but in an embodied and situated way? 'How is climate change me?'[15]

By weathering in this expansive way, we aim to sense which agencies need to be revered and which ones need to be resisted. From this place we can surrender to what is actually beyond our control, sense the heat and sense the cool, and ask what it does, while refusing the way powerful regimes try to mimic the weather, protect their interests and oppress us in the name of nature. This is a difficult reckoning.

If one state feels better than another, we can use it to help guide us, but we must be careful. Some weather is nothing if not change beyond our control. Some weather is the effects of fascism. Agencies that seek to control change may say they have our best interests at heart because they care for our losses, while they might just be monetizing the chaos.

And so we want to finish this all by talking about pleasure. Weathering also means redistributing pleasure as a specific kind of shelter. In particular, we want a redistribution of 'the pleasure of those most impacted by oppression',[16] but we don't want disposable luxury. As adrienne maree brown warns us in *Pleasure Activism*, 'moderation is key'. We need 'not be in a heady state of ecstasy at all times, but rather [to] learn how to *sense* when something is good for you, to be able to feel what enough is'.[17] If the weather were 'perfect' all the time, we'd get bored. And anyway, too much heat causes heat stroke, and too much cold shuts down our vital systems.

Sitting on a jetty with people and twilight and wind and histories we don't really know, beside waters that will nurse us all if we let them, under a sky that can shelter us all if we let it, on a wildly spinning planet that will outlast us all, breathing in, sinking down, breathing out, floating up, we are all simultaneously big and powerful and small and insignificant. We pursue the pleasure of this paradox. Of breath entering and exiting. Of bodies sharing. Of weather, of weathering, always.

Notes

1. Alexis Pauline Gumbs, *Undrowned: Black Feminist Lessons from Marine Mammals*, Emergent Strategy Series, no. 2 (Chico, CA, and Edinburgh: AK Press, 2020), 7.
2. Gumbs, *Undrowned*.
3. Jazz Money, 'Some Generosities', *Cordite Poetry Review*, 12 May 2024, http://cordite.org.au/poetry/treat/some-generosities/.
4. Toni Cade Bambara, 'On the Issue of Roles', *The Black Woman: An Anthology* (New York, NY: Mentor Books), 1970, 101–10.
5. Jennifer Hamilton, 'Affect Theory and Breast Cancer Memoir: Rescripting Fears of Death and Dying in the Anthropocene', *Body & Society* 27, no. 4 (2021): 3–29.
6. The desire to work through anxiety and find different feeling states to guide climate change responses is the premise of Sarah Jaquette Ray's *A Field Guide to Climate Anxiety: How to Keep Your Cool on a Warming Planet* (Berkeley, CA: University of California Press, 2020).
7. Astrida Neimanis, *Bodies of Water: Posthuman Feminist Phenomenology* (London and New York, NY: Bloomsbury Academic, 2017).
8. Lawrence Buell, *The Environmental Imagination: Thoreau, Nature Writing, and the Formation of American Culture*, 2nd print (Cambridge, MA: Belknap Press of Harvard University Press, 1996), 104.
9. Neimanis, *Bodies of Water*.
10. Susan Reid, 'Solwara 1 and the Sessile Ones', in *Blue Legalities: The Life and Laws of the Sea*, ed. Iris Bravurman and Elizabeth R. Johnson (Durham, NC: Duke University Press, 2020), 31.
11. Anna Lowenhaupt Tsing, *The Mushroom at the End of the World: On the Possibility of Life in Capitalist Ruins* (Princeton, NJ: Princeton University Press, 2015), 37.
12. You can read one version of this story in Catriona Sandilands, 'Some "F" Words for the Environmental Humanities: Feralities, Feminisms, Futurities', in *The Routledge Companion to the Environmental Humanities*, ed. Ursula K. Heise, Jon Christensen and Michelle Niemann (London and New York, NY: Routledge, 2017).

13. These challenges of feminist embodied methods are discussed in Blanche Verlie and Astrida Neimanis, 'Breathing Climate Crises: Feminist Environmental Humanities and More-than-Human Witnessing', *Angelaki* 28, no. 4 (4 July 2023): 117–31, https://doi.org/10.1080/0969725X.2023.2233810.
14. Personal communication.
15. Neimanis and Loewen Walker, 'Weathering: Climate Change and the Thick Time of Transcorporeality'.
16. adrienne maree brown, *Pleasure Activism: The Politics of Feeling Good* (Chico, CA: AK Press, 2019), n.p.
17. brown, *Pleasure Activism*, np.

Bibliography

Abhayawickrama, Natasha, Eve Mayes and Dani Villafaña. 'White Audacity and Student Climate Justice Activism.' In *Planetary Justice*, edited by Michele Lobo, Eve Mayes and Laura Bedford, 213–31. Bristol: Bristol University Press, 2024.

Adams, Carol J., and Lori Gruen. *Ecofeminism: Feminist Intersections with Animals and the Earth*. 2nd edn. London: Bloomsbury Academic, 2022.

AdaptNSW. 'Home Grown Climate Resilience'. https://www.climatechange.environment.nsw.gov.au/stories-and-case-studies/home-grown-climate-resilience (accessed 6 February 2025).

'Agricultural Land Use Survey in the Sumas River Watershed Report.' BC Environment, 1994. https://publications.gc.ca/collections/collection_2015/ec/En83-6-1994-21-eng.pdf (accessed 19 February 2025).

Ahmed, Sara. 'Introduction: Sexism – A Problem With a Name', *New Formations* 86, no. 86 (2015): 5–13.

Ahmed, Sara. *Living a Feminist Life*. Durham, NC: Duke University Press, 2017.

Ahmed, Sara. 'Open Forum Imaginary Prohibitions: Some Preliminary Remarks on the Founding Gestures of the "New Materialism".' *European Journal of Women's Studies* 15, no. 1 (2008): 23–39.

Ahmed, Sara. 'Resignation.' *feministkilljoys* (blog), 30 May 2016. https://feministkilljoys.com/2016/05/30/resignation/ (accessed 20 April 2024).

Ahmed, Sara. *The Cultural Politics of Emotion*. 2nd edn. Edinburgh: Edinburgh University Press, 2014. https://www.jstor.org/stable/10.3366/j.ctt1g09x4q.

Ahmed, Sara. 'The Nonperformativity of Antiracism.' *Meridians* 7, no. 1 (2006): 104–26.

Ahmed, Sara. *The Promise of Happiness*. Durham, NC: Duke University Press, 2010.

Ahmed, Sara. 'Willful Stones.' feministkilljoys (blog), 29 January 2016. https://feministkilljoys.com/2016/01/29/willful-stones/ (accessed 20 February 2022).

Alaimo, Stacy. *Bodily Natures: Science, Environment, and the Material Self*. Bloomington, IN: Indiana University Press, 2010.

Alaimo, Stacy. *Exposed: Environmental Politics and Pleasures in Posthuman Times*. Minneapolis, MN: University of Minnesota Press, 2016.

Alaimo, Stacy. 'Wanting All the Species to Be: Extinction, Environmental Visions, and Intimate Aesthetics.' *Australian Feminist Studies* 34, no. 102 (2019): 398–412.

Alaimo, Stacy, and Susan J. Hekman, eds. *Material Feminisms*. Bloomington, IN: Indiana University Press, 2011.

Aldred, Terri-Leigh, Charis Alderfer-Mumma, Sarah de Leeuw, May Farrales, Margo Greenwood, Dawn Hoogeveen, Ryan O'Toole, Margot W. Parkes and Vanessa Sloan Morgan. 'Mining Sick: Creatively Unsettling Normative Narratives about Industry, Environment, Extraction, and the Health Geographies of Rural,

Bibliography

Remote, Northern, and Indigenous Communities in British Columbia.' *Canadian Geographies / Géographies Canadiennes* 65, no. 1 (2021): 82–96. https://doi.org/10.1111/cag.12660.

Allan, Sujata, and Jennifer Hamilton. 'On Property Prices, Colonisation and Climate Change.' *Overland literary journal*, 30 March 2022, https://overland.org.au/2022/03/on-property-prices-colonisation-and-climate-change/ (accessed 30 March 2022).

Allon, Fiona, and Zoë Sofoulis. 'Everyday Water: Cultures in Transition.' *Australian Geographer* 37, no. 1 (2006): 45–55.

Anderson, Katharine. *Predicting the Weather: Victorians and the Science of Meteorology*. Chicago, IL: University of Chicago Press, 2005.

Araluen, Evelyn. *Dropbear*. Brisbane: University of Queensland Press, 2022.

Araluen, Evelyn. 'Snugglepot and Cuddlepie in the Ghost Gum,' 11 February 2019. https://sydneyreviewofbooks.com/snugglepot-and-cuddlepie-in-the-ghost-gum-evelyn-araluen/ (accessed 20 March 2024).

Armstrong, Jeannette. 'Syilx-Led Climate Justice in a Global Context.' UBC Okanagan, November 4, 2024. https://climatejustice.ubc.ca/news/armstrong-klein-syilx-led-climate-justice-in-a-global-context/ (accessed 24 June 2024).

Arnold, Jnr, Chester L., and C. James Gibbons. 'Impervious Surface Coverage: The Emergence of a Key Environmental Indicator.' *Journal of the American Planning Association* 62, no. 2 (1996): 243–58.

Åsberg, Cecilia, and Rosi Braidotti, eds. *A Feminist Companion to the Posthumanities*. Cham, Switzerland: Springer, 2018.

Austin, John Langshaw. *How to Do Things with Words*. Cambridge, MA: Harvard University Press, 1975.

Australian Government Department of Health and Aged Care. 'About Coronavirus Disease 2019 (COVID-19).' https://www.health.gov.au/topics/covid-19/about (accessed 28 October 2024).

Bacon, Francis. *The New Atlantis*. Project Gutenberg, [1626] 2008. https://www.gutenberg.org/files/2434/2434-h/2434-h.htm (accessed 4 August 2024).

Barad, Karen Michelle. *Meeting the Universe Halfway: Quantum Physics and the Entanglement of Matter and Meaning*. Durham, NC: Duke University Press, 2007.

Barry, Kaya, Maria Borovnik, and Tim Edensor, eds. *Weather: Spaces, Mobilities and Affects*. Milton Park: Routledge, 2020.

Barthes, Roland. *New Critical Essays*. Los Angeles, CA: University of California Press, 1990.

Bavyka, Ju. *Rest Your Identity*. 2023–ongoing, art project. Performative facilitations at various galleries and spaces.

Bawaka Country, Sarah Wright, S. Suchet-Pearson, K. Lloyd, L. Burarrwanga, R. Ganambarr, M. Ganambarr-Stubbs, B. Ganambarr, and D. Maymuru. 'Gathering of the Clouds: Attending to Indigenous Understandings of Time and Climate through Songspirals.' *Geoforum* 108 (2020): 295–304.

Belcourt, Billy-Ray. *A History of My Brief Body*. Toronto: Penguin Canada, 2021.

Benjamin, Walter. *The Arcades Project*. Translated by Rolf Tiederman. Washington, DC: Library of Congress, 1999.

Bibliography

Berlant, Lauren. *Cruel Optimism*. Durham, NC: Duke University Press, 2011.

Berlant, Lauren. *On the Inconvenience of Other People*. Durham, NC: Duke University Press, 2022.

Berlant, Lauren. 'The Commons: Infrastructures for Troubling Times*.' *Environment and Planning D: Society and Space* 34, no. 3 (2016): 393–419.

Bigger, Patrick, and Sophie Webber. 'Green Structural Adjustment in the World Bank's Resilient City.' *Annals of the American Association of Geographers* 111, no. 1 (2021): 36–51.

Bladow, Kyle A., and Jennifer K. Ladino, eds. *Affective Ecocriticism: Emotion, Embodiment, Environment*. Lincoln: University of Nebraska Press, 2018.

Bloch, Sam. 'Shade.' *Places Journal*, 23 April 2019. https://placesjournal.org/article/shade-an-urban-design-mandate/ (accessed 24 April 2019).

Bodyweather Lab. 'ABOUT.' BODY WEATHER LABORATORY. https://www.bodyweather.org/about (accessed 7 February 2025).

Bracke, Sarah. 'Bouncing Back: Vulnerability and Resistance in Times of Resilience.' In *Vulnerability in Resistance*, edited by Judith Butler, Zeynep Gambetti and Leticia Sabsay. Durham, NC: Duke University Press, 2016.

Briggs, Gabi, and Callum Clayton-Dixon. *Mugun & Gun: Resisting New England – Frontier Wars (Edition One)*. Anaiwan Country: Anaiwan Language Revival Program, 2018.

Britton, Clare. 'A Week on the River.' A Week on the River, 2021. http://clarebritton.net/a-week-on-the-river (accessed 18 January 2025).

Brough, Aaron R., James E. B. Wilkie, Jingjing Ma, Mathew S. Isaac, and David Gal. 'Is Eco-Friendly Unmanly? The Green-Feminine Stereotype and Its Effect on Sustainable Consumption.' *Journal of Consumer Research* 43, no. 4 (1 December 2016): 567–82.

brown, adrienne maree. *Pleasure Activism: The Politics of Feeling Good*. Chico, CA: AK Press, 2019.

brown, adrienne maree. 'Living through the Unveiling,' https://adriennemareebrown.net/2017/02/03/living-through-the-unveiling/ (accessed 1 November 2024).

Brown, Wendy. 'Suffering Rights as Paradoxes.' *Constellations* 7, no. 2 (2000): 208–29.

Brunoro, Michele. '"We Can't Wait": B.C. Spending $76.6M on Pump Station to Protect Sumas Prairie from Future Flooding.' *CTV News*, 14 February 2024. https://bc.ctvnews.ca/we-can-t-wait-b-c-spending-76-6m-on-pump-station-to-protect-sumas-prairie-from-future-flooding-1.6769137 (accessed 10 January 2025).

Buchanan, Brett, Michelle Bastian, and Matthew Chrulew. 'Introduction: Field Philosophy and Other Experiments.' *Parallax* 24, no. 4 (2018): 383–91.

Buell, Lawrence. *The Environmental Imagination: Thoreau, Nature Writing, and the Formation of American Culture*. Cambridge, MA: Belknap Press of Harvard University Press, 1996.

Butler, Judith. *Gender Trouble: Feminism and the Subversion of Identity*. New York, NY: Routledge, 1990.

Bibliography

Butler, Judith. *Bodies That Matter: On the Discursive Limits of "Sex."* New York, NY: Routledge, 1993.

Butler, Judith. *Who's Afraid of Gender?* 1st edn. New York, NY: Farrar, Straus and Giroux, 2024.

Byrne, Denis. 'Weathering in Common.' In *Feminist, Queer, Anticolonial Propositions for Hacking the Anthropocene: Archive*, edited by Jennifer Mae Hamilton, Astrida Neimanis, Susan Reid and Pia van Gelder. London: Open Humanities Press, 2021.

Cade Bambara, Toni. 'On the Issue of Roles.' Ed. Toni Cade Bambara. *The Black Woman: An Anthology*, New York, NY: Mentor Books, 1970, 101–10.

Cameron, Laura. *Openings: A Meditation on History, Method, and Sumas Lake*. Montreal & Kingston, London, Buffalo: University of British Columbia, Academic Women's Association, McGill-Queen's University Press, 1997.

Card, Kenton. *Geographies of Racial Capitalism with Ruth Wilson Gilmore*. Documentary. BFD Productions, 2020. https://www.youtube.com/watch?v=2CS627aKrJI (accessed 19 February 2025).

Carroll, Lewis. *Alice's Adventures in Wonderland and Through the Looking Glass*. New York, NY: Simon & Schuster, 2010.

Castañeda, Rafael Ruiz de, Jennifer Villers, Carlos A. Faerron Guzmán, Turan Eslanloo, Nicole de Paula, Catherine Machalaba, Jakob Zinsstag, Jürg Utzinger, Antoine Flahault and Isabelle Bolon. 'One Health and Planetary Health Research: Leveraging Differences to Grow Together.' *The Lancet Planetary Health* 7, no. 2 (2023): e109–11.

CBC Arts. 'What Would the Wind Write If It Could Write Poetry?' *CBC Arts*, November 6, 2018. https://www.cbc.ca/arts/exhibitionists/what-would-the-wind-write-if-it-could-write-poetry-1.4892750.

Chen, Mel Y. 'Feminisms in the Air.' *Signs*, Feminists Theorize Covid: A Symposium. Accessed October 27, 2024. https://signsjournal.org/covid/chen/.

Clare, Eli. *Brilliant Imperfection: Grappling with Cure*. Durham, NC: Duke University Press, 2017.

Clare, Eli. *Exile and Pride: Disability, Queerness, and Liberation*. Durham, NC: Duke University Press, 2015. https://doi.org/10.1215/9780822374879.

Clare, Eli. 'Meditations on Natural Worlds, Disabled Bodies, and a Politics of Cure.' In *Material Ecocriticism*, edited by Serenella Iovino and Serpil Oppermann. Bloomington, IN: Indiana University Press, 2014.

Clayton-Dixon, Callum. *Surviving New England: A History of Aboriginal Resistance and Resilience Through the First Forty Years of the Colonial Apocalypse*. Anaiwan Country: Newara Aboriginal Corporation, 2019.

Clement A. Price Institute. *Hacking the University: Reckoning with Racial Equity, Climate Justice, and Global Warming-Day 1*, 2020. https://www.youtube.com/watch?v=5yWiwftqI9c.

Cook, Garry, Andrew Dowdy, Juergen Knauer, Mick Meyer, Pep Canadell and Peter Briggs. 'Australia's Black Summer of Fire Was Not Normal – and We Can Prove It.' CSIRO. https://www.csiro.au/en/news/All/Articles/2021/November/bushfires-linked-climate-change (accessed 30 October 2024).

Bibliography

Correia, Maria, Sarah Alexis and Aleksandra Dulic. 'Bringing the Salmon Home: A Study of Cross-Cultural Collaboration in the Syilx Okanagan Territory of British Columbia.' *Ecology and Society* 29, no. 1 (2024): art15.

Cowen, Deborah. 'Infrastructure, Jurisdiction, Extractivism: Keywords for Decolonizing Geographies.' Edited by Shiri Pasternak, Robert Clifford, Tiffany Joseph, Dayna Nadine Scott, Anne Spice and Heidi Kiiwetinepinesiik Stark. *Political Geography* 101 (1 March 2023): 102763.

Coyne, Taylor. 'Listen Deep to Subterranean Kinfrastructures.' *Swamphen: A Journal of Cultural Ecology* (ASLEC-ANZ) 9 (2023): np.

Crandon, Tara J., James G. Scott, Fiona J. Charlson and Hannah J. Thomas. 'A Social–Ecological Perspective on Climate Anxiety in Children and Adolescents.' *Nature Climate Change* 12, no. 2 (2022): 123–31.

Cronon, William. 'Introduction.' In *Uncommon Ground: Rethinking the Human Place in Nature*, edited by William Cronon, 1st edn, 23–68. New York, NY: W. W. Norton & Company, 1996.

Crosby, Alexandra, and Ilaria Vanni. 'Green Square Water Stories (2021–2023).' Mapping Edges. https://www.mappingedges.org/projects/water-stories-activating-water-civic-ecologies-in-green-square/ (accessed 15 January 2025).

Cunsolo, Ashlee, Sherilee L. Harper, Kelton Minor, Katie Hayes, Kimberly G. Williams and Courtney Howard. 'Ecological Grief and Anxiety: The Start of a Healthy Response to Climate Change?' *The Lancet Planetary Health* 4, no. 7 (2020): e261–63.

Cvetkovich, Ann. *An Archive of Feelings: Trauma, Sexuality, and Lesbian Public Cultures*. Durham, NC: Duke University Press, 2003.

Cvetkovich, Ann, Kathry Garcia, Catherine Lord and Martabel Wasserman. 'Cruising the Archive with Ann Cvetkovich.' *Recaps Magazine*, 2011. http://recapsmagazine.com/rethink/cruising-the-archive-with-ann-cvetkovich (accessed 19 February 2025).

Daggett, Cara. 'Petro-Masculinity: Fossil Fuels and Authoritarian Desire.' *Millennium: Journal of International Studies* 47, no. 1 (2018): 25–44.

Daly, Mary. *Gyn/Ecology: The Metaethics of Radical Feminism*. Berkeley, CA: Beacon Press, 1978.

Daniek, Michel. *Do It Yourself 12 Volt Solar Power*. 3rd edn, revised & updated. East Meon: Permanent Publications, 2016.

Dawson, Ashley. *Extreme Cities: The Peril and Promise of Urban Life in the Age of Climate Change*. London: Verso Books, 2017.

Debord, Guy. 'Theory of the Dérive.' Trans. Ken Knabb. *Les Lèvres Nues* 9 (November 1956).

Deer, Sarah, and Elizabeth Kronk Warner. 'Raping Indian Country.' *Columbia Journal of Gender & Law* 38 (2019): 31–95.

Depledge, Duncan. 'Low-Carbon Warfare: Climate Change, Net Zero and Military Operations.' *International Affairs* 99, no. 2 (6 March 2023): 667–85. https://doi.org/10.1093/ia/iiad001.

Dickinson, Adam. *Anatomic*. 1st edn. Toronto: Coach House Books, 2018.

Dixon-Grovenor, Rhonda. *Aunty Rhonda's Walk*. Video, 2021. https://www.youtube.com/watch?v=3YtI605bGD4.

Bibliography

Donald, Madeline. 'Littoral Listening 2021-2022 in Practice: An Archive.' *FEELed Notes* (blog), 30 August 2022. https://thefeeledlab.ca/2022/08/30/littoral-listening-2021-2022-in-practice-an-archive/ (accessed 30 June 2024).

Donald, Madeline, and Astrida Neimanis. 'Sema:Th X'otsa: Fringe Natures as Decolonial Feminist-Queer-Trans Water Imaginaries.' In *Routledge Handbook of Gender and Water Governance*. London: Routledge, 2024.

Dyer, Sophie, and Sasha Engelmann. 'When I Image the Earth, I Imagine Another.' *Ecoes* #3 (10 August 2022). https://sonicacts.com/archive/engelmann-dyer-when-i-imagine-the-earth (accessed 20 January 2025).

Eaubonne, Francoise d'. (1974) *Feminism or Death: How the Women's Movement Can Save the Planet*. London: Verso Books, 2022.

'Ecofeminism, *n*. Meanings, Etymology and More | Oxford English Dictionary.' https://www.oed.com/dictionary/ecofeminism_n (accessed 29 October 2024).

Engelmann, Sasha, Sophie Dyer, Lizzie Malcolm, and Daniel Powers. 'Open-Weather: Speculative-Feminist Propositions for Planetary Images in an Era of Climate Crisis.' *Geoforum* 137 (1 December 2022): 237–47.

Ensor, Sarah. 'Queer Fallout: Samuel R. Delany and the Ecology of Cruising.' *Environmental Humanities* 9, no. 1 (2017): 149–66.

Ensor, Sarah. 'The Ecopoetics of Contact: Touching, Cruising, Gleaning.' *ISLE: Interdisciplinary Studies in Literature and Environment* 25, no. 1 (2018): 150–68.

Environmental Encyclopedia. 'Littoral Zone.' https://www.encyclopedia.com/earth-and-environment/geology-and-oceanography/geology-and-oceanography/littoral-zone#3404800887 (accessed 10 October 2024).

Erman, Alvina, Kayenat Kabir, Stephan Fabian Thies, Sophie Anne De Vries Robbe and Mirai Maruo. 'Gender Dimensions of Disaster Risk and Resilience: Existing Evidence.' Report. World Bank Group, 2021.

Etti, Melanie, MyMai Yuan and Jesse B. Bump. 'Sun, Skin and the Deadly Politics of Medical Racism.' *BMJ Global Health* 8, no. 8 (August 1, 2023): e013616.

European Centre for Constitutional and Human Rights. 'Gaza and the Matter of Genocide: Q&A on the Law and Recent Developments', December 2024. https://www.ecchr.eu/fileadmin/Q_As/ECCHR_Q_A__Gaza_and_Genocide_20241210.pdf.

Evers, Clifton Westly. 'Polluted Leisure.' *Leisure Sciences* 41, no. 5 (September 3, 2019): 423–40.

Frank, Adam J., and Elizabeth A. Wilson. *A Silvan Tomkins Handbook: Foundations for Affect Theory*. Minneapolis, MN: University of Minnesota Press, 2020.

Frazier, Chelsea Mikail. 'Black Feminist Ecological Thought: A Manifesto.' *Atmos*, 1 October 2020.

Freeman, D. C., E. D. McArthur and K. T. Harper. 'The Adaptive Significance of Sexual Lability in Plants Using Atriplex Canescens as a Principal Example.' *Annals of the Missouri Botanical Garden* 71, no. 1 (1984): 265–77.

Frenkel-Brunswik, Else. 'Intolerance of Ambiguity as an Emotional and Perceptual Personality Variable.' *Journal of Personality* 18, no. 1 (1949): 108–43.

Gaard, Greta. 'Toward a Queer Ecofeminism.' *Hypatia* 12, no. 1 (1997): 114–37.

Bibliography

Gardiner, James, Hayley Singer, Jennifer Hamilton, Astrida Neimanis and Mindy Blaise. 'Reading Group as Method for Feminist Environmental Humanities.' *Australian Feminist Studies* 37, no. 113 (July 3, 2022): 296–316.

Geronimus, Arline T. 'The Weathering Hypothesis and the Health of African-American Women and Infants: Evidence and Speculations.' *Ethnicity & Disease* 2, no. 3 (1992): 207–21.

Geronimus, Arline T. *Weathering: The Extraordinary Stress of Ordinary Life in an Unjust Society*. 1st edn. New York, NY: Little, Brown Spark, 2023.

Gibson-Graham, J. K., and Kelly Dombroski, eds. *The Handbook of Diverse Economies*. Cheltenham: Edward Elgar Publishing, 2020.

Gibson-Graham, J. K., Ann Hill and Lisa Law. 'Re-Embedding Economies in Ecologies: Resilience Building in More than Human Communities.' *Building Research & Information* 44, no. 7 (October 2, 2016): 703–16.

Gibson-Graham, J.K. *The End of Capitalism (as We Knew It): A Feminist Critique of Political Economy*. Minneapolis, MN: University of Minnesota Press, 2006.

Girvan, Anita. *Carbon Footprints as Cultural-Ecological Metaphors*. London: Routledge, 2017.

Golinski, Jan. *British Weather and the Climate of Enlightenment*. Chicago, IL: University of Chicago Press, 2010.

Gómez-Barris, Macarena. *The Extractive Zone: Social Ecologies and Decolonial Perspectives*. Durham, NC: Duke University Press, 2017.

Grealy, Liam, Tess Lea, Astrid Lorange, Andrew Brooks, and Christen Cornell. 'Introduction: Tending a Social Infrastructure.' *Infrastructural Inequalities*, no. 1 (2019). https://infrastructuralinequalities.net/issue-1/introduction/ (accessed 7 November 2024).

Green, Steve. 'Day Zero for Armidale Water Supply Now Known.' The Armidale Express, 17 July 2019. https://www.armidaleexpress.com.au/story/6279056/day-zero-for-armidale-water-supply-now-known/ (accessed 19 September 2024).

Grosz, Elizabeth. 'The Future of Feminist Theory: Dreams for New Knowledges.' In *Undutiful Daughters: New Directions in Feminist Thought and Practice*, edited by H Gunkel, C Nigianni, and F Soderback, 74–87. Durham, NC: Duke University Press, 2012.

Groupe d'experts intergouvernemental sur l'évolution du climat, ed. *Climate Change 2014: Mitigation of Climate Change Working Group III Contribution to the Fifth Assessment Report of the Intergovernmental Panel on Climate Change*. New York, NY: Cambridge University Press, 2014.

Gumbs, Alexis Pauline. 'Heat Is Not a Metaphor.' *Harper's Bazaar*, 2023. https://www.harpersbazaar.com/culture/features/a44819303/climate-crisis-maui/ (accessed 12 October 2024).

Gumbs, Alexis Pauline. 'In Case You Wanted to Save the Planet.' *Transition* 129, no. 1 (2020): 46–54.

Gumbs, Alexis Pauline. *Survival Is a Promise: The Eternal Life of Audre Lorde*. 1st edn. London New York, NY: Allen Lane, 2024.

Bibliography

Gumbs, Alexis Pauline. 'This Is What It Sounds like (an Ecological Approach).' *The Scholar & Feminist Online* 8, no. 3 (August 12, 2010).

Gumbs, Alexis Pauline. *Undrowned: Black Feminist Lessons from Marine Mammals*. Emergent Strategy Series, no. 2. Chico, CA, and Edinburgh: AK Press, 2020.

Gunaratnam, Yasmin, and Nigel Clark. 'Pre-Race Post-Race: Climate Change and Planetary Humanism.' *Darkmatter* 9, no. 1 (2012).

Hamilton, Jennifer. 'Tears, Rain, and Shame: King Lear, Masculine Vulnerability, and Environmental Crisis.' In *Water and Cognition in Early Modern English Literature*, edited by Nicolas Helms and Steve Mentz, 157–76. Amsterdam: Amsterdam University Press, 2024.

Hamilton, Jennifer. *Walking in the Rain*. 2011. Performance Space.

Hamilton, Jennifer, Matthew Allen, Felicity Joseph, Christina Kenny and Daz Chandler. 'Volume 1: Coda – Misogyny and the Anesthetic Affect (Conversation with Samantha Pinson Wrisley).' *The Heteropessimists*. https://www.theheteropessimists.com/podcast (accessed 23 September 2024).

Hamilton, Jennifer, and Gabrielle Briggs. 'Gabi Briggs: Long Version on the Vital Process of Centring Indigenous Sovereignty in Climate Action.' Community Weathering Station: SoundCloud, 17 December 2021. https://soundcloud.com/weatheringstation (accessed 23 September 2024).

Hamilton, Jennifer Mae. 'Affect Theory and Breast Cancer Memoirs: Rescripting Fears of Death and Dying in the Anthropocene.' *Body & Society* 27, no. 4 (1 December 2021): 3–29.

Hamilton, Jennifer Mae. 'On Bucketing Water – and a Response to Jonathan Franzen.' *Overland literary journal*, 13 September 2019. https://overland.org.au/2019/09/on-bucketing-water-and-a-response-to-jonathan-franzen/ (accessed 24 March 2024).

Hamilton, Jennifer Mae. 'The Future of Housework: The Similarities and Differences Between Making Kin and Making Babies.' *Australian Feminist Studies* 34, no. 102 (2 October 2019): 468–89.

Hamilton, Jennifer Mae. *This Contentious Storm: An Ecocritical and Performance History of King Lear*. London: Bloomsbury Publishing, 2017.

Hamilton, Jennifer Mae, and Nicolette Larder. 'Making Time to Care Differently for Food: The Case for the Armidale Food School.' *Critical Studies in Teaching and Learning* 10, no. SI (2022).

Hamilton, Jennifer Mae, and Astrida Neimanis. 'Composting Feminisms and Environmental Humanities.' *Environmental Humanities* 10, no. 2 (1 November 2018): 501–27.

Hamilton, Jennifer Mae, and Astrida Neimanis. 'Five Desires, Five Demands.' *Australian Feminist Studies* 34, no. 102 (2 October 2019): 385–97.

Hamilton, Jennifer Mae, Tessa Zettel, and Astrida Neimanis. 'Feminist Infrastructure for Better Weathering.' *Australian Feminist Studies* 36, no. 109 (July 3, 2021): 237–59.

Hamilton, Jennifer, and Astrida Neimanis. 'Nature / Culture – Fields of Difference – Composting.' In *Informatics of Domination*, edited by Zach Blas, Melody Jue, and Jennifer Rhee. Durham, NC: Duke University Press, 2025.

Bibliography

Hamraie, Aimi. '(Ir)Resistible Stairs: Public Health, Desiring Practices, and Material-Symbolic Ableism.' *Journal of Architectural Education* 76, no. 1 (January 2, 2022): 49–59.

Haraway, Donna. 'Situated Knowledges: The Science Question in Feminism and the Privilege of Partial Perspective.' *Feminist Studies* 14, no. 3 (1988): 575–99.

Haraway, Donna. *The Companion Species Manifesto: Dogs, People, and Significant Otherness*. 6th print. Paradigm 8. Chicago, IL: Prickly Paradigm Press, 2012.

Haraway, Donna. *Manifestly Haraway*. Minneapolis, MN: University of Minnesota Press, 2016.

Haraway, Donna. *Staying with the Trouble: Making Kin in the Chthulucene*. Durham, NC: Duke University Press, 2016.

Haraway, Donna. *When Species Meet*. Minneapolis, MN: University of Minnesota Press, 2008.

Harney, Stephano, and Fred Moten. *The Undercommons: Fugitive Planning and Black Study*. Brooklyn, NY: Minor Compositions, 2013.

Hayward, Eva. 'More Lessons from a Starfish: Prefixial Flesh and Transspeciated Selves.' *WSQ: Women's Studies Quarterly* 36, no. 3–4 (2008): 64–85.

Hazard, Cleo Wölfle. *Underflows: Queer Trans Ecologies and River Justice*. Feminist Technosciences. Seattle, WA: University of Washington Press, 2022.

'Heat Vulnerability Project – WACOSS.' https://www.wacoss.org.au/heat-vulnerability-project/ (accessed 23 October 2024).

Hickel, Jason. *Less Is More: How Degrowth Will Save the World*. New York, NY: Random House, 2020.

Hird, Myra J. 'Naturally Queer.' *Feminist Theory* 5, no. 1 (2004): 85–89.

Hochschild, Arlie Russell. *Strangers in Their Own Land: Anger and Mourning on the American Right*. Paperback edition. New York, NY, and London: The New Press, 2018.

Holmgren, David, and Bill Mollison. *Permaculture One: A Perennial Agriculture for Human Settlements*. Hepburn, Victoria: Melliodora Publishing, 2021.

Holzhey, Christoph F. E., and Arnd Wedemeyer. *Weathering: Ecologies of Exposure*. ICI Berlin Press, 2020.

Hoogeveen, Dawn, Clifford G. Atleo, Lyana Patrick, Angel M. Kennedy, Maëve Leduc, Margot W. Parkes, Tim K. Takaro and Maya K. Gislason. 'On the Possibility of Decolonising Planetary Health: Exploring New Geographies for Collaboration.' *The Lancet Planetary Health* 7, no. 2 (February 1, 2023): e179–83.

hooks, bell. *Feminism Is for Everybody: Passionate Politics*. 2nd edn. New York, NY: Routledge, 2015.

Horn, Roni. *You Are the Weather*. Scalo in collaboration with Fotomuseum Winterthur, 1997.

Houser, Heather. *Ecosickness in Contemporary U.S. Fiction: Environment and Affect*. Literature Now. New York, NY: Columbia University Press, 2014.

Humphreys, William F. 'Diversity Patterns in Australia. In *Encyclopedia of Caves*, edited by W. B. White and D. C. Culver, 203–19. Chennai: Academic Press.

Bibliography

Ingold, Tim. 'Earth, Sky, Wind, and Weather.' *Journal of the Royal Anthropological Institute* 13, no. s1 (2007): S19–38.

Ingold, Tim. *The Life of Lines*. London: Routledge, 2015.

Jackson, Zakiyyah Iman. *Becoming Human: Matter and Meaning in an Antiblack World*. 1st ed. Sexual Cultures Ser, v. 53. New York, NY: New York University Press, 2020.

James, Robin. *Resilience & Melancholy: Pop Music, Feminism, Neoliberalism*. Winchester: Zero Books, 2015.

Jay, Ollie, Anthony Capon, Peter Berry, Carolyn Broderick, Richard de Dear, George Havenith, Yasushi Honda et al. 'Reducing the Health Effects of Hot Weather and Heat Extremes: From Personal Cooling Strategies to Green Cities.' *The Lancet* 398, no. 10301 (21 August 2021): 709–24.

Jay, Ollie, Roman Hoelzl, Jana Weets, Nathan Morris, Timothy English, Lars Nybo, Jianlei Niu, Richard de Dear and Anthony Capon. 'Fanning as an Alternative to Air Conditioning – A Sustainable Solution for Reducing Indoor Occupational Heat Stress.' *Energy and Buildings* 193 (15 June 2019): 92–98.

Judd, Bettina. *Feelin: Creative Practice, Pleasure, and Black Feminist Thought*. Evanston, IL: Northwestern University Press, 2023.

Judith, Kate. 'The Other Alongside: Suburban Mangroves and the Postcolonial Swampy Gothic.' In *Gothic in the Oceanic South*. London: Routledge, 2023.

Jung, Kiju, Sharon Shavitt, Madhu Viswanathan and Joseph M. Hilbe. 'Female Hurricanes Are Deadlier than Male Hurricanes.' *Proceedings of the National Academy of Sciences* 111, no. 24 (June 17, 2014): 8782–7.

Kanngieser, Amer. 'Listening as Taking Leave.' *The Seed Box* (blog), 15 January 2021. https://theseedbox.mistraprograms.org/blog/listening-as-taking-leave/ (accessed 15 June 2024).

Kassouf, Susan. 'Thinking Catastrophic Thoughts: A Traumatized Sensibility on a Hotter Planet.' *The American Journal of Psychoanalysis* 82, no. 1 (2022): 60–79.

Kelley, Lindsay. 'Kitchen Futures: Participatory Taste Workshops and the Battle for Together.' *Australian Feminist Studies* 38, no. 115–116 (3 April 2023): 85–102.

Kim, Clare Jean. 'Michael Vick, Race, and Animality' In *Ecofeminism: Feminist Intersections with Other Animals and the Earth*, 2nd edn, edited by Carol J. Adams and Lori Gruen. New York, NY: Bloomsbury, 2022.

Kimmerer, Robin Wall. *Braiding Sweetgrass*. 1st edn. Minneapolis, MN: Milkweed Editions, 2013.

Kirby, Vicki. *Quantum Anthropologies: Life at Large*. Durham, NC: Duke University Press, 2011.

Kirby, Vicki, ed. *What If Culture Was Nature All Along?* New Materialisms. Edinburgh: Edinburgh University Press, 2017.

Klein, Naomi. 'Dancing the World into Being: A Conversation with Idle No More's Leanne Simpson.' *Yes! Magazine*, 6 March 2013. https://www.yesmagazine.org/social-justice/2013/03/06/dancing-the-world-into-being-a-conversation-with-idle-no-more-leanne-simpson (accessed 15 January 2025).

Bibliography

Klein, Naomi. *Doppelganger: A Trip into the Mirror World*. London: Allen Lane, 2023.

Klein, Naomi. *This Changes Everything: Capitalism vs. the Climate*. New York, NY: Simon & Schuster, 2015.

Klein, Naomi, and Judith Burr. *The Right to Feel*. Podcast. Future Ecologies, 2024. https://www.futureecologies.net/listen/the-right-to-feel (accessed 15 January 2025).

Klinenberg, Eric. *Heat Wave: A Social Autopsy of Disaster in Chicago*. Chicago, IL: University of Chicago Press, 2015.

Knox, Hannah, and Evelina Gambino. 'Infrastructure.' *Cambridge Encyclopedia of Anthropology*, March 1, 2023. https://www.anthroencyclopedia.com/entry/infrastructure (accessed 5 October 2024).

Kolbert, Elizabeth. 'The Political Climate.' *The New Yorker*, 22 August 2022.

Kuznetski (née Tofantšuk), Julia, and Stacy Alaimo. 'Transcorporeality: An Interview with Stacy Alaimo.' *Ecozon@: European Journal of Literature, Culture and Environment* 11, no. 2 (20 September 2020): 137–46.

LaDuke, Winona, and Deborah Cowen. 'Beyond Wiindigo Infrastructure.' *South Atlantic Quarterly* 119, no. 2 (April 1, 2020): 243–68.

Lakoff, George. 'The Contemporary Theory of Metaphor.' In *Metaphor and Thought*, edited by Andrew Ortony, 201–51. Cambridge: Cambridge University Press, 1993.

Larder, Nicolette, Kristen Lyons and Geoff Woolcock. 'Enacting Food Sovereignty: Values and Meanings in the Act of Domestic Food Production in Urban Australia.' *Local Environment* 19, no. 1 (January 2, 2014): 56–76.

Larkin, Brian. 'The Politics and Poetics of Infrastructure.' *Annual Review of Anthropology* 42, no. 1 (2013): 327–43.

Le Guin, Ursula K. *Dancing at the Edge of the World: Thoughts on Words, Women, Places*. 1st edn. New York, NY: Grove Press, 1989.

Lea, Tess. *Wild Policy: Indigeneity and the Unruly Logics of Intervention*. Anthropology of Policy. Stanford, CA: Stanford University Press, 2020.

Lewis, Sophie. *Enemy Feminisms: TERFs, Policewomen, and Girlbosses Against Liberation*. Chicago, IL: Haymarket Books, 2025.

Liboiron, Max. 'There's No Such Thing as "We".' *Discard Studies* (blog), 12 October 2020. https://discardstudies.com/2020/10/12/theres-no-such-thing-as-we/.

Liboiron, Max. *Pollution Is Colonialism*. Durham, NC: Duke University Press, 2021.

Liljeström, Marianne. 'Feminism and Queer Temporal Complexities.' *SQS–Suomen Queer-Tutkimuksen Seuran* 13, no. 1–2 (2019): 23–8.

Lorange, Astrid, and Andrew Brooks. 'Endless Study, Infinite Debt: On Study Inside and Outside the University Classroom.' *Critical Studies in Teaching and Learning* 10, no. 1 (2022): 1–20.

Lorde, Audre. 'Coal.' *Transatlantic Review* 41 (1972): 47.

Lorde, Audre. 'The Uses of Anger: Women Responding to Racism.' In *Sister Outsider: Essays and Speeches by Audre Lorde*, 124–33. Berkeley, CA: Crossing Press, 2007.

Lorde, Audre. 'Uses of the Erotic: The Erotic as Power.' In *Sister Outsider: Essays and Speeches by Audre Lorde*, 53–59. Berkeley, CA: Crossing Press, 2007.

Bibliography

Lorde, Audre. *Zami: A New Spelling of My Name*. London: Sheba Feminist Publishers, 1984.

MacGregor, Sherilyn. 'Making Matter Great Again? Ecofeminism, New Materialism and the Everyday Turn in Environmental Politics.' *Environmental Politics* 30, no. 1–2 (23 February 2021): 41–60.

MacGregor, Sherilyn. 'Reclaiming and Reframing Ecofeminist Politics in the Face of Continuous Global Crises.' Humboldt University, Berlin, 4 May 2023.

Mallin, Samuel B. *Art Line Thought*. Contributions to Phenomenology, v. 21. Dordrecht and Boston: Kluwer Academic Publishers, 1996.

Martin, Craig. *Renaissance Meteorology*. Baltimore, MD: Johns Hopkins University Press, 2011. https://doi.org/10.1353/book.1763.

Masco, Joseph. 'Bad Weather: On Planetary Crisis.' *Social Studies of Science* 40, no. 1 (2010): 7–40. https://doi.org/10.1177/0306312709341598.

Mayes, Christopher. *Unsettling Food Politics: Agriculture, Dispossession and Sovereignty in Australia*. London: Rowman & Littlefield Publishers, 2018. http://ebookcentral.proquest.com/lib/usyd/detail.action?docID=5497698.

Maynard, Stella. 'Weaponised Weathers: Heat, Don Dale, and 'Everything-Ist' Prison Abolition.' *Right Now*, 13 August 2019. https://rightnow.org.au/opinion/weaponised-weathers-heat-don-dale-everything-ist-prison-abolition/.

McFetridge, Christine. 'An Inconvenient Curve: Unlearning Settler Colonial Representations of Birrarung.' PhD, RMIT, 2024.

McKittrick, Katherine. *Dear Science and Other Stories*. Errantries. Durham, NC, and London: Duke University Press, 2021.

McKittrick, Katherine, and Sylvia Wynter. *Sylvia Wynter: On Being Human as Praxis*. Durham, NC: Duke University Press, 2015.

McLauchlan, Laura. 'Dr Laura McLauchlan: Hedgehogs, Conservation and Attachment to Other Animals: Embodied Approaches to Anti-Polarisation for Our Shared Worlds.' University of Oregon. Accessed October 28, 2024. https://calendar.uoregon.edu/event/dr-laura-mclauchlan-hedgehogs-conservation-and-attachment-to-other-animals-embodied-approaches-to-anti-polarisation-for-our-shared-worlds, https://www.uoregon.edu/.

McLauchlan, Laura. *Hedgehogs, Killing, and Kindness: The Contradictions of Care in Conservation Practice*. Cambridge, MA: The MIT Press, 2024.

Mellick Lopes, Abby, and Stephen Healy. 'Cultivating the Habits of Coolth.' In *Assembling and Governing Habits* Eds. Tony Bennett, Ben Dibley, Gay Hawkins, Grey Noble, London: Routledge, 2021.

Mellick Lopes, Abby, Katherine Gibson, Louise Crabtree and Helen Armstrong. 'Cooling the Commons: Pilot Research Report,' 2016.

Merleau-Ponty, Maurice. *Phenomenology of Perception*. Trans. Colin Smith. Reprint edn. London and New York, NY: Routledge and K. Paul, 1981.

'METEOROLOGY ACT 1955.' https://classic.austlii.edu.au/au/legis/cth/consol_act/ma1955160/ (accessed 7 August 2024).

Mies, Maria, and Vandana Shiva. *Ecofeminism*. London: Zed Books, 2014.

Mol, Annemarie. *The Body Multiple: Ontology in Medical Practice*. Science and Cultural Theory. Durham, NC: Duke University Press, 2002.

Bibliography

Money, Jazz. 'Some Generosities.' *Cordite Poetry Review*, 12 May 2024. http://cordite.org.au/poetry/treat/some-generosities/.

Murphy, Jamieson. 'The Leader Launches Its Water Pressure Campaign.' *The Northern Daily Leader*, June 2, 2019. https://www.northerndailyleader.com.au/story/6193564/the-leader-launches-its-water-pressure-campaign/ (accessed 23 September 2024).

Myers, Natasha. 'Ungrid-Able Ecologies: Decolonizing the Ecological Sensorium in a 10,000 Year-Old NaturalCultural Happening.' *Catalyst: Feminism, Theory, Technoscience* 3, no. 2 (October 19, 2017): 1–24.

Myles, Eileen, and Annamarie Jagose. 'Eileen Myles: To Dig a Hole in Eternity – Sydney Writers' Festival.' (2018) https://omny.fm/shows/sydney-writers-festival/eileen-myles-to-dig-a-hole-in-eternity (accessed 29 October 2024).

Myles, Eileen, and Maggie Nelson. 'Eileen Myles in Conversation with Maggie Nelson.' *Women's Studies* 51, no. 8 (November 17, 2022): 880–98.

Neimanis, Astrida. *Bodies of Water: Posthuman Feminist Phenomenology*. Environmental Cultures Series. London and New York, NY: Bloomsbury Academic, 2017.

Neimanis, Astrida. 'Stygofaunal Worlds.' *Cultural Politics* 19, no. 1 (1 March 2023): 18–38.

Neimanis, Astrida. 'Toxic Erotics and Bad Ecosex at Windermere Basin.' *Environmental Humanities* 14, no. 3 (1 November 2022): 699–717.

Neimanis, Astrida. 'Weather Writing (Out of the Classroom).' In *Teaching with Feminist Materialisms*, edited by Rachel Loewen Walker and Pat Treusch. AtGender Teaching With Series. Budapest: CEU Press, 2015.

Neimanis, Astrida, Aunty Rhonda Dixon, and Claire Britton. *The River Ends as the Ocean: Walk the Tide Out*. 2021. Walkshop.

Neimanis, Astrida, and Jennifer Hamilton. 'Falling Out Together.' *Feral Feminisms*, no. 10 (Fall 2021): 114–31.

Neimanis, Astrida, and Jennifer Hamilton. 'The Weather Is Now Political.' *The Conversation* (blog), 21 May 2017. https://theconversation.com/the-weather-is-now-political-77791.

Neimanis, Astrida, and Jennifer Mae Hamilton. 'Weathering.' *Feminist Review* 118, no. 1 (2018): 80–4.

Neimanis, Astrida, and D. R. Koukal. 'Introduction: Back to the Things Themselves!' *Phaenex: Journal of Existential and Phenomenological Theory and Culture* 3, no. 2 (2008).

Neimanis, Astrida, and Rachel Loewen Walker. 'Weathering: Climate Change and the 'Thick Time' of Transcorporeality.' *Hypatia* 29, no. 3 (2014): 558–75.

Neimanis, Astrida, and Laura McLauchlan. 'Composting (in) the Gender Studies Classroom: Growing Feminisms for Climate Changing Pedagogies.' *Curriculum Inquiry* 52, no. 2 (15 March 2022): 218–34.

Nelson, Maggie. *On Freedom: Four Songs of Care and Constraint*. Minneapolis, MN: Graywolf Press, 2021.

Neumayer, Eric, and Thomas Plümper. 'The Gendered Nature of Natural Disasters: The Impact of Catastrophic Events on the Gender Gap in Life Expectancy,

Bibliography

1981–2002.' *Annals of the Association of American Geographers* 97, no. 3 (2007): 551–66.

Ngai, Sianne. *Ugly Feelings*. Paperback edn. Cambridge, MA, and London: Harvard University Press, 2007.

Nikiforuk, Andrew. 'What Is Facism.' *The Tyee*, 5 November 2024. https://thetyee.ca/Analysis/2024/11/05/What-Is-Fascism/ (25 January 2025).

Norgaard, Kari Marie. *Living in Denial: Climate Change, Emotions, and Everyday Life*. New York, NY: MIT Press, 2011.

'Number of Cattle.' *Our World in Data*. https://ourworldindata.org/grapher/cattle-livestock-count-heads (accessed 24 September 2024).

O'Gorman, Emily, James Beattie, and Matthew Henry. 'Histories of Climate, Science, and Colonization in Australia and New Zealand, 1800–1945.' *WIREs Climate Change* 7, no. 6 (2016): 893–909.

Okanagan Nation Alliance. 'Okanagan River Restoration.' https://syilx.org/projects/okanagan-river-restoration-initiative-penticton-channel-spawning-beds/ (accessed 27 October 2024).

Out of the Woods Collective. 'Infrastructure Against Borders.' In *Hope Against Hope: Writings on Ecological Crisis*. New York, NY: Common Notions, 2020.

paperson, la. *A Third University Is Possible*: Vol. 19. Forerunners. Minneapolis, MN: University of Minnesota Press, 2017.

Papertalk-Green, Charmaine, and John Kinsella. *False Claims of Colonial Thieves*. Broome, WA: Magabala Books, 2018.

Parkinson, Debra, and Claire Zara. 'The Hidden Disaster: Domestic Violence in the Aftermath of Natural Disaster.' *The Australian Journal of Emergency Management* 28, no. 2 (April 1, 2013): 28–35.

Parson, Sean, and Emily Ray. 'Drill Baby Drill: Labor, Accumulation, and the Sexualization of Resource Extraction.' *Theory & Event* 23, no. 1 (2020): 248–70.

Pasley, And, Tommy Hamilton, and Jaimie Veale. 'Transnormativities: Reterritorializing Perceptions and Practice.' In *Rethinking Transgender Identities*, edited by Petra L. Doan and Lynda Johnston. London: Routledge, 2022.

Patrick, Wanta Steve Jampijinpa. 'Pulya-Ranyi: Winds of Change.' *Cultural Studies Review* 21, no. 1 (May 12, 2015).

Phillips, Perdita. 'Walk 'til You Run Out of Water.' *Performance Research* 17, no. 2 (2012): 97–109.

Phillips, Perdita, and Astrida Neimanis. 'Postcards from the Underground.' *Journal of Public Pedagogies*, no. 4 (2019): 127–39.

Piepzna-Samarasinha, Leah Lakshmi. *Care Work: Dreaming Disability Justice*. Vancouver: Arsenal Pulp Press, 2018.

Pinson Wrisley, Samantha. 'Heteropessimism and the Pleasure of Saying No.' *Capacious Journal* 3, no. 2 (2024).

Plevey, Tom. "On Our Own Terms': Anaiwan People Look to Buy 240 Hectares of Bushland to Reclaim Country.' *The Guardian*, 22 February 2022, sec. Australia news. https://www.theguardian.com/australia-news/2022/feb/23/on-our-own-terms-anaiwan-people-look-to-buy-240-hectares-of-bushland-to-reclaim-country (accessed 8 February 2025).

Bibliography

Plumwood, Val. *Feminism and the Mastery of Nature*. London: Routledge, 2002.

Probyn-Rapsey, Fiona, and Lynette Russell. 'Tools, Troops or Escapees? Cattle Trafficking in the Early Years of the Colony of New South Wales, Australia.' *Environment and History*, 17 October 2024, 1–22.

Protevi, John. 'Katrina.' *Symposium* 10, no. 1 (1 April 2006): 363–81.

Puar, Jasbir. 'Intersectionality, Anti-Imperialism, Anti-Semitism, and the Question of Palestine.' In *The Routledge Companion to Intersectionalities*, edited by Jennifer Christine Nash and Samantha Pinto, 529–36. London and New York, NY: Routledge, 2023.

Qualmann, Clare, and Claire Hind, eds. *Ways to Wander*. 1st edn. Axminster: Triarchy Press, 2015.

Randerson, Janine. *Weather as Medium: Toward a Meteorological Art*. Leonardo (Series). Cambridge, MA: The MIT Press, 2018.

Randerson, Janine, Jennifer Salmond and Chris Manford. 'Weather as Medium: Art and Meteorological Science.' *Leonardo* 48, no. 1 (1 February 2015): 16–24.

Rankine, Claudia. 'Weather.' *The New York Times*, 15 June 2020, sec. Books. https://www.nytimes.com/2020/06/15/books/review/claudia-rankine-weather-poem-coronavirus.html (accessed 20 August 2024).

Ray, Sarah Jaquette. *A Field Guide to Climate Anxiety: How to Keep Your Cool on a Warming Planet*. Oakland, CA: University of California Press, 2020.

Ray, Sarah Jaquette, and Jay Sibara. *Disability Studies and the Environmental Humanities: Toward an Eco-Crip Theory*. Lincoln, NE: University of Nebraska Press, 2017.

Redvers, Nicole, Yuria Celidwen, Clinton Schultz, Ojistoh Horn, Cicilia Githaiga, Melissa Vera, Marlikka Perdrisat et al. 'The Determinants of Planetary Health: An Indigenous Consensus Perspective.' *The Lancet Planetary Health* 6, no. 2 (1 February 2022): e156–63.

Reid, Susan. 'Ocean Justice.' *Cultural Politics* 19, no. 1 (March 1, 2023): 107–27.

Reid, Susan. 'Solwara 1 and the Sessile Ones.' In *Blue Legalities: The Life and Laws of the Sea*, edited by Irus Braverman and Elizabeth R. Johnson. Durham, NC: Duke University Press, 2020.

Reimer, Chad. *Before We Lost the Lake: A Natural and Human History of Sumas Valley*. Halfmoon Bay, BC: Caitlin Press, 2018.

'Resilience, n.' In *OED Online*. Oxford University Press. https://www.oed.com/view/Entry/163619 (accessed 19 August 2020).

Rice, Natalie. 'Without End.' *FEELed Notes* (blog), 29 March 2023. https://thefeeledlab.ca/2023/03/29/without-end/ (accessed 19 February 2025).

Rich, Adrienne. 'Notes towards a Politics of Location (1984).' In *Blood, Bread, and Poetry: Selected Prose 1979–1985*, 210–31. New York, NY: W. W. Norton & Company, 1994.

Rooney, Tonya, and Mindy Blaise. *Rethinking Environmental Education in a Climate Change Era: Weather Learning in Early Childhood*. London: Routledge, 2022.

Roughgarden, Joan. *Evolution's Rainbow: Diversity, Gender, and Sexuality in Nature and People*. Berkeley, CA: University of California Press, 2004.

Ruskin, John. 'Modern Painters, Volume 3 (of 5).' https://www.gutenberg.org/files/38923/38923-h/38923-h.htm (accessed 30 October 2024).

Bibliography

Sage, Daniel, Pete Fussey, and Andrew Dainty. 'Securing and Scaling Resilient Futures: Neoliberalization, Infrastructure, and Topologies of Power.' *Environment and Planning D: Society and Space* 33, no. 3 (1 June 2015): 494–511.

Salazar, Juan. *The Bamboo Bridge*. Documentary. Matadora Films, 2019.

Salleh, Ariel. *Ecofeminism as Politics: Nature, Marx and the Postmodern*. London: Zed Books, 2017.

Sandilands, Catriona. 'Desiring Nature, Queering Ethics.' *Environmental Ethics* 23, no. 2 (1 May 2001): 169–88.

Sandilands, Catriona. *Good-Natured Feminist: Ecofeminism and the Quest for Democracy*. Minneapolis, MN: University of Minnesota Press, 1999.

Sandilands, Catriona, and Erickson Bruce, eds. *Queer Ecologies: Sex, Nature, Politics, Desire*. Bloomington: Indiana University Press, 2011.

Sandilands, Catriona. 'Some "F" Words for the Environmental Humanities: Feralities, Feminisms, Futurities.' In *The Routledge Companion to the Environmental Humanities*, edited by Ursula K. Heise, Jon Christensen and Michelle Niemann. Routledge Companions. London and New York: Routledge, 2017.

Sasser, Jade. *Climate Anxiety and the Kid Question: Deciding Whether to Have Children in an Uncertain Future*. Berkeley, CA: University of California Press, 2024.

Saussure, Ferdinand de. *Course in General Linguistics*. London: Duckworth, 1983.

Schuller, Kyla. *The Biopolitics of Feeling: Race, Sex, and Science in the Nineteenth Century*. Durham, NC: Duke University Press, 2018.

Sedgwick, Eve Kosofsky. *A Dialogue on Love*. Boston, MA: Beacon Press, 1999.

Sedgwick, Eve Kosofsky. 'Making Things, Practicing Emptiness.' In *The Weather in Proust*, edited by Jonathan Goldberg. Durham, NC: Duke University Press, 2011.

Sedgwick, Eve Kosofsky, *Touching Feeling: Affect, Pedagogy, Performativity*. Durham, NC: Duke University Press, 2003.

Serres, Michel. *La Distribution*. Paris: Editions de Minuit, 1977.

Seymour, Nicole. *Bad Environmentalism: Irony and Irreverence in the Ecological Age* Minneapolis, MN: University of Minnesota Press, 2018.

Sharp, Hasana, and Chloë Taylor. *Feminist Philosophies of Life*. Montreal: McGill-Queen's University Press, 2016.

Sharpe, Christina. *In the Wake: On Blackness and Being*. Durham, NC: Duke University Press, 2016.

Shove, Elizabeth. 'Infrastructures and Practices: Networks beyond the City.' In *Beyond the Networked City: Infrastructure Reconfigurations and Urban Change in the North and South*, edited by Olivier Coutard and Jonathan Rutherford, 242–58. London: Routledge, 2015.

Shove, Elizabeth, Mika Pantzar, and Matt Watson. *The Dynamics of Social Practice: Everyday Life and How It Changes*. London: SAGE, 2012.

Siemiatycki, Matti, Theresa Enright, and Mariana Valverde. 'The Gendered Production of Infrastructure.' *Progress in Human Geography* 44, no. 2 (1 April 2020): 297–314.

Simmons, Kristen. 'Settler Atmospherics — Cultural Anthropology.' https://culanth.org/fieldsights/1221-settler-atmospherics (accessed 3 February 2019).

Singer, Hayley. *Abandon Every Hope: Essays for the Dead*. Perth, WA: Upswell, 2023.

Bibliography

Singer, Hayley, Tessa Laird, Stephanie Lavau, Blanche Verlie, and Anna Dunn. 'Do-It-Together (DIT): Collective Action in and Against the Anthropocene.' *Feral Feminisms*, no. 10 (Fall 2021): 7–21.

Sobecka, Karolina. *Thinking Like a Cloud*. 2014. Installation. https://karolinasobecka.com/thinking-like-a-cloud (accessed 15 June 2024).

Solnit, Rebecca, Thelma Young Lutunatabua, and David Solnit, eds. *Not Too Late: Changing the Climate Story from Despair to Possibility*. Chicago, IL: Haymarket Books, 2023.

Somerville, Margaret, and Frances Bodkin. 'Featherlines: Becoming Human Differently with Earth Others.' In *Becoming Earth*, 65–83. Leiden: Brill, 2016.

Springgay, Stephanie, and Sarah E. Truman. *Walking Methodologies in a More-than-Human World: WalkingLab*. Routledge Advances in Research Methods. Abingdon and New York: Routledge, 2018.

Sprinkle, Annie, Beth Stephens, Jennie Klein, Una Chaudhuri, Linda Montano and Paul B. Preciado. *Assuming the Ecosexual Position: The Earth as Lover*. Minneapolis, MN, and London: University of Minnesota Press, 2021.

Star, Susan Leigh. 'The Ethnography of Infrastructure.' *American Behavioral Scientist* 43, no. 3 (1999): 377–91.

Stephens, Elizabeth. 'Bad Feelings: An Affective Genealogy of Feminism.' *Australian Feminist Studies* 30, no. 85 (3 July 2015): 273–82.

Stevens, Lara, Peta Tait, and Denise Varney, eds. *Feminist Ecologies*. Cham, Switzerland: Springer International Publishing, 2018.

Stryker, Susan. *Transgender History: The Roots of Today's Revolution*. 2nd edn. Berkeley, CA: Seal Press, 2017.

Sultana, Farhana. 'The Unbearable Heaviness of Climate Coloniality.' *Political Geography* 99 (2022): 102638.

Supran, Geoffrey. 'The Fossil Fuel Industry's Invisible Colonization of Academia.' *The Guardian*, 13 March 2017. https://www.theguardian.com/environment/climate-consensus-97-per-cent/2017/mar/13/the-fossil-fuel-industrys-invisible-colonization-of-academia (accessed 12 October 2024).

SURJ Toronto. '. . . Until Everyone Is Free,' n.d. https://www.surjtoronto.com/blog/-until-everyone-is-free (accessed 31 January 2025).

Sustainable Living Armidale. 'FREE: Public Water Forum — Armidale Town Hall » Sustainable Living Armidale.' Accessed 24 September 2024. https://slarmidale.org/2020/02/15370.

Swain, Rachael. 'A Meeting of Nations: Trans-Indigenous and Intercultural Interventions in Contemporary Indigenous Dance.' *Theatre Journal* 67, no. 3 (2015): 503–21. https://www.jstor.org/stable/24582544.

Sydney Environment Institute. *Jan Zalasiewicz: The Anthropocene as a Potential New Unit of the Geological Time Scale*. Public Lecture, 2014. https://www.youtube.com/watch?v=y_FbbXlgkgE (accessed 23 January 2025).

TallBear, Kim. 'Making Love and Relations Beyond Settler Sex and Family.' In *Make Kin, Not Population*. Chicago, IL: Prickly Paradigm Press, 2018.

Tan, Kynan. 'Kynan Tan Meditation Teacher.' Kynan Tan Meditation Teacher. https://kynanmeditation.net/ (accessed 18 February 2025).

Bibliography

The Piddock Clam Collective. 'Wrack Writing (Selections).' *Feminist Review* 130, no. 1 (2022): 115–19.

The University of British Columbia. 'UBC Vision, Purpose and Values.' https://www.ubc.ca/about/vision-values.html (accessed 28 October 2024).

The University of Sydney. 'Hot in the City: Climate and Health in Urban Environments.' https://www.sydney.edu.au/news-opinion/news/2017/04/06/-hot-in-the-city--climate-and-health-in-urban-environments.html (accessed 4 April 2023).

The Weathering Collective. 'The Weathering Map of Microclimates and Approximate Watery Bodies.' The Weathering Station, 18 December 2017. https://weatheringstation.net/2017/12/18/the-weathering-map-of-microclimates-approximate-watery-bodies/ (accessed 23 August 2024).

Thompson, Charis, and Sherilyn MacGregor. 'The Death of Nature.' In *Routledge Handbook of Gender and Environment*, edited by Sherilyn MacGregor. Milton Park: Taylor & Francis, 2017.

Tippett, Krista. 'Ada Limón — 'To Be Made Whole' | The On Being Project,' 2023. https://onbeing.org/programs/ada-limon-to-be-made-whole/.

Todd, Zoe S. 'An Indigenous Feminist's Take on the Ontological Turn: 'Ontology' Is Just Another Word for Colonialism.' *Journal of Historical Sociology* 29, no. 1 (2016): 4–22.

Truman, Sarah E. *Feminist Speculations and the Practice of Research-Creation: Writing Pedagogies and Intertextual Affects*. London: Routledge, 2021.

Tschakert, Petra, and Krishna Karthikeyan. 'Embodied Thermal Insecurity and Counter-Hegemonic Heat Mapping.' *Antipode* 57, no. 1 (2025): 433–54.

Tsing, Anna Lowenhaupt. 'On Nonscalability.' *Common Knowledge* 18, no. 3 (August 1, 2012): 505–24. https://doi.org/10.1215/0961754X-1630424.

Tsing, Anna Lowenhaupt. *The Mushroom at the End of the World: On the Possibility of Life in Capitalist Ruins*. Princeton, NJ: Princeton University Press, 2015.

Tuana, Nancy. 'Viscous Porosity: Witnessing Katrina.' In *Material Feminisms*, eds. Stacy Alaimo and Susan J. Hekman, 188–213. Bloomington, IN: Indiana University Press, 2008.

Tuck, Eve, and K. Wayne Yang. 'Decolonization Is Not a Metaphor.' *Decolonization: Indigeneity, Education & Society* 1, no. 1 (2012): 1–40.

Tyrrell, Ian. *River Dreams: The People and Landscape of the Cooks River*. Sydney: NewSouth, 2018.

'Untreated Water for Tomato Farm – Guyra Gazette.' https://www.guyragazette.com.au/news/untreated-water-for-tomato-farm.php (accessed 24 September 2024).

Vakoch, Douglas A., ed. *Transecology: Transgender Perspectives on Environment and Nature*. Routledge Studies in Gender and Environments. London and New York, NY: Routledge, 2020.

van Dooren, Thom. *Flight Ways: Life and Loss at the Edge of Extinction*. New York, NY: Columbia University Press, 2014.

van Gelder, Pia. *Relaxation Circuit*. 2015. Mixed Media Performance. https://westspace.org.au/program/relaxation-circuit (accessed 18 February 2025).

Bibliography

van Neerven, Ellen. 'The Country Is Like a Body.' *Right Now: Human Rights in Australia*, 26 October 2015. https://rightnow.org.au/creative-works/the-country-is-like-a-body/.

van Neerven, Ellen. *Personal Score: Sport, Culture, Identity*. St Lucia: University of Queensland Press, 2023.

van Patter, Lauren E., Julia Linares-Roake and Andrea V. Breen. 'What Does One Health Want? Feminist, Posthuman, and Anti-Colonial Possibilities.' *One Health Outlook* 5, no. 1 (10 March 2023): 4.

Vergès, Françoise. *A Decolonial Feminism*. Trans. Ashley J. Bohrer. London: Pluto Press, 2021.

Verlie, Blanche. 'Climate Justice in More-than-Human Worlds.' *Environmental Politics* 31, no. 2 (21 September 2021): 297–319.

Verlie, Blanche. 'Feeling Climate Injustice: Affective Climate Violence, Greenhouse Gaslighting and the Whiteness of Climate Anxiety.' *Environment and Planning E: Nature and Space* 7, no. 4 (2024): 1601–19.

Verlie, Blanche. *Learning to Live with Climate Change: From Anxiety to Transformation*. New York, NY: Routledge, 2022.

Verlie, Blanche, and Astrida Neimanis. 'Breathing Climate Crises: Feminist Environmental Humanities and More-than-Human Witnessing.' *Angelaki* 28, no. 4 (4 July 2023): 117–31.

Vincent, Eve, and Timothy Neale, eds. *Unstable Relations: Indigenous People and Environmentalism in Contemporary Australia*. Crawley, WA: UWA Publishing, 2017.

Vizenor, Gerald. *Survivance: Narratives of Native Presence*. Lincoln, NE: University of Nebraska Press, 2008.

Walker, Jeremy, and Melinda Cooper. 'Genealogies of Resilience From Systems Ecology to the Political Economy of Crisis Adaptation.' *Security Dialogue* 42, no. 2 (1 April 2011): 143–60. https://doi.org/10.1177/0967010611399616.

Warren, Jeff. 'Practices Are the Habits We Choose.' Home Base With Jeff Warren. Accessed 31 October 2024. https://www.homebasewithjeff.com/p/practices-are-the-habits-we-choose ://substack.com/channel-frame.

'Water Conservation – Armidale Regional Council.' Accessed 24 September 2024. https://www.armidaleregional.nsw.gov.au/environment/water-usage-and-supply/water-conservation.

Watts, Vanessa. 'Indigenous Place-Thought and Agency Amongst Humans and Non Humans (First Woman and Sky Woman Go On a European World Tour!).' *Decolonization: Indigeneity, Education & Society* 2, no. 1 (4 May 2013).

'Weather, *n*. Meanings, Etymology and More | Oxford English Dictionary.' https://www.oed.com/dictionary/weather_n (accessed 6 August 2024).

'Weathering, *n*. Meanings, Etymology and More | Oxford English Dictionary.' https://www.oed.com/dictionary/weathering_n. (accessed 7 June 2024).

Whittaker, Alison. *Blakwork*. Broome, WA: Magabala Books, 2018.

Widders, Uncle Steve, and Jennifer Hamilton. *Anaiwan Elder Uncle Steve Widders Yarns about Climate and Colonisation*. Audio recording. Anaiwan Country, 2021. https://soundcloud.com/weatheringstation/steve-widders-and-jen-hamilton (accessed 6 December 2024).

Bibliography

Wiegman, Robyn. *Object Lessons*. Durham, NC: Duke University Press, 2012.

Willard, Tania. *Liberation of the Wind*. 2018. Custom-made windsocks, flatscreen TV, weather data, and poetry software. https://www.blackwoodgallery.ca/projects/liberation-of-the-chinook-wind-lwc (accessed 18 December 2024).

Williams, Raymond L. *Marxism and Literature*. Repr. Marxist Introductions. Oxford: Oxford University Press, 2009.

Wilson, Elizabeth A. *Gut Feminism*. Durham, NC: Duke University Press, 2015.

Wilson, Elizabeth A. *Psychosomatic: Feminism and the Neurological Body*. Durham, NC: Duke University Press, 2004.

Wind, Maya. *Towers of Ivory and Steel: How Israeli Universities Deny Palestinian Freedom*. London and New York, NY: Verso, 2024.

Woelfle-Erskine, C., and J. Cole. 'Transfiguring the Anthropocene: Stochastic Reimaginings of Human-Beaver Worlds.' *TSQ: Transgender Studies Quarterly* 2, no. 2 (1 January 2015): 297–316.

Wright, Judith. *The Coral Battleground*. Sydney: Harper Collins, 1977.

Wright, Kate. 'Survival Day 2018 Exhibition.' *Armidale Aboriginal Community Garden* (blog), 16 April 2018. https://armidalecommunitygarden.org/exhibitions-and-public-events/survival-day-2018-exhibition/ (accessed 24 September 2024).

Wright, Sarah. *Becoming Weather: Weather, Embodiment and Affect*. London: Taylor and Francis, 2024.

Wright, Sarah, and Matalena Tofa. 'Weather Geographies: Talking about the Weather, Considering Diverse Sovereignties.' *Progress in Human Geography* 45, no. 5 (1 October 2021): 1126–46.

Yusoff, Kathryn. *A Billion Black Anthropocenes or None*. Minneapolis, MN: Minnesota University Press, 2018.

Yusoff, Kathryn. 'Queer Coal: Genealogies in/of the Blood.' *philoSOPHIA* 5, no. 2 (2015): 203–29.

Zettel, Tessa. 'OuMoPo – Workshop for Potential Worlds.' https://oumopo.com/ (accessed 7 February 2025).

Acknowledgements

Weathering, as a project, has evolved across different places over a decade, for a long time existing only as iterative fragments. Writing this book helped us realize that something quite specific has emerged out of this exploratory process. Substantial research time in our academic jobs has given us considerable creative and intellectual freedom to work in this way. Without it, the book would not be possible. Although research is a fundamental aspect of academic work, we do not take this for granted.

We are daunted by trying to acknowledge everyone who has supported this work, because our gratitude is wide and deep, but also because of the fragmented and durational nature of the projects constelled here. In writing the book, we cite wherever possible colleagues and friends whose work has influenced us, even if we could not engage with it deeply in these pages. We also have noted the transient facilitators, co-organizers and supporters of weathering activities along the way. Endnotes are part of our citational practices but are also a deliberate mode of acknowledgement, even if frustratingly partial.

We want to first thank members of the Weathering Collective's earliest iterations: Tessa Zettel, Rebecca Giggs ('Bush Google!'), Stephanie Springgay, Sarah Truman and Kate Wright. Although the project eventually ceased being a larger collective pursuit, these early experiments (camping, walking, playing, talking, reading, making, meeting, swimming, writing) were foundational for everything that has come after. We're immensely grateful to Tessa for her steady work and ongoing commitment to the project from that first camp through to this book.

Various opportunities have been pivotal to weathering's development. Thank you to *The Seed Box: a MISTRA FORMAS Environmental Humanities Collaboratory* for firstly funding Jen's two-year part-time post-doc at the Department of Gender and Cultural Studies at the University of Sydney (2016–18), which seeded this collaboration between Jen and Astrida; and secondly, for funding 'Weathering Early Childhood Education' on Rindö in the Stockholm archipelago in 2017. Here, we prototyped many practices that form the backbone of this book (including 'Weathering with or without' and 'Cosmic weathering'). This workshop also helped us sense the scope and

Acknowledgements

potential of the work, and conceptualize its applications beyond our own academic disciplines. Thank you especially to the Common Worlds Collective (Mindy, Veronica, Affrica, Tonya) and Mia for organizing this event. Many years later, in 2023, Leila Harris invited us to share our weathering collaboration work with audiences at UBC Vancouver's Gender, Race and Social Justice Institute (GRSJ) and at the UBC Institute for Resources, Environment and Sustainability (IRES), as well as with the members of Leila's EDGES Lab. In preparing for those events, we realized that we had actually compiled a coherent body of practice-led research and research led-practices through this project, but questions and responses from the audiences, and students outside of our own humanities disciplines in particular, convinced us of the value of sharing this work in a more comprehensive and accessible form. As the project unfolded over the last decade, opportunities to continue collaborating with Tessa affirmed the important role that the weathering activities themselves have played, as specifically derived and facilitated social art practices. Two notable collaborations with Tessa were the Weathering Everything Symposium in Armidale at UNE in 2020 and a Weathering Workshop as part of Water Lessons at *rīvus* (23rd Biennale of Sydney) at the invitation of Lleah Smith in 2022. The illustration component of this book was supported by the NSW Government through a Create NSW Quick Response Grant and a UBC Support to Scholarly Publications Grant.

We are grateful to Ben Doyle and Leigh Collins at Bloomsbury for their trust and enthusiastic responses to our very particular requests as this book became the thing you are now reading. Big thanks also to friends and colleagues who provided early feedback on draft chapters: Laura McLauchlan, Blanche Verlie, Lindsay Kelley, Sujata Allan, Aleksija Neimanis, Erin Delfs, Lola Melchior.

From Astrida:
Thank you to Rachel Loewen Walker for co-authoring that first weathering article on a lark and a hunch, after hearing a talk I gave in Copenhagen in 2012 and to Cecilia Åsberg and the Posthumanities Hub for the rich gestational community for weather writing workshops as early as 2011. Thanks to participants (Jaya, Grace, Rill, Lindsay, Hannah and others) at my first Australian weathering workshop at the Somatechnics Conference in Byron Bay in 2015, where 'Lucky Dip' was born, and to Yasmin Gunaratnam and Catriona Sandilands for supporting workshops in London and Toronto, respectively, in 2018, where I continued this activity's development. Talks and workshops at The Anthropocene Campus in Venice (thanks Ifor Duncan) and The Bartlett School of Architecture at UCL in 2021 (thanks Peg Rawes); the Centre for

Acknowledgements

Interdisciplinary Studies in Society and Culture at Concordia University in Montreal in 2023 (thanks Erin Robinsong and Mark Sussman); the 'Nature-Society Relations and the Global Environmental Crisis' conference at Humboldt University in Berlin in 2023 (thanks Christine Bauhardt); and the Sonic Acts festival in Amsterdam in 2024 (thanks Hannah Pezzack) were all important opportunities to keep thinking and practising these ideas, in particular with folks from other disciplines and professions. And thanks to my students in Australia and Canada, whose curiosity keeps expanding what weather can and might mean. Support from the Canada Research Chairs programme and the Faculty of Creative and Critical Studies at UBC Okanagan have made the FEELed Lab possible practically and financially, while the creativity, labour, good humour and fierce hearts of students and visiting researchers make the Lab possible in all the ways that matter: Dani, Rina, Madeline, Emma, Daisy, Grace, Natalie, Tara, Julia, Nela, Tom, Yazdan, Chhavi, Judee, Xiaoxang, Yuji, Lola, Erin, Sierra, Claude, *Sybille, Alex*, Therese, Jasmijn, Rebecca, Laura, Sue, Liz. And big respect and gratitude to all of the students of the People's University for Gaza UBCO for leading the way. To UBCO colleagues and friends Natalie, Jenica, Matt, Erin, Michael V., Cole, Onyx, Heather, Anita, Tania and others who have collaborated on FEELed Lab project magic. Thanks also to UBC's Centre for Climate Justice, UBCO's Office of the Vice-President for Research and Innovation (especially grant wizard Brianna) and my home departments (CCGS and ECS) for their ongoing support to this work. Funders and key supporters of the walkshops mentioned in this book include: the University of Sydney, Shanghai Biennale, Create NSW, the Henry Art Gallery (thanks to Mita Mahato and Nina Bozicnik); my fabulous co-organizers include: Perdy Phillips; Clare Britton and Aunty Rhonda Dixon-Grovenor; Aleksija Neimanis, Patty Chang, Jamie Wang, and Anne Bourne. Thanks to the Poppies for blooming when needed. To Tess for wisdom, to Norah for art. And to my co-author Jen, who has made me a more careful scholar and a more accountable and thoughtful person; I would not and could not have done this with anyone else! I owe an unrepayable debt to Jeanette Armstrong, Carrie Terbasket, Kelly Terbasket and Coralee Miller, and others from whom I continue to learn what it means to be a living and breathing being on syilx lands: limləmt. To my sisters (plus entourages) and my mom who are everything; to my dad who is everywhere. To my people for all weathers: Kim, Krusa, Hugo, Mars.

From Jen:
Thank you to Astrida for their radical and seemingly endless enthusiasm for creative and scholarly collaboration, and their specific collaborative style!

Acknowledgements

It is unique and special. Working with Astrida is one of the greatest privileges and joys of my life/career. More soberly, I'd like to thank Professor Jane Edwards, Huw Nolan and the Faculty of Humanities, Arts, Social Sciences and Education at the University of New England for AUD 5000 research seed funding in 2019 for the development of the Community Weathering Station (CoWS); my Head of Department and Head of School, Sarah Lawrence and Alistair Noble, for really supporting my work; AdaptNSW for the grant for the first phase of the Armidale Climate and Health Project; UNE's Internal Funding Scheme for funding for Phase 2 of this project, and in particular Sujata Allan and Nicolette Larder for their ongoing contributions to ACHP. The first installment of CoWS was supported by Kandos School of Cultural Adaptation at Groundswell in Bingara. Thanks to KSCA, and especially Lucas Ihlein, Imogen Semmler and Laura Fisher; and also to Diana Barnes for including CoWS in the 'Compassion, a Timely Feeling' conference. At work, the small feminist reading group and our ambitious research and teaching projects is a lifeline: Felicity Joseph, Christina Kenny, Matt Allen, Daz Chandler and Stevie Howson. Also members of the virtual un/earthing affect reading group: Laura McLauchlan, Blanche Verlie, Susie Pratt and everyone else who shows up. I'm thankful for my connections with Anaiwan leaders Uncle Steve Widders, Gabi Briggs and Callum Clayton-Dixon; I don't take what I've learned for granted and plan to keep working at doing the work.

The wider Armidale community has been so supportive of and influential for both CoWS and ACHP in numerous ways. Sustainable Living Armidale (SLA) and the community connected with this grassroots organisation have been important local champions, thanks specifically to Bar, Patsy, Tanya, Annette, Jo, Iain, Maxine and Helen. The garden tours and community meal collaborations in Food Group has been inspiring, fun and energizing; thank you Suj, Nikki, Imo, Kade, Lauren, Craig and Mac. The exhibition at New England Regional Art Museum (NERAM) and its potential afterlives would not be possible without Rachel Parsons. I'm also deeply grateful for the friends and chosen family on the ground in Armidale. The Crumpets (Jhana, Sujata, Maxine, Frida and Crumpet), the Larder-Corcoran for housing us during the majority of the writing period (Nikki, John, Edie, Finn, Maggie and Coco), The Street Gangs (Nic, Michelle, Dominic & Damian), the Bumpkins, Cold Water Swimmers, Easy Jam Group, the Mandarins, Sauna Fridays, School Parents, Running Mostly (you all know who you are; identified here via groupchat name!) for the deep community and next-level accountability to each other in a small place. Sometimes other

Acknowledgements

people are very inconvenient, but learning to (being forced by proximity to) show up and work through the rifts rather than fleeing into another corner of the big city has been life changing for me. I'm also grateful for the love and powerful enthusiasm of my mother, Maggie Hamilton, the inspiration and energy of my son Stanley Fox and the support, grounded connection and care of my life partner, CMJ.

Index

#haircutsforplanetarysurvival 114

ableism 57, 131
Aboriginal Cultural Centre and Keeping Place 200, 201
academic research 233
academics 7, 26, 115, 126, 128, 139, 171, 199, 218, 233
accountability 32, 33, 136, 137, 138, 163
accumulations 79
activism (*See also* protest) 83, 126
    climate change 24, 26
    pleasure 10, 241
    queer 52, 132
adaptation (*See* climate change adaptation)
affects (*See also* feeling) 23, 30, 32, 66, 158
agency 86, 130, 203, 215
agribusiness 201
agriculture 54, 172, 200
agrifood system (*See also* food) 172
Ahmed, Sara 35, 83, 131, 197
AI (*See* Artificial Intelligence)
Airconditioning (aircon) 80, 110
Alaimo, Stacy 26
Alberta Tar Sands 161
Alice in Wonderland 10
Allan, Sujata 198, 200, 204
ambiguity tolerance and intolerance 182
ambivalence 82, 110, 215, 221, 236,
Anaiwan Country 79, 172–3, 176, 180, 193, 199–200, 224
Anaiwan Language Revival Program 179
Anaiwan land buy-back 200–2
anatomy 240
Angelo, Claude 160
anger 31, 55, 151
animal/s (*See also* cows; multibeing; multispecies) 33, 34, 84, 151, 159, 173, 174, 184 n. 3, 199
    animal health as planetary health 193–4
    movement 51

Anishinaabe lands 142
anthotype printing 156
Anthropocene 197, 206 n. 14,
    Anthropocenomania 102
    colonial Anthropocene 216
    Hacking the Anthropocene 64
anthropocentrism 26, 37, 51. 59. 172, 239
anti-2SLGBTQ 216
anti-Blackness 57, 58, 80
anti-capitalist work 177
anticolonial (*See also* decolonial) 22, 27, 29–30, 61, 66, 130, 152, 154, 157–8, 171, 179–80, 194, 196, 202–5, 207, 233, 241
anticolonialism 8
antifascism 8, 234
antifascist 8, 21, 22, 25, 27
anxiety 22
    climate 55, 65, 151, 239, 241
    health 238–9
aquifer levels 219
archive 4, 204
    Cvetkovic's "archives of feeling" 158, 164
    body as 88
    butcher's paper as 135
    feminist 132
    lakeshore as material archive 240
Armajun Aboriginal Health services 204
Armidale 10, 114, 125–8, 135, 160, 171–7, 224
Armidale Aboriginal Community Garden 173
Armidale Climate and Health Project (ACHP) 180, 193, 198, 200–1, 268
Armidale Community Farmer's market 180
Armstrong, Jeannette 85, 133
Artificial Intelligence 66
artists 1, 4, 9, 15 n. 24, 29, 50, 115, 134–5, 154, 162, 178, 184 n.1, 214, 218, 233,
arts festival 178, 224
arts of noticing 240

Index

arts-led practices (*See* practice: arts-led)
Attention Deficit Hyperactivity Disorder (ADHD) 164
atmospheres of comfort and conviviality 163
attune 11, 214, 219, 226
Aunty Helen (*See* Riley, Aunty Helen)
Aunty Rhonda (*See* Dixon Grovenor, Aunty Rhonda)
Australia Day 173
Australian Bureau of Meteorology (BOM) 51, 57
Australian Research Council (ARC) 133

Bacon, Francis 69
Baltic Sea 237
bamboo bridge 99, 106, 108
Barad, Karen 217
barometer 3
Barthes, Roland 53
Bavyka, Ju 15
Bawaka Country collective 69
BC (*See* British Columbia)
Bees Nest fire 185
Belcourt, Billy-Ray 226
Bellevue Creek 154
Benjamin, Walter 53
Berlant, Lauren 100, 109, 113, 158, 176, 193, 221
Betasamosake Simpson, Leanne 142
Bidjigal Country 1, 13, 225
Biennale of Sydney (2022) *rīvus* 11
big infrastructure (*See also* infrastructure) 100, 103, 104, 175, 179, 216,
binarization 216
binary thinking (*See also* gender: binary) 85, 132
Bingara 176, 178
Bingara's Living Classroom 178
Biripi 180
Black Gully Festival of environment and arts 180
Black Lives Matter 58
Black slavery 58
Black Summer 158, 174, 180
Blaise, Mindy 136
Blast Furnace Park 219
Blue Mountains 219
bodies (*See* embodiment)
bodies of water 105, 225, 239
bodily limitation 88 (*See also* heat: stress)

bodily vulnerability (*See* vulnerability)
body hermeneutics (*See also* embodiment) 12, 239
Bodyweather 63, 64
Boscacci, Louise 219
both/and 33
Bourne, Anne 162, 267
breakfast 85, 125, 126, 127, 174, 180, 220
breath 35, 116, 235, 237, 240, 242
bridges (*See* Infrastructure)
Briggs, Gabi 31, 52, 67, 132, 179
British Columbia 103, 104, 152, 225
British and European Imperialism and Enlightenment 53
Britton, Clare 105, 225
Brooks, Andrew 130
bucketing water 177
buckets 222, 223, 224
Buddhism (*See* secular buddhism)
Buell, Laurence 239
building materials 235
bushfire smoke 65
Butler, Judith 14 n. 14, n. 21, 26–8, 86, 89,
Butoh 64

Cade Bambara, Toni 234
campus (*See* university: campus)
Canada Research Chairs 163
cancer 238
Capon, Anthony 194
care (*See also* community: housework; health: care; housework) 63, 99, 109, 115, 142, 151, 173, 196, 213, 241
  Care for the Stranded 221–3
  ethos of 113
  gender-affirming 204
  for land 224, 226
  privatization of 24
Carney Pond 218
carrier bag 214
catchment 172
cattle farming 172
Cham, Kampong 99
Chance 181, 194, 163
Chang, Patty 222
Chen, Mel Y 88
choice 83, 86, 142, 158, 163
Christmas Climate Change Variety Hour 184
cis-heteropatriarchal colonial capitalism 138

272

Index

citational practices 138
Clare, Eli 88
Clark, Nigel 87
class 23, 33, 80, 86, 115, 131, 153, 158
classism 131
classroom 35, 109, 125, 130, 137, 139, 140, 178, 222
Clayton-Dixon, Callum 179, 180, 199
cleaving 217
climate
    emergency 108, 116, 157, 234
    feeling (s) 151, 153, 157, 159, 239
    justice 24, 26–7, 35, 81, 125, 132, 151, 193
    mitigation infrastructure 101, 110
    science 3, 31, 63, 129, 161–2
climate change 1–5, 7–10, 176
    adaptation 5, 9, 24, 34, 79, 80, 87, 89–90, 106, 114, 161, 173, 176–8, 193, 200, 233
    and antifascist feminism 22–5
    in bodies 37, 60, 63–7
    climate/weather distinction (*See also* weather, weathering) 60–2, 137
    denial of 23, 61, 114, 162, 182
    and ecofeminism 25–9
    as feminist issue 21–2
    feminist & feeling based inquiry as climate change research 128, 140, 152, 153, 157, 159
    mitigation strategy 216
    at scale of the body 29–35, 233–42
    as symptom 137
climatology 240
    racist 87–8
'Close Meteorology' (*See also* reading: close) 10, 59, 60, 61, 140
close reading (*See* reading)
Cold War science 129
collaborations 138, 221
colonial institutions (*See also* university) 24, 234
colonial meteorology (*See* meteorology: colonial)
colonialism (*See also* anticolonial, anticolonialism) 26, 30–3, 49–52, 54, 57, 113, 118, 131, 136, 180, 202
common situation, being in common (*See also* Berlant) 112, 142, 215
common feeling (*See also* feeling) 158
Common Worlds 238

community 10, 115–6, 155, 158, 171, 175–83, 197–200
    critical engagement with 5, 7, 171
    economies (*See also* diverse economies) 185, 187
    facilitation in 35
    feeling 3
    gardens 173, 202
    health 202–5
    housework 10, 115, 125, 200
    Indigenous 57, 138–9, 200
    markets 5, 177
    regional 171
Community Weathering Station (CoWS) 171–3, 176, 182–3, 198, 224, 268
community-scaled agriculture 179
community-scaled response 177
composting 24, 90
Composting Feminisms 9, 134–7, 141, 154
concepts 7, 29, 30, 78, 80, 100, 106
concrete bridges 100, 109, 110, 111
consent 32
conservation biologists 162
consumer capitalism 24
consumption and conserving water 175
contact zone 213, 214, 221
control 3, 126, 175, 226
    climate control 5, 116
    desire for & dream of 54, 129, 182
    failure of 57
    feminist surrendering of 115, 241
    of nature for cultural ends 9, 52–4
    of weather 9
controlled 52, 54, 116, 126, 155
Cooks River (*See also* Goolay'yari) 1, 103
coolth 80
Conference of Parties 200
COP26 Climate Conference (*See* Conference of Parties)
Copernican revolution 53
cops (*See also* police) 116, 140
Coronavirus (*See* COVID) 125
cosmic weathering 239–40
cosmologies 240
country
    access to Country 200, 201
    Country (Indigenous concept) 2, 67, 68–9 fn8, 105, 129, 137–8, 200–5, 208, 213–5, 225–6
    the country 180

273

Index

COVID 59, 88, 125, 135, 199, 200, 204, 217, 225
   lockdowns in Australia 225
   pandemic 58, 59, 106, 125, 152, 199, 225
CoWS (*See* Community Weathering Station)
cows 172, 201
Coyne, Taylor 143
Craft-a-strophe! 158, 161, 162
creative and community-engaged feminist methods 7
creative methods 10, 164
creativity 29, 86, 267
creeks 172, 218, 224, 225
Crosby, Alexandra 143
cross-domain mapping 56, 61, 66
crip (*See also* justice: disability) 28, 196
   ecologies 29
critical race 80
cultural healing work 200
cultural imaginaries 55
cultural scholarship on weather 50
culture (*See* nature/culture)
cure 196, 238,
curiosity 2, 3, 159, 181, 182, 216, 267
Cvetkovich, Ann 157
Cyborg Manifesto 129

D'Eaubonne, Françoise 250
dam wall 175, 177
dance party 156
De Sassure, Ferdinand 49, 68
dead, the 224
death 25, 59, 140, 195, 222
decolonial (*See also* anti-colonial; feminism: decolonial; power: decolonial) 67
   desires 126, 198
   responses to climate change 52
decolonization 132, 160, 179, 204, 205
decolonizing waterways 224
Deep Listening 222
deep time (*See also* time) 77, 78, 88, 236, 237, 241,
Defence Force (*See also* Israel Defence Force) 57, 128, 130
definition 8, 12, 25, 38, 55, 56, 67, 77, 78, 107, 134, 196
   of weathering (*See* weathering: definition of)
   of weather (*See* weather: meaning of weather words)

Delaney, Samuel 113
Delfs, Erin 160
denial 23, 55, 61, 114, 153, 162, 182 (*See also* climate change: denial)
Derrida, Jacques 68, 184
desire (*See also* control: desire for & dream of; decolonial: desires) 22, 28, 32–3, 54, 56, 61, 82, 112, 126, 133, 140, 142, 198, 202, 204–5
Diversity Equity and Inclusion (DEI) (*See* Equity Diversity and Inclusion)
difference 8, 21, 52, 67, 80, 87–9, 111–2, 142, 152, 157, 160, 182, 194, 200, 202, 213–5, 221, 234
   embodied 37, 79, 111
   gender 5, 111
   in language 28–30, 49
   non-hierarchical 86
   race 5
   in scale 106
   solidarity in 32–3, 82
disability justice (*See* justice: disability)
disciplined extrospection 239
DIT (*See* Do-it-Together)
diverse economies (*See also* community: economies) 114, 177
diverting 141, 185
Dixon Grovenor, Aunty Rhonda 105, 225–6
Do-It-Together (DIT) 135, 145, 163, 261
Do-it-yourself (DIY) research methods conference 160
Do-it-yourself (DIY) tools 61
Do-it-yourself 12-volt Solar Power 179
Doctors for Environment Australia (DEA) 198
dolphin 234
domestic violence 22, 24
Donald, Madeline 155, 217
double negative 33
doubled university 128
drought-friendly hairstyles 141, 179,
downscaling 193, 195, 197, 199, 201, 203, 205
drain/s & drainage 90, 101, 103, 125, 155, 175, 215, 226
drawing 9, 50, 110, 160, 217
drinking-water reservoirs 172
drought 126, 155, 171–81, 224
dualistic thinking 54
duration 6, 77, 78, 79, 100

Index

duty of care 196, 213
Dyer, Sophie 61
dykes and levees 216
dynamic process of weathering 51

echolocation 33
eco-poetry readings 153
eco-social weathers 234
ecocide 140
ecocriticism
ecofacism 24
ecofeminism (*See* feminism)
econationalism 24
economic growth 128, 195
economics (*See also* community: economies; diverse economies) 80
ecotone 213
edges 213, 215
Elders 163, 201, 214
embodied (*See also* body hermeneutics)
    bodies (*See also* climate change: in bodies) 1, 3, 6, 9
    difference (*See also* difference: gender) 21–3, 25–8, 30–2, 34–8
    'Embodied Imagination' 36
    'Imaginative Embodiment' 36
    imagination 37
    experience 2, 35, 52, 197, 219
    extrospection 219, 239, 240
    politics of solidarity 8, 22, (29–35), 111
    trauma 80
emplaced relation 215
encampments 128, 139, 140
endings 135, 222, 225
enemy 129, 172
enemy feminisms (*See* feminism: enemy)
engineering 6, 54, 103, 104, 126, 154
Englemann, Sasha 61
English (*See also* languages: English) 49–55, 159
Ensor, Sarah 113
entropic process 197
envelopes 36
environmental
    assessments 220
    determinisms 87
    health (*See also* health; community: health; planetary health; one health) 194, 196, 197, 198, 202

    humanities (*See also* Feminist Environmental Humanities) 134
    justice 77, 80, 81,195
epidemiological studies of illness and health 194
Equity Diversity and Inclusion (EDI) 131
erasure of the meteors 53
erosion 6, 78, 85, 197
erotics 43
essentialism 25, 37, 87
experimentation 106, 108, 159
expertise 3, 61
exposure (*See also* vulnerability) 68, 78, 82, 84, 89, 108, 116, 138, 220
exquisite corpse 160
extraction 22, 23, 27, 31, 161, 219
extreme heat 195

facilitation infrastructure 173
far-right 23, 162
farmer 103, 175, 178,180
fascism 38, 241
fatigue 89, 237
fear 2, 27, 28, 177, 181, 182
FEELed (*See also* field)
    Lab 81, 137, 138, 145 n. 40, 151–64, 217–8, 267
    Library 155
    notes 165
    work 163
feeling (*See also* affect; archive: Cvetkovic's "archives of feeling"; climate: feeling(s); common feeling; community: feeling) 3, 10, 99, 108, 159–62, 179, 226, 232,
    bodies 111, 138
    climate 151–2, 173
    feminism and 31–2, 35
    as political 70 n40, 157
    as research method 3, 162–3
    uncertain and ambiguous 82, 180–3
    weathering as 8, 55, 79, 83
feet 58, 222, 235, 236
feminism (*See also* feminist; queer)
    academic 22
    antifascist and antipolarizing 23–4, 29
    Black 29, 40 n. 30, 57, 66, 197, 234
    decolonial, Indigenous 29, 68
    as descriptive 4
    ecofeminism

Index

as embodied politics of solidarity
enemy 23
as fit-for-purpose 21, 27, 33, 35
and nature 8
neo-poststructuralist, neo-ecofeminism 29–35
as prefigurative 4, 22, 25–59, 40–1 fn34,
posthuman 27, 21, 27
poststructuralist 25–9, 41, 68
queer 31, 32, 34, 53, 216
trans-exclusionary reactionary 28
white 23
Feminist Antifacist Weather Front 63
feminist
  archive 132
  classrooms 109
  climate justice 151
  literary and cultural studies 6
  new materialism 26
  political economy 177
  posthumanities 26
  science and technology studies (Feminist STS) 26
  theory (See also feminism; queer; theory; theory-practice distinction) 35, 131–2, 179
  theory is feminist practice 22, 35
Feminist environmental humanities 5, 25, 28–9, 125, 128, 133, 138, 152, 154, 158
femme 172
field (See also FEELed)
  lab 158
  philosophy 158
  work 12
Floyd, George 58
flying foxes 2
food 1, 27, 85–6, 90, 112, 128, 135, 155, 172, 183, 200–1
Food School 207
footbridge over the river east of Wardell Road 105
forecasting 57, 63, 128, 129
forecasting weather 57
forest fires 89
forever chemicals 197
fossil fuel corporations 143
Frank, Adam 182
Friends of Woodhaven 155
Fringe Natures 155, 213, 216, 217, 218

fringe 214–8, 220
fringey zones 214–5
fuchsia orb sun 153

Gadigal 1, 12, 13, 225
Galiano Island 77
Gamilaraay Country 176, 180
Ganza, Ella 204
garbage 215
Garcia Chua, Rina 157
Gardiner, James 136
Gaza 34, 128, 139–43, 160
gazebo 2, 178
gender (See also difference) 25–9, 34
  abundance 22, 216
  binary 26, 57, 84, 86
  essentialism 87
  gender studies 6, 30, 125
  gendered division of labour 24
  genders 34, 53, 216
  hierarchy 54
  performativity 6, 26
  sex and 25, 26
  stereotypes 32
genetic predispositions 1
genocidal violence 34, 140
genocide 23, 51, 128, 139, 140, 160
gentrification 113
geographer/s 61, 108, 153, 202
geological feature 77
geology 6, 82
Geronimus, Arline 80, 86, 197
gerund 6, 78, 159
Gibson-Graham, J.K. 114, 177, 178
Giggs, Rebecca 239
Gilmore, Ruth 114
ginkgo 216
Girvan, Anita 56
glitchy 221
glitchfrastucture 221
Going Underground 218, 219
Gondwana rainforest 79, 174
Goolay'yari (See also Cooks River) 1, 4, 103, 104, 105, 225
grand theory 217
grazing 172
Green Square 143
Greenies 220, 221
Greywater 176
Grief 151, 152, 157, 181

Groundswell festival 176, 178, 198
groundwater 219, 220
Guerilla gardens 154
Gumbaynggirr 79, 180
Gumbramorra Swamp 13, 103
Gumbs, Alexis Pauline 33, 65, 218
Gunaratnam, Yasmin 87
gut 65, 236
Guyra 175

habit/s (*See also* practice/s) 12, 61, 86, 100, 103–4, 118 fn19, 130, 135, 138, 142, 155, 164, 175, 215–6, 235, 240
Hacking the Anthropocene (*See* Anthropocene)
hands 22, 60,61, 158, 159, 202, 223, 224, 226, 236
Haraway, Donna 85, 129, 184
Harney 115, 134
Harney, Stefano 134
Hayward, Eva 217, 226
Healing 193, 197, 200, 202, 224
healing justice 197
health (*See also* environmental health, community health, planetary health, one health) 80, 86–92, 193–207
 anxiety about (*See also* anxiety) 239
 public 6, 80, 197
 sciences 195
heat 14 fn15, 53–5, 65–6, 172–3, 241
 Heat and Health research Incubator 194
 heatwaves 54, 80, 195
 mapping 80
 stress 195–6, 199
Henry Art Gallery 222, 223
heteronormative Aboriginal health services 203
heteronormative family constructs 53
heteropatriarchal settler colonial capitalism 233
heteropatriarchy 23, 34, 59
historical trauma 183
historical violence 224
holding containers 215
Home Grown Garden Tour 200
hooks, bell 23, 24, 179
Horn, Roni 65, 66
housework (*See also* care; community: housework) 10, 115, 125, 163, 200

Huggins, Jessie 222
human rights 33, 139
human-weather relations 1
human/non-human binary 52
Humans are weather makers 59
Humphreys, Bill 220
Hunt, Victoria 64
Hurricane Katrina 22, 57, 58
Hurricanes 22, 32
hydrological cycle 239
 fear of the other 182

Inconvenience 115, 183
Increasing Resilience to Climate Change Community Grant 199
IndigenEYEZ 155
Indigenous
 researchers 133, 158,
 people 157, 201, 203, 208 fn28
 feminisms (*See* feminism: decolonial, Indigenous)
 community (*See* community: Indigenous)
 intimacy 113
 kinship 23, 113
 naming 1
 healthcare services 197
 ontology 129
 knowledges 51, 85, 129, 132, 193–4, 199, 200, 203
 literacy programmes under settler colonialism 52, 83
 sovereignty 30, 31, 52–3, 132–3
 views of season and weather 51
 weather knowledge 51, 53, 66–7, 137, 139
individual change 102
inefficiencies 233
Infrastructural Inequalities collective 102, 115, 134
infrastructure (*See also* big infrastructure; glitchfrastructure; mega dams) 9
 bridges 99–101, 108–9, 117
 dams 101, 104
 design of 101
 digital infrastructure 56
 feminist infrastructure 89–90, 111–6, 162, 220
Infrastructural Turn 101
Inset C as Infrastructure 80–1

277

Index

Judith Butler on 86
for managing the meanwhile 108–11, 215
meteorological infrastructure 57
mobile infrastructure 214
physical infrastructure 56
public Works 101
reading group as 133–6
for redistributing shelter and vulnerability 116, 220
resilience 106–8
of resistance 100
seawalls 101
social (*See also* practice: social practice theory) 29, 105, 115, 152, 158, 215, 221
weathering 106–8
university as 142
inheritance 49, 61, 67, 78, 107
inner-urban 171
Intergovernmental Panel on Climate Change 2, 13
international airport 104, 226
interpersonal dynamics 183
Invasion Day 173
IPCC (*See* Intergovernmental Panel on Climate Change)
Israel Defence Forces (IDF) 139, 140

Jaquette Ray, Sarah 242
Jay, Ollie 194, 206
Jean Kim, Claire 34
jobs 66, 115, 131, 142
Johnson, Craig 184
joyful 7, 21, 28
justice 7, 21, 24, 28, 37, 108, 139, 140
climate 24, 26–7, 35, 81, 125, 132, 151, 155, 160, 193
disability 88, 107
social 77, 197
environmental 77, 81, 195, 197
reproductive 23
feminism as theory and practice of 25, 37

k'emcnitkw floodplain 109
Kandos 178, 268
Kandos School of Cultural Adaptation (KSCA) 178, 268
karst systems 219

Kelley, Lindsay 119
Kelowna 10, 109, 152, 153, 154, 157, 162, 218
kelp 223
Kenny, Christina 204
Keogh, Therese 161
kin (*See also* kinship; Indigenous: kinship) 102, 241
King Lear 6
Kinsella, John 179
kinship 23, 53, 63,113, 179, 203
Kirby, Vicki 85
Klein, Naomi 153, 162
Klúsxnítkw (*See* Lake Okanagan)
Kuch, Declan 185

la paperson 126, 130, 198
labour 24, 27, 82, 102, 108, 115, 133, 145, 195, 220, 222, 267
LaDuke, Winona 104
Lake Madgwick 125–7
Lake Okanagan 152, 218
Lake Pillans 219
Lake Sludgewick 126
Lake Zot 200, 224
Lakes 103, 126, 172
Lakoff, George 55
Lakshmi Piepzna-Samarasinha, Leah 89
Lammi, Sierra 160
Land 2, 34, 51, 67, 71, 129, 142, 151, 161, 163, 193, 202, 224, 240–1
Landback 200
language (*See also* metaphor) 5–7, 15 fn24, 26–8, 35, 51–3, 55–6, 59, 67, 68, 83–4, 128–9, 226
Ferdinand de Saussure's theory of 68 fn2
as inherited 49
as mutable/immutable 49
as social contract 59
unlearning a 52, 83
using and hacking 7
as world building 4, 27
languages
French 78
Spanish 78
Anaiwan 179, 199
nsyilxcən 85
English (*See also* English) 51
Larder, Nicolette 202
Larkin, Brian 102
Le Guin, Ursula 214

Index

Lea, Tess 117, 118
Leander, Caolan 241
Learning Endings 222
Leigh Star, Susan 102
Leki 204
Leota Lu, Amao 204
Leutwyler, Kim 204
Lewis, Sophie 23
LGBTQ 240
Liberation of the Chinook Wind 66
Liboiron, Max 30, 33, 158
library 131, 155, 178, 179, 180
lifestyle 90, 197, 202
Limon, Ada 58
Lincoln Park 222
linguistic turn 6
listening 2, 12, 34, 66, 155, 222
listicle 22, 29, 30, 35
literary festivals 153
literary studies 6, 7, 12, 27, 30, 50, 125
Lithgow 219, 220, 225
Littoral Listening 155
littoral zone 214, 215
livestock 172, 199
loaf of white bread 85
local paper 174
Loewen Walker, Rachel 5, 78, 266,
Lorange, Astrid 130
Lorde, Audre 151, 159, 197
Louisiana 58
Love 8, 83, 102, 132, 157, 179, 225, 226, 233
low-carbon warfare 129
Lucky Dip 10, 22, 35, 36, 37, 60, 61, 64, 140, 237, 240, 266
lunch 152, 156, 200, 226
luxury 241
Lytton 152

Macklin, Rebecca 161
Macleod, Janine 91
Madgwick, Sir Robert 126
maintenance 114, 115
Making Time 14
Mallin, Sam 239
man-camps 22
managing the meanwhile 100, 104, 108, 110, 114, 176, 215
mangroves 1, 105, 226
Manhattan 113
Maori meteorologists 234

Maree Brown, Adrienne 142, 241
margins 112, 214, 216, 218,
marine biologist 222
Marine mammals 222, 223
market stall 10, 173, 177, 178, 183, 193
Marrickville 103
Masco, Joseph 129
masculinist 30, 31, 159
masculinity 23, 31, 187
master model (*See also* Val Plumwood) 34
mastery 23, 31, 34, 67
materiality 6, 27, 83, 86, 87, 88, 89, 102, 206, 224
materiality of bodies (*See also* bodies; embodied) 27, 87
MacGregor, Sherilyn 26
McClure, Rod 198
McFetridge, Christine 52
McGiffin, Emily 91
McLauchlan, Laura 8, 162
McManus, Emma 184
measurement(s) 3, 54, 63, 65
meditation 10, 12, 15, 235, 237, 238, 241
mega dam (*See also* infrastructure: dam) 177
Mekong river 99
Melchior, Lola 160
memory 79
menopausal 65, 66
Merleau-Ponty, Maurice 5
metaphor 4, 9, 29, 30, 50, 55–6, 58–9, 61, 66, 106, 114, 128, 213
meteorology 8, 10, 51, 54, 57, 59, 60, 61, 83, 128, 129, 137, 140, 193
  colonial 83, 193
  meteors (e.g. thunder, lightning, wind, rain) 7, 8, 49, 53, 54, 55, 56, 60, 67
  Meteorological Act 1955 57, 128
  science of 128
Métis 132, 157, 161
Money, Jazz 234
micro-commons 215
micro-poetry 161
microplastics 197, 240
Middle Passage 58
Mies, Maria 27
militarism 129
military 57, 128, 129, 137
Milpirri 213, 215, 221, 226
mindfullness-based stress reduction (MBSR) 238

279

Index

mines 24, 220
Mishra, Pankaj 141,
misogyny 24, 57, 131, 182
mobility 88, 103, 107 215, 216, 218
more-than-human 102, 116, 154, 214, 239
more than meteorological 9, 50, 55, 56, 57, 59, 66, 82, 89
Morris, Kyla 155
Moss, Lauren 178
Moten, Fred 115, 134
mouth 64, 226
moving line 213, 214, 215, 217,
multibeing 22, 29, 37, 222
multiscalar 241
multispecies 65–6, 184
multispecies drag workshop 162
Mumford, Lisa 184
mundane 2, 5, 79, 90, 106, 114, 115, 140, 173, 193, 234
municipal dam 175
Myers, Natasha 161
Myles, Eileen 30, 33
myth of information deficit' 31

Nafisi, Golrokh 62
NAIDOC week (*See* below)
National Aboriginal and Islanders Day Observance Committee (NAIDOC) week 201
national media 176
National Party (Australia) 181
National Tertiary Education Union 131
natural disasters 22, 195
natural intelligence (NI) 66
natural/innate; social/constructed 88
nature (*See* nature/culture)
nature/culture (*See also* feminism: and nature) 27, 63, 78, 84–7, 89, 92, 102–3, 106, 111
    nature/culture debate within feminism 86
    naturecultures 85
Neimanis, Aleksija 222, 266, 267
Nelson, Maggie 162
New Atlantis, The 54
New England Regional Art Museum (NERAM) 203, 268
new materialist 85
New Orleans 57, 58
New South Wales 173

NI (*See* natural intelligence) 66
Nicholson, Tara 156, 162
non-scalability 138
normal 89, 103, 183, 195, 196
normativity 194, 196
nostalgia 28, 79, 108
Nowra 204
nsyilxcən 85, 155, 161
NTEU (*See* National Tertiary Education Union)
nuclear fallout (*See also* queer: fallout) 113, 129

objectivity 2, 31, 151
obligations 30, 31, 57, 128, 158, 163, 164
    of time to weather 77
Oliveros, Pauline 222
One Health (*See also* planetary health) 193, 194
Open Mic Creek Walks 224
open-weather 61, 62, 63

Pacific Northwest 77
Pacific Ocean 221, 225
paddocks 172
Paen, Koh 99
Palestine 139
Palestinian 139,160
Palestinian struggle for freedom 139
Papertalk Green, Charmaine 179, 180
paradox 116, 132, 240, 242
Parsons, Rachel 204, 268
participatory taste workshops 119
pastoral fantasy 172
Patrick, Steven Wanta Jampijinpa 213
pattern(s) 51, 61, 63, 129, 130, 157, 215
Pay the Rent 208 fn 28
pedagogy 125, 136,237
pelicans 1, 215
People's University for Gaza at the University of British Columbia (Okanagan) 141, 142, 143, 160, 267
performativity 6, 12, 26, 86
phenomenology 10
phenomological 239
Phillips, Perdita (Perdy) 218
philosophy 5, 27, 50, 158, 239
physiology 195, 196, 240
picnic table 1
Pierson, Dani 151, 157, 160

Index

pigmentation 87, 88
Pinson Wrisley, Samantha 182
pipes 134, 215
piss-yellow sky 153
place-thought 51
placenta-eating covens 26
planetary 22, 54, 66, 70, 78, 102, 199, 241
planetary health (*See also* health; one health) 166, 193–6, 199, 201–3
    healthcare 205
    psychology of 166
pleasurable 84, 115, 234
pleasure 10, 12, 32, 204, 241, 242
pleasure activism 10, 241
Plumwood, Val 27
podcast(s) 175, 201
poetry 3, 6, 58, 66, 153, 155, 161, 204, 233
polar ice caps 197
polarization 8, 23, 28, 112, 160, 182
police 58, 59, 137, 240
police violence 59
politician(s) 84, 175, 181
pollinator 164
pollution 27, 215, 241
pop-up 114, 154, 180
portal 222
postcard art 221
poststructuralist 25–9
poverty 57
power 6, 22–4, 31–2, 34, 52–4, 63, 82–5, 101, 104, 111, 126, 130, 132, 137
    decolonial 126, 130, 132
    as energy (e.g. solar and coal) 31, 179
    hierarchical 177
    feminist politics as about 31
    redistribution of 24
    in resistance and solidarity 82–5
    settler colonial 104, 132, 198
    structures and systems of 31, 58–9, 66, 111, 202
powerful men 23
practice (*See also* methods, Insets A-J) 3–5, 7, 9–12, 59, 84, 102–3, 110, 125, 127–8, 135–8, 160–5, 208 fn 28, 234–5, 237
    arts-led 60
    creative 60–1, 64–6
    feminist 21–2, 24, 34–5, 37, 49–50, 78, 80, 90, 111–9, 127, 173–7, 193, 220, 234
    as feminist infrastructure 112
    as habits we choose 12, 15 fn24, 135, 235
    insets as instructions for 10–12, 37,
    performativity as 14 fn21
    poetic 70
    social practice theory 102
    theory and 101, 125, 194, 217, 233,
    as weathering 7, 21, 90, 111, 140, 217, 219–20, 237
practice-led research 4, 12, 152, 266, 219
pragmatism 116
prediction(s) 3, 54, 63
Princes Highway 105
private domestic home 175, 177
productivity 195, 196, 199,
promiscuity 29
property 24, 59, 112, 113, 154, 201
protest 10, 58, 59, 67, 83, 84, 109, 125, 132, 139, 173, 221
Protevi, John 58
Protocols 135, 163, 164
public health (*See* health: public)
pumping stations 103, 104
purity politics 173
pussy-grabers 23

q̓awsitkw (Okanagan River) 109
queer (*See also* feminism: queer feminism)
    activism 52, 132
    AF healthcare 203–5
    closeted life 152
    ecogothic portraiture 162
    ecologies (*See also* trans-: ecologies; crip: ecologies) 28, 216
    feminism 216
    feminist environmentalisms 53
    infrastructure 114
    joy 109
    kinship 179
    fallout (*See also* nuclear fallout) 113, 116
    feminist infrastructures 114, 120
    ways of life 113
    phobia 131
    queerness 33, 85
quick-fix 237

race 26, 33, 80, 87–8, 131, 157
racism 57, 58, 59, 88, 131, 157, 173, 197
rain (*See also* meteors) 2, 3, 7, 8, 49, 53, 55, 56, 57, 67, 71 fn115, 78, 79, 82, 83, 103, 104, 175–7

Index

rainforests of Gondwana 54, 174
Rankine, Claudia 58, 61, 197
reading 11, 30, 35, 50, 51, 84, 113, 127, 161
   close 60
   Close Meteorology as close reading 60
   group/s 8, 10, 128, 133–4, 136–7, 152
   for difference 28
Reading and Listening Groups 121
reading groups (*See* reading: group/s)
reckoning 31, 182, 241
redistribution of shelter and vulnerability (*See* shelter; vulnerability)
Reid, Susan 37, 91, 240,
relational traction 8
relationship/s 10, 22, 29, 51, 59, 102, 108, 114, 115, 126, 138, 142, 155, 157, 171, 215, 220, 234
   between meteorology and national security 128
   between words and worlds 5, 49, 60, 68
   repairing and re/building 7, 200
   between people and the world 7, 195, 201
   human-nonhuman 59, 69 fn8
   time-weather-body relationship 78
   between feminism and 'nature' 8, 26
   with weather 79
   with nature 22, 25, 28
repair 8, 28, 115, 183, 202
representations 86, 128
reproduction 23, 102
reproductive justice 23
research lab 154, 155
resilience 9, 88, 100, 101, 106–8, 114, 116, 193
resilient 85, 86, 107, 176, 238
Rest as Resistance 157
Rice, Natalie 70, 155
Rich, Adrienne 30
right-wing media 171
rights of 'nature' 33
Right to Feel (podcast) 165
rigorous imagination 240
Riley, Aunty Helen 219
River Ends as the Ocean, the 12, 105, 225
rivers 84, 85, 104, 172,
rocks 37, 77, 78, 82, 215
round goby 216

Sakr, Omar 204
Salazar, Juan 117
Salish Sea 77
saltbush 216
Sandilands, Catriona 40, 41, 242
Scalability 111, 138
scalable 109, 138, 233,
scale 60–5, 99, 101–2, 106–14, 207 n. 14
   scale and feeling 159
   community-scaled response 173–80, 201–2
   downscaling 193, 198–203
   scalability and non-scalability 111, 138
   scale of embodied experience 30, 63, 219, 235, 237, 240
scaling 111
scholasticide 140
Schuller, Kyla 166
sciences 3, 54, 100, 154, 158, 161, 195, 240,
scientific objectivity 31
scientific positivism 54
scientists 3, 29, 33, 66, 151, 153, 157, 178, 214, 218, 222
script(s) 235, 237, 240
scyborg 130, 137, 198
Seattle 222
secular buddhism 15
secularization 53
Sedgwick, Eve 14, 15
self-identity 171
Semá:th X_ó:tsa 104
Semmler, Imogen 178
sensory attunement 220
sensory experience 219
Serres, Michel 53
settler imaginaries 216
sex positivity 32
sexual rights 23
sexual violence 22
sexuality 33, 63, 80, 82, 113
Seymour, Nicole 173
shame 136, 157, 173,
Shanghai Art Biennale 225
Sharpe, Christina 57, 197
shelter (*See also* vulnerability) 5, 8, 9, 34, 37, 64, 68, 82, 100, 110, 116, 145, 183, 233–4, 242
   redistribution of shelter and vulnerability 5, 9, 11, 21, 24, 29, 32,

Index

82, 88, 90, 109–10, 112, 116, 131, 138, 141, 157, 162, 198, 220, 223,
  for the vulnerable 84
  as protection (feminist, anti-colonial) 132–4
  temporary 193
  pleasure as 241
Shiva, Vandana 27
shoreline(s) 83, 215, 221, 222, 225, 223, 240
Singer, Hayley 136
singing 220
skilling up 12, 164
skin 3, 8, 32, 37, 57, 87–9
skin pigmentation 87–8
Sky Country 241
slow process 81–4, 233
slowness 79, 235
small-talk 1
smell 1, 3, 36
Smith, Kade 178
smoke inhalation 174
snacks 2
Sobecka, Karolina 65
social atmospheres 66, 215
social infrastructure 29, 115, 152, 158, 215, 221
spcial practice theory (*See* practice)
social justice 64, 77, 151, 197
social media 38, 174
social support 102
social work 6
soil 6, 37, 79, 172, 178, 199, 202, 235
soil science 6
solidarity 9, 21, 27, 29, 35, 37, 53, 82, 84, 111, 112, 136, 138–9,
  feminism as embodied politics of 8, 22, 29, 30–5, 111
songlines 214
Sooke Potholes 77
speculative fiction 54, 63, 214
speech act theory 6
speed-zining 10, 125, 160, 161
Springgay, Stephanie 13, 227
State Mine Heritage Park and Railway 219
Steve Widders, Uncle 199, 201, 202, 224
Stó:lō people 103, 104
stories 29, 33, 68, 88, 214, 224
stormwater lake 126
stormwater ponds 224
stranger intimacy (ies) 112, 114, 181, 215, 220,

stratigraphy 240
structure of feeling 158
structures of power 58, 66, 111, 157
Stryker, Susan 216
student encampments 128, 139, 140
student intifada 140
stygofauna 220
submerged perspectives 216
subterranean 102, 219, 241
sulphur-crested cockatoos 2
Sultana, Farhana 153
Sumas Valley
  Prarie 103, 104
  flood 104
survival 10, 31, 51, 83, 88, 173, 201
Survival Day 173
Sustainable Living Armidale 200, 268
sweat 1, 2, 60
Sweden 237 238
swim(s)(ming) 1, 77, 79, 152, 172, 174, 226
Sybille Mueller, Hanna 162
Sydenham 103
Sydney 1, 10, 103–4, 135, 143, 152, 173, 178, 219, 221, 225–6,
Sydney Harbour Bridge 99
syilx (*See also* nsyilxcən) 85, 109, 133, 152, 155–7, 161, 163
system we call climate 3

T'souke Nation 77
tablelands 172
tactics 21, 30, 34, 114, 142, 162
TallBear, Kim 113
Tan, Kynan 15
Tanaka, Min 64
Taylor, Affirca 238
temporarily 80, 106, 133, 154, 214, 215, 221
tensions 26, 114, 140, 221
terms of transition 104, 110, 193
terrifying 153, 234
theory (*See also* practice) 15, 35, 37, 77, 86, 90, 100–1
  of language 49
  of metaphor 56, 59
  theory=boring/practice=interesting equation 100
  theory-practice distinction 12
thermometer 3
thermoregulation 195
thermoregulatory physiology 195, 196

283

Index

Thompson, Claris 26
thunder (*See also* weather: meteors) 8, 49, 55, 67
time (*See also* deep time) 3, 9, 14, 77–84, 116–7, 132, 203, 205, 207 fn26, 214–8, 234–7
Times Square 113
Todd, Zoe 67, 132,
Tomkins, Silvan 182
tongue 3
Too Rude 184
town hall meetings 175
Traditional Chinese Medicine (TCM) 197
traffic 1, 102, 215
training 5, 6, 12, 64, 67, 115, 142, 154, 198, 215
trainshop 135, 218, 219, 220
trans-
    ecologies 28, 216, 217
    exclusionary radical feminism (TERFs) 23
    experience 216
    inclusive feminisms 216
    phobia 86, 131
    -ing 216
transforamtive justice 108
transition economy 178
transways 217, 226
Truman, Sarah E. 13 fn6
Tsing, Anna 138, 240,
Tūpoupou 234

University of British Columbia (UBC) Okanagan 133, 151, 152, 155
University of British Columbia (UBC) Centre for Climate Justice 160
Uncle Steve Widders (*See* Steve Widders, Uncle)
Undercliff 105
underground 215, 218, 219
Unearthing Armidale's Diverse Food Economy 202
university (*See also* scholasticide) 9–10, 130, 221
    campus 127, 141, 143, 154, 155, 160, 214, 218
    as colonial establishment 130
    hypocrisy of the neoliberal 140
    management 125
    neoliberal 9, 133

    as paradox 132, 160, 198
    as research institution 127–9
    as site of potential liberation and transformation 128, 130, 132
    union (*See* National Tertiary Education Union)
    as workplace 125–6, 130–1, 221
    as world-building technology 130
University of British Columbia 133, 141–6, 151–2, 155, 160
University of New England 125, 135, 174, 178, 180, 266,
University of Sydney 134, 135, 154, 194
unlearning 15, 50–3, 57, 60, 64, 83, 85, 137, 193
    colonial weather 50, 57, 60, 64, 85, 137
urban heat mapping 80
US military (*See also* Defence Force; IDF; military; militarism) 129

Vakoch, Douglas A. 227
van Gelder, Pia 15
van Neerven, Ellen 51, 137, 203
Vanni, Ilaria 149
Vergès, Françoise 23, 25
Verlie, Blanche 65, 153, 162
vulnerability (*See also* shelter)
    bodily 111, 233
    low-stakes 11, 145 n. 37, 183

walk the tide out 105, 225
walking 79, 83, 115, 214, 217–9, 222–6
walkshops 4, 10, 135, 140, 214–25
Waminda 204
Wangal 13, 225, 1
Warner, Michael 113
Warren, Jeff 12
Water + Fire 157, 161
water quality 104, 172
water scarcity 176
Waters, Rob 204
waterways 13, 103, 172, 201, 215, 224,
Watts, Vanessa 51
we 33, 34, 134,
weapons manufacturers 233
weather 2–4, 6, 7, 8–10, 36, 49–68
    as ambient backdrop 50
    as boring small talk 53
    and climate change 3, 35
    as colonial knowledge to unlearn 50–52

Index

epistemology of weather knowledge(s) 51, 52, 53, 60, 66, 67, 128, 130, 137, 139
forecasts 3, 57
fronts 10, 63, 128, 130, 213, 215, 226
Indigenous weather knowledge 51
meaning of weather words (*See also* definitions) 49–50
as multispecies event 65
research 50, 128
settler weather services 51
as e.g. thunder, lightning, wind, rain (*See* meteors)
weather-makers 4, 59, 66, 128, 163, 233
weathering
　as accumulated and embodied weathers (*See also* embodied; bodies) 79
　as ambivalent and slow 81–4
　better 89, 90, 101, 111, 114, 152, 177
　as bridge between theory and practice 7
　concept(s) 5, 9 90, 157, 219
　as connecting weather and climate 78
　definition of 6–7, 78, 87
　difference 213
　enabling of the redistribution of vulnerability and shelter 29
　in engineering 6
　as eroding nature/culture binary 84–9
　as feminist concept for climate change 9, 78
　'A Field Guide to Weathering' 179
　games 140
　in geology 6
　as methodology 5, 31, 214, 215, 217, 22
　as politics of solidarity and resistance 81–4
　as practice 21
　as process-oriented tool 80
　in public health 6, 80
　specific feminism required for 21–2, 24–5
　in soil science 6
　report(s) 60, 61
　weather as 67
Weathering Collective, the 1, 4, 7, 10, 11, 35, 60, 115, 160, 171, 214, 221, 239

'Weathering Everything' symposium 114, 125, 127, 180, 198
Weathering Map of Microclimates and Approximate Water Bodies, the 80
'Weathering with and without' 10, 80, 140, 237,
weathervane 3
West Seattle Fauntleroy Ferry 222
Westbank First Nation 155
Western epistemologies 151
white feminism (*See* feminism: white)
white supremacy (ist) 34, 54, 58, 59, 84, 111, 87, 136,
White, Maria 184
Whittaker, Alison 179
wicking bed 178, 179
Wiegman, Robyn 33
wildfire smoke 88
Willard, Tania 66
Williams, Raymond 158
Wilson, Elizabeth 182
Winter Blooming Festival 203, 224
Wirajuri 219, 221, 234
Wölfe-Erskine, C. 227
Wölfle Hazard, Cleo 151, 158, 217
Wolli Creek 2, 13, 105,
Wollongong 103
Woodhaven Eco Culture Centre 153, 155, 163,
Woodhaven Regional Park 153
workers 7, 29, 115, 125, 140, 195, 205
Workman, Ken 222
workplace/s 11, 112, 125, 130, 131, 195
World Bank 106
wormholes 120
wrench 126, 136
Wright, Judith 179, 180
Wright, Kate 13
Wright, Sarah 51
Wright's Lookout 79
Wukun 69

youth 157

Zettel, Tessa 5, 10, 11, 89,
zine/s 14, 141, 151, 154, 160, 161, 179,
Zoom 134, 135, 142